OBSCENITY

LAW IN CONTEXT

Editors: Robert Stevens (Haverford College, Pennsylvania), William Twining (University of Warwick) and Christopher McCrudden (Balliol College, Oxford)

Obscenity

*An Account of Censorship Laws and their
Enforcement in England and Wales*

GEOFFREY ROBERTSON B.A., LL.B., B.C.L.
Of the Middle Temple, Barrister

WEIDENFELD AND NICOLSON
London

© 1979 Geoffrey Robertson

Weidenfeld and Nicolson
91 Clapham High St London sw4

ISBN 0 297 77213 9 cased
ISBN 0 297 77459 x paperback

Printed in Great Britain by
Butler & Tanner Ltd, Frome and London

CONTENTS

TABLE OF CASES

TABLE OF STATUTES AND TREATIES

PREFACE

Books about obscenity law are rarely law books. More often they take the form of partisan accounts of their authors' preference for more or less rectitude in the public presentation of erotic themes. The very mention of obscenity law has become inseparable from the desire for obscenity law reform. Each major trial acts as a signal for renewed demands for a change in the definition of the crime. During the second decade of its operation, the 1959 Obscene Publications Act suffered more criticism than any other contemporary piece of legislation, although no alternative formulation of the offence commanded sufficient support to displace the elusive 'tendency to deprave and corrupt' as the criterion and test of guilt. A dispassionate exposition of the present state of the law relating to obscenity, indecency and assorted rudery will not begin to shake the moral certitude of those who know what is good (or bad) for others: it may, however, dispel the belief that the criminal process can be relied upon either to make value judgements on literature or to punish the purveyors of poor taste.

The chief object of this book is to give some coherent impression of the workings of the Obscene Publications Act and of its relationship with other statutory and common-law prohibitions upon offensive publications. The looseness of legislative language and the vagueness of judicial dicta makes this area of law particularly prone to definition in terms of what officials do in fact, and consequently details are given of police routines, trial tactics, and the behaviour of those publishers for whom prosecution is an occuaptional hazard. The rule of obscenity law is very much the rule of the Director of Public Prosecutions' thumb, and although Messrs Weidenfeld & Nicolson have baulked at a pictorial approach to the subject, some attempt has been made to describe the DPP's operational taboos. Courts are enjoined to reflect in their verdicts 'the contemporary climate of publishing' and 'current standards of morality' – imponderables which require an excursion into the pornographic market-place and an analysis of the censorship forces at work in those media institutions which have an impact on popular taste. Although this study focuses upon the law

of England and Wales, comparisons have been made with other jurisdictions to demonstrate alternative methods of coping with a subject-
matter which acknowledges no national frontiers. The final chapter
outlines a system of administrative control which would take much
of the uncertainty and some of the passion out of a debate which an
overworked system of criminal justice has been unable to adjudicate
with any satisfactory degree of fairness, efficiency or consistency.

This book grew out of the weariness of one occasional participant
with the periodic moral flashpoints which pass for obscenity trials.
I am indebted to the series editors for their encouragement and their
patience; to Clare Sieradzki, Christine Booker and Tim Robertson
for their work on the manuscript, and to Andrew Nicoll for compiling
the table of cases and the index. It remains to thank John Mortimer
for the challenge of Voltaire and the companionship which accompanied his leadership in the lists, and Bel Mooney and Jane Cousins
for their reminders that it is not always necessary to fight to the death
for the right to debase others.

'Today I finished Book III Chapter I [of *Brideshead Revisited*] – the most difficult part of the book so far and in spite of some passages of beauty I am not sure of my success. I feel very much the futility of describing the sexual act; I should like to give as much detail as I have to the meals, to the two coitions – with his wife and Julia. It would be no more or less obscene than to leave them to the readers' imaginations which in this case cannot be as accurate as mine. There is a gap in which the reader will insert his own sexual habits instead of those of my characters.'

Evelyn Waugh, Diary entry for 9 May 1944

I
Obscenity in context

In the beginning is the word, or the picture. It offends somebody, who complains to the police. The police apply to a magistrate for a warrant to search for and seize any offensive book, magazine or film from the suspected premises. The haul is examined by the office of the Director of Public Prosecutions, which decides, sometimes on the advice of treasury counsel, whether to launch a criminal prosecution, apply for a civil forfeiture order, or throw the catch back, like a disappointed fisherman, into the turbulent pool of marketable erotica.

Censorship laws in Britain fall into two distinct categories: those which prohibit 'obscene' articles likely to corrupt readers or viewers, and those which permit the authorities to confiscate 'indecent' material which merely embarrasses the sexual modesty of ordinary people. Obscenity, the more serious crime, is punished by the 1959 Obscene Publications Act, either after a trial by judge and jury, or by 'forfeiture proceedings' under a law which authorizes local justices to destroy obscene articles discovered within their jurisdiction. Disseminators of 'indecent' material which lacks the potency to corrupt its readers are within the law so long as they do not despatch it by post, or seek to import it from overseas, or flaunt it openly in public places. Both 'obscenity' and 'indecency' are defined by reference to vague and elastic formulae, permitting forensic debates over morality which fit uneasily into the format of a criminal trial. These periodic moral flashpoints may edify or entertain, but they provide scant control over the booming business of sexual delectation. Occasional forfeiture orders, based upon the same loose definitions, are subject to the inconsistent priorities and prejudices of local constabularies in different parts of the country, and offer no effective deterrent to publishers with access to a printing press and a ready supply of paper. The deep division in society over the proper limits of sexual permissiveness is mirrored by an inconsistent and ineffective censorship of publications which may offend or entertain, corrupt or enlighten, according to the taste and character of individual readers. The problem of drawing a line between moral outrage and individual freedom has become intractable at a time when one person's obscenity is another person's bedtime reading.

A joke went the rounds of the Old Bailey after a series of inconclusive obscenity trials in the mid-1970s: 'What's the best way to open the prosecution in an obscenity case?' a barrister asks a more experienced colleague. 'You stand up and say "I offer no evidence."' It reflected increasing frustration at the difficulty of convicting even the most desolating pornography, after trials which wasted large amounts of public money and conferred lucrative publicity upon defendants. Prosecutors began with prejudice firmly on their side: the exhibits were shocking, unpleasant and sometimes stomach-turning, and jurors would undoubtedly classify them as 'obscene', in the colloquial sense, as soon as they saw them. But in strict legal theory, the Crown had to *prove*, and prove to the normal criminal standard, 'beyond a reasonable doubt', that the material would tend to deprave and corrupt its likely customers. Policemen never managed to discover evidence that it had actually harmed anybody. Jurors were obliged to speculate, and if they speculated honestly they would have to admit at least to some doubt about whether the trash on their table would seriously effect the moral fabric of their society. At a time when social scientists had failed to establish causal connections between literature and depravity, while European neighbours survived and flourished after legalizing pornography, jurors had to be a little dubious about its corrupting potential for British adults. There is always a prima facie case against the pornographer, but it cannot be proven beyond reasonable doubt in a society which is genuinely ambivalent about the effects of sexually explicit material.

The preamble to the 1959 Obscene Publications Act declares a legislative intention 'to provide for the protection of literature; and to strengthen the law concerning pornography'. A book is obscene only if, taken as a whole, it would tend to deprave and corrupt likely readers to an extent which could not be redeemed by its literary or scholarly qualities. The first cases emphasized that the law is concerned with a real prospect of social harm. The *Lady Chatterley's Lover* case (*R*. v. *Penguin Books* 1960) established that a tendency to corrupt is a stronger concept than a tendency to shock or disgust, and implies the spread of moral perversion.[1] Corruption is not confined to the consequences of sexual indelicacy: it extends to promoting the pleasures of drug taking (*Calder* v. *Powell* 1965)[2] and to conditioning young children to engage in violence (*DPP* v. *A.&B.C. Chewing Gum Ltd* 1968).[3] The Act adopts a variable definition of obscenity: the presence or absence of this criminal quality depends upon the circumstances of distribution. Articles which would be obscene if placed on general sale could lawfully be sold to respectable or experienced individuals who took care not to expose them to more vulnerable members of the public (*R*. v. *Clayton & Halsey*[4] 1962, and *R*. v. *Barker*[5] 1962). The Court of Appeal quashed the conviction of the publishers of *Last Exit to Brooklyn* because the jury might have mistaken revulsion for corruption: authors are entitled to turn their readers' stomachs for the purpose of arousing concern or condemning the corruption explicitly described. Obscenity is concerned with seduction, not aversion. This decision (*R*. v. *Calder & Boyars*[6] 1967) confirmed that the 'public good' defence extended to ethical and sociological merits, and the *A.&B.C. Chewing Gum* case indicated that arguments about the impact of publications on the mind of special classes of readers might also be canvassed. Material which facilitated corrupt behaviour, such as resort to prostitutes through contact advertisements, could still be prosecuted as a common law conspiracy,[7] and non-obscene material merchandised so as to cause offence by public display or unsolicited mailing was subject to the lesser test of 'indecency'.[8] Prosecution of genuine if avant-garde literature was discouraged by the Divisional Court[9] at the same time as Parliament abolished pre-censorship of the theatre in favour of an obscenity law which appeared, by 1968, to have achieved its object of protecting art and suppressing pornography. The first decade of the Act's operation seemingly produced a conceptually neat and sophisticated control, confining punishment to those whose publishing activities caused demonstrable harm to others. The broad police powers of search and seizure, afforded 'to strengthen the law concerning pornography', aroused surprisingly few complaints. Pornographers always pleaded 'guilty', and generally received small fines in the lower courts. As the sixties drew to a close, even Soho seemed under reasonable control. What the public eye did not see, the public heart did not grieve over.

The first shock came from the revelation that pornography might not deprave and corrupt after all. Between 1965 and 1969 Denmark lifted all restraints on sexual explicitness, without suffering any moral decline discernible from crime statistics or standards of public behaviour. Lurid magazines of the glossiest quality and the hardest core began to enter England in bulk, carried in private planes or beneath consignments of Danish bacon. In 1970 the 'Danish experiment' received weighty endorsement from an American Presidential Commission on Obscenity and Pornography, which recommended abolition of all censorship for adults.[10] Sexual orientation, it argued, was too deep-seated to be adversely affected by reading matter. Pornography was not merely harmless: it conferred therapeutic benefits by 'enhancing marital communication', providing pleasure for the ugly and forlorn, and acting as a 'safety valve' substitute for potential rapists and child molesters. Emboldened by these apparently scientific claims, the publishers of erotica abandoned their low courtroom profile and paraded expert testimonials to the benefits of their masturbatory fantasies. Between 1971 and 1976, at trials throughout the country, a troupe of doctors, psychiatrists, psychologists and sociologists proclaimed that publication of obscene material was justified, under section 4 of the 1959 Obscene Publications Act, because it served 'an object of general concern' – namely the mental health and physical happiness of a community plagued by 'sexual dysfunction'. 'Softcore' magazines were regularly acquitted after *R.* v. *Gold* in 1972; *Jolly Hockeysticks* and other heterosexual blue movies survived a major prosecution (*R.* v. *Lindsay*) in 1974; and *Inside Linda Lovelace* was launched with the priceless publicity of an Old Bailey trial in 1976. These acquittals of 'good clean pornography' caused less public criticism than the inability of juries to convict sado-masochistic material, in even the most extreme of which some experts were prepared to discern some merit. The courts reacted by strengthening the law: in *DPP* v. *Whyte* the House of Lords ruled that 'depravity and corruption' was a condition of the mind, and books which aroused erotic fantasy without stimulating overtly antisocial behaviour could nonetheless be declared obscene.[11] In *DPP* v. *Jordan* a stop was put to 'therapeutic effect' evidence by limiting the 'public good' defence to material with intrinsic merit as literature or learning.[12] These decisions shortened trials but had no immediate effect on conviction rates or on the volume of publicly marketed erotica: a law, once proven an ass, could not be transformed into a milk-white steed by judicial cross-breeding.

If pornography did not corrupt its readers, it certainly corrupted some of those charged with enforcing the law against it. The 1959

Act had 'strengthened the law concerning pornography' by vesting a broad discretion in policemen to search premises and seize stock without issuing receipts. They operated, largely without account-ability, a law which hinged on subjective assessment, and the tempta-tion to share in the spoils from a commodity of dubious danger proved too great. Throughout the 1960s certain Scotland Yard officers main-tained an unofficial licensing system in Soho, permitting the surrepti-tious sale of hard-core material by favoured booksellers who bribed heavily for police protection. Newspaper exposures and the advent of Sir Robert Mark as Metropolitan Commissioner of Police led to the suspension of twenty officers and the trial for corruption of a further fifteen. Twelve of them were jailed for a total of eighty-four years in 1977, convicted of 'an evil conspiracy which turned the Obscene Publications Squad into a vast protection racket'.[13] That racket had at least provided a measure of ad hoc control – porno-graphy was distributed, but only to a limited number of booksellers who could be trusted to keep it under the counter. The reformed Obscenity Squad had little success in achieving consistent restraint, and in 1973 Sir Robert Mark complained that its task 'was at times made more difficult because the demarcation line between what is and is not obscene in law is becoming more obscure. That this is so is demonstrated by the fact that a half of the contested cases dealt with on indictment during the year resulted in acquittals.'[14] The sub-jective element became apparent as different provincial police forces applied varying standards and priorities: in Manchester in 1977 the local force was seizing *The Sun Book of Page 3 Girls*, while in Portsmouth police tolerated the sale of anything short of child porn, bestiality or torture. Between these two extremes a wide range of standards were inconsistently and arbitrarily applied. Through the widening gaps in the law crept a host of purveyors of 'adult reading', prospering by satisfying public demand but constantly vulnerable to the shifting sands of police discretion.

But it was neither the special pleading of pornographers nor the wholesale corruption of a police department that caused a re-evalua-tion of the obscenity law, so much as its use against the apostles of radical change. The trials of the underground press – *I.T.* (1970), *Oz* (1971) and *Nasty Tales* (1973) – assumed at one stage the proportions of a cultural collision, souring the respect of those who had no truck with exploitation of sex and raising false hopes in those who foolishly looked to the law for protection against political unorthodoxy. *Oz* was neither literature nor pornography, although it combined elements of both to attack hypocrisy and repression. Those forces rose to the bait, with the result that the *Oz* editors occupied for six weeks a privileged platform from which they propagated their allegedly corrupt philosophy. Their struggle was celebrated by a book, a play and a pop record, and is said to have provoked more letters to *The Times* than the Suez crisis. The tumult and shouting died away after the Court of Appeal quashed the obscenity conviction,[15] and subsequently an Old Bailey jury acquitted the editors of *Nasty Tales*. But the episode damaged respect for a law which could apparently be used for political purposes, and served to crystallize concern over 'the problem of pornography'. In 1971 a private committee was set up by Lord Longford to lobby for a more effective and more stringent censorship. The *Oz* trial brought a short-term advantage to commercial exploiters by arousing the hostility of a younger generation of jurors to obscenity prosecutions, but liberal circles became uneasy about 'men's magazines' which pandered to violent and chauvinistic fantasies. Sexual emancipation entails the abandonment of oppression and manipulative treatment of women – in literature as well as in life. If all you need is love, aggressively sexist pornography is spurious. *Time Out*, one magazine which emerged from the underground to bask in the sunlight of commercial success, banned sexist advertisements for men's magazines and massage parlours. The 'new obscenities' were violence, racism and sex discrimination, and civil libertarians were increasingly reluctant to tolerate the intolerant.

One test of liberal democracy is the extent to which it allows minorities to find happiness in behaviour of which the majority, were it ever asked, might disapprove. But the utilitarian purpose of punishment – the prevention of harm to others – begs the question of what conduct amounts to 'harm'. Incitements to rape and violence, obtaining children for purposes of prostitution, disseminating inaccurate medical information, all endanger the reader by encouraging him to damage himself or others. But the harm caused by colour picture-books of copulating couples is of a much more questionable kind. Whether such articles constitute a real and appreciable danger to their readers is a matter of opinion, not a question of fact which can be decided by evidence of the kind which courts of law are accustomed to receive. Criminal trials are mechanisms for deciding who is telling the truth, but in obscenity trials there is no truth to tell – only a clash of opinions, as a captive audience is invited to score a polite debate between bewigged protagonists. Traditional courtroom trappings,

with the publisher in the dock and his witnesses put to their proof
by oath and interrogation, only serve to conceal how the wide words
of the obscenity laws require magistrates and juries to reach value-
judgment verdicts.

Disaffection with the law of obscenity is now entrenched in the law
itself. Lord Widgery has described it as unsatisfactory, Lord Denning
says it has misfired, and Lord Wilberforce has proclaimed it illogical
and unscientific. In 1959 pornography was assumed to deprave and
corrupt; in 1979 it is expected to do many things, pleasant and unpleasant, which fall short of depravity and corruption. Its only proven
casualties have been dishonest policemen, whose successors have had
little success in achieving any systematic control over prurient publications. The real 'problem of pornography' is the problem of finding
any reasonably acceptable legal alternative to the Obscene Publications Act. Prosecutors have resorted to common-law charges and to
statutes embodying the broader test of 'indecency', but these are of
restricted application and make no distinction between the meritorious and the meretricious. Private pressure-groups have conducted
courtroom crusades against permissiveness, meeting with judicial
sympathy but little success, except for the revival of blasphemy to
punish the indecent treatment of sacred subjects. Parliament has been
reluctant to intervene while social attitudes are polarized and votes
may be lost by a major shift either way. One legislative initiative to
curb indecent public displays foundered in 1974 over the impossibility
of giving a meaningful definition to 'indecency'. Ironically, the most
significant reform of the seventies has been to extend the much-
maligned Obscene Publications Act to cover the cinema, after common-law prosecutions had miscarried. In 1978 a measure to protect
children from involvement in pornography production was passed,
although it added little to existing legal controls. In 1977 a Home
Office Committee on Obscenity and Film Censorship, chaired by
Professor Bernard Williams, was asked 'to review the laws concerning obscenity, indecency and violence in publications, displays and
entertainments in England and Wales, except in the field of broadcasting, and to review the arrangements for film censorship....'

The markets for sexually explicit literature – open in respect of borderline 'soft porn' and black in connection with 'hard-core' material –
boomed in the 1970s. The trend was noticed in 1971 by the Metropolitan Commissioner of Police, who concluded that 'The profitability
of this trade has undoubtedly led to its precipitated growth.' He

overlooked the consumer demand which must exist before any trade can prosper. In 1972 over two million 'hard porn' books and magazines were seized by Customs. The Deputy Director of Public Prosecutions has estimated that 'the police and Customs are lucky if, between them, they manage to seize more than one in every half-dozen imported into this country' – which would suggest that at least ten million articles were illegally imported for sale in Britain in that year alone.[16] In 1973 the Court of Appeal was shocked to discover that 'soft porn is sold at sweet shops and other shops, where magazines can be bought, at innumerable places in London – there is one close to the offices of Lord Longford in Piccadilly and others as far away as Hammersmith and Chiswick'.[17] In 1977 an authoritative marketing survey estimated that this 'soft porn', dispensed by four hundred wholesalers through a national network of over 20,000 newsagents and bookshops, is consumed by twenty-seven million men and women throughout the country.[18] The profitable sale of many millions of sexually explicit books and magazines in Britain each year indicates a significant degree of popular acceptance, and makes it difficult to postulate any current community consensus on whether, and to what extent, the distribution of erotic material should be regulated. The Metropolitan Commissioner of Police, when accused of dereliction of duty for tolerating Soho pornshops, replied, 'The comparative absence of public complaint suggests that pornography causes less public unease than most other breaches of the law.'[19]

'Hard porn', imported in bulk from Scandinavia and America, is usually available through 'adults only' shops in major cities, supplied by anonymous men in fast cars. It has been graphically described by Lord Denning:

Prominent are the pictures. As examples of the art of coloured photography, they would earn the highest praise. As examples of the sordid side of life, they are deplorable. There are photographs showing young men and women who appear to have worked themselves up into a state of extreme lust for the sake of the photographers. In their lust these young people have adopted positions natural, and positions unnatural.... The photographers have crouched close – inches close – to them and to their most private parts. They have photographed them apparently in the very act in the utmost detail. They have taken these photographs in bright colours. They have enlarged them. Then the printers have multiplied them in their thousands and hundreds of thousands. To add to it, there is letterpress. It tells of it all, gloatingly, without shame, as if to commend the readers to do likewise or worse....[20]

The profits of pornography are legion. 'Borderline' and 'soft-core' material, selling from 40p to £2, and *What The Butler Saw* home movies selling at £7, gross at least a hundred million pounds each year. The Longford Committee discovered retailers who made eighty per cent profit on cost, under sale-or-return agreements with publishers ('only publishers with enormous confidence that their products will sell can afford to offer terms like these'[21]). 'Hard-core', sold at £7 a magazine and £16 to £20 per eight-millimetre film, has been conservatively estimated to earn ten million pounds a year for people who do not declare it on tax returns. The Inland Revenue is not the only loser from the illegality of the trade: purchasers suffer mark-ups as high as two thousand per cent of production price.[22] The weekly gross of a police-protected Soho shop was estimated at £10,000 and one bookseller who was actually prosecuted in 1971 had been netting a weekly profit of £2,000 during his two years of operation, beside which his £2,500 fine appeared derisory. Life beneath the law has its overheads, and increasing stock seizures have occasioned much loss of capital and some loss of liberty. But raids are inevitably arbitrary and sporadic, and the trade has continued, with increasing competition from overground 'men's magazines' and from massage parlours and escort agencies which offer more tangible forms of corruption. The paradox of pornography is that it enables a man to watch a woman do to another that which, for much the same price, he could have done to himself.

Who buys pornography? Few readership surveys have been undertaken in Britain, but studies of sex-shop patrons in America and Copenhagen coincide in describing the average customer as white, middle-aged, middle-class, married, male, wearing a business suit and shopping alone. The American Presidential Commission noted: 'The patrons were almost exclusively male. Almost three-quarters were estimated to be in the age range of 26–55, while twenty-two per cent were 21–25, and four per cent were over 55. Less than one per cent were possibly under 21. Over half the sample were casually dressed, twenty-six per cent wore suits and ties, thirteen per cent were blue-collar workers; the remainder were soldiers, students, tourists, hippies and clergymen ... well over half of these patrons were probably married.'[23] Dirty old Americans appear at first blush to be a better class of person than their counterparts in Britain, where legal mythology has it that pornshop patrons are 'inadequate, pathetic, dirty-minded men seeking cheap thrills'. That, at least, was the assumption in one leading obscenity case, *DPP* v. *Whyte*.[24] Southampton police kept watch on a bookshop situated opposite Southampton Technical College, in an area dotted with council flats. The customers were described in evidence as 'principally men of middle-age and upwards, who came there regularly to make purchases, what are commonly known as dirty old men'. The police swooped and seized, but the magistrates reasoned that once the majority of customers had already been depraved and corrupted they could not be corrupted further: 'We see regular customers as inadequate, pathetic, dirty-minded men, seeking cheap thrills – addicts to this type of material, whose morals were already in a state of depravity and corruption. We consequently entertained grave doubt as to whether such minds could be said to be open to any immoral influence which the said articles were capable of exerting.'

When the case reached the House of Lords, it was decided that dirty old men *could* be depraved more than once:

> It takes time for a man to become depraved (*Nemo repente fuit turpissimus*). The regular customers of this shop whom the justices found to be now in a state of depravity and corruption may have been far less corrupted when they first saw books of this sort exposed for sale in the respondent's shop. Similarly, a middle-aged or elderly man who was not yet an addict of pornography might at any time see these books in the shop, be attracted to them, become a recruit to the band of regular readers and in time become as depraved as the others.[25]

In other obscenity cases, patrons of adult bookstores questioned by police have turned out to be ordinary citizens from all walks of life. Doctors doubt whether pornography can be addictive, and the image of the dirty old man underwent a distinct improvement with the publication in 1975 of Mr Gladstone's diaries, revealing that eminent Victorian as a reader of pornography (albeit in Latin and Greek). Indeed, Gladstone advocated pornography as a method of avoiding sexual temptation – the very argument which was for a time advanced under the 'public good' defence of the 1959 Obscene Publications Act. In 1975 an old Harrovian stood in the dock at the Old Bailey, guilty of supplying hard-core Danish porn to a highly select clientele, including directors of the city's leading merchant banks, and vicars and schoolteachers who were pillars of their local communities. A survey of four thousand readers of *Forum* revealed a predominantly sober, middle-class and highly educated readership. Newsagents interviewed as witnesses for the *In Depth* trial in 1973 indicated that most of their clientele for that 'sex education' magazine and its competitors were married people between twenty-five and thirty-five. Most correspondents were married persons seeking advice about sexual incompatibility, or reassurance about their indulgence in unorthodox sexual practices. *Libertine*, a magazine tried for obscenity in 1977, paraded an ambulance driver, a lay preacher, a film director, a psychiatrist, a travelling salesman and a civil servant to testify, as regular readers, to its entertainment value. It seemed that when the dirty mackintosh was opened, as often as not a pin-striped suit was underneath.

In 1977 one market-research firm discovered for its advertising clients a £20-million market in 'the exciting world of men's magazines ... about the same value as more traditional Mintel markets, like marmalade or lavatory cleansers'.[26] It found a wealthy, young-executive readership, attracting respectable advertisers of cars, hi-fi, liquor and other manifestations of modern luxury living. Presidential candidate Carter allowed himself to be interviewed by *Playboy* in 1976; at the same time *Penthouse* in England was offering interviews with Enoch Powell, wine hints from Kingsley Amis and motoring reports from Stirling Moss. 'The myth of the dirty old man is finally destroyed,' announced the *Financial Times*. 'It is the younger, richer males who fall into this category.' Magazines carrying articles and pictorials which would once have been judged grossly obscene are now thought fit to propagandize on behalf of the most respectable manufacturers of cigarettes and alcohol. Television's *Till Death Do Us Part*, a prime target of 'clean-up' campaigners, topped the ratings for all but one week of its 1972 series, and a detailed study of the BBC Audience Research Department failed to find any evidence that the programme had caused social harm. There are more than sixty cinema clubs for blue film *aficionados*, and although the major film distributors protest concern with family entertainment most of their offerings are 'X'-rated. J. Arthur Rank's interest in the cinema was originally to make religious films, but by September 1975 eighty per cent of Rank cinemas in London were showing 'X' films, with titles like *Nurse on the Job* (St Albans), *Red Hot in Bed*, *The Reluctant Virgin* (Hounslow), *Suburban Wives* (Wimbledon), and *Before and After Sex* (Dalston).[27] Nudity and four-letter words have ceased to raise eyebrows in West End theatres in the wake of *Oh Calcutta*. Fleet Street sub-editors no longer blue-pencil vulgarity, at least in appropriate contexts, and in 1972 even *The Times* published a full-page advertisement featuring the profile of a naked model. The arts pages of the *Guardian* and the *Observer* have offered full-frontal nudity, and the circulation battle between the *Sun* and the *Mirror* is waged partly in terms of provocative page-three 'spreads' and investigative probes of wife-swapping in the provinces. Some local pubs offer lunch-time strip shows, and 'sex shops' have become almost as common as Mothercare. The most comprehensive opinion poll on public attitudes to permissiveness, conducted in December 1973, revealed that seventy-four per cent agreed with the proposition that, 'Adults should be allowed to buy whatever indecent or erotic books and magazines they like, as long as they are not on public display.'[28]

The realities of popular permissiveness are reflected in the law, because material charged as obscene must be tested by 'the current standards of ordinary decent people'.[29] The jury, as a 'microcosm of democratic society',[30] must first identify the contemporary standards of its society, and then apply them to the publication at issue. The problem with this approach is that the notion of 'community standards' is ambiguous. There are 'standards' in the sense of precepts, laid down by the good and the wise, which most people respect but less manage to follow. Precepts such as premarital chastity and religious observance remain social standards, although they may be more honoured in the breach than the observance. Articles in many books and magazines attack moral precepts, but are nevertheless acceptable to a large segment of the population. This material falls within the tolerance of 'popular standards': what the ordinary person is prepared to accept, and what a significant portion of the population wishes to consume. Citizens of high purpose and moral rectitude may be shocked and disgusted by Alf Garnett, yet his foul-mouthings were compulsive viewing in millions of homes. Jurors will doubtless be aware of popular standards, and of the climate prevailing in publicly available entertainment, and this awareness will influence their response when they are invited, at an obscenity trial, to set the lowest standard of all: the standard above which a man is entitled to publish without going to prison.

A different problem emerges when the issue is viewed, not in terms of the right of the individual to dilate over pornographic fantasies, but from the perspective of a community which requires a limited social cohesion to secure equal and civilized treatment for all its members. Does a commitment to toleration entail a licence for intolerance? The 'good way of life' sought by the majority in the 1980s may well be a social life which is free from prejudice and discrimination. That freedom is challenged by propaganda designed to stir hatred against blacks, women, homosexuals, Christians or any other group defined in discriminatory terms. A law against moral corruption may be incompatible with a free market-place of ideas, but without it a society which wishes to tolerate minorities may be powerless to protect them against verbal or written assault by degradation, humiliation or defamation. Propaganda *in favour* of homosexuality only has effect, if at all, on private sexual behaviour, which is ultimately a matter of personal choice in which the state can have no legitimate interest. But propaganda *against* homosexuals, if it reaches the degree of virulence shown in the US campaign to 'Kill a queer for Christ', is a matter of public concern, because it exploits the emotion of hatred to destroy the happiness of a particular group of law-abiding citizens.

The traditional proponents of civil liberties are increasingly prepared to draw the line at writing which promotes anti-social attitudes – or, at least, attitudes that find no place in their own ideal society. There are strains of pornography which glamorize the degradation and maltreatment of women, and assert their subordinate function as mere receptacles for male lust. Some self-avowed 'men's magazines' feed the traditional fantasy of the female as nymphomaniac – saying 'no' when she really means 'yes', willing to surrender, weeping but inwardly excited, to swaggering sexual machismo. Young models are encouraged to wink and blush and masturbate so that the vaselined lenses of 'glamour photographers' may capture their humiliation for mass titillation of prurient-minded men. A jury which is really concerned to reflect 'progressive' thinking might find that such magazines would 'tend to corrupt' by perpetuating false and degrading sexual stereotypes. If intolerant writing *does* harm society by threatening social cohesion and infringing the rights of particular people to fair and equal treatment, if it is designed to make miserable the lives of otherwise law-abiding classes defined only in terms of their colour or sex, then it tends precisely to that kind of harm which is the declared target of section 1 of the Obscene Publications Act. What is truly corrupting is not sexual explicitness in itself, or even the suggestion that people should do whatever they like with a consenting partner, but the idea that they should overbear the will of another. 'Seduction manuals' which suggest that women should be plied with drink or drugs to make them more complaisant, or publications which stir up racial hatred, feature pictures of children in indecent poses, give erroneous medical advice on sexual hygiene or exploit the female body to sell alcohol and cigarettes, may all do more damage than the ideologically vapid fantasies which change hands in the pornographic market-place.

The only generalization it seems safe to make about community standards is that they cannot be the subject of generalizations. The law at least recognizes that they change over time. In 1936 a Bow Street magistrate declared that Radclyffe Hall's novel *The Well of Loneliness* was obscene because it dealt with lesbianism. In 1974 it was read over the airwaves as a BBC *Book at Bedtime*. It may be that much of the leering salacity presently dispensed on street corners will prove unacceptable when society becomes genuinely concerned to uphold the dignity of women. The real question is whether the law, at a time of transition in moral values, should allow attitudinal changes to work themselves out through jury applications of broad definitions of obscenity, or whether, consonant with the standards of certainty and clarity prized in criminal jurisprudence, the ambit of taboo should be precisely determined. One alternative may be to decriminalize the publication of tasteless books, films and magazines, and to rely instead upon administrative regulation to contain public offence. It must be doubted whether criminal laws relating to obscenity and indecency, however much they may be amended, will be workable unless or until a community consensus emerges to support their application.

2
Obscenity law in the making

THE ORIGINS OF CENSORSHIP

The history of English censorship is the story of one society's inability
to solve a problem posed by the invention of printing. Centuries were
to pass before the initial fear of subversive literature was supplanted
by concern over erotic writing, and pornography finally replaced sedition as the prime target of the laws which regulate publishing. By
1650 the subject-matter of pornography was settled: the sexual imagination of subsequent generations added new words and novel settings,
but discovered no fundamental variation on the finite methods of
coupling. Geographically, London's libido-land moved but a mile,
from Holywell Street (now the Aldwych) to modern Soho. The scarlet
woman, pornography's picaresque and picturesque prop, gained one
dimension with the development of photography and another with
the abolition of stage censorship, but the modern exploits of Linda
Lovelace were old hat to Fanny Hill. The Society for the Suppression
of Vice was born again in the Festival of Light, but its modern victims
were to prove as incorrigible as those jailed and vilified by moral guardians of the past. Even the rhetoric has remained constant. The first
Obscene Publications Act, in 1857, was sponsored by a Lord Chancellor who equated pornography with poison. In 1928 *The Well of
Loneliness* was destroyed on the theory that it would prove more
dangerous than a phial of prussic acid. In 1974 at the Old Bailey a
book about homosexuality was described by treasury counsel as
'a sugar coated pill of poison', and the metaphor has found a fashion-
able resting-place in current crusades against the spread of 'moral
pollution'. The rationale of censorship has not changed: protection

is demanded for the young and for the working classes, groups feared throughout history for their susceptibility to unorthodox sexual or political propaganda. The central irony of the courtroom crusade is still with us – seek to suppress a book by legal action because it tends to corrupt, and the publicity attendant upon its trial will spread that assumed corruption far more effectively than its quiet distribution. The only lesson we learn from the legal history of censorship is that the more the law changes, the more the social reality remains the same.

The first person on record to be corrupted by ocular suggestion was Aholibah, in the Old Testament story of Ezekiel.[1] She 'increased her whoredom' when she saw pictures of Chaldean warriors chalked in vermilion on a wall. They were 'girded with girdles upon their loins, exceeding in dyed attire upon their heads, all of them princes to look to . . . and as soon as she saw them with her eyes, she doted upon them, and sent messengers unto them'. The Chaldeans were nothing loath to accept her invitation: they 'came unto the bed of love, and they defiled her with their whoredom, and she was polluted with them'. The sexual licence of ancient Greece is legendary, and survives today in priapic statuary, explicit paintings on terracotta, and the plays of Aristophanes. Pornography was written, sex toys were manufactured, and only a few philosophers showed concern. Plato argued that passages 'not conducive to self-restraint' should be expunged from *The Odyssey* to make it more suitable for schoolboys, and Socrates worried over the excessive horror in some of the stories about descents into Hades.[2] In Rome, at least until the Empire was overwhelmed by Christianity, writers and playwrights enjoyed similar freedom, and such classics as Ovid's *Ars Amatoria* and the *Satyricon* of Petronius emerged to bedevil the censors of subsequent centuries. In Britain the *Exeter Book*, one of the earliest surviving examples of Anglo-Saxon literature, contains coarse anatomical riddles, enthusiastically compiled by the cathedral monks, and fourteenth-century Europeans digested without demur the writings of Chaucer and Boccaccio. The *Canterbury Tales* was published by Caxton in unexpurgated form shortly after he commenced printing at Westminster in 1476. Editions of the *Decameron* were soon available, and one translation was specifically licensed in 1620.[3] In the first dawn of the printed word, little apprehension was felt about the impact of sexual writing upon the few men of the age who might entertain themselves with such a study. Children and workers could not read.

The first licensing decree was issued by the Star Chamber in 1538, although it was not enforced until the incorporation of the Stationers' Company in 1557. Members of the Company enjoyed a monopoly of printing books in England, and to enforce their privilege they were entitled to seek out and destroy unlicensed presses, and to fine and imprison unlicensed printers. The Royal Charter was avowedly 'a suitable remedy' for suppressing 'certain seditious and heretical books, rimes and treatises ... daily published and printed by divers scandalous, malicious, schismatical and heretical persons'.[4] It was a device for the political censorship of subversive literature, and decreed instant execution for anyone who spread rebellious words. In 1559 the Charter was confirmed by Queen Elizabeth: no serious book was to be published without the approval of the Queen or her Privy Council, the Archbishops of Canterbury, York or London, or the Chancellors of Oxbridge or Cambridge University. Licensing fees were to be paid to the Stationers' Company, which kept a register of permissible books. This decree included the forerunner of today's 'public good' defence: the system was not to apply to classical authors and foreign language works which had been formerly used in the universities. Overwhelmingly, Elizabethan censorship was concerned with books which challenged faith or government. Many dissidents were hanged, drawn and quartered for publishing Catholic propaganda, but there is scant evidence that the licensing system was operated to suppress either popular or bawdy literature.[5] One contemporary writer was moved to complain of delays in the licensing of serious works, 'whilst other bookes full of all filthiness, scurrility, bawdy, dissoluteness, cosinage, conycatching and the like ... are either quickly licensed or at least easily tolerate'.[6]

The one great curiosity to emerge from Elizabethan censorship was the country's first Obscene Publications Bill, drafted in 1580 by William Lambard, a lawyer and magistrate. It seems to have been prompted less by prudery than by concern for the commercial interests of the licensed publishers, who looked greedily upon the printers of popular squibs exempt from licensing requirements. The 'Act to restrain the licentious printing, selling and uttering of unprofitable and hurtful English books' declared in its preamble a pious concern

For the better control of poesies, sundry books, pamphlets, ditties, songs and other works and writings of many sorts and names serving (for a great part of them) to none other end (what titles soever they bear) but only to let in the main sea of wickedness and to set up an art of making lascivious ungodly love, to the high displeasure of God, whose gifts and graces be pitifully misused thereby, to the manifest injury and offence of the godly-learned, whose praiseworthy endeavours and writings are therefore the less read and regarded, to the intolerable corruption of common life and manners, which pestilently invades the minds of many that delight to hear or read the said wanton works, and to no small or sufferable waste of the treasure of this realm which is thereby consumed and spent in paper, being of itself a foreign and chargeable commodity....

The Bill aimed to establish censorship by lawyers, rather than politicians or divines, and to embrace popular as well as serious literature. Eight Benchers of the Inns of Court were to form a censorship board, with powers to fine any who disobeyed their rulings. The scheme was never presented to Parliament, although its draftsman was subsequently celebrated for standing 'at a crossroads in the history of English literature, pointing vainly in the direction he wanted us all to take and using in this context, for the first time, the explosive word "corruption"'.[7]

In the seventeenth century licensing came and went. The system existed on paper until 1640, although the increase in the range of printed books made it difficult to enforce. In 1637 the Lord Chief Justice was permitted to license law books, and histories were to be approved by a Secretary of State. The cost of licence fees alone deterred many publishers from submitting their books, and in 1640 the whole system fell with the abolition of the Star Chamber. In 1643, however, it was reintroduced by Cromwell, moving Milton to utter his immortal cry for freedom of the Press, the *Areopagitica*:

Promiscuous reading is necessary to the constituting of human nature. The attempt to keep out evil doctrine by licensing is like the exploit of that gallant man who thought to keep out the crows by shutting his park gate.... Lords and Commons of England, consider what nation it is whereof ye are: a nation not slow and dull, but of a quick, ingenious and piercing spirit. It must not be shackled or restricted. Give me the liberty to know, to utter and to argue freely according to conscience, above all liberties.

Milton's plea fell on deaf ears, and the country was saddled with no less than twenty-seven censors, chosen from 'the good and the wise' – schoolmasters, lawyers, ministers of religion, doctors – those very professions reflected in the composition of the Home Office Committee on censorship established in 1977. They seem to have been no more effectual than their predecessors, although one of their victims was, predictably, Milton himself (his 'Defensio' was burned by the public hangman). The Lord Protector's protection was designed to save his subjects from political error rather than lusty thoughts, and the first statutory reference to censorship of erotica came in the early years of the Restoration, in the Licensing Act of 1662, which enjoined the licensers to refuse books 'contrary to good life or good manners'.[8] Milton's *Paradise Lost* almost fell victim in 1667, but only because it suggested that an eclipse of the sun 'with sudden fear of change perplexes monarchs'.[9] Licensing survived in a series of enactments until 1695, but the power to suppress 'offensive' books was rarely used against indecency. 'Chapbooks' – cheap and coarse tales sold on the London streets – readily received an imprimatur, and the robust works of Rochester, Dryden, Sedley and Congreve were not seriously impeded. Although Robert Stephens, the egregious 'Messenger of the Press' charged with ferreting out unlicensed publications, occasionally made bonfires of imported salacity, the whole force of the licensing system was aimed at subversion and irreligion. Political offenders were tortured, flogged, pilloried and executed.[10] But the licensing system, even when backed by such barbaric punishments, notably failed to stem the tide of subversive literature. A large black market developed, and in the reign of Charles II the Privy Council heard that two hundred thousand banned publications were in circulation. Some courageous publishers were even moved to complain on behalf of a reading public which was buying unlicensed books at a black-market rate of three times their value.[11] Moreover, by the time the system was abolished in 1695, the common-law courts were punishing blasphemy, sedition, heresy and criminal libel with such severity that the additional system of prior restraint was an unnecessary duplication. Licensing finally ended when Parliament uncovered widespread corruption in its operation. Fraud, extortion, favouritism and intimidation by licensers and their agents had made the whole system a scandal.[12]

The mid-sixteenth century saw the classic themes of hard core pornography committed to print. A new wave of literature written for the single purpose of titillation by means of erotic fantasy originated in Europe with the rise of 'Libertinism' in political thought, as a challenge to established authority. The emerging attacks on religious and social conventions produced explicit writing, obsessed with sexual orgies in mock-religious settings and with desecrating family life by using the theme of incest. Pornography

. . . had a well-defined starting-point and a very rapid development. We begin with *La Puttana Errante* about 1650 which turns the dialogue between whores from Aretino's satiric realism to an exposition of the means of sexual pleasure; but it is still based on the brothel. *L'Ecole des filles* in 1655 brings the subject into the private house, relating it to the realities of family life and also tying it to romantic love as against the conventions of society. By 1660 with Chorier's *Satyra sotadica* almost all the themes of later pornography are present; within a completely amoral attitude, in which all perversions are welcome if they gratify the senses, we have lesbian love, sodomy, seduction of the young and innocent, multiple copulation, flagellation and more subtle forms of sadism. But above all, these take place within a tightly-knit family circle, with the shocking suggestions that all the conventional relationships of society are merely a façade for personal gratification, into which even the local priest enters. This attempt to include the Church within the pattern is made explicit in *Venus dans le Cloître* of 1683 and other contemporary works.[13]

The Puritans may not have made their morality the law of England, but they left a legacy of shame and guilt about sexual pleasure which was never quite eradicated from the national conscience and which created consumer demand for the new pornography. Soon the first 'dirty old man' made his appearance, none other than Samuel Pepys, the diarist. On 13 January 1668, 'homeward by coach and stopped at Martin's, my bookseller, where I saw the French book which I did think to have had for my wife to translate, called *L'escholle des filles*, but when I came to look in it, it is the most bawdy lewd book that ever I saw, rather worse than *La Puttana errante*, so that I was ashamed of reading in it'. Curiosity soon got the better of indignation, however, and a few weeks later Pepys returned to the bookshop, and after browsing an hour, doubtless to pluck up courage, bought 'the idle, rogueish book ... in plain binding, because I resolve, as soon as I have read it, to burn it, that it may not stand in my list of books, nor among them, to disgrace them if it should be found'. The next day he was reading it avidly, excusing himself with the rationalization of many a subsequent researcher into the problem of pornography: 'a rightly lewd book, but yet not amiss for a sober man once to read over to inform himself in the villainy of the world.' That evening, after partaking of a 'mighty good store of wine' the diarist returned the task of educating himself about world villainy, a course of instruction which soon prompted him to masturbate, an activity which he recorded for posterity in guilty shorthand, and 'after I had done it, I burned it, that it might not be among my books to my shame'.[14] It was the classic reaction of a tired twentieth-century businessman: shock, curiosity, a surreptitious purchase, an eager perusal as soon as circumstances permit (with hypocritical self-justification about seeing how the other half lives), sexual excitement, masturbation, and then a sense of shame and embarrassment and a desire to disassociate –

at least for the present. The puritan legacy had ensured that pornography, if not strictly illegal, was frowned upon by those in authority.[15] Popular writers fulminated against the licentiousness of the stage, and in 1692 a society was founded, with royal patronage, pledged to the reformation of manners. It lauched a series of prosecutions for prostitution, drunkenness and breach of the Sabbath. There was still no law against written obscenity, but the groundswell had begun.

THE COMMON LAW

During the reign of Charles ii, the king's judges wrested control over disorderly conduct from the moribund ecclesiastical courts. To do so they asserted an inherent power, independent of Parliamentary or ecclesiastical authorization, of superintending public morality by punishing deviations from what they considered to be desirable standards of conduct. The watershed case, in 1663, involved the poet Sir Charles Sedley, who had been responsible for a breach of the peace one night in Covent Garden. Sedley and his fellow revellers, 'inflamed by strong liquors', had climbed to the balcony of the Cock Tavern, 'and putting down their breeches they excrementiz'd in the street: which being done, Sedley stripped himself naked, and with eloquence preached blasphemy to the people'.[16] A riot almost ensued, and some windows were broken – evidence of a breach of the King's Peace, and therefore appropriately tried by the Court of the King's Bench. But in rejecting Sedley's demands to be dealt with by the more lenient church courts, the Court of King's Bench announced that it possessed an inherent power to punish moral subversion, whether or not there was a judicial precedent or any law in force against the particular brand of immorality alleged. 'This court is the custodian of the morals of all the king's subjects,' the court ruled, 'and it is high time to punish such profane conduct.'[17] The poet was heavily fined, which allegedly moved him to complain that 'he thought he was the first man that paid for shitting'.

The surviving reports of the case are short and conflicting, and the evidence of public disturbance provided a settled ground for punishment without the need to create new law. Yet *Sedley's* case was to become the precedent for the creation by English judges of the offence of obscenity and the crime of conspiracy to corrupt public morals. In 1707 James Read was tried for publishing *The Fifteen Plagues of a Maidenhead*, a set of poetic variations on the theme that chastity was just another form of malnutrition. His conviction was quashed by the Court of King's Bench, where Mr Justice Powell reasoned that:

> This is for printing bawdy stuff, that reflects on no person, and a libel must be against some particular person or persons, or against the Government. It is stuff not fit to be mentioned publicly. If there is no remedy in the spiritual court, it does not follow there must be a remedy here. There is no law to punish it: I wish there were: but we cannot make law. It indeed tends to the corruption of good manners, but that is not sufficient for us to punish. As to the case of Sir Charles Sedley, there was something more in that case than shewing his naked body in the balcony.[18]

But twenty years later, the Court of King's Bench did a complete volte-face, and declared, on the authority of *Sedley*, that obscene libel *was* a crime at common law.

The man whose activities pushed the judges to overrule *Read's* case was Edmund Curl, the grubbiest publisher in Grub Street. Curl's bookshop, over a period of forty years, stocked many important literary and scientific works, as well as countless volumes of pornography, deceit and quackery written for him by badly paid hacks who 'lay three in a bed at the Platter Inn in Holborn'.[19] He ran London's first 'sex shop', vending patent medicines with miraculous properties, which he puffed in a book entitled 'The Charitable Surgeon. Being a new way of Curing (without Mercury) the several degrees of the venereal distemper in both sexes. . . . With a new discovery of the true seat of Claps in Men and Women. . . . Likewise the most certain easy way to escape infection, tho' never so often accompanying with the most polluted Companion.' Curl was execrated by Alexander Pope for his piracy of copyright, sharp practice and fraud, and for his mean treatment of his hacks, while Daniel Defoe raged against his 'lewd abominable pieces of bawdry. . . . What can be the reason why such a criminal goes unpunished?'[20] The reason, of course, was *Read's* case, in which the court had refused to recognize an offence of obscene libel. Curl replied to Defoe in a pamphlet, *Curlicism Displayed*, which constitutes the first reasoned defence of pornography on the grounds of public good. If vice exists, Curl argued, it was better to be open about it instead of sweeping it under the carpet, because forewarning forearmed the young against temptation. The extravagant detail in his *Treatise on the Use of Flogging in Venereal Affairs* was justified, he claimed, in the interests of science and learning, while his other studies in deviancy taught tolerance of minorities. Books were not obscene if they treat 'only of matters of the greatest importance to society', or conduce to 'the mutual happiness of the nuptial state' or are 'directly calculated for antidotes against debauchery and unnatural lewdness'.[21] For all his cocksure hypocrisy Curl might never have made his fateful contribution to English law had he been more politically astute. Twice he was personally reprimanded by the House of Lords for publishing unauthorized works which dealt with matters of state, and finally, in 1725, he was prosecuted for publishing an erotic book entitled *Venus in the Cloister, or The Nun in her Smock*. In the course of a long adjournment in the proceedings, Curl made the mistake of returning to publishing. A purported biography of a French prelate who had raped 133 virgins passed without notice, but the memoirs of a Government spy brought about his re-arrest for sedition. In 1727 he became the first Englishman to be convicted for publishing erotica, although his seditious words earned a heavier punishment.[22]

Curl's judges created a law of obscenity. They overruled *Read's* case and accepted the Attorney-General's submission that *Sedley* was authority for judicial legislation against any activity which 'tends to corrupt the morals of the King's subjects'. One judge, Mr Justice Fortescue, demurred: 'There should be a breach of the peace, or something tending to it, of which there is nothing in this case.' But the Attorney, Sir Philip Yorke, replied that the 'King's Peace' included 'good order and Government', which would be broken by disseminating immoral ideas without actual force. 'I do not insist that every criminal act is indictable, such as telling a lie . . . but if it is destructive of morality in general, if it does, or may, affect all of the King's subjects, it then is an offence of a public nature.' The court agreed: *Venus in the Cloister* was a book which tended to 'weaken the bonds of civil society, virtue and morality', and its publication was a common-law misdemeanour.[23]

At first the new crime brought no new prosecutions: it was not activated again until a much more serious political radical than Curl took the stage. In 1763 John Wilkes, whose popular polemics excoriated George III and his Ministers, privately circulated a robust parody of Pope, on the theme that '. . . life can little more supply/Than just a few good fucks, and then we die', and the misdemeanour of obscenity provided a ready-made excuse to silence him. This *Essay on Woman* was solemnly read to the House of Lords by Lord Sandwich, a casualty of the publisher's polemics, and when one peer protested the others shouted 'Go on, go on'. They ultimately resolved that the poem was 'a most scandalous, obscene and impious libel'. In the same year the principle of *Curl's* case, namely that the courts had an inherent power to punish immorality, was reasserted in a case in which Sir Francis Deleval was convicted of conspiring to debauch a consenting eighteen-year-old girl apprenticed to him for music lessons. Lord Mansfield ruled: 'This court is the *custos morum* of the people, and has the superintendency of offences *contra bonos mores*, and upon this ground both Sir Charles Sedley and Curl, who had been guilty of offences against good manners, were prosecuted here.'[24] In 1774, while holding that a wager laid on the result of an appeal to the House of Lords was not contrary to 'good manners or policy' Lord Mansfield repeated that, 'Whatever is against good morality and decency, the principles of our law prohibit, and the King's Court as the general censor and guardian of the public morals is bound to restrain and punish.'[25]

These statements of judicial policy lay dormant in ancient law reports until 1961, when the House of Lords judges disinterred them as precedents for punishing a man named Shaw, who had published a *Who's Who* of London prostitutes.[26] But at the same time that Lord Mansfield was asserting this egregious doctrine, directories of prostitutes were freely circulating in London. The Egon Ronay, so to speak, of these guides was Harris, who published an annual *List of Covent Garden Ladies*. His *Man of Pleasure's Kalender for the year 1788*, for example, was a work 'containing the Histories and some curious anecdotes of the most celebrated Ladies on the Town, or in Keeping, and also Many of their Keepers'. Harris was nothing if not critical. Mrs Howard, of No. 14 Moors Place, Lambeth, had 'contracted such an habit of intimacy with the gin bottle, that unless a person is particularly partial to it, it is almost intolerable to approach her', while Miss Clicamp, of 2 York Street, was at least 'fortunate for the true lovers of fat, should fate throw them into the possession of such full-grown beauties'. But his connoisseur's eye was not blind to the charms of such ladies as Miss Wilkinson, of 10 Bull-and-Mouth Street, which included

a pair of sweet pouting lips that demand the burning kiss, and never receive it without paying with interest; a complexion that would charm the eye of an anchorite ... Descend a little lower and behold the semi-snow-balls ... that want not the support of stays; whose truly elastic state never suffers the pressure, however severe, to remain, but boldly recovers its tempting smoothness. Next take a view of nature *centrally*; no *folding lapel*, no *gaping orifice*, no *horrid gulph* is here, but the *loving lips* tenderly kiss each other, and shelter from the cold a small but easily stretched passage, whose *depth* none but the *blind boy* has liberty to fathom; She is a native of Oxfordshire, and has been a visitor on the town about one year, is generally to be met with at home at every hour excepting ten at night, at which time she visits a favourite gentleman of the Temple.

Shaw's *Ladies' Directory* of 1959 was coy and pallid by comparison. Potential customers of 'Miss Fetishe', who plied her trade from an address in the Charing Cross Road, were laconically informed: 'Age 24. 43-25-37. Theatrical wardrobe available. Shoes, rubber hosiery, etc.' None the less, Shaw was sentenced to nine months in prison for conspiring to corrupt the morals of a public which was assumed to be a good deal more intolerant of prostitution than the gentlemen of Lord Mansfield's days.

The law of obscene libel created by the judges in 1727 failed to make an impact on the circulation of erotica. Sexual deviations which now attract prosecution if detailed in print were openly discussed. As early as 1676 an elderly libertine in Thomas Shadwell's play *The Virtuoso* is questioned about his bent for flagellation: 'I wonder that should please you so much, that pleases me so little?' asks his ingenuous strumpet. 'I was so us'd to't at Westminster School I could never leave it off since', comes the first recorded explanation of *le vice anglais*. By the middle of the eighteenth century the classic of English pornography, *Fanny Hill*, was on sale, with its lurid, if decorous, descriptions of rape, sodomy, flagellation and most other forms of sexual deviation. John Cleland (another Westminster graduate) wrote the book in debtors' prison, and it passed through several editions before it was noticed by certain influential bishops, who secured the arrest of author, printer and publisher. Cleland excused his work as the necessity of 'my present low abject condition, that of a writer for bread', and reminded his ecclesiastical persecutors that 'more clergymen bought it, in proportion, than any other distinction of men'. He pleaded sensibly for his co-accused, who had been misled by the absence of four-letter words: 'they certainly were deceived by my avoiding those rank words in the work, which are all that they judge of obscenity by, and made them think the line was drawn between them, and all danger of law whatever'. Cleland also pointed to a moral which the Director of Public Prosecutions would have done well to remember before seeking to destroy the book two hundred and fifteen years later: 'they can take no step towards punishing the Author that will not powerfully contribute to the notoriety of the Book.... Why slept this zeal so long? and waked not but till the Book had had its run, and is dying of itself, unless they choose to give it new life?'[27]

Social change, not legal action, was ultimately to proscribe porno-graphy. By the end of the eighteenth century shame and guilt about sex, inculcated by the Puritans and emphasized in the sermons of the evangelical revival, had caused a Christian recoil from sensual pleasure. The spread of literacy meant that books were no longer the entertainment of a sophisticated elite: the middle classes were read-ing, and more alarmingly, so were their wives and children. Violence and vulgarity had run their course, and now virtue and sentimentality were in vogue. 'Good manners' were offended by licentious writing. Macaulay summed up the change since the abolition of licensing in 1695:

> During a hundred and sixty years the liberty of our press has been becoming more and more entire; and during those hundred and sixty years the restraint imposed on writers by the general feeling of readers has been becoming more and more strict. At length even that class of works in which it was formerly thought that a voluptuous imagination was privileged to disport itself, love songs, comedies, novels, have become more decorous than the sermons of the seventeenth century. At this day (1855) foreigners, who dare not print a word reflecting on the government under which they live, are at a loss to understand how it happens that the freest press in Europe is the most prudish.[28]

The stage was now set for this improvement in 'good manners' to receive its expression in the courts. Political power was slowly devolv-ing to the new middle class, the hard-working Christians who had chartered an Industrial Revolution which required sobriety, toil and obedience from the working classes. 'Propriety' became a watchword, and prudishness meant a determination to enforce propriety. In 1787 George III issued a proclamation against vice, which urged the sup-pression of 'all loose and licentious prints, books, and publications, dis-pensing poison to the minds of the young and unwary, and to punish the publishers and the vendors thereof'. William Wilberforce founded the Proclamation Society, replaced in 1802 by the Society for the Sup-pression of Vice – dubbed by Sydney Smith as 'a society for suppress-ing the vices of those whose incomes do not exceed £500 per annum'.[29] Its formation marks the turning point in the history of English obscenity law, and ushers in one hundred and seventy-five years of unremitting legal battles against the purveyors of 'corruption'.

THE VICTORIAN LEGACY

Between 1802 and 1857 the Society for the Suppression of Vice in-stituted 159 prosecutions, all but five of them successful, which

brought jail sentences averaging eight months to a variety of Holywell
Street booksellers and publishers.[30] In 1824 it secured the passing of
the Vagrancy Act, which penalized the public sale or display of
obscene or indecent material. The Society and its officers served as
an amateur Obscene Publications Squad, their puritan zeal overcom-
ing the procedural difficulties which hampered routine police action.
The Society was convinced that Britain stood in peril of continental
pollution. Its Secretary, testifying before a Parliamentary Committee
in 1817, described how pornography was dispersed to the provinces
by no less than six hundred hawkers, chiefly Italian. The Society's
evidence was heard with respect: its campaign at the time was against
indecent snuff-boxes, which were apparently being circulated in the
best boarding schools for young ladies, rendering 'the wholesome
seminaries of female education the scenes of pollution and vice'.[31] The
Society had no doubts that pornography caused sex crimes, at least
when it fell into the hands of the working class. Prosecuting John Rich
in 1809 for selling *The Quintessence of Birch Discipline*, counsel claimed
that the effect of the book would be 'to incite and encourage (readers)
to indecent practices and the commission of crimes against nature and
particularly the crime of bestiality'.[32] Lord Ellenborough agreed, and
sentenced Rich to stand in the pillory and then to serve a term of
two years' imprisonment. The Society courted some adverse publicity
for its obsession with blasphemy, but obscenity prosecutions met with
official favour. Unlike blasphemy cases, they were in the main
directed at worthless books, and full-blooded defences were rare. The
Society's worst defeat came in 1822, when it prosecuted William
Benbow for publishing the popular *Rambler* magazine. Benbow's
counsel secured an acquittal by excoriating the hypocrisy of private
prosecutors:

It was the bounden duty of the gentlemen of the jury to put a stop to these
self-elected prosecutors, and to teach them that Englishmen were not to be
treated thus with impunity. In the name of God! where were the law officers
of the Crown? Were they so careless of their duty, that they left the scrutiny
of these works to the Vice Society? These were your Christian champions!
These were your pretenders to Christianity! It would be well if they opened
the sacred volume, and perused it; and they would there learn that it teaches
forgiveness – not persecution. Christians! – Pharisees! These were your vice.
suppressors, who had joined their funds to drag to the bar of justice poor
men, who, even if acquitted, must be ruined by the enormous expense of the
law.... Let him that was not guilty throw the first stone; but let not men
whose only virtue was in their purse, assume to themselves a power the law

gave them not. In the hands of the Jury he left his client, for they were the only protectors of the poor man against the powerful coalition of the rich.[33]

The Society for the Suppression of Vice, despite its success with judges and magistrates, failed to suppress pornography, or even to keep it from public view. In Holywell Street twenty bookshops were flourishing in 1857. In that year a new champion of virtue intervened, and secured the first Parliamentary action against obscene publications. It was in the course of a debate on the Poisons Act that the Lord Chief Justice, Lord Campbell, announced his intention of bringing in an Obscene Publications Bill:

> He was happy to say that he believed that the administration of poison by design had received a check. But from a trial which had taken place before him on Saturday, he had learned with horror and alarm that a sale of poison more deadly than prussic and strychnine or arsenic – the sale of obscene publications and indecent books – was going on.[34]

His Obscene Publications Bill contained no definition of obscenity, and was primarily concerned with establishing a procedure for the destruction of obscene literature. Magistrates were empowered to issue search warrants on being shown a suspicious book; the prosecutor, armed with the warrant, was entitled to raid the premises of printer, publisher or bookseller, seize any books he could find, and bring them back to the magistrate, who could order their destruction if he felt that publication would be 'a misdemeanor proper to be prosecuted'. These 'forfeiture' proceedings were not strictly criminal – no penalty could be imposed on the vendor other than the cost of the literature destroyed – and the burden of proving that the material was not obscene lay on the bookseller.[35] Because the magistrate who heard the case was usually the magistrate who had issued the summons, destruction orders were in practice virtually impossible to resist, as the publishers of *The Rainbow* and *The Well of Loneliness* discovered to their cost in the next century. The new system was a boon to prosecuting authorities and the vice-suppression societies, who could thereafter proudly boast of the tonnage of literature which had been consigned to the flames by their efforts. But to put a pornographer in prison, the prosecutor had to give the publisher the option of trial by jury and had to prove the obscenity of his books beyond a reasonable doubt. The House of Commons inserted two further safeguards before enacting the Bill: a right of appeal to a judge at Quarter Sessions and a requirement that the prosecutor prove that the offending book was actually for sale to the public. Lord Campbell acquiesced in these amendments, and looked forward to a time 'when Holywell Street would become the abode of honest, industrious handicraftsmen and a thoroughfare through which any modest woman might pass'. The dirty booksellers gradually moved north, to Leicester Square, Charing Cross Road, and finally to Soho. Holywell Street became in time the premises of the Australian High Commission.

Lord Campbell's Act encountered strong opposition in both Houses of Parliament. Lords Lyndhurst and Brougham thought the existing law adequate, and feared for the fate of Restoration dramatists, Renaissance art and the poetry of Ovid at the hands of benighted magistrates. One Scottish MP condemned it as 'an attempt to make people virtuous by Act of Parliament. A man who had a taste for the class of prints and publications referred to in the Bill would get them in spite of all the laws they could pass.'[36] In an attempt to satisfy his critics, Lord Campbell assured the House that the measure was not intended to apply to works of art or literature, but 'exclusively to works written for the single purpose of corrupting the morals of youth and of a nature calculated to shock the common feelings of decency in a well regulated mind'. Not only would it apply exclusively to salacious material, but only to the work of authors who deliberately set out to corrupt – 'people who designedly and industriously manufactured books and prints with the intention of corrupting morals ...'[37] Lord Lyndhurst wisely reminded him that an act of Parliament does not mean what its sponsors intend it to mean, but what later generations of judges want it to mean. Predictably, the literature repressed in leading cases proved to be the very stuff which Lord Campbell had disclaimed any desire to censor.

The task of defining obscenity fell to his successor as Lord Chief Justice, Sir Alexander Cockburn, in an 1868 case, *R.* v. *Hicklin*, which arose from religious bigotry rather than commercial greed. The Protestant Electoral Union, pledged to the abolition of the 1828 Catholic Emancipation Act, had encouraged the publication of a work entitled *The Confessional Unmasked* – a crude piece of anti-Popish propaganda which purported to reveal techniques used by priests to extract erotic confessions from female penitents, with the usual wealth of collaborative detail. Copies of this work (bound in a cover which depicted the Pope unleashing a dragon upon chaste Britannia) were seized from the premises of an evangelical Wolverhampton metal broker, who purposed to sell them without profit to like-minded Anglicans. The Quarter Sessions recorder found that the volume was obscene because its indiscriminate circulation would injure public morals, but he considered that the defendant's actions were redeemed by his innocent motive. This ruling was reviewed, as a point of law, by the Queen's Bench Division of the High Court, which decided that a man who publishes a book in circumstances where he must reasonably know that it is obscene commits an offence, even if his motive is pure. But the case of *R. v. Hicklin* owes its epoch-making quality to one passing judicial comment which has survived the passage of time and which returns regularly to plague the courts and parliaments of England, America and the common-law world:

> I think the test of obscenity is this, whether the tendency of the matter charged as obscenity is to deprave and corrupt those whose minds are open to such immoral influences, and into whose hands a publication of this sort may fall.[38]

Armed at last with a definition of obscenity, Victorian prosecutors proceeded to destroy many examples of fine literature and scientific speculation. The sting of the new definition was in its tail: depravity and corruption were to be judged, not by a book's effect on its most likely readership, but upon those susceptible persons – children, psychopaths, women, the working class – whose minds were assumed to be open to immoral literature, and into whose hands any publication might one day conceivably fall. This extended test could be applied to purple passages in great literature, as well as to respectably written passages in scientific or philosophical criticism of accepted truths. The impact of the *Hicklin* test was demonstrated by the fate of *The Fruits of Philosophy – An Essay on the Population Problem*, a work which had been freely available since 1834. It offended Victorian moral precepts because it advocated birth control, rather than chastity, as the remedy for overpopulation. In 1876 a destruction order was made, lest its argument convince some susceptible reader to practice birth control. James Bradlaugh and Annie Besant republished it and dared the Government to indict them: 'since progress can only be made through discussion, we claim the right to publish all opinions so that the public may have the material for forming a sound judgement'.[39] The Solicitor-General, Sir Hardinge Giffard, obliged, and told the jury that the book 'tended to create morbid feelings and lead to unlawful practices' – particularly amongst the poor, who could obtain it at 6d a copy. The Chief Justice thought the prosecution ill-advised and counter-productive: 'Here is a work which has been published for more than forty years and which appears never to have got into general circulation and which by these injudicious proceedings has got into large circulation so that the sale has suddenly risen by thousands.'[40] But he repeated his *Hicklin* view that however well-intentioned the defendants, their guilt was established if they must have known that publication would challenge the moral fabric of Victorian society.[41] The jury did not understand the import of the Chief Justice's summing-up, and returned with a 'special plea', which they had not intended to operate as a conviction: 'We find that the book is calculated to corrupt public morals, but we entirely exonerate the defendants from any corrupt motives in publishing it.' 'That,' announced Lord Cockburn, 'is a verdict of guilty.' Two mortified jurors sent contributions to the defence costs, and the conviction was subsequently quashed by the Court of Appeal on a technicality: the prosecution had omitted to set out the offending passages in the indictment, and 'the only result of the prolonged proceedings was that the circulation of *The Fruits of Philosophy* rose from a few hundred a year to one hundred and twenty thousand'.[42]

The Court of Appeal's verdict did have, however, the result of spoiling the summer of a future Liberal Prime Minister. Mr Asquith, in 1888 an eager junior prosecuting counsel, recalls how he spent 'the best part of a fortnight in the Long Vacation, with scissors and a pot of paste at hand, in a diligent quest for the most objectionable passages in M. Zola's voluminous works'.[43] His zeal was at the request of the National Vigilance Association, an organization which combined puritanism with xenophobia in its efforts to suppress French classics. Its target was Henry Vizetelly, an eminent bookseller who had brought the work of Longfellow and Edgar Allan Poe to the British public. He was duly charged with 'uttering and publishing certain obscene libels, to wit, certain books entitled *La Terre* by Emile Zola, *Madame Bovary* by Gustave Flaubert, *Sappho* by Alphonse Daudet, *Bel-Ami* by Guy de Maupassant, and *Mademoiselle de Maupin* by Théophile Gautier, against the peace of Our Sovereign Lady the Queen, her Crown and Dignity'. A fortnight before the trial Zola was appointed to the French Legion of Honour for his services to literature and freedom, but this failed to assuage the injured dignity of the English Crown. 'A voluminous French author,' sneered the Solicitor-General. 'A *popular* French author,' remarked the judge. Asquith's summer of smut-spotting won the day: his purple passages, set down out of context in the indictment, so offended one juryman that he jumped to his feet and demanded that they should not be read in open court. Confronted with this depth of prejudice before the trial had even begun, Vizetelly threw in his hand and pleaded guilty, receiving a £100 fine. *The Times* gloated that 'In future, anyone who publishes translations of Zola's novels and works of similar character will do so at his peril, and must not expect to escape so easily as Mr Vizetelly.'[44] It was right, of course. Next year Mr Vizetelly himself, a sick man of seventy, was jailed for three months for publishing further books by Zola and de Maupassant.

The rabid fears engendered by the trials of Oscar Wilde deprived Havelock Ellis of a reputable British publisher for *Sexual Inversion*, his pioneering study of homosexuality, although a Leipzig edition had been critically acclaimed in Europe. In 1897 the work was accepted by a pornographer named de Villiers, working under the dubious imprint of 'The Watford University Press'. Reputable booksellers were also running scared, and only a radical named Bedborough was prepared to stock the book. His ensuing prosecution rallied progressive thinkers, and a defence committee which included George Bernard Shaw, George Moore and Edward Carpenter raised funds to brief a leading counsel and to provide expert medical evidence of the book's undoubted scientific value. At the door of the court Bedborough panicked at the prospect of a prison sentence and agreed to a deal with the police: in return for a bind-over order, he would plead guilty. The Recorder, Sir Charles Hall, approved: it would be impossible to contend that the book was not 'filthy and obscene – you might at the first outset perhaps have been gulled into the belief that somebody might say that this was a scientific work. But it is impossible for anybody with a head on his shoulders to open the book without seeing it is a pretence and a sham. . . .'[45] The eminent scientists waiting in the corridor were not given their chance to gull an Old Bailey jury – and the contentious issue of the admissibility of expert testimony was left to another generation of judges.

The suppression of *Sexual Inversion* completed the legal edifice of Victorian moral hypocrisy. The obscenity law forbade any work of literature, science or art in which any isolated passage would arouse sexual desire or challenge prevailing public morality. The Victorian 'cordon sanitaire' was rounded off by the Vagrancy Act of 1824, the Post Office Act of 1853 and the Customs Consolidation Act of 1876, which collectively prohibited the display, posting or importation of 'indecent' material. In 1888 press reports were shrouded by the cloak of the Law of Libel Amendment Act, which rendered newspapers liable to prosecution if they quoted blasphemous or obscene passages which had been read in open court. These laws were in turn bolstered by suffocating institutional censorship exercised by lending libraries and the book distributors. Charles Mudie's monopoly of libraries and W.H. Smith's control of railway bookstalls endowed them with formidable powers of commercial censorship. No new novel was worth publishing if they refused to stock it – and they were particularly sensitive to complaints from old ladies in the provinces. This was the very reason given to George Moore by Smith himself (described by Lord Campbell in the debate on the 1857 Act as 'a truly Christian gentleman utterly incapable of doing an unworthy act') for the refusal to stock his books. Moore was furious:

> Let us renounce the effort to reconcile these two irreconcileable things – art and young girls ... all I ask is that some means may be devised by which the novelist will be allowed to describe the moral and religious feeling of his day as he perceives it to exist, and to be forced no longer to write with a view of helping parents and guardians to bring up their charges in all the traditional beliefs.[46]

While the eyes of the nanny were looking over the shoulder of the serious novelist, the ugliest pornography was flourishing behind her back. Lord Campbell's hopes for the rehabilitation of Holywell Street were shortlived: eleven years later the *Saturday Review* noted that 'the dunghill is in full heat, seething and steaming with its old pestilence', as bookshops openly displayed obscene publications. Despite the new law, pornography thrived in the Victorian underworld as never before. Repression was all on the surface, and even the Vice society was moved to lament that 'unfortunately a long experience has shown that, though the vigorous enforcement of the law is for a time attended with the best effects, offences of this class always have a tendency to revive'.[47] This was the time of the great *œuvres* of Victorian prurience: *The New Lady's Tickler* (1860), *Lady Bumtickler's Revels* (1872), *Colonel Spanker's Experimental Lecture* (1879), *The Story of a Dildoe* (1880), *My Secret Life* (1885), not to mention one classic entitled *Raped on the Railway: A True Story of a Lady who was first ravished and then flagellated on the Scotch Express* (1894). Such titles found a new and avid readership as illiteracy declined from thirty per cent in 1861 to an estimated five per cent in 1893. These new readers required the protection of the obscenity law. In the first twentieth-century obscenity case, the Common Sergeant of the Old Bailey could confidently assert that a book which sold at 1s 11d would 'clearly tend to the corruption of morals ... In the Middle Ages things were discussed which if put forward now for the reading of the general public would never be tolerated.'[48]

TWENTIETH-CENTURY CASES

The twentieth century began hopefully, with a Joint Select Committee reporting in 1908 in favour of rational law reform.[49] The various censorship statutes should be replaced with one consolidated Act, carrying graduated penalties: a fine of £30 or three months' imprisonment for a first offence, and in the case of sale to persons under sixteen or a second offence, a penalty of £100 or six months' imprisonment. An exception was recommended for any book of genuine merit or high repute. The report was ignored, however, and in 1915 one thousand copies of D.H. Lawrence's *The Rainbow* were destroyed by a Bow Street magistrate who regretted that Methuen & Co. 'should have allowed their reputation to be soiled as it had been by the publication of this work'.[50] Methuen did not even bother to defend the book, but abjectly apologized to the court for the author's tastelessness. Lawrence was dogged by the timidity of his patrons – in 1929 fourteen verses were excised from his poetry book *Pansies* at the insistence of the Director of Public Prosecutions, and in the same year the police seized thirteen of his pictures, in which they had descried some traces of pubic hair.[51] This episode stimulated Lawrence's remarkable essay on *Pornography and Obscenity*. Recalling those 'dainty policemen in a picture show', who ignored the meaning of art in their search for 'a fragment of human pudenda', he railed against 'the shadow of the grey elderly ones who belong to the last century, the eunuch century, the century of the mealy-mouthed lie, the century that has tried to destroy humanity, the nineteenth century. All our grey ones are left over from this century. And they rule us.' They extended their rule into the civil courts when the maxim 'he who comes to Equity must come with clean hands' was applied to deny protection to Miss Elinor Glyn's copyright in her book *Three Weeks*:

> The episode depicted in the plaintiff's novel, which she alleges has been pirated by the defendants, is, in my opinion, grossly immoral both in its essence, its treatment and its tendency. Stripped of its trappings, which are mere accident, it is nothing more nor less than a sensual, adulterous intrigue ... it is enough for me to say that to a book of such a cruelly destructive tendency no protection will be extended by a court of equity.[52]

Another 'elderly grey one' was Sir Archibald Bodkin, the DPP from 1920 to 1930. He described a work by Freud as 'filth', and threatened Allen & Unwin with prosecution unless its circulation was restricted to those doctors, lawyers and university dons who were prepared to give their names and addresses when purchasing the book.[53] *Ulysses* was another work of 'indescribable filth', and police were ordered to investigate a young Cambridge don named F.R. Leavis who had presumed to request importation of a copy for teaching purposes. They infiltrated his lectures, with instructions to note the number of women in attendance.[54] In 1923 Bodkin was the British delegate to a League of Nations conference on the international traffic in pornography, where he argued heatedly against any definition of the material which the nations of the world were pledging themselves to suppress. He boasted that under his own country's supple definition of obscenity he had secured the imprisonment of two people who had merely swapped pornography between themselves.

The most celebrated obscenity case of the period was instituted by Bodkin and the Home Secretary, Sir William Joynson-Hicks. It involved *The Well of Loneliness*, a novel by Radclyffe Hall which described lesbian attraction. The book was published by Jonathan Cape in 1928, and received glowing reviews: it was 'sincere, courageous, high-minded and often beautifully expressed' (*Times Literary Supplement*) and 'honest, convincing and extremely courageous' (Arnold Bennett). More courageous, in the event, than its publishers, who took fright when the pompous sensationalist James Douglas in his *Sunday Express* column condemned it as 'a seductive and insidious piece of special pleading designed to display perverted decadence as a martyrdom ... I would rather put a phial of prussic acid in the hands of a healthy girl or boy than the book in question....' Cape wrote to the Home Secretary and offered to withdraw the book if he so desired. The desires of Joynson-Hicks, president of the National Church League which was engaged at the time in a crusade against a new Anglican prayer book, were predictable, and Cape cravenly complied. But then, in a fit of bravado, or perhaps a wish to make some money out of the publicity, the publishers sent the plates to a Parisian subsidiary, so that copies might appear in Britain under a different imprint. They did so, and were duly seized by order of the Bow Street magistrate, Sir Charles Biron. The defence rallied some serious literary figures, although the defence solicitor later remarked how most popular writers 'almost with one accord made it clear that they were not going to risk their reputations by showing sympathy with an unpopular cause'.[55] The trial itself was forensically notable for a rare display of incompetence by Norman Birkett KC, who opened dishonestly for the defence by claiming that the book was not about lesbianism at all. The relations between the women 'repre-

sented a normal friendship'. Over the luncheon adjournment he was
assailed by Radclyffe Hall, weeping 'tears of heart-broken anguish'
at his legal perversion of her theme.[56] That afternoon Birkett made
his second blunder. Instead of calling his experts to testify to the merit
of the book, he asked his first witness 'In your view is it obscene?'
This question was inadmissible on any view of the law, because it
entailed an answer to the very question that the court had to decide.
The magistrate rightly excluded it, and Birkett was not allowed to
call thirty-nine other eminent writers. The book was duly declared
obscene because it 'glorified unnatural tendencies ... there is not
one word which suggests that anyone with the horrible tendencies
described is in the least degree blameworthy. All the characters are
presented as attractive people and put forward with admiration.
What is even more serious is that certain acts are described in the
most alluring terms.'[57] In the magistrate's eyes, Miss Prism's dictum
was to be the legal straitjacket for the modern novel: 'The good end
happily, and the bad unhappily. That is what Fiction means.'[58]

The Government was committed to the book's suppression, and the
Attorney-General led for the prosecution when the Appeal came to
Quarter Sessions. Sir Thomas Inskip could think of only one other
reference in English literature to the 'vile affection': St Paul's epistle
to the Romans. The *Hicklin* test, he argued, was conclusive: 'the young
of either sex' and some 'persons of advanced years' would be struck
by 'thoughts of the most impure character' when they considered the
one sentence in the book which actually suggested sexual behaviour:
'And that night they were not divided'. 'What does this *mean*?', he
asked rhetorically. 'Imagine a poor woman or young man reading
it. What is the picture conjured up at once? The man would ask:
"What does this woman mean?" It corrupts him, conjures up a
picture, which the writer of the book intends.... The book seeks to
glorify a vice or to produce a plea of toleration for those who practise
it.... It is propaganda.' The conviction was confirmed, and the
book was not published in England until 1949. Three other well-
reviewed novels were declared obscene in its wake: *Sleeveless Errand*
(1929), *Boy* (1931) and *Bessie Cotten* (1935). In the last two cases,
defence lawyers advised their clients to plead guilty and accept fines,
rather than run the risk of imprisonment. Outlining the case against
Heinemann at the Old Bailey over *Bessie Cotten*, the Attorney-General
explained that, 'the book deals with what everybody will recognize
as an unsavoury subject – gratification of sexual appetite'.[59]

The most bizarre defendant to an obscenity charge in this period was the eccentric bohemian poet Count Geoffrey Wladislas Vaile Potocki de Montalk, who claimed to be the uncrowned King of Poland. In 1932 he sought to publish privately, for the amusement of his friends, a few parodies of Verlaine entitled *Here Lies John Penis*, but his shocked printer reported him to the police. His rhymes had the misfortune to be considered by the Old Bailey Recorder, Sir Ernest Wild, who had the previous year himself published verses of 'unbelievable banality' entitled *The Lamp of Destiny*.[60] After an altercation over the oath (de Montalk insisted upon swearing by Apollo, an affirmation never heard before or since in English courts) the Recorder asked the jury: 'Are you going to allow a man, just because he calls himself a poet, to deflower our English language by popularizing these words? A man may not say he is a poet and be filthy. He has to obey the law just the same as ordinary citizens, and the sooner the highbrow school learns that, the better for the morality of our country.' The jury took the hint, and convicted. But what penalty fitted the crime of raping the English language?

SIR ERNEST WILD: 'Can't you suggest what punishment you think you deserve?'

DE MONTALK: 'Yes, My Lord. I think I deserve to be sentenced to several years in Buckingham Palace.'[61]

The poet was indeed made a guest of Her Majesty, but in the less exalted confines of Wormwood Scrubs prison. The Court of Appeal saw no reason to interfere with his six months' sentence, despite the intercession of T.S. Eliot, Laurence Housman, Aldous Huxley, Walter De la Mare, J.B. Priestley, Hugh Walpole and H.G. Wells. The highbrow school had been warned.

There were other straws in the legal wind, however, which presaged a more rational approach to the obscenity law. In *Montalk's case*, the Recorder had at least acknowledged that: '... it would be a defence in this case if the thing was done for the public good. ... as an advancement of literature. ...'[62] and in 1935, when a destruction order was sought against a sex education text, *The Sexual Impulse*, Professors Malinowski, J.B.S. Haldane and Julian Huxley were permitted to testify to its medical and psychological value. (Their evidence did nothing to dispel the bigotry of the magistrate, a Mr Rowland Powell, who found that the book was 'reckless of desirable convention' and not 'fit and decent for people of the working class to read'.) In 1936 a new Attorney-General, Sir Donald Somerville KC, interpreted the law in a much more liberal fashion than strict precedent would justify when he directed the DPP and the postal and Customs authorities to take no action against James Joyce's *Ulysses*. (He may have been influenced by the fact that a sumptuously bound copy of the book had been found among the personal effects of a former Lord Chancellor, Birkenhead, on his death in 1930, and only the intervention of a High Court judge had prevented its sale at public auction.) According to the official minutes of the meeting between the Attorney and the Director,

In his (Somerville's) view the question of intention has to be taken into account as in criminal law generally: the context has also to be considered. No one today would, he thought, be found to hold that such books as those of Havelock Ellis on sexual matters were obscene, nor any medical book dealing with sexual aberrations. Standards in these matters were constantly changing – as conventions and taste changed.

If he were challenged in the House of Commons his answer would be on the line that it was a well established principle of law that the intention of a writer had to be taken into account as well as the general setting or context of the book. On applying these tests to *Ulysses* he was of the opinion that the book was not obscene and having regard, in addition, to its established position now in literature he had decided to take no action.[63]

This act of administrative enlightenment removed one masterpiece from the list of 'The Obelisk Press', founded in Paris in 1931 by Jack Kahane with the object of republishing all worthwhile books which had been declared obscene in England, together with others (such as Cyril Connelly's *The Rock Pool*, Lawrence Durrell's *The Black Book*, the novels of Henry Miller and Frank Harris's *My Life and Loves*) which timid British publishers had turned down. 'Hard-core' pornography continued its clandestine availability, but the wisdom of censoring it was gradually being called into question. For example in 1929 Bertrand Russell announced that 'Even frank pornography would do less harm if it were open and unashamed than it does when it is rendered interesting by secrecy and stealth. . . . Nine-tenths of the appeal of pornography is due to indecent feelings concerning sex which moralists inculcate in the young; the other tenth is physiological, and will occur in one way or another whatever the state of the law may be.'[64]

In 1942 came the first 'modern' obscenity trial. It concerned a book about sex written for working people by Dr Eustace Chesser, a psychiatrist and gynaecologist who had practised during the Depression in the slum area of Manchester. *Love without Fear* was a straightforward explanation of sexual behaviour, together with common-sense reassurance about practices which Chesser had found to be common among his patients, but productive nonetheless of debilitating guilt, shame and neurosis. After five thousand copies had been sold, the DPP ordered his arrest, with the object not merely of destroying the book – any magistrate would have obliged in that course, as *The Sexual Impulse* case had shown – but of branding Chesser and his publishers as criminals, and placing them at risk of a jail sentence. Chesser stood and fought, with the assistance of three medical witnesses who, like himself, had been engaged in giving sexual counsel to the poor. The prosecutor was Mr Byrne (later the judge in the *Lady Chatterley* trial), and the outcome hinged upon the effect of Chesser's own evidence.

What had caused him to write *Love without Fear*? 'One cannot be in practice for long without realizing that the physical ailments of most people are nothing as compared with mental troubles and difficulties. A large proportion, if not the greatest proportion, of these mental difficulties are the direct result of sexual difficulties.' In his industrial practice, he had discovered 'an utter lack of knowledge ... I felt that these sexual difficulties would, in a great many cases, never have arisen if there had been anything like a proper amount of sex teaching or sex books ... my whole object was to make this understandable by the ordinary man'. Why had he included information about sexual deviations, like flagellation, lesbianism and what the prosecutor delicately termed 'kissing extended down to the thighs'? 'None of us like to feel that we are absolutely unique, and that we stand alone in possibly having a sex deviation or abnormality. If, on the other hand, on reading a book like this, patients find that there are quite a large number of people suffering from it, they are much more likely to seek aid than they might otherwise be.' But was it really necessary to be so explicit, and so down to earth? 'If I use Latin words, then you do not even know what part of your anatomy it refers to. You must be given something which describes your sexual organs to you and describes what happens during congress.'[65]

The jury took less than an hour to acquit, and the verdict proved a landmark in the struggle of sex education against the obscenity laws. For the next three decades Dr Eustace Chesser wrote books which brought sexual enlightenment to millions of ordinary people. In 1972, exactly thirty years after his own ordeal, he took his revenge on obscenity law and the Director of Public Prosecutions. He became the first expert to stand in a witness box and testify to the therapeutic effect of pornography. The case, *R.* v. *Gold*, was a prosecution under the 1959 Act of four 'soft porn' magazines, whose colourful fantasies were alleged to 'put ideas in readers' heads, and encourage them to experiment with sex techniques they might otherwise never have considered'. In vain did the judge remind the jurors of the fate of the Roman Empire: the defendants were acquitted on all counts.[66] Chesser's evidence, which substantially repeated his 1942 arguments, ushered in a short but significant era in which British courtrooms resounded to the claim by doctors and psychiatrists that publication of pornography was 'for the public good' under section 4 of the 1959 Act, because of its liberating and therapeutic effect on readers.

THE MOVE FOR REFORM

The 'modern' attitude towards sexuality dawned with the *Kinsey Report*, published in 1948.[67] Lionel Trilling placed the new art of intimate opinion polling in cool perspective:

> The Report will surprise one part of the population with some facts and another part with other facts, but really all that it says to society as a whole is that there is an almost universal involvement in the sexual life and therefore much variety of conduct. This was taken for granted in any comedy that Aristophanes put on the stage.[68]

That is as maybe, but exhaustive tabulations of private morality force recalculations of public morality. The behavioural statistics of Kinsey, followed by the laboratory researches of Masters and Johnson, demonstrated that the unmentionable was not necessarily the unconventional. Censorship of writing about sexual practices had not stopped individuals from practising, although it had engendered some neurosis and many feelings of guilt and anxiety. Some 'perversions' were so widespread that they could not longer be objectively classified as 'perverse'. Clandestine availability of erotica could hardly be blamed: according to Kinsey only two per cent of boys obtained sexual knowledge from printed matter, while over ninety per cent received their information from conversations with male companions. A scientific imprimatur was accorded to the blindingly obvious by one solemn survey of American college girls. When asked what they found most sexually stimulating, the majority replied 'Men'.

What was the DPP to make of the discovery that so many of his efforts had been directed to keeping knowledge of sexual deviations from a public which had surreptitiously been practising them all the while? He immediately applied for a destruction order on the *Kinsey*

Report, at the unlikely venue of Doncaster Magistrates Court. To his surprise, the Doncaster magistrates declined the proffered place in the history of obscurantism. But in 1953 an Interpol Conference in Oslo decided that pornography was one cause of sex crimes, and British police responded with a 'purge' of cheap 'novelettes', including the works of a certain Hank Jansen, whose publisher sought to argue that Jansen's prose was no more explicit than that which could be found between the covers of books carrying the imprint of Britain's most reputable publishers. He handed a sample to the judge, who refused to allow the jury to read and compare them.[69] This ruling was upheld by the Court of Appeal, but not before Lord Goddard had caught a glimpse of these recent novels from the houses of Heinemann, Hutchinson and Secker & Warburg. The Lord Chief Justice intimated that the DPP should look at them, 'and that' the DPP later recalled in his evidence to a Parliamentary Select Committee, 'is not an intimation which I can ignore'.[70] And so it came to pass that in 1954 four of Britain's leading publishers were arraigned at the Central Criminal Court, in proceedings which left the obscenity law in total confusion, and led directly to the passage of the 1959 Obscene Publications Act.

Secker & Warburg, charged with publishing *The Philanderer*, was fortunate to be tried by Mr Justice Stable, whose preference for an acquittal was evident from the outset when he rescued Mr Frederick Warburg from the dock and invited him to sit with his solicitors in the well of the court. The judge declared that 'deprave and corrupt' meant more than merely 'to shock or disgust'. The book had to be judged by its effect on an intelligent adult, and not a fourteen-year-old schoolgirl, otherwise English literature would be confined to nursery rhymes. Nature, not books, put ideas into young heads. The act of sexual passion was the greatest motive force in the history of the human race. The duty of the writer was to hold up a mirror to the reality of his time, and not to sweep embarrassing facts under the carpet.[71]

Hutchinson, the next publisher to come up for trial, was not so lucky with its judge. The Recorder of London kept the director in the dock, and his summing up was virtually a point-by-point rebuttal of Mr Justice Stable. The jury could convict if they found the book repugnant. The obscenity law was to protect sex and marriage from being dragged in the mud. They had to consider whether it might deprave or corrupt 'a callow youth or a girl just budding into womanhood'. Not surprisingly the jury convicted, whereupon the Recorder fined the defendants a total of £1,000 and chilled the publishing world with his sentencing homily:

> I should have thought that any reader, however inexperienced, would have been repelled by a book of this sort, which is repugnant to every decent emotion which ever concerned man or woman ... it is a very comforting thought that juries from time to time take a very solid stand against this sort of thing and realize how important it is for the youth of this country to be protected, and that the fountain of our national blood should not be polluted at its source.[72]

A less comforting thought was that juries might reflect the disparate prejudices of the judges who happened to instruct them, and a widespread protest about the uncertainty and oppressiveness of the law ensued in the wake of the 1954 prosecutions (which had ended with two juries deadlocked over Heinemann's book *The Image and the Search*). A committee chaired by Sir Alan Herbert was set up by the Society of Authors, and its demands for law reform were powerfully articulated by Norman St John-Stevas and C.H. Rolph. In 1955 Mr Roy Jenkins introduced a draft Bill, which drew all-party support, and in 1957 it was referred to a Select Committee of the House of Commons. The reform movement had three basic criticisms of the definition of obscenity:

> 1. Under the *Hicklin* test, the possible effect of the article on the most vulnerable members of society was crucial.
> 2. The definition took no consideration of the literary merit of the article, and expert evidence of such merit was usually excluded. (In the 1954 trials the defence had packed the public benches with famous literary figures, in the hope that the jury would recognize them as silent supporters.)
> 3. The definition made it unnecessary to consider the overall impact on the normal reader. Prosecuting counsel could, and usually did, read isolated words and passages, out of context, as indicating the obscenity of the whole work.[73]

'It is the accepted function of government,' began the Home Secretary's memorandum to the Select Committee, 'to suppress pornography.'[74] The deliberations of the Committee, the debates in the House of Commons, and subsequent judicial pronouncements, all proceeded on the basis that obscene material was of two clear and discernible kinds: 'pornography' and 'literature'. The latter should be jealously protected unless it seriously threatened the public good; the former should be vigorously suppressed, for reasons which were generally articulated in terms of personal revulsion. The British

Society of Authors wanted to roast the pig without burning its own house, as Sir Alan Herbert frankly admitted:

> It is the other man you want to get after, the man who sits down and thinks 'I want to make my readers as randy as I can, as often as I can.' That is the man you are after always. He is not bothering whether he corrupts anybody. He is frankly marketing lust, he is marketing something he knows he can sell. The problem you have to face is to distinguish, shall we say, between myself and the other fellow.

At times the proceedings smacked of a horse-trade: Mr Roy Jenkins, MP offered the Commissioner of Metropolitan Police 'a more effective means of proceeding against the really filthy stuff' if, in return, the police would take no action against 'borderline stuff'. The Commissioner promised an attitude of 'complete indifference',[75] and the Select Committee duly recommended a saving clause for 'literature', counter-balanced by a strengthening of police search and seizure powers in relation to 'pornography' (defined as that which 'makes no pretence to literary or artistic merit, but exists solely in order to pander to depravity.'). The horse-trade was reflected in the preamble to the 1959 Obscene Publications Act, which described the measure as 'an Act to amend the law relating to the publication of obscene matter; to provide for the protection of literature; and to strengthen the law concerning pornography.'

The 1959 Obscene Publications Act emerged from a simplistic notion that sexual material could be divided into two classes, 'literature' and 'pornography', and the function of the new statutory definition of obscenity was to enable juries and magistrates to make that distinction. The tendency of a work to deprave or corrupt its reader was henceforth to be judged in the light of its total impact, rather than the arousing potential of 'purple passages', and the readership to be considered was the actual or at least predictable reading public rather than the precocious fourteen-year-old schoolgirl into whose hands it might perchance fall – unless it were in fact aimed at or distributed to fourteen-year-old schoolgirls, by whose vulnerability to corruption it should then be judged. It was recognized that a work of literature might employ, to advance its serious purpose, a style which resembled, or had the same effect as, the pornographer's: here the jury was to be assisted to draw the line by experts who would offer judgments as to the degree of importance the article represented in its particular discipline. All pornography was unjustifiably obscene, so its publication was criminal. Works of art or literature might be obscene (i.e. depraving or corrupting) but their great significance might outweigh the harm they could do, and take them out of the prima facie criminal category established by section 1 of the Act.

In so far as the 1959 legislation was an endeavour to isolate 'pornography' as the class of writing which should be proscribed, it paralleled the objective of the United States Supreme Court two years before in *Roth's* case.[76] There the court decided that material which appealed predominantly to prurient interests, and which was devoid of intellectual content, did not qualify as 'speech' to which constitutional protection could be afforded. But on both sides of the Atlantic the distinction between 'pornography' and 'literature' was found to be much more elusive than had been imagined. The old formulae broke down entirely in the following decade when confronted by *Playboy* magazine's modish appeal to both intellect and instinct, by 'soft-core' journals offering medical and psychiatric advice on sexual problems in a deliberately titillating but arguably therapeutic style, and by the underground press with its flamboyant revolutionary celebration of sex as a means of baiting a prudish political establishment. These publications were neither 'pornography' nor 'literature', and whilst they did not particularly edify the public, there was not much evidence that they were prone to deprave or corrupt either. In consequence they flourished in this grey area between pornography and literature, between public good and public corruption, and when lawyers sought to intervene they often made an ass of the law. Pornography of the hardest core slipped effortlessly through the thin blue line and took a stand in Soho, while much that was undoubtedly serious writing was harassed and persecuted at vast public expense. The first trial – that of *Lady Chatterley's Lover* – was a case in point. Mr Roy Jenkins wrote to the *Spectator* claiming that the prosecution was a betrayal of an implied promise given by the police to the Select Committee that under the new Act they would confine prosecutions to 'pornography'.[77] But the Commissioner of Police had only promised indifference to 'borderline stuff', and the Select Committee had given him complete discretion to stake out the border. It should have known better: the police had catalogued *Lolita* and *The Ginger Man* as 'pornography' in a list submitted to the Committee as 'appropriate for prosecution'.

3
The definition of obscenity

A TENDENCY TO DEPRAVE AND CORRUPT

'Obscenity, Members of the Jury, is like an elephant. You cannot define it, but you know it when you see it.' With this despairing judicial aphorism, Old Bailey juries retired to consider their verdict on books and magazines in the 1970s. In 1959 Parliament *had* purported to define the indefinable: 'obscene' means 'having a tendency to deprave and corrupt'. But what, in turn, did that mean? In the forensic free-for-all which developed when pornographers pleaded 'not guilty', it meant whatever ten out of twelve arbitrarily selected jurors could be convinced that it meant by lawyers whose advocacy was unfettered by scientific or sociological footnotes. The consequences were unpredictable and often conflicting, as publications resoundingly condemned in one court were triumphantly vindicated in another. Reviewing the results from the vantage point of the House of Lords, Lord Wilberforce was moved to remark of the 'depravity or corruption' test that

... these alternatives involve deep questions of psychology and ethics; how are the courts to deal with them? Well might they have said that such words provide a formula which cannot in practice be applied ... I have serious doubts whether the Act will continue to be workable in this way, or whether it will produce tolerable results. The present is, or in any rational system ought to be, a simple case, yet the illogical and unscientific character of the Act has forced the justices into untenable positions.[1]

The results were not tolerable for any rational system of law, because they were uncertain and incompatible, largely hinging on the sexual outlook of the particular jurors who happened to be empanelled to try each case. The formula of 'depravity and corruption' was loyally applied by the courts, but not without considerable confusion over the appropriate gloss which the English language could provide to assist jurors and justices in their task. In consequence, the definition has in recent years become a focus for law reformers; anti-pornography campaigners demand a change from the metaphysics of moral corruption to what seems to them to be the more comprehensible concept of sexual embarrassment or infringement of community standards, while the libertarian lobby, when it is not agitating for complete repeal of the laws, argues for a test which makes demonstrable harm a prerequisite of criminal liability. Meanwhile the pressure of new cases spins the definition like a catherine wheel, sparking off new irrationalities.

The Oxford English Dictionary offers 'filthy', 'repulsive', 'loathsome', 'indecent' and 'lewd' as synonyms for the word 'obscene'. Colloquially the word usually denotes images, not necessarily sexual, which shock or disgust. In law, however, the meaning is governed by the statutory definition, 'a tendency to deprave or corrupt'. The repulsive content of an article, which characterizes it as 'obscene' in the normal usage of that word, is insufficient to justify conviction. The 1959 Act paved the way for the courts to rule that any judicial reversion to the ordinary meaning of 'obscene' ('repulsive', 'filthy', 'loathsome', 'lewd', etc.) would amount to a misdirection of such gravity as would vitiate the conviction. The definition of obscenity originated in *Hicklin's* case, when Chief Justice Cockburn enunciated the test of 'whether the tendency of the matter charged as obscenity is to deprave and corrupt those whose minds are open to such immoral influences, and into whose hands a publication of this sort may fall'.[2] The House of Commons Select Committee hoped that the definition in the 1959 Act would give legislative force to the jury direction by Mr Justice Stable in *The Philanderer* case.

Remember the charge is a charge that the tendency of the book is to corrupt and deprave. The charge is not that the tendency of the book is either to shock or to disgust. That is not a criminal offence. Then you say: 'Well, corrupt or deprave whom?' and again the test: those whose minds are open to such immoral influences and into whose hands a publication of this sort may fall. What exactly does that mean? Are we to take our literary standards as being the level of something that is suitable for a fourteen-year-old schoolgirl? Or do we go even further back than that, and are we to be reduced to the sort of books that one reads as a child in the nursery? The answer to that is: Of course not. A mass of literature, great literature from many angles is wholly unsuitable for reading by the adolescent, but that does not mean that the publisher is guilty of a criminal offence for making those works available to the general public.[3]

The complete statutory definition of obscenity is contained in section 1 (A) (1) of the Obscene Publications Act:

For the purposes of this Act an article shall be deemed to be obscene if its effect or (where the article comprises two or more distinct items) the effect of any one of its items is, if taken as a whole, such as to tend to deprave and corrupt persons who are likely, in all the circumstances, to read, see or hear the matter contained or embodied in it.

Although the Select Committee wanted 'a tendency to deprave and corrupt' to mean more than 'a tendency to shock and disgust', it was at least open to the courts to read 'shock and disgust' back into the legal interpretation of the statute, by imparting notions of 'contrary to community standards' or 'offensive to right-thinking persons' which had been frequent judicial glosses on the *Hicklin* test prior to 1959. Indeed, the first case to come before the High Court, *R*. v. *Clifford*, did not bode well for the utilitarian view that a 'tendency to deprave and corrupt' must involve a reasonable prospect of harm. The publisher of an illustrated booklet called *Scanties* appealed against his conviction on the ground that the trial judge had not told the jury that they should be satisfied the article was 'something more than shocking or vulgar'. Lord Goddard said that it did not matter what the judge had or had not told his jury: one had only to pick the book up to feel 'quite certain that no jury could conceivably have failed to convict'.[4]

A few months later, in the *Lady Chatterley* prosecution, Mr Justice Byrne took care to include the sought-after instruction: 'the mere fact that you are shocked or disgusted, the mere fact that you hate the sight of the book when you have read it, does not solve the question as to whether you are satisfied beyond reasonable doubt that the tendency of the book is to deprave or corrupt'.[5] He declined, however, to echo defence counsel's contention that 'deprave and corrupt' necessarily included a tendency to change a reader's character for the worse in some *demonstrable* sense, e.g. to impel him to do something wrong which he would not otherwise have done, an approach which sought verifiable harm as justification of the criminal sanction. He adopted instead the Oxford English Dictionary definition of 'deprave' ('to make morally bad, to pervert, to debase or corrupt morally') and 'corrupt' ('to render morally unsound or rotten, or destroy the moral purity or chastity of, to pervert or ruin a good quality, to debase, to defile').[6] Of the cases decided before the passing of the Act, he selected a passage from Mr Justice Devlin's remarks in 1954 when Hutchinson had been prosecuted for publishing *The Image and the Search:*

> Just as loyalty is one of the things which is essential to the well-being of a nation, so some sense of morality is something that is essential to the well-being of a nation, and to the healthy life of the community; and, accordingly, anyone who seeks by his writing to corrupt that fundamental sense of morality is guilty of obscene libel.... Of course, there is a right to express oneself, either in pictures or in literature. People who hold strong political views are often anxious to say exactly what they think, irrespective of any restraint, and so too a creative writer or a creative artist, one can well understand, naturally desires complete freedom with which to express his talents or his genius. But he is a member of the community like any other member of the community. He is under the same obligation to other members of the community as any other is, not to do harm, either mentally or physically or spiritually, and if there is a conflict between an artist or writer in his desire for self-expression, and the sense that morality is fundamental to the well-being of the community, if there is such a conflict, then it is morality which must prevail.[7]

This direction introduces the difficult question of locating a moral consensus in the community, but it does emphasize that harm – physical, moral or spiritual – was the mischief at which the law was directed.

Some years later the test of obscenity was considered by the Court of Appeal in two cases of major significance – *R.* v. *Calder & Boyars* (*Last Exit to Brooklyn*, 1967)[8] and *R.* v. *Anderson* (*Oz* magazine, 1971)[9]. In the *Last Exit* appeal the court confirmed that 'the essence of the matter is moral corruption'. It declined a defence initiative to define 'moral corruption' as making a reader *behave* worse than he would otherwise have done, on the pragmatic ground that otherwise 'it would perhaps be difficult to know where the judge ought to stop'. This does not, of course, preclude counsel from advancing it as a rational interpretation of the section. The court added the warning that 'when, as here, a statute lays down the definition of a word or phrase in plain English, it is rarely necessary and often unwise for the judge to attempt to improve upon or redefine the definition.'[10] This view proved fatal to the conviction in the *Oz* trial, in which the trial judge widened the definition by suggesting that the original Greek meaning of 'obscene' – something not fit to be shown on the stage – might still be retained in the Act, and that the statutory connotation of 'obscene' might include what is 'repulsive', 'filthy', 'loathsome', 'indecent' and 'lewd'. The Lord Chief Justice ruled that this constituted 'a very substantial and serious misdirection': for the future, there must be no widening of the formula to introduce colloquial notions of obscenity, or concepts imported from the less serious 'indecency' offences.[11]

By this time Mr Justice Stable's direction in *The Philanderer* was clear law in relation to the irrelevance of reactions such as shock or dismay. It then became the turn of judges in the House of Lords to consider further the ambit of depravity and corruption. The first case, *Knuller* v. *DPP* (1972), was an appeal by the editors of the underground newspaper *International Times*, who had been convicted of a conspiracy to corrupt public morals when they published contact advertisements by and for homosexuals. The Law Lords considered that the word 'corrupt' implied a powerful and corrosive effect, which went further than one suggested definition, 'to lead morally astray'. Lord Simon warned: 'Corrupt is a strong word. The Book of Common Prayer, following the Gospel, has "where rust and moth doth corrupt". The words "corrupt public morals" suggest conduct which a jury might find to be destructive of the very fabric of society.'[12] Lord Reid agreed that 'Corrupt is a strong word and the jury ought to be reminded of that.... The Obscene Publications Act appears to use the words "deprave" and "corrupt" as synonymous, as I think they are. We may regret we live in a permissive society but I doubt whether even the most staunch defender of a better age would maintain that all or even most of those who have at one time or in one way or another been led astray morally have thereby become depraved or corrupt.'[13] These dicta in *Knuller* emphasize that the effect of publication must be to produce real social evil, going beyond immoral suggestion or persuasion, and constituting a serious menace to the community.

Prosecutors derived more comfort from *DPP* v. *Whyte* (1973), a case involving a bookshop which dispensed pornography to 'dirty old men'.[14] The House of Lords asserted that erotic material might corrupt if its only influence was to stimulate sex fantasies which have no issue in overt sexual activity, but merely arouse 'thoughts of a most impure and libidinous character'. Depravity may be all in the mind, without ever causing anti-social behaviour. Lord Wilberforce thought that '... influence on the mind is not merely within the law but is its primary target....'[15] Lord Pearson added: '... in my opinion, the words "deprave and corrupt" in the statutory definition, as in the judgement of Cockburn CJ in *R.* v. *Hicklin*, refer to the effect of

pornographic articles on the mind, including the emotions, and it is
not essential that any physical sexual activity (or any "overt sexual
activity", if that phrase has a different meaning) should result.'[16]
Lord Cross agreed that depravity and corruption were conditions
of the mind, although he thought that 'evidence of behaviour may
be needed to establish their presence'. It was a question for the jury
to decide whether elderly men were corrupt when they bought erotic
books in order to arouse sexual fantasies, and then proceeded to relieve
themselves by masturbation in the privacy of their homes.[17]

The decision in *Whyte's* case meant that although corruption implies
some change for the worse in the character of likely readers, that
change need not be manifested in anti-social conduct. It can consist
in some new mental orientation, such as a preoccupation with sexual
fantasies, which need not be permanent nor necessarily result in delin-
quent behaviour. Most books published today would be obscene if
'corruption' meant merely the provocation of erotic imaginings; no
books would be obscene if 'corruption' meant destroying the fabric
of society. In *Whyte's* case the House of Lords was not laying down
a hard-and-fast rule that all books which stimulated sex fantasies are
obscene, but merely rejecting the opinion of local justices that
'depravity and corruption' must *necessarily* mean that readers will
engage in anti-social behaviour. It leaves to the jury the almost un-
answerable question of whether, in the circumstances of the particular
case, erotic material may cause social, moral, psychological or spiritual damage.

THE AVERSION THEORY

One important corollary of the decision that obscene material must
have more serious effects than arousing feelings of revulsion is the doctrine that material which in fact shocks and disgusts may *not* be obscene,
because its effect is to discourage readers from indulgence in the
immorality so unseductively portrayed. Readers whose stomachs are
turned will not partake of any food for thought. The American judge
and philosopher Jerome Frank first noted the irony: 'if the argument
be sound that the legislature may constitutionally provide punishment for the obscene because, anti-socially, it arouses sexual desire
by making sex attractive, then it follows that whatever makes sex disgusting is socially beneficial'.[18] In other words 'one vindicates a book
by its capacity to induce vomiting'.[19] The argument, however para-

doxical it sounds – and Lord Denning has described it as 'a piece of sophistry'[20] – has frequently found favour as a means of exculpating literature of merit. Publication in the United States of James Joyce's *Ulysses*, for example, was permitted by the courts in 1933 on the grounds that 'whereas in many places the effect of *Ulysses* upon the reader undoubtedly is somewhat emetic, nowhere does it tend to be aphrodisiac'.[21]

In England, too, the aversion argument first emerged in the defence of books of substantial merit. It was publicly propounded in 1949 by the Attorney-General, Sir Hartley Shawcross QC, when explaining to the House of Commons his decision not to prosecute Norman Mailer's war novel *The Naked and the Dead*: 'While there is much in this most tedious and lengthy book which is foul, lewd and revolting, looking at it as a whole I do not think its intent is to corrupt or deprave, or that it is likely to lead to any other result than disgust at its contents.'[22] In the trial of *The Philanderer*, Mr Justice Stable reminded the jury, as a point in the book's favour, that: 'the theme of this book is the story of a rather attractive young man who is absolutely obsessed with his desire for women. It is not presented as an admirable thing, or a thing to be copied. It is not presented as a thing that brought him happiness or any sort of permanent satisfaction. Throughout the book you hear the note of impending disaster.' If the good end happily, and the bad unhappily, no offence will be taken: the problem with scarlet women like Lady Chatterley, Fanny Hill and Linda Lovelace was that they failed to repent by the end of their stories. In 1974 treasury counsel explained that the most obscene passage in *Street Boy*, a book about the adventures of a London homosexual prostitute, was a suggestion that the hero had achieved greater fortune and happiness through a life of vice than he could have earned by remaining in his honest but unrewarding trade as assistant catering manager at a Midlands hotel.

Last Exit to Brooklyn presented horrific pictures of homosexuality and drug-taking in New York. Defence counsel contended that its only effect on any but a minute lunatic fringe of readers would be horror, revulsion and pity. It made the reader share in the horror it described and thereby so disgusted, shocked and outraged him that, being aware of the truth, he would do what he could to eradicate those evils and the conditions of modern society which allowed them to exist. Instead of tending to encourage anyone to homosexuality, drug-taking or brutal violence it would have precisely the reverse effect. The failure of the trial judge to put this defence before the jury in his summing up was the major ground for upsetting the conviction. The Court of Appeal stressed that

> With a book such as this, in which words appear on almost every page and many incidents are described in graphic detail which in the ordinary, colloquial, sense of the word anyone would rightly describe as obscene, it is perhaps of particular importance to explain to the jury what the defendants allege to be the true effect of those words and descriptions within their context in the book....[23]

The aversion argument was extracted from its literary context and elevated into a full-blown defence of crudity in the *Oz* case. The magazine contained a number of savage cartoon caricatures depicting unpleasant people engaging in deviate activities. The defence called a distinguished psychologist, who likened these drawings to the pictures which he used in aversion therapy to make patients feel disgust at anti-social activities to which they had hitherto been attracted. Once again the trial judge misunderstood the argument and failed to remind the jury of it, and once again the Court of Appeal was obliged to quash the conviction. The Lord Chief Justice accepted that 'the aversion theory', as he termed it, could be a complete defence under section 1 of the Act:

> One of the arguments was that many of the illustrations in *Oz* were so grossly lewd and unpleasant that they would shock in the first instance and then would tend to repel. In other words, it was said that they had an aversive effect and that, far from tempting those who had not experienced the acts to take part in them, they would put off those who might be tempted so to conduct themselves ... the learned trial judge never really got over to the jury this argument of aversion, in other words, never put over to the jury that the proposition central to the defence case was that certain illustrations could be so disgusting and filthy that they would not corrupt and deprave but rather would tend to cause people to revolt from activity of that kind.[24]

Legal recognition of the psychological fact that behaviour will often react against, rather than strive to emulate, perceived actions is welcome, although paradoxically the court held that the very psychological evidence by which the aversion argument was explained to the jury in the *Oz* case was in fact inadmissible, so that it must henceforth be expounded by counsel as a matter of common sense rather than science. Since *Oz* it has been adopted as a defence for bizarre forms of hard-core pornography, on the basis that those who view grotesqueries will be 'averted' from the conduct depicted. But while it is fair to make the point that ordinary readers may be revolted, and

that their feelings of revulsion will confirm their existing moral outlook rather than work any undesirable change, such material is not
produced for the average reader, but for minorities with the morbid
curiosity or fetishistic desire to dilate over it. In *Mishkin* v. *New York*
it was argued that sado-masochistic books would disgust and sicken,
rather than stimulate, the average reader, and so would not appeal
to his prurient interest. The US Supreme Court pointed out the fallacy: 'Where the material is designed for and purely disseminated
to a clearly-defined sexual group, rather than the public at large, the
prurient appeal requirement of the *Roth* test is satisfied if the dominant
theme of the material taken as a whole appeals to the prurient interest
in sex of members of that group.'[25]

Just as there is concern in some quarters about aversion therapy,
one assumption of the aversion defence needs to be questioned. If the
grotesque sexual caricature repels its viewer, and confirms his pre-
existing prejudices, no harm has been done to him. But if its repulsive-
ness causes anxieties or neurosis or tends to put the viewer off healthy
sex, there is a real prospect of harm. There is a difference between
ugliness which is merely shocking or savagely satirical, and ugliness
which can be mentally damaging to readers of a certain psychological
make-up.[26] Material which arouses unwarranted fears and anxieties
about sex may indeed cause harm, but not the sort of harm prohibited
by the Obscene Publications Act.

The most valuable aspect of the aversion defence is its emphasis
on the context and purpose of publication. Writing which sets out
to seduce, editorials which exhort and pressurize the reader to indulge
in immorality, are to be distinguished from those which present a
balanced picture, and do not overlook the pains which may attend
new pleasures. For over a century prosecutors thought it sufficient
to point to explicitness in the treatment of sex, on the assumption that
exposure to such material would automatically arouse the libidinous
desires associated with a state of depravity. Now they must consider
the overall impact, and the truthfulness of the total picture. Books
which present a fair account of corruption have a defence denied to
glossy propaganda. In deciding whether material depraves and corrupts, the jury must lift its eyes from mere details and consider the
tone and overall presentation. Does the material glamorize sex, or
does it 'tell it like it is'?

THE TARGET AUDIENCE

The Act defines obscenity as that quality in a publication which would tend to corrupt 'persons who are likely, having regard to all relevant circumstances, to read, see or hear the matter contained or embodied in it'. The importance of considering this target audience was stressed by Lord Wilberforce in *DPP* v. *Jordan*:

> The main point to be noticed about this section is ... that it is directed at relative obscenity – relative, that is, to likely readers. (I use 'readers' to include other types of recipients.) In each case it has to be decided who these readers are and so evidence is usually given as to the type of shop or place where the material is, and as to the type of customer who goes there. When the class of likely reader has been ascertained, it is for the jury to say whether the tendency of the material is such as to deprave or corrupt them.[27]

The prosecution will normally adduce evidence of the circumstances in which the article was seized, of the location in cases of bookshops or cinema clubs, or of distribution arrangements in the case of a publisher. Police officers will have kept observation on the defendants' premises, and may give evidence of the kind of customer who frequented them, in terms of age, sex and social class. The environment is important: the prosecution may point to the likelihood of casual passers-by being attracted to the shop, or to the presence in the vicinity of schools, youth clubs or residential accommodation. The selling price of the article, the place and prominence of its display, and the composition of its cover or container are also factors for the jury to weigh in deciding the type of customer who might be minded to make a purchase. The defendant is entitled to describe his patrons, and to explain any restrictions he may have placed either on the availability of the article in question, or on access to his premises by members of the public. Evidence of his good repute may assist his contention that he has merchandized it responsibly to mature adults who have sought it out, and a sample of his clientèle may be called to explain their reasons for patronising his business. A publisher may give evidence of a book's sales, of his distribution system, and of any advertisements or reviews which may have brought it to public notice. Although expert evidence of the likely effect of an article is inadmissible, expertise may assist the jury to establish potential readership. The conclusions of a readership survey conducted by a magazine publisher prior to his arrest, an analysis of the social make-up of patrons of a cinema club, or evidence of custom and distribution patterns in the book trade would be relevant in appropriate cases.

The need to ascertain the target audience in prosecutions under the 1959 Act effects the most important shift in emphasis from the common-law definition, which looked not to the likely readership, but to the impact of the article on the most vulnerable members of society. In *R*. v. *Hicklin* the court considered that *The Confessional Unmasked* was obscene precisely because the book 'is sold at the corners of streets, in all directions, and of course it falls into the hands of persons of all classes, young and old, and the minds of those hitherto pure are exposed to the danger of contamination and pollution from the impurity it contains'.[28] Similarly, in the 1954 case of *Reiter*, the Lord Chief Justice stressed how, 'when one is considering the test of obscenity, one's mind naturally turns to depraving and corrupting young people into whose hands (these books) may fall. There are, no doubt, dirty-minded elderly people, but it is not to be expected that many elderly people would read these books. Younger people are more likely to, and we are told that they circulate in the Armed Forces.'[29]

The common law's concern for the young, the sexually immature and the psychologically abnormal loaded the dice against defendants, who were hard put to convince juries that erotic writing would not affect some little boy or girl, or some mentally disturbed adult, into whose hands it might conceivably fall. In *R*. v. *Martin Secker & Warburg*, Mr Justice Stable devoted much of his exculpatory summing up to offering the jury an answer to this dilemma:

> You have heard a good deal about the putting of ideas into young heads. Really, is it books that put ideas into young heads, or is it nature? ... it is the natural change from childhood to maturity that puts ideas into young heads. It is the business of parents and teachers and the environment of society, so far as is possible, to see that those ideas are wisely and naturally directed to the ultimate fulfilment of a balanced individual life.... The literature of the world from the earliest times when people first learned to write so far as we have it today – literature sacred and profane, poetry and prose – represents the sum total of human thought throughout the ages and from all the varied civilizations the human pilgrimage has traversed. Are we going to say in England that our contemporary literature is to be measured by what is suitable for the fourteen-year-old schoolgirl to read? You must consider that aspect of the matter.[30]

The fourteen-year-old schoolgirl, however, was precisely the person whom the common law sought to protect, and Mr Justice Stable's rhetoric, however much it represented common sense, was out of line with the decisions of higher courts in *Hicklin* and *Reiter*. The 1959 Act gave legislative sanction to the Stable approach by adopting a relative definition of obscenity – relative, that is, to the 'likely' rather than the 'conceivably possible' readership. This was further emphasized by section 2 (6) of the Act, which provides that in any prosecution for publishing an obscene article, 'the question whether an article is obscene shall be determined without regard to any publication by another person, unless it could reasonably have been expected that the publication by the other person would follow from the publication by the person charged'. Similarly the 1964 legislation which created the offence of possession of obscene articles for publication for gain, requires that 'the question whether the article is obscene shall be determined by reference to such publication for gain of the article as, in the circumstances, it may reasonably be inferred he (the defendant) had in contemplation, and to any further publication that could reasonably have expected to follow from it, but not to any other publication' (section 1 (3) (b)).

These statutory provisions ensure that the publication in question is judged by its impact on its primary audience – those people who, the evidence suggests, would be likely to seek it out and to pay the asking-price to read it. They reject the 'most vulnerable person' standard of *Hicklin*, with its preoccupation with those members of society of the lowest level of intellectual or moral discernment. They also reject another standard employed frequently in the law, that of the 'average' or 'reasonable' man, and focus on 'likely' readers and proven circumstances of publication. A work of literature is to be judged by its effect on serious-minded purchasers, a comic book by its effect on children, a sexually explicit magazine sold in an 'adults only' bookstore by its effect on adult patrons of that particular shop.

In *R*. v. *Penguin Books* Mr Justice Byrne pointed out that the paperback price of 3s 6d would, in these days of 'high wages and high pocket money', put the book within the grasp of a vast mass of the population.[31] In that case, the jury had to consider the effect of the book on a reading public which would purchase it at a paperback price. The converse situation was met in *R*. v. *Barker*, where an explicit picture was sent to a photographer who kept it in a locked drawer. In that case the obscenity of the picture had to be judged by its effect on the individual concerned. The Court of Criminal Appeal emphasized that the issue was

Whether the effect of the article is such as to tend to deprave and corrupt the individual to whom it is published ... a jury should obviously take into account the article itself and in addition they should have regard to the age and occupation of the person to whom the article is published, if such age and occupation is proved in evidence.... In many cases the person accused of publishing an obscene article may be wholly unaware of the age or occupation of the individual to whom it is published. In our judgment this factor is irrelevant. A person who sells potentially obscene matter to an unknown applicant takes the risk that the latter is someone whom the article would tend to deprave and corrupt. On the other hand, if the unknown applicant is not of that type, the accused's ignorance of the applicant's character cannot make the article obscene.[32]

The publisher was acquitted, because his customer was not the sort of man to be corrupted by the photograph. *Barker's* case was applied in *R. v. Clayton & Halsey*, where the proprietors of a Soho bookshop were charged with selling obscene material to two experienced members of Scotland Yard's Obscene Publications Squad. These officers conceded that pornography had ceased to arouse any feelings in them whatsoever. The prosecution argument that the pictures were 'inherently obscene', and tended of their very nature to corrupt all viewers, was rejected:

This court cannot accept the contention that a photograph may be inherently so obscene that even an experienced or scientific viewer must be susceptible to some corruption from its influence. The degree of inherent obscenity is, of course, very relevant, but it must be related to the susceptibility of the viewer. Further, while it is no doubt theoretically possible that a jury could take the view that even a most experienced officer, despite his protestations, was susceptible to the influence of the article yet, bearing in mind the onus and degree of proof in a criminal case, it would, we think, be unsafe and therefore wrong to leave that question to the jury.[33]

Although judges sometimes loosely talk of material which is 'inherently obscene' or 'obscene *per se*', it is clear that this concept is irreconcilable with the legislative definition of obscenity. The quality of obscenity inheres whenever the article would tend to corrupt its actual or potential audience; the degree of that corruption becomes relevant when it is necessary to balance it against the public interest, if a 'public good' defence has been raised under section 4 of the Act. The rulings in *Barker* and *Clayton & Halsey* remain good law, and were confirmed by the Court of Appeal in *Attorney-General's Reference (No. 2 of 1975)* when it held that publication of *Last Tango in Paris* to the licensee of a cinema, who was not a person likely to be corrupted by the film, provided insufficient evidence to be left to the jury on an obscenity charge.[34]

The concept of 'relative obscenity' adopted by the Act received careful elucidation from Lord Wilberforce in *Whyte's case*:

One thing at least is clear from this verbiage, that the Act has adopted a relative conception of obscenity. An article cannot be considered as obscene in itself: it can only be so in relation to its likely readers. One reason for this was no doubt to exempt from prosecution scientific, medical or sociological treatises not likely to fall into the hands of laymen, but the section is drafted in terms wider than was necessary to give this exemption, and this gives the courts a difficult task. For, in every case, the magistrates, or the jury, are called on to ascertain who are likely readers and then to consider whether the article is likely to deprave and corrupt them.[35]

Evidence of factual relevance to this question included the site of the bookshop (it was in an ordinary shopping-area, opposite a technical college, and near a block of council flats), the nature of other wares sold from the shop (it offered books of general interest, although no newspapers or comics), the arrangement of the offensive material (it was marked 'adults only' and confined to a special section of the shop, but it was on open display rather than in a closed cupboard) and the age and class of the customers (men of middle age and upwards, many of whom were regulars). These facts were all relevant to the issue of identifying likely readership in the circumstances of the case. This was required by 'the principle of relative "obscenity"'; certainly the tendency to deprave and corrupt is not to be estimated in relation to some assumed standard of purity or some reasonable average man. It is the likely reader. And to apply different tests to teenagers, members of men's clubs, or men in various occupations or localities would be a matter of common sense.'[36]

The notion of 'variable' or 'circumstantial' obscenity has been developed along similar lines in the United States. In *US* v. *31 Photographs* the Kinsey Research Institute had imported Scandinavian pornography for research purposes. The court held that in the possession of the Institute the pornography was not obscene, even though identical material would have been held to be so had an ordinary citizen attempted its importation. The Government contention that some erotic material is 'obscene *per se*' was expressly rejected.[37] A corollary of this decision was the Supreme Court's refusal of constitutional protection to newsagents who sell soft-core erotica to children. One such unscrupulous merchandiser was upbraided by Justice Brennan: 'The "girlie" picture magazines included in the sales here are not obscene for adults.... The concept of obscenity ... may vary according to the group to whom the questionable material is directed or from whom it is quarantined. Because of the State's exigent interest in preventing distribution to children of objectionable material, it can exercise its power to protect the health, safety, welfare and morals of its community by barring the distribution to children of books recognized to be suitable for adults.'[38]

The mere fact the pornographic material is merchandised only to adults does not mean that a bookseller is entitled to an acquittal. It is simply one of the circumstances to be taken into account by the tribunal. It was argued in *Shaw* v. *DPP* that purchasers of *The Ladies Directory*, on sale in Soho and Paddington, were likely to be already depraved, but the Court of Appeal pointed out 'the fallacy of this argument is that it assumes that a man cannot be corrupted more than once'.[39] In *Whyte's case*, the House of Lords accepted that the same fallacy had misled local justices when they acquitted a bookseller who peddled pornography to 'dirty old men' on the assumption that they were so far gone in corruption that another dose would make no difference. 'The Act is not merely concerned with the once-for-all corruption of the wholly innocent, it equally protects the less innocent from further corruption, the addict from feeding or increasing his addiction.'[40] If the target audience are 'addicts' of pornography, impelled to buy the books and feed their appetite, and their reading habits had been corrupted by the books in the first place, the tribunal could interpret this as evidence of guilt.

THE SIGNIFICANT PROPORTION TEST

The 1959 Act requires a tendency to deprave and corrupt 'persons' likely in the circumstances to read or hear the offensive material. But how many persons must have their morals affected before the test is made out? There is always a lunatic fringe of readers who might conceivably be damaged by exposure to particular works of literature, and any book or magazine circulating in the community could possibly fall into the hands of a child or a psychopath. The answer was given by the Court of Appeal in *R.* v. *Calder & Boyars*: the jury must be satisfied that a significant proportion of the likely readership would be guided along the path of corruption:

> The only possible criticism that can be validly made of this part of the summing-up is that the judge gave no guidance to the jury on the difficult question as to what section 1 meant by 'persons' who were likely to read that book. Clearly this cannot mean all persons; nor can it mean any one person, for there are individuals who may be corrupted by almost anything. On the

other hand, it is difficult to construe 'persons' as meaning the majority of persons or the average reader, for such a construction would place great difficulties in the way of making any sense of section 4. The legislature can hardly have contemplated that a book which tended to corrupt and deprave the average reader or the majority of those likely to read it could be justified as being for the public good on any ground. This court is of the opinion that the jury should have been directed to consider whether the effect of the book was to tend to deprave and corrupt a significant proportion of those persons likely to read it. What is a significant proportion is a matter entirely for the jury to decide. It has been persuasively argued by Mr Mortimer that in the absence of such a direction the jury may have thought that they were bound to hold the book obscene if they came to the conclusion that it tended to corrupt and deprave perhaps only four or five of the 13,000 persons who bought it. On the other hand, the jury may have thought that they could convict only if the book tended to deprave and corrupt the average reader or the majority of its readers.[41]

The 'significant proportion' test has been applied at obscenity trials ever since. It protects the defendant in that it prevents the jury from speculating on the possible effect of adult literature on a young person who may just happen to see it, but it does not put the prosecution to proof that a majority, or a substantial number, of readers would be adversely affected. This was emphasized by the House of Lords in *Whyte's* case, where local justices had mistakenly interpreted 'significant proportion' to mean 'the great majority'. Lord Cross accepted that the 'significant proportion' test was the standard which the justices were required to apply, but stressed that 'a significant proportion of a class means a part which is not numerically negligible but which may be much less than half'.[42]

Lord Simon remarked, 'It is true that the expression "significant proportion" does not appear in the statute, but was taken from *R.* v. *Calder & Boyars*. But the statute must be explained to a jury, and to use expressions like "*de minimis*" would merely confuse them. For the reasons given in the judgment of the Court of Appeal in that case, with which I respectfully agree, "significant proportion" is a helpful and accurate gloss on the statute.'[43]

Lord Salmon, who had given the judgement in *Calder & Boyars*, agreed with Lord Simon. The 'significant proportion' test is, in consequence, incorporated by judicial interpretation into section 1 of the Act.[44]

'TAKEN AS A WHOLE'

In obscenity trials before the 1959 legislation it was unnecessary for juries to consider the overall impact of the subject matter on its likely readers. Prosecuting counsel could secure convictions merely by drawing attention to isolated 'purple passages' taken out of context. If one passage was obscene, the whole book was condemned. In *Paget Publications Ltd.* v. *Watson*, the Divisional Court held that where a magistrate had found that a book's cover was obscene, although its contents were innocuous, the contents must be destroyed along with the cover.[45] 'A publication may be obscene because part of it is obscene,' and a magistrate who had stumbled across one obscene page needed to read no further.

The Select Committee on the Obscene Publications Act had stressed the importance of considering the 'dominant effect' of the whole work:

> The contrary view, under which a work could be judged obscene by reference to isolated passages without considering the total effect, would, if taken to its logical conclusion, deprive the reading public of the works of Shakespeare, Chaucer, Fielding and Smollett, except in expurgated editions. We therefore recommend that regard should be paid in any legislation to the effect of a work as a whole.[46]

This recommendation was duly embodied in the 1959 statute, which provided that 'an article shall be deemed to be obscene if its effect or (where the article comprises two or more distinct items) the effect of any one of its items is, if taken as a whole, such as to tend to deprave and corrupt....'

In *R.* v. *Penguin Books* Mr Justice Byrne instructed his jury to consider the total effect of the work after reading it from cover to cover. 'You will read this book just as though you had bought it at a bookstall and you were reading it in the ordinary way as a whole.'[47] Less satisfactory was the trial judge's direction in *R.* v. *Calder & Boyars*, where he told the jury to 'read the book and read it as nearly as possible all the way through. I know we all do a bit of skipping and scamping, and some of us are better at it than others. But remember you are to form a view as a whole, and read it all, and do not form any opinion about it until you have heard the evidence.' Defence counsel took objection to the hint that 'skipping and scamping' was permissible, and the judge recalled the jury to direct them to read the book thoroughly: 'I certainly hope none of you thought that we expect you to skip any of it.'[48]

In 1971 the Court of Appeal discovered a serious defect in the draft-ing of the Act, which negatived the recommendation of the Select Committee in relation to magazines and anthologies. The case was *R. v. Anderson*, and the subject matter was *Oz* magazine, which com-prised forty-eight pages of variations on the theme of 'schoolkids' liberation', interspersed with advertisements. The court decided that the effect of the disjunction in section 1 (i.e. '. . . or (where the article comprises two or more distinct items) the effect of any one of its items . . .') was that when magazines were prosecuted a single item, no matter how inconspicuous, could be plucked out and, if obscene when examined in isolation, would poison the whole issue:

> It is in our view quite clear from section 1 that where one has an article such as this comprising a number of distinct items the proper view of obscenity under section 1 is to apply the test to the individual items in question. It is equally clear that if, when so applied, the test shows one item to be obscene, that is enough to make the whole article obscene. Now that may seem unfair on first reading but it is the law in our judgment without any question. A novelist who writes a complete novel, and who cannot cut out any passages without destroying the theme of the novel, is entitled to have his work judged as a whole, but a magazine publisher who has a far wider discretion as to what he will, and will not, insert by way of items is to be judged under the 1959 Act on what we call the 'item by item' basis . . . the proper course to be taken in future is the 'item by item' approach for magazines and other articles comprising a number of distinct items.[49]

This 'item by item' approach was elaborated in the *Oz* case because of the Lord Chief Justice's concern that one particular item – an advertisement for *Suck*, a sex newspaper produced in Holland – was so obscene that no reasonable jury could find it otherwise. Yet this item was printed in 6 point type in an inconspicuous 4 inch by $1\frac{1}{2}$ inch box buried in an 8 inch by 11 inch page of classified advertisements. Most readers would have missed it entirely; all in all, it took up one seven-hundred-and-twentieth of the whole magazine. The 'item by item' test gives rise to a number of practical difficulties:

(a) Most editions of magazines and newspapers are conceived and produced as a totality by a regular staff, for a reasonably identifi-able audience and with a distinctive character, theme and format. Very few are a potpourri of totally unconnected items. The overall 'tone' of the magazine – satirical, ironic, polemic etc. – will often govern the effect of any one item, whose message will be received and acted upon (if at all) in a way conditioned by the tone of the whole magazine. Thus the 'item by item' approach is unfair to the psychological realities of reading the magazine, in that it ignores the item's effect on the reader's mind *after* he has finished reading the whole magazine. In practice, whether the item will be memorable or not may also be conditioned by its prominence, the readability of its type face, the layout, whether it is promoted on the cover, in the editorial, or the table of contents, the quality of other articles in the same magazine, which may overshadow it, and so on. The crucial question in judging an item's potential for corruption should not be 'what will the reader think and do after reading the "item"' but rather 'what will the reader think and do after reading the *magazine* in which the item is published?'

(b) What is a 'distinct item' for the purposes of the section? Is the illustration to an article an 'item' to be judged in isolation from the article itself, or a single cartoon panel an 'item' to be judged without reference to the whole strip cartoon? The Court of Appeal judgment in *Anderson* gives no guidance. The 'item by item' approach must be adopted for newspapers, magazines and anthologies; it might arguably extend to a non-fiction work by a single author dealing with a number of distinct subjects, or to manuals with separate chapters on different aspects of sex. Unresolved difficulties were met in this respect during *R. v. Gold*, the trial of *In Depth* magazine in October 1972. The magazine boasted a regular feature entitled 'Sexual Arena', where readers' letters were published and answered by doctors or psychiatrists. The prosecution singled out one letter and claimed it constituted an 'item'. The defence insisted that the whole feature – the introduction, all the letters and all the answers – was the only 'item' involved. The judge, however, favoured a third interpretation: the single letter, in conjunction with the answer which it received, constituted an 'item'. Each of the three different approaches involved reasonable interpretations of the Court of Appeal's ruling. In 1971 the 'item by item' approach was applied to *The Little Red Schoolbook*, a 228 page instruction manual mainly concerned with educational issues. The book was found obscene because of a twenty-three-page chapter on sex, which had been considered in isolation. The court accepted the prosecution argument that, because the book had an itemized table of contents, readers would tend to select chapters which interested them rather than read the whole book from beginning to end. Such results mark a substantial inroad on the 'dominant effect' principle established so confidently in the minds of legislators in 1959.

(c) It is not at all clear how the 'public good' defence could relate to a work which has been subjected to the 'item by item' approach. If a magazine is held obscene because of one obscene cartoon, can experts be called to testify that publication of the whole magazine was justified for the public good, or will they be confined to an opinion about the artistic merit of the single cartoon? If *The Times* published a classified column of London prostitutes, could it escape an obscenity conviction by pleading that it is for the public good to publish *The Times*? The wording of section 4 of the Act, which refers to the public good of 'articles', not 'items', forced the court in *R*. v. *Gold* to accept that the answer must be 'yes'.[50] Publication of magazines which contain worthwhile material as well as obscene items may thus be justified by expert testimony under section 4. In America, one enterprising publisher reprinted a boring Obscenity Commission Report interleaved with the most explicit Scandinavian pornography. Who could deny the public interest in reading the 'Illustrated Longford Report'?

(d) The Indictment Rules provide that 'Every indictment shall contain ... such particulars as may be necessary for giving reasonable information as to the nature of the charge.'[51] It follows that in charging a magazine publisher with an offence under the Obscene Publications Act, the prosecution should particularize those sections of the magazine which it alleges to be obscene. In cases involving dozens, or even hundreds, of different magazines, this would be a major undertaking and is rarely insisted upon by the defence, no doubt because it would only serve to draw the Court's particular attention to more salacious items which might otherwise be glossed over by normal reading. Highlighting 'purple passages' only emphasizes the unsatisfactory nature of the 'item by item' test, which denies to newspapers and magazines one of the most important protections afforded to books by the 1959 Act, and is likely to cause great confusion in the juryroom. Suppose the twelve-man jury is unanimous that a magazine is obscene, but the jurors are hopelessly split on which of its items contains the moral poison – three jurors think an item on drugs is likely to corrupt, three different jurors conclude that the classified advertisements are the only objectionable feature, while the remainder are convinced that some salacious pictures are obscene but that the rest of the magazine is tolerable. Although each juror believes the magazine is obscene, the verdict must be an acquittal, because there is not a sufficient majority agreement on the obscenity of any one item. Properly applied, the 'item by item' test would involve the trial judge taking a special verdict on every item singled out by the prosecutor – although even this approach would not exhaust the possibilities, because the jury would have a constitutional right to find an item obscene even though the prosecution made no complaint about it. The 'special verdict' procedure should be adopted in any case for the benefit of the defendant, at least if he is the publisher of a regular monthly magazine, because he is entitled to know the nature of his transgression so that he can edit his magazine accordingly in the future.

THE DEFENDANT'S INTENTION

The Obscene Publications Act is an exception to the general rule that criminal offences require a specific mental element. The *intention* of the writer, publisher or bookseller is beside the point. It matters not whether his purpose was to educate or edify, to corrupt or simply to make money. The *effect* of his work on the reading public is all that matters. In this respect the 1959 Act may be harsher for the defendant than the common law, which required an intention to corrupt, although this intention was normally inferred from the presumption that a publisher would appreciate the natural and probable consequences of his publication.[52]

In 1961 the Court of Appeal in *Shaw* ratified the change:

If these proceedings had been brought before the passing of the Obscene Publications Act 1959, in the form of a prosecution at common law for publishing an obscene libel, it would no doubt have been necessary to establish an intention to corrupt. But the Act of 1959 contains no such requirement and the test of obscenity laid down in section 1 (1) of the Act is whether the effect of the article is such as to tend to deprave and corrupt persons who are likely to read it. In other words obscenity depends on the article and not upon the author.[53]

That obscenity is an offence of strict liability was confirmed by the Court of Appeal in *R. v. Calder & Boyars*. Lord Justice Salmon remarked that 'the intent with which the book was written was irrelevant. However pure or noble the intent may have been, if, in fact, the book taken as a whole tended to deprave and corrupt a significant proportion of those likely to read it, it was obscene within the meaning of that word in the Act of 1959.'[54] These comments, of course, relate only to section 1 of the Act. Under section 4, the 'public good' defence, the author's intention may be highly relevant, and it may be discussed in evidence by experts called to make out or to rebut that defence. In *R.* v. *Penguin Books* Mr Justice Byrne directed that 'as far as literary merit or other matters that can be considered under section 4 are concerned, I think one has to have regard to what the author was trying to do, what his message may have been, and what his general scope was'.[55]

A limited defence is provided by the Obscene Publications Act for those defendants who act merely as innocent disseminators of obscene material. Section 2 (5) of the 1959 Act reads:

A person shall not be convicted of an offence against this section (i.e. the offence of publishing obscene material) if he proves that he had not examined the article in respect of which he is charged and had no reasonable cause to suspect that it was such that his publication of it would make him liable to be convicted of an offence against this section.

Similarly, in proceedings for the offence of possessing an obscene article for publication for gain, section 1 (3) (a) of the 1964 Act provides that a defendant 'shall not be convicted of that offence if he proves that he had not examined the article and had no reasonable cause to suspect that his having it would make him liable to be convicted for an offence against that section'.

The onus of proof is placed on the defendant under these sections. He must show, on the balance of probabilities, both that he did not examine the article and that he entertained no suspicions about the nature of its contents. There has been no judicial interpretation of 'examine': is it sufficient to negative the defence to show that the defendant merely handled the book, or caught sight of its cover, or must the prosecution go further and show that the defendant actually read some of the contentious pages or even that he read it, as the Act requires, 'as a whole'? It is often possible to judge pornographic books by their covers, and a bookseller would probably fail if he admitted to catching sight of a provocative cover-picture or suggestive title. In *R.* v. *Love* the Court of Appeal quashed the conviction of a director of a printing company, who had been absent at the time a print order for obscene books was accepted, and who had no personal knowledge of the contents of those books.[56] Even though he had accepted general responsibility for his company's operations, and would probably have agreed to print the books had the decision been referred to him, he could not be convicted unless he had been given specific notice of the offensive material. A defendant who had not 'examined', in the sense of personally inspected, the offending items might nonetheless be given reasonable cause to suspect obscenity by clandestine or unorthodox behaviour on the part of his supplier. Any evidence that, for example, a printer has specially increased his profit margin to cover a risk factor, would be fatal to a section 2 (5) claim. Conversely, if the accused can show that the material came to him in the normal course of business from a reputable supplier, he may have a defence. Cases on the liability of distributors for libels in newspapers emphasize the importance for this defence of establishing that the business – of printing, distributing or retailing – was carried on carefully and properly. The test is whether the unwitting distributor *ought* to have known that the material would offend.[57]

In practice, prosecuting authorities frequently distinguish between flagrant and deliberate breaches of the law and those where the defendant may not have intended offence, by prosecuting the former under section 2 of the Act but merely launching forfeiture proceedings against books stocked by innocent disseminators. There is no basis in the Act for this distinction: it is entirely a matter of prosecutorial discretion, and it is not always exercised in the manner suggested by the Solicitor-General in 1964, when he undertook to bring criminal proceedings only against those publishers who manifested an intention to publish irrespective of forfeiture orders.[58] Juries invariably take intention into account: they realize that individuals, not books, are on trial, and display a sympathy for genuine crusaders for sexual enlightenment which is notably lacking in verdicts on commercial traffickers. In the United States the concept of 'pandering', in the sense of aggressively salacious advertising to maximize profits, has been applied by the Supreme Court to deny constitutional protection to defendants who have deliberately and publicly exploited prurience.[59] It would be better to recognize reality by importing *mens rea* into the offence, and permitting the prosecution to adduce evidence of profiteering or anti-social motivation.

COMMUNITY STANDARDS – CURRENCY AND COMPARISONS

Juries at obscenity trials are enjoined to 'keep in mind the current standards of ordinary decent people'.[60] They 'must set the standards of what is acceptable, of what is for the public good in the age in which we live'.[61]

If jurors embody or represent the standards of decency, they must be presumed to know, or at least to be able to identify, current community standards, without the assistance of evidence. The collective experience of twelve people, however arbitrarily chosen, should provide a degree of familiarity with popular reading trends, what is deemed acceptable on television and at cinemas, and the degree of explicitness which can be found in publications on sale at local newsagents. Judge and counsel can invite them to take notice of changes in the contemporary climate, and even point out that the test of obscenity was settled in 1868 by a court which had been told that nothing could be more obscene than the statue of Venus in the Dulwich Gallery.[62] But in considering the question of obscenity juries are not permitted to hear evidence about other publications, at least when it is introduced for the purpose of comparison. A defendant may not argue that he should be acquitted because his publication is less obscene than others which are freely circulated.

This rule was imposed by the Court of Appeal in *R. v. Reiter*,[63] which adopted the reasoning of the High Court of Justiciary in *Galletly v. Laird*:

... the character of the offending books or pictures should be ascertained by the only method by which such a fact can be ascertained, viz., by reading the books or looking at the pictures. The book or picture itself provides the best evidence of its own indecency or obscenity or of the absence of such qualities.... The character of other books is a collateral issue, the exploration of which would be endless and futile. If the books produced by the prosecution are indecent or obscene, their quality in that respect cannot be made any better by examining other books, or listening to the opinions of other people with regard to these other books.[64]

The 1959 Act does, however, provide for two situations in which comparisons are both permissible and highly relevant. Under section 2 (5), it may be that a defendant has 'no reasonable cause to suspect' the obscenity of a book which he has not personally examined because books with similar or identical titles or themes have been acquitted, to his knowledge, in previous proceedings. And under section 4 it may be highly relevant to the jury's task of evaluating the merit of a particular book to compare it with other books of the same kind, and to hear expert evidence about the current climate of permissiveness in relation to this kind of literature. This exception was recognized by Mr Justice Byrne in *R. v. Penguin Books*, when he permitted expert witnesses to compare *Lady Chatterley's Lover* with works by Lawrence and other twentieth-century writers, and to discuss the standards for examining sexual matters reflected in modern literature. At one point in the trial he agreed that 'other books may be considered, for two reasons, firstly, upon the question of the literary merit of the book which is the subject matter of the indictment, ... (where) it is necessary to compare that book with other books upon the question of literary merit. Secondly ... other books are relevant to the climate of literature.'[65] This ruling considerably mitigates the severity of the rule in *Reiter's case*. Where a 'public good' defence is raised, juries may be asked to make comparisons in order to evaluate the real worth of the publication at stake, and they may be told by experts about the state of informed contemporary opinion on subjects dealt with in those publications.

In cases where no 'public good' defence is raised, jurors must be guided by their own knowledge of the world outside the courtroom and by observations about contemporary standards which fall from judge and counsel. There have been occasions when judges have dismissed the 'current climate' as simply a creation of licentious artistic imaginations. In the 1971 trial of Paul Ableman's book *The Mouth and Oral Sex*, Judge King-Hamilton maintained that the real climate was not set by media fashions:

> They set the trend. The author may put four-letter words into his book, a play may have nude scenes, and a film may show an act of sexual intercourse. The fact that many people buy such a book, or see such plays and go to such films, does not necessarily mean that the general standard is set by these people.

The judge asked one witness if he knew 'as a historical fact' that 'Rome fell because of many years of decadence and immorality', and suggested that the British Empire might suffer a similar fate. Jeremy Hutchinson QC enjoined the jury to apply a different perspective.

> Was it permissive books that brought the Empire down, or was it something more important, something called Christianity? Was it an Empire we all want to preserve? People held in bondage without any rights, without any freedom? In Victorian times, what was the position? ... There were industrialists going to church, very proper and moral, when in their factories children were working fourteen to sixteen hours a day at the age of ten. In Leicester Square – you talk now about prostitutes – there were hundreds of prostitutes outside the theatres when the gentlemen came out of their reputable and honourable clubs in the evening.

When it is said that now we are decadent, therefore you, the jury, should stand up and find this gentleman here guilty of publishing this book, not because of the book's obscenity but because it will be in some way a protest against the decadence of our society, I ask you, first, not to act on that basis and, secondly, not to accept what is perhaps the inference as to whether this world we live in, in England, is in fact more decadent than it was a little while ago.[66]

The relevance of judicial nostalgia was firmly rejected by Lord Reid in *Knuller*:

We may regret that we live in a permissive society but I doubt whether even the most staunch defender of a better age would maintain that all or even most of those who have at one time or in one way or another been led astray morally have thereby become depraved or corrupt. I think that the jury should be told in one way or another that although in the end the question whether matter is corrupting is for them, they should keep in mind the current standards of ordinary decent people.[67]

The law of evidence prevents defence counsel from introducing comparative material, so jurors must draw on their own knowledge of the frontiers of permissiveness. Some of their decisions have acquitted purveyors of hard-core pornography, and in 1977 the Court of Appeal was driven to admit:

The difficulty, which becomes ever increasingly apparent, is to know what is the current view of society. In times past there was probably a general consensus of opinion on the subject, but almost certainly there is none today. Not only in books and magazines, on sale at every bookstall and newsagent's shop, but on stage and screen as well society appears to tolerate a degree of sexual candour which has already invaded a large area considered until recently to lie within the forbidden territory of the obscene. The jury's formidable task, with no other guidance than section 1 of the Act gives them (and that is precious little), is to determine where the line should be drawn. However conscientiously juries approach this responsibility, it is doubtful, in the present climate of opinion, whether their verdicts can be expected to maintain any reasonable degree of consistency.[68]

PUBLICATION

There are two separate charges which may be brought in respect of obscene publications. It is an offence to *publish* an obscene article contrary to the Obscene Publications Act of 1959, and it is an offence to *have an obscene article for publication for gain*, contrary to the Obscene

Publications Act of 1964. A charge under the 1959 Act requires some *act* of publication, such as sale to a customer or giving an obscene book to a friend. There must be some evidence connecting the defendant with movement of the article into another's hands. Mere possession of an obscene book will not satisfy the definition of publication in section 1 (3) (b) which governs both Acts:

> For the purposes of this Act a person publishes an article who (a) distributes, circulates, sells, lets on hire, gives, or lends it, or who offers it for sale or for letting on hire; or (b) in the case of an article containing or embodying matter to be looked at or a record, shows, plays or projects it....

Commercial gain is irrelevant to the 1959 offence. The Act specifically refers to 'any person who, *whether for gain or not*, publishes an obscene article'. Gain is a prerequisite, however, for prosecution under the 1964 Act, which widens the ambit of the law by penalizing *possession* of an obscene article, without evidence that it has actually been distributed, provided that the defendant has the article in his ownership, possession or control with the intention of publishing it for gain. It matters not whether the profit goes to him or to some other person, and 'gain' includes advantages in kind as well as in cash. Private possession of obscenity remains legal, so long as the defendant intends to keep it solely to himself. Both crimes require the prosecution to prove that the defendant *intended* to publish – he cannot be convicted if obscene articles kept in a private drawer are stolen and find their way into general circulation. The 1964 Act was designed to close a loophole in the 1959 legislation revealed in the case of *Mella* v. *Monahan*, where it was held that a bookseller who displayed an obscene article in his shop did not thereby 'publish' it: he was merely inviting the public to treat, rather than offering it for sale.[69] The present legal position with regard to publication may be stated as follows:

1 Retention of obscene articles solely for personal use incurs no liability.

2 If those articles are deliberately disclosed, without charge, to sex partners, friends, business associates or any other restricted group, prosecution may be brought under the 1959 Act, but the jury will be confined to considering whether the articles have tended to corrupt that restricted class of persons.

3 If the articles are sold to others, prosecution may follow under either the 1959 or 1964 legislation.

4 If obscene articles are found in the defendant's possession in sufficient quantity to give rise to the inference of an intention to sell,
but there is no actual evidence of distribution, prosecution may only
proceed under the 1964 Act.

5 The defence may be raised, to both charges, that there was no intention of publishing the articles to any other person. It is a defence
to the 1959 charge that no act of publication can be proven to have
taken place, or if it can, that such publication was neither to the
defendant's knowledge nor within his intention. It is a defence to
the 1964 charge that the articles were not in fact in the defendant's
possession or under his control, or that if they were, that he had
no intention to take any form of commercial advantage from their
distribution to others.

The statutory definition of 'publishing' goes on to exclude 'anything
done in the course of television or sound broadcasting'. What is unclear is the point at which 'the course of' television or broadcasting
begins. The protection, to be effective, should run from the time a
writer commences work on a television or radio script: but the courts
may limit the scope of the exemption to those responsible for putting
the material on the airwaves 'in the course of' an actual broadcast.
Writers, directors and actors would be protected, however, if at the
time of their participation their intention was to produce an article
which would not be 'published' in a way which could attract liability
under the Act. An analogous defence succeeded for United Artists
when that company was privately prosecuted for releasing the film
Last Tango in Paris. The evidence established that the company had
'let on hire' a copy of the film to the licensee of a London cinema,
who had in turn screened it to audiences made up of ordinary
members of the public. At the time, the Obscene Publications Act
provided an exemption for commercial film shows, as well as for television and broadcasting. The Court of Appeal, in *Attorney General's
Reference (No. 2 of 1975)*, confirmed that the act of screening a film
in a public cinema was not a 'publication' for the purposes of the
Obscene Publications Act, because the proviso then excluded cinematograph exhibitions.[70] United Artists had 'published' the film by
'letting it on hire', but only to the licensee of the cinema, who was
not a person susceptible to corruption. The thousands who had
flocked to his cinema had, of course, seen the film, but not as the result
of any 'publication' to them within the meaning of the Act, and
although they may have been in danger of corruption from this oppor-

tunity to 'see or hear the matter contained or embodied in it', they had not seen or heard it as a result of a 'publication'. This exemption for cinema films was subsequently repealed by section 53 of the 1977 Criminal Law Act.

Those who participate in or promote obscene publications are entitled to acquittal if they intend their work to be 'published' in a manner which falls outside the Act, either specifically (in the course of television or radio transmissions) or because they genuinely believe that distribution will be confined to a select group immune from corruption, or to those countries which do not have laws against obscene publications. A film producer, for example, who makes a 'blue movie' in England and then takes the negative to Denmark for development and ensuing commercial distribution commits no offence under English law, unless he is aware of plans to re-import copies for sale in Britain. Major English studios sometimes make two versions of feature films, a 'hard' edition for continental distribution and a 'soft' version suitable for home consumption. But the prosecution is not put to specific proof that obscene material is intended for publication in a manner which will infringe the Act, if such publication is a common-sense inference from the circumstances of production. In *R. v. Salter and Barton*, two actors were charged with aiding and abetting an offence under the 1964 Act by performing in an obscene movie. They had been paid £25 for their day's work, and they denied any knowledge of the producer's purpose or his distribution plans. The Court of Appeal held that ignorance could not avail them, although positive belief in a limited publication would have provided a defence:

... common sense says that if the evidence showed that these films were to be distributed generally for gain the vast majority of purchasers would be those who were either addicted to pornography or out of curiosity thought they would buy some pornographic films. If that was the market, inevitably there must have been some in that market who, if they bought the films, were likely to be depraved and corrupted ... Neither of (the defendants) sought to say that they thought the films were being used for the purpose of sociological research, medical investigation or anything of that kind, nor did they say that they thought the films were going to be shown in places where such showings did not come within the ambit of the Obscene Publications Act, 1959. Ignorance was the basis of their defence. In this case what the jury had to be satisfied about was that these two appellants both knew that the film was going to be distributed generally for gain, and, if they knew that, then such distribution was likely to bring the film to the notice of some who might be depraved and corrupted.[71]

In *Attorney General's Reference (No. 2 of 1975)* the Court of Appeal confirmed that: 'The Act is not concerned with the obscenity of articles which are not published or intended or kept for publication. In a general sense to read, to see and to hear involve the publication of what is read, seen or heard to the person who reads, sees or hears.'[72] But the Act *does* concern itself with articles which are circulated in the most private and restricted circumstances. Anyone who 'gives' an article to another commits a 'publication'. A husband who shows his wife an obscene book, a couple who invite neighbours to watch erotic home movies, friends who swap their porn collections, are all within the ambit of the law. A prohibition on private distribution would be justified in cases where the defendant's purpose is to corrupt, but, since motive is irrelevant, the Act extends into personal areas which might be thought beyond the province of the criminal law. Canadian courts, defining the word 'publication' unfettered by statutory definitions, have ruled that its meaning does not cover non-commercial screenings of obscene films to guests in private houses.[73] An American statute similar to section 3 of the English Act, authorizing seizure of pornography from private houses, has been struck down by the US Supreme Court with Justice Marshall's forceful reminder that dislike of obscenity provides 'insufficient justification for such a drastic invasion of personal liberties . . . a State has no business telling a man, sitting alone in his own house, what books he may read or what films he may watch. Our whole constitutional history rebels at the thought of giving Government the power to control men's minds.'[74]

TIME LIMIT ON PROSECUTIONS

A limitation on prosecutions is contained in section 2 (3) of the 1959 Act, which stipulates that 'A prosecution on indictment for an offence against this section shall not be commenced more than two years after the commission of the offence.' One object of this provision was to avoid the uncertainty of some nineteenth-century cases, in which books circulating for decades were suddenly and arbitrarily selected for prosecution. The section is inadequately drafted for this purpose, because an offence is 'committed', not by first exposure of a book, but by an individual defendant, who may first stock the work many years after its initial publication. The Court of Appeal has now interpreted the section in a way which renders it inapt as a protection for writers, performers and publishers who have assisted in putting an article into circulation originally, but whose contribution to its publication has effectively ceased more than two years prior to their arrest. The offences of 'publishing' and 'possessing for publication for gain' are *continuing* offences, and an individual contribution stays alive for as long as the article remains on the market. In *R.* v. *Salter and Barton*, the defendants' actual participation in the project of publishing obscene films had ended when they were paid at the conclusion of their performance, and more than two years elapsed before their arrest. Over that period they had made no contact with the film's producer, and were unaware of its wide distribution. The Court of Appeal held that section 2 (3) did not apply to bar their prosecution, because the defendants' original purpose had been to assist in the commission of an offence which they knew would be committed after their own contribution had concluded, and would continue for some time thereafter.

On behalf of the Crown it was said that the offences charged against the principals, namely having for publication for gain and publishing for distribution for gain, were continuing ones and that they continued to be committed over a period of time. In relation to film production that must be so. When a film is made it is intended not only that it should come into existence for the purpose of publication when it is made but as long as that film is held it is being held for the purpose of showing it at a later date ... those who aid and abet an offence which is a continuing one commit this offence on the same dates as the principals.... Those who help someone to commit a continuing offence run the risk, until they dissociate themselves from that continuing offence, that they may be found guilty of aiding and abetting its commission.[75]

How can actors, cameramen, writers, printers or publishers 'disassociate themselves' from a continuing publication? The Court of Appeal gave no guidance, other than indicating, by its decision, that some positive act of renunciation is required. The defendants had no further involvement with film production from the moment they were paid, so 'disassociation' must mean more than 'not associated with'. Would it have sufficed for them to request the producer to destroy the film, or were they obliged to go further and report the matter to the police? Does 'disassociation' imply an element of mind-change, satisfied by public recantation? Must they go further, in order to claim the protection of section 2 (3), and produce evidence that more than two years before their arrest they had endeavoured to destroy all available copies of the film? The decision in *R.* v. *Salter and Barton* requires legislative action if any force is to be given to section 2 (3) other than as a mandate for police to keep articles seized under the Act for up to two years while deciding whether to prosecute.

DOUBLE JEOPARDY

It is a fundamental principle of criminal jurisprudence that a man must not be placed in 'double jeopardy' by suffering second trial for an offence of which he has previously been acquitted or convicted. Similarly, it is undesirable that an issue settled by one trial should be litigated over and over again. The Obscene Publications Act provides a stark exception to both of these basic precepts. A man who is acquitted of publishing an article to customers in one part of the country may subsequently be indicted for publishing the same article elsewhere. This result follows from the 'relative' concept of obscenity: an article is not obscene in itself, but only in relation to its particular audience, and every separate act of publication involves a separate set of circumstances and gives rise to the prospect of a different jury verdict. A defendant who is prosecuted a second time cannot avail himself of the plea of 'autrefois acquit', because he has been charged with a different offence – publishing the same article, but at a different time or place. Nor can he rely upon the doctrine of 'issue estoppel', a rule of civil law which precludes one party to litigation from raising any issue which has been conclusively determined in earlier proceedings. The House of Lords in *DPP* v. *Humphrys* held that this rule has no place in criminal law, with the consequence that the acquittal of one publisher for distributing a particular book does not stop the prosecution from proceeding against another in respect of the same work.[76]

Lord Salmon has suggested that trial judges possess an inherent power to halt prosecutions which are oppressive and vexatious, or which may 'smack of an attempt by a disappointed prosecution to find what is considered to be a more perspicacious jury or tougher judge'.[77] But it is unlikely that the court would exercise this power on behalf of a defendant who would be perceived simply as an inveterate pornographer who has been once lucky. 'Those who skate on thin ice', Lord Morris has warned, 'cannot be heard to complain if they fall in.'[78] Their only real protection lies in the sense of fair play exhibited by prosecuting authorities, who are generally unwilling to breach the spirit of the convention against double jeopardy. Their largesse is sorely strained in obscenity cases, because they suffer from reverse handicaps. 'Autrefois convict' is not available, and 'issue estoppel' will not run against an incorrigible defendant. A long and costly trial, which results in the conviction of one individual for publishing an obscene book, does not preclude another individual from putting the prosecution to proof all over again, by republishing the same book. A defendant convicted in one town, or at one time, may recommence publication in another place, or in the same place at a later time, and argue that circumstances have changed in the interim. A book declared obscene in one year may be published in a more permissive climate a few years later. A conviction marks the beginning, and not the end, of the struggle.

These problems have been exemplified in litigation over the activities of a film director named John Lindsay. In 1972 he made a batch of blue movies which were sold through commercial outlets in Birmingham and London. In 1974 he was charged with conspiracy to publish obscenity, but was acquitted by a Birmingham jury. He returned to Soho, where he opened a shop which sold only those films which were the subject matter of the Birmingham indictment. His activities came to the notice of the Attorney-General who decided to waive the convention against double jeopardy and to direct another prosecution, this time against Lindsay alone for direct infringement of the Obscene Publications Act. At the trial it was argued that the judge should invoke his residual power to halt oppressive and vexatious proceedings, because Lindsay was effectively being tried a second time on the same allegation which had not been proved against him in Birmingham. This was rejected, because the relative definition of obscenity required the London jury to assess the consequences of Lindsay's new distribution arrangements. The prosecution moved that no reference should be made to the Birmingham proceedings, but Lindsay had packaged his films in boxes which referred to his previous acquittal, and had decorated his shop with posters made up from press coverage about the Birmingham trial. This publicity material was present to the eyes and minds of potential customers, and the judge ruled that it was admissible in evidence. Lindsay was again found 'not guilty', a verdict he celebrated by placing his twice-acquitted films on continuous show at a Soho cinema club, where he now awaits a third prosecution.

COMPLICITY

Those who agree to publish obscenity may be charged with conspiracy to contravene the Act, and those who facilitate publication (for example, by advertising books known to be obscene) are guilty of aiding and abetting the offence. In every case where two or more persons are involved in possessing or publishing obscene articles it is theoretically possible to charge conspiracy as well as substantive offences under the 1959 and 1964 Acts, although the Court of Appeal has discouraged the addition of conspiracy counts in such cases unless 'charges of substantive offences do not adequately express the overall criminality'.[79] In 1977 the Court issued a Practice Direction requiring prosecutors to justify any inclusion of a conspiracy count overlapping with substantive charges, a tactic which would only be upheld where 'the interests of justice demand it'.[80] It follows that statutory conspiracy should only be resorted to in cases involving distribution networks which have operated over a long period of time, or to incriminate 'behind the scenes' organizers who have never taken obscene books into their possession, or else to catch pornography enterprises which have not commenced publication at the time of police action.

Those who knowingly assist the production or distribution of obscene articles – by procuring models, taking or processing photographs, printing magazines, or warehousing material – may be charged as aiders and abetters. In *R.* v. *De Marney* the Court of Appeal upheld the conviction of a magazine editor who had published advertisements for obscene books, thereby facilitating the advertiser's offence of publishing obscenity, although the advertisements were themselves unexceptionable.[81] Section 2 (4) of the Obscene Publications Act 1959 provides:

> A person publishing an article shall not be proceeded against for an offence at common law consisting of the publication of any matter contained or embodied in the article where it is of the essence of the offence that the matter is obscene.

Although conspiracy was, until 1977, a common-law offence, the Court of Appeal in *R.* v. *Clayton & Halsey* ruled that section 2 (4) did not preclude a charge of conspiracy to contravene the Act, because the essence of such a conspiracy count is not the *publication* of obscenity but the *anterior agreement* to publish.[82] Actual publication is not a necessary element in the offence. The only effect of section 2 (4) is to abolish prosecutions for the common-law offence of obscene libel: publishers may still be charged with conspiracy to contravene the 1959 or 1964 Acts, or with conspiracy to commit the common-law offences of corrupting public morals or outraging public decency. In *Shaw* v. *DPP* the House of Lords rejected an argument that section 2 (4) barred such prosecutions: 'The offence at common law alleged, namely, conspiracy to corrupt public morals, did not "consist of the publication" of the magazines, it consisted of an agreement to corrupt public morals by means of the magazines, which might never have been published.'[83] This analysis was approved, albeit reluctantly, in *R. v. Knuller*, where Lord Reid commented that 'technically the distinction ... is correct but it appears to me to offend against the policy of the Act, and if the draftsman of the Act of 1959 had foreseen the decision in *Shaw's* case he might well have drafted the subsection differently'.[84] Draftsmen of subsequent legislation, with hindsight of *Shaw's* case, have specifically excluded common-law conspiracies in respect of plays and films,[85] and the Law Officers have given Parliamentary undertakings that conspiracy to corrupt public morals would not be used so as to deprive publishers of the 'public good' defence.[86] It has been held that this defence may be raised by a defendant accused of conspiring to contravene the Act,[87] although it is difficult to see how it could operate if no 'article' were in existence, because the merits of any projected publication would be entirely hypothetical.

The decision to charge conspiracy rather than a substantive obscenity offence will provide some tactical advantage to the prosecution. Hearsay evidence may be received to suggest that the defendant agreed to commit the crime, and convictions may more readily be achieved through 'guilt by association'. The particularity normally required in criminal indictments does not affect conspiracy charges: they may refer to 'divers dates' over many years, and to agreement 'with persons unknown'. But these advantages may be more apparent than real. There is increasing evidence that conspiracy counts are counter-productive in the fight against crime. They tend to lengthen the trial, confuse the issues, and bewilder the jury. In some respects charges of conspiracy to contravene the Obscene Publications Act will be more difficult to prove than substantive counts of publishing or possessing obscenity for gain. The latter charges do not require proof of an intention to corrupt, but conspiracy does demand knowledge of the criminal consequence of the agreement. A defendant to a conspiracy charge would be entitled to argue that at the time he entered into the agreement to publish he believed that the articles concerned would not corrupt readers, or else that they would only be published in circumstances where they would have no deleterious effect. Participants in initial stages of obscenity conspiracies are not guilty if they believed any obscenity would be edited out prior to publication, or else was intended for publication outside the jurisdiction of English courts, in countries where obscenity laws are more lax. Although they may have been aware that the finished product could corrupt, they would not have the requisite criminal intent if they genuinely believed that any obscenity would be redeemed by its literary or artistic value. These defences to conspiracy charges are left open by section 1 (2) of the 1977 Criminal Law Act, which provides that

> Where liability for any offence may be incurred without knowledge on the part of the person committing it of any particular fact or circumstance necessary for the commission of the offence, a person shall nevertheless not be guilty of conspiracy to commit that offence by virtue of subsection (1) above unless he and at least one other party to the agreement intend or know that that fact or circumstance shall or will exist at the time when the conduct constituting the offence is to take place.

Even if the defendants agree to publish an article which they hope or expect will be obscene, they cannot be convicted of conspiracy if the article, when published, turns out to be within the law.[88]

An individual commits no crime merely by deciding, on his own initiative, to publish a sexually explicit book. Thought is free. But if two or more persons put their heads together and come to the same decision, their mere agreement may be made the subject of a charge of conspiracy to publish or to possess obscene articles. Two heads, in conspiracy theory, are guiltier than one. This is an irrational result, but it has long been embedded in the common law, and is now given statutory life by the Criminal Law Act of 1977. Conspiracy theory has some social rationale in cases where criminal gangs are apprehended while planning violent crime, but it may be doubted whether publishers deserve to be prosecuted for plots which never thicken. A man on the verge of publishing an obscene article may be charged with an *attempt* to commit the substantive offence. If he organizes or encourages others to peddle obscenity, he is guilty of *inciting* the offence. If a conspiracy is nipped *after* it has budded, anyone who has aided and abetted or counselled and procured the publication may be convicted of complicity in the complete crime. Conspiracy is unnecessary, because the scope of attempt, incitement, or complicity, coupled with the wide terms of the 1959 and 1964 statutory offences, is ample for police intervention whenever public danger is realistically apprehended.

4
Enforcing the Obscene Publications Act

CASTING THE FIRST STONE

The predominant characteristic of English obscenity law is vagueness, with the consequence that a wide discretion is vested in prosecuting authorities. When books, films, or magazines have been seized by police, a decision must be made on the method of proceeding against their owner. There are two statutory alternatives: either a prosecution for a criminal offence under section 2 of the 1959 Act, or a civil forfeiture hearing under section 3. In the former case, a summons is issued against the occupier or any other person who may have assisted publication, and the trial proceeds either before a magistrate (who may sentence a convicted defendant to a maximum term of six months' imprisonment and/or a fine of £400) or, at the election of either party, before a Crown Court judge and jury, where the sentence may be as high as three years, and the fine unlimited. Section 3 forfeiture proceedings, on the other hand, involve no criminal charge or consequence other than destruction of the articles if a magistrate or a bench of lay justices is satisfied that they are obscene. The procedure differs in each case, and the decision as to which course to adopt will be made by police lawyers, in consultation with the office of the Director of Public Prosecutions.

Police action

The police formulate their own internal guidelines for action on obscenity, and these generally provide some extra-legal restraint on the powers of individual officers. In the London area, for example, a confidential memorandum was drawn up for police guidance in

1970. It was avowedly motivated by concern at the prospect of a 'bad press': whenever publicity of any sort was apprehended, a 'report before action' would be considered at senior level. But in routine cases of 'filth for filth's sake', warrants might be applied for 'following observations and information' – in other words, on mere suspicion. The only safeguard was that all search warrants required approval from a Detective Inspector of the Obscene Publications Squad – or 'the dirty squad' as it is generally known. This regulation was designed to achieve uniformity, although at the time it had the effect of consolidating the corrupt monopoly of that Squad over Soho bribery and protection rackets. The directive records that

> The special difficulties in policing the delicate field of pornography/ obscenity are appreciated.... Routine observations, enquiries and subsequent search and seizure of unquestionably 'hard-core' pornography from the 'dirty bookshops' do not attract very much publicity or any real protest. Clearly, in this field it is relatively simple to assert that the seized articles are 'filth for filth's sake' ... However, it is clear that there is a level of pornography which is exceptionally delicate, where any police action will obviously attract much publicity, subsequent analysis and criticism. It is impossible to set out an exhaustive list but obvious examples are:
> (a) Displays in recognized galleries and books expensively published
> (b) Works of alleged or real masters
> (c) Exhibitions of famous, infamous or notorious individuals
> (d) Films at private clubs and associations, etc.
> In any such case which is likely to be the source of more than average publicity, it is necessary to establish and determine police action with proportionate care.
>
> Police will not seek out such displays or exhibitions to discover possible obscenity offences. Only when the weight of complaints makes it necessary to determine what police action, if any, should be taken will we trouble ourselves with such matters....[1]

In the absence of more explicit official guidance, the squad makes do with its own rules of thumb for identifying 'filth for filth's sake'. In 1978, erections, labial, anal, oral, child, animal, and group sexual depictions were the main taboo subjects. The politics and racial origins of the borderline bookseller have not been entirely ignored: Marxists and coloureds have figured disproportionately over the years as victims of bookshop raids. The 'dirty squad's' finesse at spotting hippie needles in haystacks of hard-core commercial pornography was frequently displayed in the early seventies: because of deep personal antipathy to the 'alternative society', police took liberties against underground press editors which they would not have inflicted upon professional criminals and commercial photographers. More recently the Squad's targets have shifted to pornography imported from the Continent, especially that featuring violence, and to the less prepossessing class of English men's magazines. In the first five months of 1978 articles worth more than £1 million were seized in London alone.[2]

If pornography does contaminate, its first victims ought logically to be those who handle it most. Policemen usually deny feeling any glimmers of sensation at perusing erotica, although one officer admitted to suffering 'a general dirtying of the mind' from the ordeal of reading *Oz*.[3] A more common problem is boredom – the satiation effect.[4] One 'dirty squad' detective who had viewed ninety pornographic movies in the course of investigating a case in 1973, admitted in court that work had caused him to lose interest in 'normal marital sex'.[5] After this cri de cœur, the Commissioner announced that officers would be transferred from the squad after two years' service – a measure which had less to do with solicitude for marital harmony than with concern that longer exposure might enure officers not to porn but to protection rackets. At least life in the 'dirty squad' circa 1972 amused one of its members, who survived to tell the tale:

Much of our labour turned out to be a waste of time in the changing moral climate. But we did everything we were required to do with a will, and lightened the sordid aspect of our task with all measure of japes and jollification. The dirty squad were a great bunch of fellows to work with and I had more laughs with them than at any other time. It was probably the right attitude. If we'd taken a serious interest in everything we saw we'd have ended up like the dirty old men whose fun we were out to spoil. Basically we were the DPP's runners, as far as obscene publications were concerned.... I saw some very odd sights. I wasn't shocked and I stopped being amazed. After all there's a physical limit to what can be done in the sex act, and basically, when you've seen one dirty book you've seen them all. Even the action with animals – pigs, donkeys, horses and dogs – was so remote from the real thing as to be idiotic. If that was what people liked, that was their problem. 'Chacun a son blue' as one wit remarked. It wasn't for me. And it didn't bother me, as long as they didn't do it in the road. What I didn't like were the scenes showing beatings, cuttings, and burnings, really vicious stuff that made me feel quite ill. Most of the time the material we saw was just a source of rude comments, comparisons, and cues for jokes. This particularly applied to the films.... Occasionally on a Friday evening we might have a special showing for selected friends and acquaintances in CI – a sort of stag party. During the week we had a bit of fun with the tea ladies, accidentally exposing them to something spicy and giving them the giggles. Whichever way you looked at the dirty squad – dull it wasn't.[6]

The Director of Public Prosecutions

The 'dirty squad' and its provincial equivalents devote life on the beat to reading, raiding and reporting to the DPP, who must be consulted over the decision on whether to prosecute or initiate forfeiture proceedings. The DPP is himself obliged by the statute establishing his office to work 'under the superintendence of the Attorney-General',[7] who is in turn responsible to Parliament for the Director's conduct. Under the Theatres Act the Attorney must personally authorize any prosecution of a stage play, and since it is normal practice for the Director to consult the Law Officers on cases of special importance or difficulty, it is inevitable that the men who must answer for it in Parliament should be consulted on general prosecuting policy in obscenity cases. The revival in 1969 of charges of 'conspiracy to corrupt public morals' to depth-charge the underground press was specifically approved by Sir Elwyn Jones, and in 1976 Mr Sam Silkin approved a decision to prosecute John Lindsay a second time in respect of films which had already been the subject of acquittal at a trial in 1974 (see page 77). These were important policy decisions and they were approved by Law Officers who could (and did) suffer public criticism when they were implemented. Routine decisions to prosecute are normally made by lawyers in the Director's office without reference to the Law Officers. After the acquittal of *Inside Linda Lovelace*, the Solicitor-General publicly denied any part in the initiation of police action against the publisher, which was taken after a complaint was received in the DPP's office from a retired barrister who had bought the book at a station bookstall in Brighton.

The DPP's officers maintain some centralized control over obscenity prosecutions by reading material seized by metropolitan and provincial police or submitted by members of the public, advising whether its publisher should be prosecuted and if so under what section of what Act, and keeping records of the results of prosecutions in attempts to identify patterns in jury verdicts. The DPP's involvement is required by section 6 (2) (d) of the Prosecution of Offenders Regulations 1946, which obliges police forces to report to the DPP 'cases of obscene or indecent publications, in which it appears to the chief officer of police that there is a prima facie case for prosecution'.[8] The regulation does not oblige police to stay all action until the Director's advice is received, although this is the usual practice for reasons of prudence. In *R. v. Metropolitan Police Commissioner, ex p. Blackburn* the Court of Appeal sympathized with official apprehension about

'what might be said of the police had they prosecuted without await-
ing the director's advice and the director then offered no evidence
in a prosecution previously launched by the police', and acknowledged the desirability of achieving a uniform standard for obscenity
prosecutions throughout the country by the system of referral to a
centralized department.[9]

The DPP acts, in effect, as custodian of public morals, although
this role is one which Directors traditionally deprecate or disavow.
In a memorandum to the Select Committee on the Obscene Publications Bill, Sir Theobald Matthew deplored the fact that his Department was forced to act as a censor of literature.[10] In evidence to the
Committee, he frankly admitted, 'I do not know, and I do not suppose anybody else knows, what corrupts.'[11] His successor, Sir Norman
Skelhorn, maintained:

> The DPP is not acting as a censor, he is not judging the moral standards
> of the day. All we try to do is predict what a jury is likely to do. We try
> to assess the prospects of conviction if we prosecute. Of course, it is not easy
> to predict what a jury is likely to do, but one is guided by the statutory defini-
> tion of obscenity and one's experience of how the courts have reacted in pre-
> vious cases.[12]

But the loose statutory definition of obscenity gives little guidance,
and jury verdicts have been too inconsistent to provide a reasonable
basis for prediction. Anxious publishers who enquire about their
wares are simply referred to the Obscene Publications Act and advised
to consult their own lawyers. In 1966, when the firm of Calder &
Boyars first submitted *Last Exit to Brooklyn* to the DPP, they received,
in the words of the Court of Appeal, 'an inconclusive reply', ending
with the sentence, 'If you find – as I am afraid you will – that this
is a most unhelpful letter, it is not because I wish to be unhelpful
but because I get no help from the Acts.'[13] Ten years later the new
Director, Sir Thomas Hetherington, was none the wiser. 'I regret that
I am unable to give you the type of advice you seek regarding the
operation of the Obscene Publications Acts,' was his stock response
to worried publishers. 'I am unable to do so because of the generally
recognized uncertainty in the operation of law in this field.'[14]

Private prosecutions

If the DPP did not know the law, there were others who thought
they did. Mrs Mary Whitehouse launched a private prosecution
against the film *Blow Out*; Mr Ross McWhirter sought to injunct the

BBC from televising a documentary on Andy Warhol; Mr Ernest Shackleton prosecuted the distributors of *Last Tango in Paris*, and Mr Raymond Blackburn indicted a number of cinema managers for showing indecent films. On only one occasion – a Blackburn prosecution of the film *More About the Language of Love* – did the DPP intervene to take over the conduct of the trial, and secured conviction of the film's exhibitors for holding an indecent exhibition. The case is the only recent example of private initiative affecting public prosecution policy: other cases failed, for the most part on technical grounds. There is no evidence that private prosecutions do more than create additional confusion over the limits of acceptability.

The right of private individuals to initiate prosecutions is a fundamental principle of English criminal law, although in 1961 the High Court of Scotland refused to allow a private prosecution of *Lady Chatterley's Lover*, ruling that 'no private complainer can be keeper of the public conscience'.[15] In 1958 the Select Committee on Obscene Publications considered whether an exception should be made in obscenity cases in order to secure some uniformity in the administration of vague and controversial laws which might otherwise be invoked vexatiously or eccentrically. The Attorney-General firmly opposed the suggestion, on the ground that 'Uniformity in the administration of the law is a matter for the courts themselves and should not, in my view, be achieved by interposing the decisions of officers of the executive between them and the law which they administer.'[16] This constitutional doctrine prevailed until 1967, when it was abandoned after the confusion over *Last Exit to Brooklyn*. The DPP at first declined to prosecute Messrs Calder & Boyars, after his experts advised that the book had literary merit and would do readers no psychiatric damage. Sir Cyril Black MP disagreed, and summoned a London bookseller to 'show cause' why his copies of the book should not be destroyed. These section 3 proceedings denied Calder & Boyars the right to trial by jury, and placed the onus on them to prove that the book was not obscene. The magistrate ordered destruction, an action which obliged the Law Officers to reverse their earlier decision and to bring criminal proceedings against the publishers. The inconvenience and confusion which might arise from conflicting decisions over the same book in different magistrates' courts in different parts of the country convinced the Government that proceedings should not be initiated by members of the public, and section 25 of the 1967 Criminal Justice Act prohibited private applications for destruction orders. In the same year the Solicitor-General warned the

Joint Committee on Censorship of the Theatre that obscenity was an area prone to attract vexatious prosecutions because 'difficulties of definition are such that the letter of the law becomes substantially wider than the spirit', and recommended that the fiat of the Attorney-General should be required for any action against stage plays.[17] This principle was embodied in the Theatres Act 1968, and similar protection was extended to the cinema by the Criminal Law Act 1977, which requires all proceedings relating to the exhibition of feature films to be initiated by the DPP.[18] After private prosecutions against *Gay News* and *Private Eye*, the Royal Commission on the Press recommended that no action for obscenity, blasphemy, sedition or criminal libel should be taken against newspapers without the consent of the DPP.[19]

POLICE SEARCH AND SEIZURE

For booksellers, the policeman on the beat is the ad hoc community censor: to ignore his advice against stocking a particular article would invite unwelcome seizures and expensive legal proceedings. Yet the wide discretion given to police forces in England makes obscenity control arbitrary and sporadic, as the zeal of any particular force to tackle the problem will vary with its manpower and make-up. In 1977 the Chief Constable of Manchester launched a 'clean-up campaign' which involved the seizure of many magazines which were freely available throughout the rest of the country. But even a determined effort by a large and disciplined unit will not avail against the wiles of determined pornographers, a fact which was dramatically illustrated in 1973, in the course of a Court of Appeal hearing of a complaint by Mr Raymond Blackburn against the inaction of Scotland Yard's eighteen-man obscenity squad. Whenever counsel for Scotland Yard mentioned the name of a shop recently raided by police, Mr Blackburn's assistants would rush to that very shop, purchase the most flagrant pornography, and carry it triumphantly into court, as proof of the ineffectiveness of police action. After this demonstration, the court was understandably cynical about police raids in Soho, but exculpated the Commissioner on the ground that the present obscenity law was difficult to enforce.[20]

The search warrant

Ironically, the sponsors of the 1959 legislation had been concerned to strengthen even further the broad powers of search and seizure contained in the 1857 Act. Any police officer may obtain a search warrant merely by telling a justice of the peace that he suspects obscene material is stored at an address within the court's jurisdiction. The power is contained in section 3 (1) of the 1959 Act, which provides:

> If a justice of the peace is satisfied by information on oath that there is reasonable ground for suspecting that, in any premises in the petty sessions area for which he acts, or on any stall or vehicle within that area, being premises or a stall or vehicle specified in the information, obscene articles are, or are from time to time, kept for publication for gain, the justice may issue a warrant under his hand empowering any constable to enter (if need be by force) and search the premises, or to search the stall or vehicle, within fourteen days from the date of the warrant, and to seize and remove any articles found therein or thereon which the constable has reason to believe to be obscene articles and to be kept for publication for gain.

The 1857 Act at least required some evidence of sale before a warrant could be issued, but the 1959 Act only requires a constable to say on oath that he has 'reasonable cause' for such a suspicion, which might be aroused by an unverified complaint from a member of the public, or by police observation that a shop sells 'adult' magazines. This extensive power might be appropriate in relation to warehouses which are closed to public inspection, but it is regularly used to mandate raids upon bookshops and newsagents where stock is on open display. In such cases, a modicum of control over arbitrary seizures could be achieved by requiring a 'test purchase' to be submitted to the magistrate as evidence that pornographic material is in fact being sold by the occupier whose shop is the object of the search warrant application. In deciding whether to issue a warrant the magistrate must act judicially, in the sense that he must be satisfied that reasonable cause has been shown,[21] but under the 1959 Act he is entitled to make his decision on the strength of one policeman's unexamined assertion. The only fetters upon police discretion are that the search must take place within fourteen days of the issue of the warrant, and that the officer who makes the application must suspect both that material on the premises is obscene *and* that it may be distributed commercially. The Act does not authorize search or seizure of private collections.

Police seizure

Once a warrant has been issued, police officers are empowered to confiscate any article they reasonably believe is obscene, and this discretion can extend to any book, film or magazine which deals with sex, violence or drugs. Most bookshops and newsagencies stock 'adult' publications on special racks, out of the reach of children – a practice which simplifies the task of police, who usually seize all articles there, irrespective of merit. Magazines like *Playboy* and *Forum*, which the DPP does not regard as appropriate for prosecution, are frequently made the subject of destruction orders after indiscriminate seizures. A magistrate has no duty to specify, on the face of the warrant, a particular title which he deems fit for seizure, so that police are given in practice an entirely free hand to remove from bookshop shelves any publication which they dislike. A general warrant is obviously suitable in the case of a pornographic bookshop with a high turnover, where the books in stock at the time of the raid may be different to those which caused offence at the time of the initial complaint or investigation. But common victims of section 3 raids are respectable High Street newsagents, who stock monthly magazines on regular supply from reputable wholesalers. A more satisfactory policy in such cases would be for police to consult beforehand with the DPP as to which periodicals were appropriate for seizure, and to specify their titles on the search warrant. This would at least avoid the unseemly spectacle, reported on several occasions, of a DPP representative requesting a court *not* to destroy a particular magazine which had been included amongst a batch of seized articles.

Police armed with a search warrant may seize additional material relating to the business of the occupier. Section 3 (2) provides that

> A warrant under the foregoing subsection shall, if any obscene articles are seized under the warrant, also empower the seizure and removal of any documents found in the premises or, as the case may be, on the stall or vehicle which relate to a trade or business carried on at the premises or from the stall or vehicle.

Business records may be relevant to a possible prosecution if they show the volume of trade conducted by the occupier, or the nature of his customers. But the section is worded so widely that it entitles police to seize *any* documents, whether or not they relate to trade in the suspected article. This is a statutory extension of the search power at common law which 'does not permit police officers, or anyone else, to ransack anyone's house, or to search for papers or articles therein, or to search his person simply to see if he may have committed some crime or other'.[22] The common law does, however, permit seizure of goods or records which are reasonably believed to provide material evidence in relation to the offence for which the warrant is issued.[23] The combination of this common-law power with the statutory authority of section 3 (2) bestows a broad mandate upon police officers to close down a publishing operation or a bookshop before any court has had an opportunity to consider the case. These powers were subjected to severe political and legal criticism in 1970, when police raided a cinema showing Andy Warhol's *Flesh*, and seized not only the film but the projection equipment and even the theatre screen.[24] At much the same time, the offices of 'underground' magazines were raided repeatedly in clumsy attempts to close them down. Quite apart from allegedly obscene magazines, seizures were made of files, artwork, records, personal address-books, invoices and even filing cabinets and pictures on the walls. It is hard to comprehend how documents relating to legitimate business could be claimed as 'material evidence' of an obscenity charge, but section 3 (2) authorizes seizure nonetheless. Another serious defect in the section is that no provision is made for police to give receipts to occupiers verifying the amount or nature of property seized, and some occupiers have complained of a shortfall in the stock which ultimately appears in court. The absence of a duty to provide receipts facilitated police corruption in Soho, when pornography seized in bulk on raids was sold back to shopkeepers by the same policemen who had confiscated it.

One handicap to effective enforcement of the law is that a search warrant may only be issued in respect of premises where obscene material is stored – normally warehouses, shops and offices. In the pornography trade, as in other vice enterprises, the central figures do not incriminate themselves by overt links with the illegal operation. 'Warehouses' are often lock-up garages leased by underlings in false names, while shops are run by men of straw who 'front' for the real criminals who collect the profits. Only fortuitously will evidence implicating major criminals be discovered on raids, and 'front men' will normally fulfil their function by taking responsibility. In most cases they will not even know the real identity of the man who pays their salaries. Those who organize importation and distribution stay far away from shop counters, although they may not be able to avoid some link with the leasehold through nominee companies. One possible method of drawing them into the police net would involve creation of an offence of knowingly permitting premises to be used for sale of obscene material, and giving police the power to search private addresses of shareholders or directors of companies with property rights in premises where obscene material has been discovered.

A complaint often voiced by publishers is that police acting in pursuance of a warrant may seize their entire stock – sometimes many thousands of copies – of a book which has at that stage not even been considered by the DPP. The 'material evidence' requirement would be satisfied by taking a handful of copies – sufficient for submission to the Director and, in the event of a prosecution, for jury and counsel to read at the trial. There are dicta in some cases which suggest that police should only take a sample sufficient for the purposes of their investigation – 'if a copy will suffice, it should be made and the original returned'.[25] It is arguable that the police have no right to take more than a few samples of each suspected title, but the point has not been directly tested, and police practice varies. It would go some way towards meeting the complaint if 'sample' copies only were seized, and the publisher was allowed to retain the rest of his stock upon entering into recognizances that it would not be distributed unless and until the matter was concluded in his favour. There is, however, a more fundamental problem: is an accused publisher entitled to continue distribution of an allegedly obscene article while court proceedings are pending? Usually more than a year will elapse between seizure and trial, and financial loss will accrue to small publishing companies which cannot sell stock in the period before the hearing. Since a defendant is presumed innocent until proven guilty, there would seem to be no objection in principle to continuing in operation, subject to the practical danger that evidence of further sale might increase the ultimate penalty. Nor can it be satisfactory that material which is finally found to have a corrupting tendency is on open distribution for a long period. Police seek to avoid the problem by confiscating all the stock they can find, but this is no solution in cases involving periodicals and cinema clubs, where persistent raids might be relied upon by the defence at the trial as evidence of police harassment, and painted as an attempt to pre-judge the issue. Even a prosecution launched by the DPP does not stop a determined defendant from protesting his innocence by republishing the article: this action, and any reaction by the authorities, is a calculated risk for either side.

The broad scope of police powers under obscenity warrants is the subject of frequent complaints. Richard Neville, the editor of *Oz* magazine, has recalled how his 'bust' turned into a search for drugs and politically subversive literature where an obscenity squad ransacked his personal belongings. 'In a previous sortie, police confiscated copies of *Oz 23*. Subsequently they decided not to prosecute it, but despite persistent requests the issues have not been returned. The excuse? "Sorry – lost in the warehouse." No receipt has been forthcoming for the items taken from my home and I will probably never know in detail exactly what was commandeered.... An Englishman's home is his castle, unless it's a pad at Notting Hill Gate.'[26]

The Obscenity Squad was a little more respectful when they raided Richard Handyside, publisher of *The Little Red Schoolbook*. Himself the son of a policeman, Handyside recollects:

No less than eight members of Scotland Yard's Obscene Publications Department invaded my tiny office.... By the time I arrived, the police already had been through all my office files and had extracted all invoices relating to the book, correspondence, copies of the manuscript, proofs, leaflets and posters. They also had all the copies of the book they could find (just over a thousand), including some already sealed in envelopes and addressed to individuals who had written in and paid for them.

Fortunately – perhaps because there were too many of them to see clearly in such a small space – the worthy officers of the law missed the bulk stock of the book elsewhere on the premises. Anyone outside the office late that night could have seen a curious procession of cars, taxis and vans being loaded with some 14,000 books and dispersing to different corners of the Home Counties. Without this timely rescue operation by many friends, the police would have definitely succeeded in driving me out of business (as one of them was later heard saying).

The following day I was honoured by a further police visit, armed with yet another search warrant. Clearly they had done their arithmetic ... [but] by this time they were too late: only some 100 copies remained....

One important detail about both raids: the police flatly refused to give any form of receipt for what they were taking. I later learned that this is quite a standard practice. A newsagent who was raided later found several publications which he had never stocked included in a list of what the police had 'taken from his premises'. To say the very least, this procedure is wide open to abuse from the police.

In the following days sales of the book naturally boomed, and in fact by a week later virtually all remaining copies had been sold (including those fortunately rescued between the two police raids). However, despite the fact that no charges had been made, the police continued to apply their own inimitable forms of pressure. I happened to be in a bookshop on the Charing Cross Road when two by now familiar obscenity squad men came in and curtly told the manager to stop selling the book, 'otherwise we'll get a warrant and search the whole place'. Similar visits were paid to other bookshops (some of which courageously declined to accept the police suggestion).[27]

Handyside's complaints were deemed sufficiently serious by the European Commission on Human Rights to merit examination by the European Court. It was unanimously held that police action was in accordance with the search and seizure provisions of the Act, and the majority decided that these provisions, however arbitrary and ineffectual, were within the discretion of member states to protect the morals of their subjects. One dissent was entered, on the ground that police action had been ineffectual and unnecessary. No action had been taken against sale of *The Little Red Schoolbook* in other parts of England, or in Wales, Northern Ireland, the Channel Islands or the Isle of Man, and the book had been acquitted of obscenity in Glasgow and Edinburgh. 'In this case it is difficult to understand why a measure that was not thought necessary outside England and Wales was deemed to be so in London.'[28]

Retention of seized goods

The DPP makes the decision whether to prosecute or whether to proceed instead to a forfeiture hearing under section 3, and occupiers and other interested parties are kept in suspense until his department has considered the matter. Delays of many months are commonly experienced while this process of consultation takes place, prolonged even further if the DPP seeks advice of Treasury counsel in a difficult or borderline case. At common law, police must not retain seized goods for longer than reasonably necessary, and it follows that they are obliged to bring seized articles before a court within a reasonable time.[29] Similarly, the European Convention on Human Rights guarantees in Article 6 (1) that 'In the determination of his civil rights and obligations or of any criminal charge against him, everyone is entitled to a fair and public hearing within a reasonable time by an independent and impartial tribunal established by law....'[30]

But what length of time is 'reasonable'? In *Cox* v. *Stinton*, a case involving a nine-month delay between seizure and summons under section 1 of the 1857 Obscene Publications Act, the Divisional Court held that the delay was not sufficient to cause the summons to be set aside. It did intimate, however, that in a case of excessive delay, the justices might decline to issue a summons. Lord Goddard said of the search and seizure provisions, which are similar to those in the 1959 Act:

it is a complete code in itself... intended not as an instrument of punishment but as preventive legislation. It was meant to give the authorities the power of seizing obscene publications before they were distributed.... Perhaps if justices thought, when the goods were brought before them, that there had been such an unexplained or unreasonable delay that it might be prejudicial to the defendant, they might be entitled to refuse in their discretion to issue a summons. . . .[31]

In the same case Devlin L.J. went further, and warned that

... the statute does, I think, contemplate that the acts which are set out in the section shall follow one another within a reasonable time, and in particular the duty to carry all the articles so seized before the justices does not mean that that can be done with any amount of delay which the police like to impose. If it were done with an unreasonable delay, and if the justices thought it right to issue a summons, it might well be that the defendant would have some cause of complaint.[32]

Where police have delayed unreasonably, an occupier whose property has been seized might obtain an order of *mandamus* directing the police to obey section 3 (3) of the Act, either by bringing all the property to court or by returning it forthwith. Subsection (3) provides that

Any articles seized under subsection (1) of this section shall be brought before a justice of the peace acting for the same Petty Sessions area as the justice who issued the warrant, and the justice before whom the articles are brought may thereupon issue a summons to the occupier of the premises or, as the case may be, the user of the stall or vehicle to appear on a day specified in the summons before a magistrates' court for that petty session area to shew cause why the articles or any of them should not be forfeited. . . . Provided that this subsection does not apply in relation to any article which is returned to the occupier of the premises.

The proviso, inserted by the 1977 Criminal Justice Act, permits police to return articles seized by mistake, although once again no time limit is imposed. Articles retained must be brought before local justices, who 'may' issue a summons. Their duty is to inspect the books which the police have seized, and either release them or mark them for destruction unless an interested party can satisfy the court that they are not obscene. If they subsequently find that the books are not obscene, they are empowered by section 3 (6) to order the police to pay the costs of any party who has intervened to contest the seizure. But if they merely decline to issue a summons and the books are returned without a hearing, or if the books have already been returned by the police, the owner has no right to claim damages for loss he has suffered by their detention, even though, in the case of periodicals, the delay may have made them unsaleable. The most unsatisfactory aspect of this procedure is that neither the owner nor any other interested party may intervene to address the justices at the stage when they consider whether a summons should be issued. In consequence, most summonses issue from seizures as a matter of course: a right to make even written representations as to the acceptability of the articles might avoid the time and expense of some forfeiture hearings.

The wording of section 3 (3) and the practice adopted pursuant to the Prosecution of Offenders Regulations means that in forfeiture cases local justices simply duplicate the function of DPP lawyers, since all seized articles are in any event submitted to the DPP for advice. A much more satisfactory method would be for police to ascertain the DPP's policy *before* applying for a search warrant, and to seize only those articles which clearly infringe it. Alternatively, the Act could be amended to make the DPP responsible for initiation of forfeiture proceedings, rather than the justices themselves. This would give effect to one recommendation of the 1958 House of Commons Select Committee which was not embodied in the final draft of the Obscene Publications Act. The Committee reported that 'all he (the DPP) would be determining would be the fitness for prosecution or proceedings, on the basis of the views currently expressed by the courts of the country as a whole. We therefore recommend that the consent of the Director should in future be required for the initiation of proceedings.'[33] Adoption of this recommendation would have avoided the embarrassment which occurred in 1976, when a Liverpool magistrate issued a summons to W.H. Smith & Sons in respect of *The Joys of Sex* a few weeks after Treasury counsel, instructed by the DPP, had stated in the course of a trial at the Central Criminal Court that this book was not, and could not be, considered obscene.

Disclaimers

One device for avoiding court scrutiny of 'borderline' publications has been for police to invite occupiers to sign forms disclaiming ownership of property seized in a raid. Faced with the DPP's disinclination to act, the police must return to the scene of the non-crime, confess to the shopkeeper that their suspicions appear to have been unfounded, and present him with by now out-of-date stock. Sometimes the shopkeeper is invited to sign a document reading 'I do hereby disclaim ownership to the above items seized from my bookshop.' This convenient but dishonest method of destroying books has been in use for decades, and drew strong criticism from the 1957 Select Committee, which recommended that no article should be destroyed without a court order. The mandatory wording of the original section 3 (3) ('Any articles seized *shall* be brought before a justice') was designed to effectuate this recommendation, but the practice continued unabated until 1973, when the Court of Appeal in *R.* v.

Metropolitan Police, ex parte Blackburn described it as undesirable and probably illegal.[34] In 1977 the section was amended to enable police to return articles instead of bringing them before the courts, and the amendment pointedly omitted to sanction the discredited 'disclaimer' system.

THE FORFEITURE HEARING

Composition of the bench

Article 6 (2) of the European Convention on Human Rights guarantees a fair hearing by an 'independent and impartial tribunal'. But in many section 3 cases the bench of justices who hear the summons comprises the same justices who inspected the material and decided to issue the summons in the first place. In so doing they have expressed a view, without hearing argument, that the material is at least prima facie obscene. The occupier, or anyone else who has intervened to defend the material, has the almost impossible task of convincing the bench in public that it was wrong in private. In *Morgan* v. *Bowker* it was argued that justices who had issued a summons after looking at allegedly obscene photographs could not be expected to approach the hearing with open minds, and the case should have been heard by a differently composed bench. Lord Chief Justice Parker rejected the suggestion that justice had not been seen to be done:

> Justices must come to a prima facie view when the articles are brought before them, as these justices did. They are not determining the matter; they are merely deciding whether a summons should issue. It seems to me quite wrong to suggest that, because they have taken a prima facie view, they are in some way biased or incapable of approaching with an open mind the hearing of the summons. I feel that there is nothing whatsoever in that objection.[35]

But it is not easy for a respondent to believe that his case will receive a fair hearing from a tribunal which has at least provisionally made up its mind against him. He feels that the hearing is really a dispute between him and the court, with the court doubling as final adjudicator. The bench is entitled to say, in effect, 'convince us we are wrong'. This is particularly anomalous in proceedings in respect of major seizures where large sums of money are at stake, or where evidence of literary merit is adduced. In 1964 *Fanny Hill* was destroyed, in the face of impressive evidence of its literary and historical merit, by a Metropolitan Chief Magistrate who had read the book before signing the search warrant, and again before issuing a summons.

Defending counsel, Mr Jeremy Hutchinson QC, was forced to confront the obvious issue of bias as politely as possible in the circumstances:

> Inevitably, you must have come into this court, being a human being, with some view about the book, before you had heard what the evidence would be. That must have made your position much more difficult ... it is no disrespect to you that we asked for a trial by jury. I am sure that personal tastes which you have to try to dismiss from your mind are bound to creep in with the greatest care that you exercise. I am sure that you would have welcomed in trying this matter the views of other people, other minds, and perhaps persons of the other sex, to assist you to come to a just conclusion.[36]

Lay justices have limited powers to fine criminal offenders, but section 3 affords them the power to deprive a respondent of his property and to destroy goods which, in large seizures, may be valued at many thousands of pounds. The apparent unfairness of these proceedings would be avoided if responsibility in law for their initiation rested with the DPP rather than with the court itself, and if they took the form of a contest between two parties, rather than a one-sided dialogue with a referee who has already blown the whistle.

The right to intervene

One improvement on the 1857 Act is section 3 (4), which accords to authors, publishers and distributors a right to intervene in forfeiture proceedings to argue that publications in which they have an interest should not be destroyed. Frequently a reputable work is seized from the premises of unprepossessing people, and the right of intervention was designed to ensure that the merits of such a work could be considered independently of booksellers who might stock it on the same shelves as indefensible pornography. The section is cast in wide terms:

> In addition to the person summoned, any other person being the owner, author or maker of any of the articles brought before the court, or any other person through whose hands they had passed before being seized, shall be entitled to appear before the court on the day specified in the summons to show cause why they should not be forfeited.

The reform was advocated by the Select Committee on the grounds that:

> Two fundamental liberties are involved. The first is freedom of expression: a reputable author will wish both to stand by what he has written and to

defend his writing against attack in any form, but he may be denied the opportunity to do so under the present law. Secondly, the writer of a book has a form of property in the continued circulation of his work, but he may find that he is unable to intervene in a trial where both his royalties and his reputation may be adversely affected. Similar considerations apply in the case of the publisher and printer.[37]

The Committee was concerned to provide the right of intervention in both forfeiture proceedings and prosecutions, but the Government was reluctant to 'tie the hands of the prosecuting authorities' and refused to extend the right to trials on indictment. A major practical drawback to the right of intervention is that the Act provides no machinery for notifying authors or publishers of the hearing date of the summons. Many books and magazines have been destroyed by provincial justices in uncontested cases of which interested parties have no knowledge. The police, the courts and the DPP refuse to accept responsibility for informing distributors or publishers, even when their addresses are printed on the contents page of the article itself. This lacuna has been raised in Parliament on several occasions, after publishers have complained of forfeitures which have taken place behind their backs, but in 1975 a Minister of State at the Home Office pointed out that 'In 1969 the Attorney-General of the day agreed that, in section 3 proceedings against booksellers, it was not the Director's responsibility to contact the publishers of any material seized and to inform them of the seizure ... in the circumstances, I think that the initiative must rest with the bookseller to inform the publisher that proceedings have been set in train.'[38] The bookseller will have no incentive to contact the publisher if he does not propose to contest the proceedings, and in such cases the very evil feared by the Select Committee will come to pass. It can only be avoided by a statutory duty upon either police or court officials to give notice to publishers in cases where they are resident in England at readily ascertainable addresses.

Burden of proof

The right of intervention under section 3 (4) is expressed as an entitlement 'to show cause why they should not be forfeited'. Before a destruction order can be made, the court must be 'satisfied' that the articles were obscene at the time that they were seized. But which party carries the burden of proving the issue to the court's satisfaction, and to what standard of proof? Obscenity is defined in section 1 of the Act, and penalized as a criminal offence in section 2 if a magistrate or jury is satisfied to the standard of proof in criminal cases – i.e., beyond reasonable doubt. Logically, the standard of proof in section 3 proceedings should be the same : any other standard could produce disparate results between the two sections in respect of identical material. If the 'satisfaction' need only be on the balance of probabilities, a magistrate who thought that a book was 'probably' but not 'certainly' obscene would be obliged to acquit the defendant and return his books in a section 2 proceeding, but obliged to destroy the same books if proceedings were taken by way of a section 3 summons. The discrepancy would be even greater if the burden of proof at a forfeiture hearing shifted to the respondent, and he had the onus of proving a negative – that the articles, on the balance of probabilities, were *not* obscene. On this interpretation of section 3, justices who merely think that books *might* be obscene, but are by no means convinced, would be entitled to make a destruction order. This burden would be virtually impossible for the respondent to discharge in cases where the same bench had made a prima facie finding of obscenity at the time of issue of the summons. This crucial matter has never been authoritatively tested, and different standards of proof have prevailed in different courts.

Although the criminal standard is consistent with the scheme of the Act and is the only interpretation which avoids inconsistent results in the application of the two sections, a test which places the burden of proof squarely on the respondent is often adopted, because of dicta in *Thomson* v. *Chain Libraries Ltd.* In that 1954 case the court rejected the argument that police who had seized books under the 1857 Act had to spell out their allegations of obscenity in an adversary procedure for forfeiture before the respondent was called upon to 'show cause'. Lord Goddard observed that, 'It does not require evidence to satisfy the justices whether or not they are obscene. The justices must look at them for themselves. . . . It is not for the prosecution to proceed to read out particular paragraphs unless the justices ask the prosecution to address them or to point out some particular thing.'[39]

Lord Goddard makes no reference to the standard by which the justices must be 'satisfied', although Mr Justice Hilbery, in the same case, placed it squarely upon the respondent:

It was contended on behalf of the respondents that this was a criminal proceeding, and that the general rule in a criminal proceeding was that the prosecutor, who affirmed, had to discharge the burden of proof in regard to what he affirmed, but . . . the Act of 1857, which is a code in itself, provides a special procedure and makes an exception to the general rule . . . if the justices thought that publications, which had been seized and brought before them, under section 1 of the Act, could not be considered as obscene, obviously they would not issue a summons. If, prima facie, the publications are obscene when they are brought into court, the justices issue a summons. In the present case they issued a summons. Section 1 of the Act provides that such summons is to call on the occupier of the house or other place which may have been so entered 'by virtue of the said warrant to appear within seven days before such police stipendiary magistrate, or any two justices in petty sessions for the district, to show cause why the articles so seized should not be destroyed....' That, plainly, in the particular circumstances, throws the onus on the person who has been the occupier of the premises where the obscene literature is on sale to show cause why those articles which are before the court should not be destroyed.[40]

Mr Justice Hilbery was construing the 1857 Obscene Publications Act, a very different piece of legislation to the 1959 statute. It contained no definition of obscenity, and no provision for prosecution, which was left to the existing common law of obscene libel. The 1959 Act abolished the common-law libel offence, replaced it with a statutory definition of obscenity, and provided two different procedures for testing that obscenity. Section 3, unlike section 1 of the 1857 Act, requires the justices to be satisfied that the articles 'at the time when they were seized ... were obscene articles kept for publication for gain'. The test of obscenity is the same for both procedures, and so, it might be argued, is the standard by which the tribunal must be satisfied that the test has been made out. Respondents and interveners 'show cause' by appearing on the return day and adducing reasons why the publications are not obscene: the 'cause' that they should be entitled to 'show' is that the articles are not obscene 'beyond a reasonable doubt'.

The likely readership

The use of section 3 proceedings to destroy books and magazines seized in bulk from warehouses has created problems for the courts in determining the identity of likely readers. Section 3 (7) provides:

For the purposes of this section the question whether an article is obscene shall be determined on the assumption that copies of it would be published in any manner likely having regard to the circumstances in which it was found, but in no other manner.

For several years after the Act was passed, many courts interpreted the words 'in no other manner' as entitling them to ignore the respondent's evidence of the nature of his business and his system of distribution. Regard was had merely to the articles and to the police evidence of seizure. This restricted interpretation of the section was rejected by the Divisional Court in 1964 in the case of *Morgan* v. *Bowker*. Justices had refused to consider the evidence of a film producer as to the ages of his customers, his policy of not selling films to teenagers, and his attempts to have the film approved by a censorship authority. Lord Parker held that

What is sought to be discovered under subsection (7) is the nature of the publication, and what publication, as defined by section 1 (3), is likely, having regard to the circumstances in which the articles were found.... Justices would be perfectly right in saying: 'We are not going to listen to what the defendant intends to do,' but at the same time the nature of his business and the method under which it has been conducted heretofore must, as it seems to me, be part of the circumstances in which the articles are found, just as much as the nature of the premises ... they should therefore consider the evidence given by the defendant in regard to the nature of his business and the methods employed by him, and, in the light of such of that evidence as they accept, determine whether the articles or any of them tend to deprave or corrupt such adults as would see them; whether it was likely that the articles would be published to persons under twenty-one; and, if so, whether those articles would tend to corrupt or deprave such persons.[41]

Procedure at forfeiture hearings

The Divisional Court has stressed that local justices hearing section 3 cases may adopt any procedure which is considered appropriate, so long as it 'will do justice to the prosecution and defence'.[42] The normal practice is for the DPP's representative to address the court on the law and to call evidence from police officers as to the circumstances in which the books were found. Defence counsel then outlines his case for saying that the articles are not obscene, and calls evidence of distribution and public good, if any. The justices will then retire to consider the material before announcing their findings. It will not invalidate the proceedings if they hear both sides argue the question of obscenity, make a finding on that issue, and then invite evidence of public good which might justify the publication of matter already determined to be obscene.[43]

Where a number of lay justices form the tribunal, it is not essential for each justice to read every word of every book, but they must all make themselves fully acquainted with each book as a whole, so that they are in a position to pass both an individual and a collective judgment on it. This principle was settled by the Divisional Court in 1974, in the case of *Olympia Press* v. *Hollis*. Thirty-four different novels had been seized from the Olympia Press premises and brought before a bench of six justices at Stony Stratford, who divided the reading task between them: at least two read every book. It was held that although not all the justices had read all the books, they had discussed and deliberated on the books as a whole so that a collective opinion could be formed and formulated into a specific decision of the bench. So long as there had been 'full and proper discussion', the Divisional Court declined to interfere.[44] This decision is contrary to the principle that every member of a tribunal must hear all the evidence in the case. Doubtless the Divisional Court was prepared to sacrifice principle to expediency in order to avoid excessive demands on the time of lay justices in cases of bulk seizures, but certain facts of the *Olympia Press* case do suggest that the discretion given to the justices is open to abuse. Olympia Press was the imprint under which maverick publisher Maurice Girodias introduced the reading public to Lawrence Durrell, J.P. Donleavy, Samuel Beckett, Jean Genet and William Burroughs. In 1972, 134,000 copies of thirty-four different books were seized, including *Moscow Nights*, which Girodias claimed was an important Russian underground novel. The six justices merely compared notes over a ninety-minute luncheon adjournment, and then declared the whole stock obscene. The 'full and proper discussion' of each book would have averaged less than three minutes per title. The result of these hasty proceedings forced the closure of Olympia Press, without the benefit of the jury trial demanded by Girodias. It is difficult to reconcile the *Olympia Press* decision with an earlier Divisional Court case, *Burke* v. *Copper*. This was an appeal by a prosecutor from 'perverse' findings of local justices who ordered certain photographs to be destroyed but returned others to the respondent. Lord Parker remarked in the course of his judgment that

> Counsel for the respondent ... ventured to suggest that maybe the justices divided up the photographs and were each responsible for a certain number, and on that basis it would be possible for one justice to take a certain view of obscenity and the other to take a different view. I am loth to think that that happened because it would have been a most improper thing. The decision is not a decision of individual justices but a decision of the whole bench.[45]

Appeal to crown court

The decision of a local bench has no impact outside its own geographical jurisdiction, and destruction orders made after routine seizures from local booksellers or newsagents make little effective contribution to the suppression of pornography. Justices are not required to give reasons for their decisions, and the only way a publisher can obtain any real guidance is to appeal a forfeiture decision to the Crown Court under section 3 (5) of the Act. It is heard by a judge, usually sitting with two justices, and normally a reasoned decision will be delivered. A recent example of such an appeal was a case heard by Her Honour Judge Lowry in respect of 235 separate magazines, which had been forfeited by order of the Newham justices after cursory deliberation and without any statement of reasons. Her Honour and her colleagues spent eighteen and three-quarter hours examining the magazines, and allowed the appeal in respect of forty-three titles. After summarizing the relevant law, she set out reasons so that both the DPP and the publisher could understand the approach adopted by the Court:

> Where normal sexual relations between a man and a woman are depicted or described, however explicitly, such as a colour photograph of oral sex, we have not found against the publication on that ground – however boring or tasteless the photograph may be.
>
> Neither have we ruled out publications concerning other acts, which, while unromantic, are within the known regions of ordinary sexual behaviour.
>
> On the other hand, we have refused the appeal where the picture or story or article may encourage or promote, first of all, illegal sexual behaviour, secondly, acts or attitudes which while not illegal are in derogation of a happy sexual life, thirdly, where what is apparently recommended and depicted is the use of an instrument – we have excluded it – and simply note that a number of the implements featured could cause a degree of physical injury.
>
> Where ninety per cent of the matter has described what we regard as tending to deprave or corrupt, but ten per cent has consisted of a pious entreaty to do otherwise, we have had regard to the ninety per cent and not to the ten per cent.
>
> Turning to the question of homosexual behaviour, we have had regard to the known situation that there are a proportion of members of our society who are not heterosexual ... where a part of a publication has been an acknowledgement, however forceful, that sexuality including physical contact does exist between members of the same sex, we have looked at the whole publication before making our decision. But where a publication has been substantially devoted to male or female homosexuality in such a manner as to advocate homosexual behaviour – possibly to the exclusion of other sexual behaviour – we have ruled it out.[46]

This intelligible approach enabled both sides to know where they stood, and to act accordingly. It would lead to greater certainty in the operation of the law if contested forfeiture proceedings were taken direct to the Crown Court, without troubling a lay bench, and if those courts were obliged to give reasons in all cases. The proliferation of local forfeiture hearings, with inevitable inconsistencies in decisions and unfairness in procedures, can neither control the dissemination of pornography nor contribute a satisfactory degree of certainty to the law.

JUSTICES OR JURIES?

Dicey's famous comment[47] that 'Freedom of discussion is, then, in England little else than the right to write or say anything which a jury, consisting of twelve shopkeepers, think it expedient should be said or written,' requires some revision: juries, since the abolition of the property-holding qualification in 1972, have comprised a much more representative sample of the spectrum of society. The most acute grievance of publishers whose books and magazines are seized under section 3 is that they have no legal right to a trial by jury. Since any censorship decision notoriously depends upon the personal prejudice of the censor, they maintain that this task should be undertaken, in disputed cases, by a jury, and not be left to the value-judgment of elderly justices whose beliefs about sex may not reflect those of the community at large. This view finds strong support in repeated House of Lords dicta which stress that a jury is the appropriate tribunal to decide questions of sexual morality, on the grounds that 'Even if accepted public standards may to some extent vary from generation to generation, current standards are in the keeping of juries, who can be trusted to maintain the corporate good sense of the community and to discern attacks upon values that must be preserved.'[48] The principle has found favour in the jurisprudence of other common law countries; as one Australian judge has explained:

People in the same community, including those who hold judicial office, vary greatly in their opinions as to what is obscene. Even the same man is seldom constant in his views. His opinion in his youth is probably not the one he will hold in his age, especially if he has daughters. I think that the net result of the approach which we are bound to use is to give far too much weight to the opinions, or rather the emotions, of one man. Thus the result must often be just the luck of the magisterial draw. I do not suggest that the position would be different if a judicial draw were substituted. It would be far better if questions of indecency or obscenity were decided by a jury of twelve.... Juries, of course, are not infallible but they are a cross-section of the community and are thus more likely to reflect its ideas....[49]

Section 3 of the Obscene Publications Act contains no provision permitting a respondent to opt for trial by jury. A defendant to a section 2 criminal charge, however, may so elect, although if he does he risks a three-year maximum sentence. The section 3 procedure, however, has no criminal consequence whatsoever. It is akin to a civil proceeding *in rem* against the allegedly obscene article itself, and permits anybody claiming an interest in the article to intercede. The section may well have been appropriate to meet the situation where a bookshop or street stall proprietor stocks only a few obscene books, perhaps inadvertently, and does not deserve to be convicted of a criminal offence. But section 3 has been exploited in a number of cases for the wholly objectionable purpose of depriving publishers of their right to trial by jury. Books – in some cases, many thousands of books – have been seized from publishers who do wish to defend them to the hilt. The ensuing forfeiture order has been more costly, in practical terms, than the maximum fine of £400 which can be imposed by a magistrates' court under section 2, and the victim has been deprived of the mainspring of his defence – an appeal to a jury. The publisher is given no choice by the DPP – a section 3 summons means trial by magistrate, or lay justices, with a maximum effective fine of the value of the books likely to be destroyed. The section 3 procedure is a cheap and convenient method of censorship only when the defendant agrees to what amounts to a quasi-criminal trial without the opprobrium of a conviction, but also without the traditional safeguards of the criminal law.

The use of section 3 against an *unwilling* publisher is a contravention of an undertaking given by the Law Officers to Parliament in 1964. During a debate on the Obscene Publications Act of that year, Mr Roy Jenkins moved an amendment which would have given publishers a specific right to elect trial by jury in respect of any seized book which was capable of a 'public good' defence. The move was prompted by the fate which earlier in the year had befallen Mayflower Books, the publishers of *Fanny Hill*. The novel had been seized from a Soho bookshop, whereupon Mayflower had requested a jury trial so that its decision to publish could be tested by a jury verdict representing contemporary public opinion. The DPP refused: because the publishers had 'acted throughout with a proper sense of responsibility ... it was decided that the prosecution would be oppressive in the circumstances'.[50] Instead, the book was brought before a magistrate who had already found it to be prima facie obscene, and who made a forfeiture order despite uncontested evidence of its literary and historical merits. The DPP's attitude was catch-22: a responsible publisher could never, by definition, obtain a fair trial – this right was reserved for those who acted irresponsibly. The Jenkins amendment was supported by members on both sides of the House, and most vigorously by Mr Leo Abse:

> Unless we have a subsection of this kind in the Bill it is almost inevitable that the question whether the book is likely to corrupt or not will be determined by a particular group of people, by a magistrate or magistrates who often have been selected, quite deliberately, not because they enjoy a ribald story or have a Rabelaisian temperament, but precisely because they have a certain rigidity and rectitude which, although it may equip them in certain respects to deal with many laws, makes them, perhaps, peculiarly unsuitable and unacceptable to deal with the question of what is or is not likely to corrupt.[51]

The Solicitor-General, Sir Peter Rawlinson, intervened to satisfy this concern, and obtain withdrawal of the amendment, by giving an assurance on behalf of the Law Officers of the Crown that publishers whose work was seized from bookshops under section 3 orders would always be given the opportunity to be charged under section 2 and tried (without the bookseller as a co-defendant) by a jury. Sir Peter stated:

> In the absence of special circumstances, and if satisfactory evidence of the offence is available, the ordinary policy of the Director of Public Prosecutions will be to proceed against the publisher by way of prosecution: first, where an article has been seized under a warrant from a retailer or printer and the publisher, before the case is brought before the justice under section 3 of the 1959 Act, indicates his intention to continue publishing whatever the result of forfeiture proceedings; and, secondly, where enquiries are being made about an article which the prosecution considers to be prima facie obscene and the publisher indicates his determination to publish, and to continue to publish, in circumstances which would constitute a criminal offence.[52]

MPs on both sides of the House understood this undertaking as a promise that the DPP would offer publishers and authors the alternative of jury trial whenever their books were in danger of destruction. They expressed confidence 'that any government of the day will honour it'.[53]

Their optimism was misplaced, and governments of later days did not honour it. In 1975 the Law Officers were criticized by MPs over section 3 proceedings which had been brought against editions of *Forum* in some provincial towns, without giving its publishers the opportunity to opt for trial by jury. These editions were regularly offered for sale as 'back issues' after destruction orders had been made, so there was no doubt of the publishers' intention to continue their sale. The Law Officers sought to distinguish the case on the basis that in 1964 'the then Solicitor-General stated that the authorities would prosecute where the publisher has demonstrated a determination to persist in publishing an article which appears obscene, and indicates his intention to do so whatever the result of forfeiture proceedings'.[54] The editor of *Forum* persisted in publishing previous issues, and would have indicated, had he ever been asked, an intention to do so irrespective of provincial destruction orders.

On this point it seems that Parliament in 1964 also misunderstood how the undertaking would operate.[55] It was assumed that before a case was brought before the justices, police would interview the publishers of the seized magazines and ascertain whether they proposed to continue publication. If they did, the DPP would then decide whether to charge them with an offence under section 2, or whether to drop proceedings entirely. Because this procedure has never been adopted, the 1964 undertaking has been nullified, and publishers are hardly ever notified by the courts or the police that their works are in danger of destruction. (The undertaking was honoured on one occasion in 1967, when copies of *Last Exit to Brooklyn* were destroyed by a London magistrate at the behest of a private complainant. The publishers demanded a jury trial, and the Law Officers complied. As a result of the *Last Exit* case the Act was amended to deny individual complainants the right to initiate forfeiture proceedings (see page 86), but nothing was done to give publishers a statutory right of jury trial if their books fell victim to police initiatives.)

To effectuate the 1964 undertaking section 3 should be amended so that booksellers or publishers who give notice of their wish for a jury trial can be re-charged under section 2 of the Act, or the forfeiture proceedings dropped entirely. Such a change would be unlikely to increase significantly the business of the Crown Courts. Publishers as a rule do not qualify for legal aid, and the economics of an Old Bailey trial would lead them to avoid it except when an issue of principle was at stake. This is exactly the sort of case where the jury is the most acceptable tribunal. Another factor militating against election for jury trial except for an issue of principle is the sentencing power of Crown Courts in obscenity cases. (As Mr Roy Jenkins put it in 1964, 'I should not have thought that to put upon somebody the right to opt to be prosecuted and to run all the risks, including the risk of prison, was conferring very excessive liberty of choice upon any individual.'[56]) This is a difficult choice for publishers to make, nevertheless *they*, and not the State, should be given the right to make it.

That, at least, was the conclusion of the Committee on the Distribution of Criminal Business, which reported in 1975 that 'It seems to us especially desirable that a person charged with an offence involving an obscene or indecent publication should have a right to have the matter decided by a jury, which can better reflect contemporary public attitudes towards obscenity and indecency than can a stipendiary magistrate or a bench of lay justices.'[57] Magistrates and justices sometimes approach their serious censorship task under section 3 in a cavalier fashion. A jury, obliged to consider carefully each article before it, will inevitably give a more thorough consideration to the question of obscenity than a magistrate's court which must slot this unusual task into its regular list of minor criminal business.

Otherwise, it is difficult to generalize about the fitness of magistrates and lay justices for the censorship function they are sometimes called upon to fulfill. Certainly they tend to be appointed from a fairly narrow class base: a survey of lay justices in 1967 showed that seventy-seven per cent were drawn from professional and managerial classes (which comprise only four per cent of the general population), ten per cent had clerical occupations and twelve per cent a skilled trade. Semi-skilled and unskilled persons were not represented at all. The average age was fifty-six, and only five per cent were under forty.[58] In 1973 a survey of the magistracy in one provincial city found it to be a tightly knit self-perpetuating clique, a 'mysterious old-boy network' wholly unrepresentative of the broad spectrum of local society. 'Only one magistrate was a manual worker, and none were drawn from the town's six thousand Pakistani citizens. Moreover, in spite of a large Roman Catholic population in the town, including six thousand regular churchgoers, there was no Roman Catholic magistrate. But twenty-nine of the forty-three were connected with the Masonic movement or Rotary or both.'[59] Given this unrepresentative make-up, it is not surprising that lay justices tend to accept an inflated view of their function as moral guardians of the community, and rarely decline the opportunity to order the destruction of salacious magazines. Sometimes local vigilance is taken to improper lengths: in Norwich in 1973 lay justices collaborated with police in drawing up an 'index' of magazines which were liable to be seized on sight. Newsagents and booksellers did not dare to stock them, although all the titles were freely available in London and several had actually been acquitted at Old Bailey jury trials.

An analysis of the inconsistencies and geographical variations in obscenity decisions by magistrates does not demonstrate their unsuitability for the task, so much as emphasize that under the present law the decision is essentially a matter of personal prejudice. For example, Croydon justices dismissed the prosecution case against *Brutus*, an illustrated account of bestial violence in ancient Rome, but the book was convicted without hesitation by a bench of justices at Clerkenwell. *The Little Red Schoolbook* was declared obscene in 1971 by a London magistrate, but prosecutions in Glasgow and Edinburgh failed. Edinburgh magistrates are hardly pillars of the permissive society: in 1967 a set of Aubrey Beardsley prints was held to be obscene, despite its exhibition at the Victoria and Albert Museum and consequent appearance in the museum catalogue, published by HMSO and available at every government bookshop. It is reasonable enough that certain localities should opt for different standards, but such variations between cities, and in the case of *Brutus* between areas of the same city, emphasize an arbitrariness in the operation of enforcement provisions which drew surprise and some criticism from the European Court of Human Rights in the *Handyside case* (see page 93).

5
Anatomy of an obscenity trial

TRIAL PROCEDURE

The obscenity trial is the formal process by which we publicly eradicate material we dislike. The crucial question is, who are 'we'? In a democratic society, the 'we' is in theory the majority of elected representatives in Parliament expressing the wishes of electors in the form of legislative orders to punish certain clearly-defined conduct. It is not the function of judges or juries to decide whether other conduct should also be made criminal: they are simply parts of the mechanism which decides whether an act, defined as criminal by the legislature, has been perpetrated by a particular defendant. They decide the strict question of whether the accused committed the crime with which he stands charged, *not* whether the actions he committed should be made criminal. Obscenity trials, while they appear to observe this convention, involve the application of a law which describes the criminal conduct in such ambiguous and emotive terms that jurors are obliged, if they are to reach a meaningful decision, to find a resolution in terms of their own moral instincts. If the legislature decreed, for example, that publication of photographs depicting oral sex was a crime, the jury's task would be to answer simple questions of fact: Did the photograph show oral sex? Did the defendant publish it? But instead the present law requires juries to decide whether oral sex pictures 'tend to deprave and corrupt' – a question impossible to answer without reference to some code of sexual morality and some understanding of the effect of these pictures on the minds of viewers. In this sense the Obscene Publications Act amounts to a delegation by Parliament of its law-making authority to an ad hoc group of jurors, empowered to declare whether certain publications placed before them at an obscenity trial should be destroyed. Juries do not apply pre-existing law, they actually make a little law by their decision in each case.

In ordinary criminal cases, the jury is called upon to decide whether or not an accused person committed an unlawful act. At obscenity trials, the accused rarely contests that he has performed the act – publication – which is alleged: the question for the jury is whether he *ought* to be punished for what he has published. This fundamental distinction is rarely acknowledged, and courts have sought to assimilate obscenity proceedings with the rules which govern other criminal matters. At virtually every stage problems have been encountered which have not been satisfactorily resolved by application of ordinary procedural principles.

COMMITTAL PROCEEDINGS

Once the DPP decides to proceed under section 2 of the Act, summonses will be issued charging the criminal offence of either publishing obscene articles, or of possessing obscene articles for publication for gain. Selection of defendants will depend upon the ambit of police enquiries: authors, publishers, printers, distributors, booksellers and even doormen and projectionists may be charged if there is evidence that they knowingly assisted the act of publication alleged. In most cases the DPP will be content with a plea of 'guilty' in a lower court where the maximum penalty is six months imprisonment or a fine of £400, but defendants who wish to contest the charge will rarely be advised to do so at this stage, since the likelihood of conviction by justices is much higher than before a jury. The normal course adopted in such cases is for the defendant to elect jury trial, and be committed to Crown Court without further examination of the charge. There may be value in committal proceedings, however, for a defendant who is only marginally involved in the publication, or who can raise a technical defence. Printers and others on the periphery of conspiracy charges have been 'let out' by magistrates who have taken the view that any jury trial should only involve defendants who are primarily responsible for the publication at issue. In such cases the right to a full committal hearing may act as a restraint upon overzealous prosecutions, and is a useful way of reducing the cost and complication of the ultimate trial. It may also enable the defendant to discover the reason why he has been prosecuted, and to learn the particular subject-matter of his publications which has caused concern.

On the other hand, contested committal proceedings do increase the time that a case takes to come on for trial, and they are open to abuse by publishers seeking to prolong proceedings in order to continue making profits from activities of dubious legality. It is wellnigh impossible to convince an examining magistrate that no prima facie case exists on the central issue of obscenity. Any publication dealing with sex, drugs or violence raises at least the possibility of a conviction, and magistrates are reluctant to usurp the function of a jury. A stark example is provided by the private prosecution of *Last Tango in Paris*. The examining magistrate expressed his personal opinion that the film might not on balance infringe the law, but committed its distributors for trial on the basis that there was at least a prima facie case, and the ultimate decision should be left to a jury. The Divisional Court confirmed his decision to commit, notwithstanding his personal feelings as to the likelihood of defence evidence exonerating the film.[1] The case illustrates the absence of any effective safeguard at committal stage against weak or marginal prosecutions.

THE ROLE OF COUNSEL

The DPP will normally instruct Treasury counsel to advise in borderline cases and to conduct prosecutions. They will not be instructed to address their minds to the question 'Should this article be prosecuted?' but rather 'Is a prosecution of this article likely to succeed?' They may advise prosecutions which are likely to succeed, but also likely to produce discriminatory, socially divisive, or counter-productive results. Because the law is unclear the yardstick for their advice is not readily apparent. One Treasury counsel told an Arts Council enquiry that he recommended prosecution if a book made him feel randy. 'Entirely subjective,' he confessed, 'but what else is there?'[2]

One result of the instruction of senior counsel (in provincial cases, QCs often lead for the Crown) is that legally-aided defendants are often granted counsel of similar status.[3] The Court of Appeal has stressed the sense in which every obscenity trial is a test case, potentially of major social significance in setting the bounds of public tolerance,[4] and legal aid officials often mark this significance by authorizing the instruction of leading counsel – a practice which increases the public expense of a trial, particularly at times of high police activity. Reputable publishers will naturally tend to rely upon Queens

Counsel, while those who have been successful in 'making money out of sex' will engage advisors of the same calibre as a routine operational expense.

A regrettable result of the 'political' nature of obscenity trials is the tendency of the press and public to identify counsel appearing on either side with the cause which they forensically espouse. Barristers are obliged to accept any briefs they are offered, irrespective of personal feelings, but the debating points they are obliged to make in obscenity cases do assume a particular moral perspective, and in many obscenity cases counsel's brief may accord to some extent with his personal sympathies. Bernard Levin criticized Mervyn Griffith-Jones QC for his conduct of the *Lady Chatterley* prosecution, because 'he felt deeply moved, not by the lawyer's indignation assumed for the sake of his brief, but by a perfectly genuine revulsion from what he regarded as an obscene book with no redeeming qualities. This feeling of his – and it is clear that the judge, with equal sincerity, shared it – stemmed not from wilfulness but from an inability to see in the book what others, of all levels of education and understanding, could see.'[5]

In similar vein, an editorial in *The Times* remarked on the difficulty of obtaining an obscenity conviction when the defence was led by Mr John Mortimer QC who 'has a particular gift for amusing irrelevance, which makes the proceedings appear absurd, combined with a passionate devotion to defence of the freedom of pornography'.[6] Mortimer quickly pointed out that, 'In all obscenity cases a person, not a book, is on trial and any barrister's duty is to be "passionately devoted" to the defence of his client. It would be a sad day if a defendant charged with an alleged crime could not be defended without his counsel being accused of devotion to murder or robbing banks.'[7] The 'taxi rank' principle established by Erskine in his unpopular defence of Thomas Paine's *Age of Reason* is one which even editors of *The Times* are prone to overlook in the gloom of disappointment at an obscenity acquittal. But the identification of counsel with cause is an inevitable result of a trial process, which invites value-judgments from all involved in its course. In 1978, the second centenary of Voltaire's death moved John Mortimer to complain:

The lack of understanding of what Voltaire was on about is so widespread nowadays that if, for instance, you oppose censorship you are taken to warmly approve of pornography. It also happens that I find modern pornography deeply depressing, the models extremely unattractive, the photography poor and the prose style appalling. At the showing of blue movies at Scotland Yard I take the precaution of removing my glasses, which reduces the whole messy business to an impressionist blur; and I can't think what I dislike more, the motorway pin-ups in *Rustler* or the awful pseudo-psychological jargon with some of the world's most boring fantasies in *Forum*. None of it at all nice; but I am sure that censorship is more dangerous. . . .[8]

Prosecutors must believe in the obscenity of an article, else they would not have advised its prosecution, and defendants naturally turn to advisors who have some sympathy with the philosophy of Voltaire. The jury verdict may depend upon which side has the more eloquent lawyer – but this is an inevitable by-product of a law which hinges upon debating points rather than verification of fact.

DRAFTING THE INDICTMENT

The Indictment Rules require that every specific offence charged shall be accompanied by 'such particulars as may be necessary for giving reasonable information as to the nature of the charge'.[9] Before the 1959 Act indictments relating to books often set out the specific passages to which objection was taken, and these were read in open court as part of the charge.[10] The 1959 Act provides that books must be judged 'as a whole', so the former method of identifying 'purple passages' is no longer permissible. Indictments should refer merely to the title of the book, and to the date and place at which it is alleged to have been published or stocked for publication for gain. The position is otherwise in cases involving magazines, which may be held obscene if one 'item' within the article as a whole is found obscene (see pages 62–5).[11] If the prosecution alleges that an individual item infringes the law, the draftsman of the indictment should make specific reference to it in the particulars of the offence, so that the defence is fully alerted to the case it has to meet.

One important practical difficulty is encountered in cases where many pornographic articles have been seized. Should their titles all be lumped together in one count, or else be made the subject of separate charges, involving perhaps several hundred counts on a mammoth bill of indictment? The sheer impracticability of the latter course, which would involve a jury spending many weeks reading through all the material, is generally avoided by some form of compromise. The prosecution is entitled to select a handful of articles – usually, the 'worst' examples – and indict them in separate counts, leaving the residue to be dealt with at a forfeiture hearing after the trial has taken place. This practice produces the anomaly that justices at the subsequent forfeiture proceeding are in no way bound by the jury verdict: if the defendant is acquitted in respect of the sample, they may nevertheless condemn the residue, and vice versa. A respondent to a forfeiture summons could hardly have better 'cause' to 'show' than that he has recently been acquitted by a jury in respect of similar material: this will be a persuasive argument, but not one which the justices are obliged in law to accept. A fairer method, which ensures final disposal of the whole case at trial, is for all the seized material to be included within one global count, whereupon the parties may agree to place a 'representative sample' before the jury. This method was approved by Mr Justice Ashworth in *R. v. Lindsay*. The jury was spared the ordeal of watching over thirty pornographic films by an agreement between counsel to show a 'representative sample' of eight: four selected by the prosecution, and four by the defence.[12] The acquittal meant the release of all films, whereas a conviction would have entailed complete destruction. The problem with this course is that it will only work satisfactorily where all the articles are of the same kind, otherwise juries may wish to make distinctions which cannot be reflected in a single verdict. The only alternative is to take a 'special verdict' – an invitation to a jury to explain its decision – so that the defendant knows which aspect of his trade has caused offence, and the judge is in a position to sentence him accordingly. 'Special verdicts' have been discouraged in ordinary criminal cases,[13] but there seems to be no other solution to a problem which was not considered by those who framed the obscenity legislation. That the problem is avoided in most cases is due to informal agreements between counsel, with the objective of making the trial as fair to both sides, and as manageable for the court, as is possible in the particular circumstances.

JURY CHALLENGES

Arguably the most important stage of an obscenity trial is the selection of the jury, because the moral outlook of ten out of those twelve randomly selected individuals will determine the defendant's fate. Judges optimistically believe that each jury will act as 'the microcosm of democratic society',[14] but no public opinion pollster would dare to draw a conclusion from a random sample of twelve. Given the deep rift in social attitudes towards sexual explicitness, juries which are truly representative would in most cases never be able to reach agreement. So the process of 'calling to the book to be sworn' will be an anxious time for all parties.

In America, prospective jurors may be questioned exhaustively by both sides in a quest for an impartial panel, and some defenders have even hired psychiatrists to observe prospective jurors and gauge the possibility of antagonism. In Britain the defence is confined to a list of the names and addresses of members of the jury panel supplied on request a few days before the trial begins. The defendant has a minute or so to decide, on a visual impression, whether to exercise any of his three challenges. Although 'there's no art to find the mind's construction in the face', there may be some indication of mental construction in reading matter carried under the arm. The hearts of obscenity defendants no doubt leap at the *Guardian*, and sink at the sight of a *Daily Express*. On one occasion, a juror was observed with a copy of a work written by Isaac Babel. A speedy check with a literary expert providentially waiting outside court established that Babel had suffered severe censorship problems in his native Russia, so the juror was not challenged. The *Oz* defendants, perusing the names of potential jurors on the evening before their trial, were overjoyed to discover that one bore the name 'William Blake'. They decided to accept him – until an elderly and severe-looking man answered to the visionary's name when it was trumpeted on the morrow by the court clerk.

In strict legal theory it should not matter whether a jury is representative, because its overriding task is not to reflect public opinion, but to decide the guilt or innocence of the individual arraigned in the dock. For this task every juror must be impartial, and should refuse to serve if he has any preconceived views about the harmful effects of sex publications. This principle was accepted by Judge King-Hamilton at the *In Depth* trial, which took place while pornophobia was sweeping the press in the wake of the *Longford Report*. Before the jury was sworn, he made this announcement to prospective members:

> If any of you hold, or have expressed, or belong to any organization which holds or expresses, strong views against publication in any form of explicit sexual matters or practices, then it would be desirable if you did not serve on this jury, because you would be going into the jury box with preconceived views about the matter which has to be decided.

After the announcement was made, one man asked to be excused. He explained later that he was married with children, had seen samples of pornography and was totally opposed to it: he could not have listened to the evidence with an open mind.[15]

This judicial formula may not be appropriate now that the Court of Appeal has emphasized that

> A jury consists of twelve individuals chosen at random from the appropriate panel. A juror should be excused if he is personally concerned in the facts of a particular case ... (but) it is contrary to established practice for jurors to be excused on more general grounds such as race, religion or political beliefs or occupation.[16]

This guidance does not cover a situation which may arise at an obscenity trial if a juror feels such physical revulsion from the exhibits that he or she is unable to pass impartial judgment on the case for the accused. Some judges inform potential jurors at the outset that the case they are about to hear entails viewing pornography, and invite them to stand down if they would be caused personal distress. A physiological reaction in the course of the trial would make a juror 'personally concerned in the facts of the particular case', and courts have been prepared to overturn verdicts in other criminal cases when personal bias has been exhibited in open court.[17] Revulsion is not the test of obscenity – indeed, it may indicate support for a defence argument that the material is so 'aversive' that it could not corrupt. The desire to make the jury representative will conflict in such cases with the principle that a defendant is entitled to be tried by people with open minds.

Obscenity trials became notorious for the number of jury challenges in the days when defendants were entitled to seven challenges apiece. The record was set in the *Nasty Tales* trial, at which forty-nine jurors were rejected – four by the crown and forty-three by the defence. The *Oz* trial defendants rejected twenty-six and their *In Depth* counterparts nineteen. In both cases the object was to fish for youthful jurors, but the makeup of the *Oz* jury panel was such that only one of the thirty-eight candidates was aged under thirty-five. Ultimately the *In Depth* jury included a stockbroker, a teacher, a research chemist, two blacks and two engineers.[18] It was an intelligent mixture, as Old Bailey juries go: certainly it compared favourably with the panel which tried *Last Exit to Brooklyn*, one of whom complained to the judge, 'You'd need an interpreter to read this.' Defence witnesses (including several professors of literature) had laboured well over five hours in reading the book, yet several jurors claimed to have finished within an hour. The exasperated (and convicted) publishers were moved to write to *The Times* urging that jurors in future obscenity cases should be selected with A-levels as a minimum educational qualification.

The abolition in 1972 of the property-holding and age qualifications for service has produced a larger proportion of women and young people on jury panels – a development viewed with mixed feelings by those who favour convictions. Mrs Mary Whitehouse maintains that 'In these days of sex equality it is surely unarguable that a jury should consist of an equal number of men and women, and that any woman juror objected to should be replaced by another woman juror.'[19] *The Times* has editorially deplored 'sympathetic-looking jurors, perhaps young men of radical appearance'.[20] Both fears seem misplaced. Radical young men might be more antagonistic to sexist pornography than their elders, and women have served on juries which have unanimously acquitted defendants in major obscenity cases. Three women were empanelled for the *Lady Chatterley* trial, and five for the trial of *Inside Linda Lovelace*. All-male gatherings have a tendency to be over-protective toward women in their absence. The power of a trial judge to exclude women from a jury was abolished in 1971: it was exercised in the *Last Exit* case, where the all-male panel convicted. Studies undertaken for the American Presidential Commission on Obscenity suggested that women are far more tolerant than men of homosexual erotica, doubtless because they feel less personally threatened by it.[21] The reality is perhaps best expressed by one experienced journalist, in reply to editorial criticisms in *The Times* of jury challenges at the *Linda Lovelace* trial:

> Those who have observed obscenity trials at the Old Bailey for several years would tell you that the majority of jurors are generally in the extremity of middle and late-middle age. If a jury is to be a cross-section of the community, and it is vital in such a case, the chances of it so being without defence challenges are small.
>
> Despite this, juries tend to be middle-aged and therefore by your facile definition 'unsympathetic' to pornography. Perhaps this is appropriate since the majority of *aficionados* interested in the kind of drivel which is contained inside Linda Lovelace are of the age of *Times* leader writers or even older.[22]

In those cases where erotic material is displayed or sold only to males, the defendant should have some residual right to be judged by jurors best able to assess its likely effect. If a man is entitled to be judged by a representative selection of his peers, the right of challenge provides a rudimentary method of leavening and cross-sampling. In most criminal cases challenges are not used at all, but in those which involve questions of conscience or lifestyle, they remain an important, albeit highly restricted, safeguard.

ORDER OF SPEECHES

In criminal trials the prosecutor opens his case with an address to the jury which sets out the crown case, and then calls his supporting evidence, placing before the jury any exhibit on which he relies. Defending counsel may then make an opening speech and call his evidence. In fairness to the defendant, two important changes in this procedure are usually made in obscenity cases: the prosecutor is restrained from reading 'purple passages' to prejudice the minds of the jury in his opening address, and defence counsel is given leave to outline his case before the jury retires to read the allegedly obscene article.

These procedural changes were approved by Mr Justice Byrne at the outset of the trial of *R.* v. *Penguin Books*, after defence counsel (Mr Gerald Gardiner QC) had intervened during the opening speech for the prosecution to object to the recitation at that stage of particular passages from *Lady Chatterley's Lover*. The argument and ruling ran as follows:

MR GRIFFITH-JONES (*for the prosecution*): Members of the Jury, the book starts with a description, or a history, rather, very briefly in Chapter 1, of how Lady Chatterley, whose name is Constance, married her husband, Sir Clifford, in 1917, and how he was wounded and, I have told you, returned from the war. They set up married life again in 1920 at his family seat, which was Wragby Hall, apparently a Victorian, rather ugly, lonely pile of a house, in a park, with woods and forests, just outside a mining village in the Midlands.

... the heroine, if I may so describe her, Lady Chatterley, and the hero, if I may so describe him, the gamekeeper, are, you may think, little more than bodies, bodies which continuously have sexual intercourse with one another. You will see on page 7 ...

MR GARDINER: My Lord, I object. I object to my learned friend drawing the jury's attention to any passages in the book before they have read it. I am not objecting to my learned friend putting before the jury the nature of the story, as he has already done, or the grounds on which the prosecution contend it is obscene, as he has already so clearly done. Nor do I object to the prosecution drawing the jury's attention to any particular passages when they have read the book. I submit the prosecution are not entitled to try and prejudice the jury's mind as to particular passages before they have read the book as a whole.

If one goes right back it was always necessary in a prosecution of this kind to set out in the indictment the parts of the book which are said to be obscene, and the question was, 'Are those parts obscene.' It was perfectly proper to say to the jury, 'You can read the rest of the book if you like, but don't bother about the rest, these are the passages which the prosecution say are obscene. . . .' This was always grossly unfair to authors, because obviously what ought to have been decided was whether the author's work as a whole was obscene. This is one of the very points which Parliament has now altered, because section one provides in express terms that that is the question, which has to be decided, whether it is obscene taken as a whole.

My respectful submission is, in a case of this kind it is really essential, in fairness to the defence, that the jury should read the book before their mind has been prejudiced either on one side or the other. It is entirely a matter for your Lordship, but the most convenient course might be after my learned friend has called formal evidence and after the defence has been opened, that that might be the point at which the jury could read the book, when they have heard the nature of the prosecution's case and the nature of the case for the defence.

MR JUSTICE BYRNE: Do you propose then the prosecution should call their evidence and you should then open your case and then the jury should read the book?

MR GARDINER: Yes, my Lord.

MR GRIFFITH-JONES: My Lord, in my respectful submission I am entitled, indeed it is my duty, to open the evidence upon which the prosecution relies in this case, to the jury. It must surely be, so long as it is properly done, in counsel's discretion as to how he does open the case. My Lord, in a case of this kind the evidence for the prosecution is the book, or parts of the book itself.

All I am seeking to do is to stress and point out to [the jury] those passages – that evidence, in other words – which the prosecution says show that this charge is a good charge and substantiate this indictment.

MR JUSTICE BYRNE: I think you have, if I may say so, very fully indicated to the jury sufficient about this book at the moment to show them what your submission is with regard to it . . . you are entitled to exercise your discretion as to how you open a case, but as this book is charged in this indictment as a whole – indeed, it would not matter whether it was so charged or not, it would have to be considered as a whole – I think the better course, which is only postponing what you will do, would be for the jury to read the book and then for you in due course to point to your particular passages. It is, after all, only postponing the event, and in my view it enables the jury to read this book just as though they had bought it from a book-stall, and no doubt they can make up their minds about it. Then you will be able to point out your passages in due course, and, of course, Mr Gardiner will deal with his suggestions.[23]

Mr Justice Byrne went on to rule that defence counsel could make his opening speech before the jury retired to read the book, and this precedent has been followed in subsequent obscenity proceedings at the Central Criminal Court, including *R. v. Calder & Boyars* and *R. v. Anderson*, where it was noted without demur by the Court of Appeal. Clearly it is fairer if the jury retire after hearing both sides of the case, rather than be obliged to read a book with the prosecution approach uppermost in mind.

READING THE EVIDENCE

How, and where, is the jury to read an allegedly obscene book? The overly serious surroundings of a courtroom hardly conduce to a realistic atmosphere, and works of literature are not usually read as if they were legal contracts, with line by line analysis. Judges have often been at pains' to instruct juries to assimilate the articles in an ordinary way, as though they had bought them at a bookstall. When trying *The Philanderer*, Mr Justice Stable requested jurors to '. . . take that book home and would you mind reading it, as I said, from cover to cover. Read it as a book. Do you follow? Not picking out bits that you think have, shall we say, a tendency here or there, or picking out bits that you think have a sort of immoral tendency, but read it as a book.' In the *Lady Chatterley* trial Mr Justice Byrne gave a similar direction: 'You won't make up your minds about it. You will read this book, you have to hear evidence and so forth, but you will read this book just as though you had bought it at a bookstall and you were reading it in the ordinary way as a whole.'

The trial will be adjourned to give the jury sufficient time to read the articles thoroughly. Usually this task is performed in the privacy of the jury room, although there have been cases where jurors have been permitted to complete their reading at home. The advantages of the bedside were strongly urged by Mr Gerald Gardiner QC in *R. v. Penguin Books*:

> First of all the jury rooms are jolly uncomfortable places. There are hard wooden seats, and anything more unnatural than twelve men and women sitting round a table on hard wooden chairs with a book is in my submission to read it in wholly different circumstances from those in which the ordinary person who bought the book would read it.

MR JUSTICE BYRNE: The learned Clerk of the Court said he cannot agree with the observation that conditions in the jury room are uncomfortable.

MR GARDINER: I am told there are hard chairs. The average rate of reading is, I think, 298 words a minute, which is rather less than a page. On that footing it will take the average reader between seven and eight hours. There are always those who read much slower and others who read much faster.

There is, as your Lordship appreciates, this vital difference between a publication on a wireless and reading a book, that the first is usually done in company. But when you read a book what you read is private to the author and you . . . no-one who bought it would read cheek by jowl, especially with someone of the opposite sex. It would save any possibility of the members of the jury being embarrassed if they were allowed to read it at home.

MR JUSTICE BYRNE: I think the jury should read the book here. I am very sorry, Members of the Jury. I don't want to condemn you to any kind of discomfort, but if you were to take this book home you might have distractions. One knows perfectly well in one's home things do happen unexpectedly. There are distractions: you are trying and carrying out a very onerous duty, and I think it would be much better if you were to read this book in your room.[24]

In ordinary criminal cases jurors examine exhibits in open court. There is no statutory provision for the jury to retire in order to do so, but the practice has now been commended in obscenity cases by the Court of Appeal, which remarked that it 'accords with common-sense: it would be a ridiculous rule which made jurors sit in the jury box hour after hour reading with the judge, counsel and the public watching them'.[25]

THE PRESS AND THE PUBLIC

It is a fundamental principle that 'Every court in the land is open to every subject of the King.'[26] Although juries retire from the court-room to inspect books and magazines, judges cannot exclude members of the public when allegedly obscene passages are read in open court by counsel or witnesses. In *Scott* v. *Scott* the House of Lords reluctantly concluded that there is no common-law power to prevent the public from hearing indecent evidence. Lord Loreburn regretted that 'However true it may be that the publicity given to obscene or bestial matter by trial in open court stimulates and suggests imitation, as many judges have learned from experience at Assizes, and however deplorable it may be that they have no power to prevent it, the remedy must be found by the legislature or not at all.'[27] The remedy has not to date been found by the legislature, save in the Official Secrets Act and the Children and Young Persons Act.

In cases involving obscene films, a makeshift projection apparatus is usually set up in the well of the court, or else the trial moves temporarily to a suitable cinema. The judge has a discretion to decide under what conditions the jury is to study exhibits, and just as he can direct them to read an allegedly obscene book in the privacy of home or jury room, so he may decide that they should view cinematic exhibits in a closed courtroom. This procedure was adopted in the case of *R.* v. *Waterfield*, apparently out of concern that 'persons with a taste for the nasty may come into court . . . and create an atmosphere of tension that results in gasps, giggling and comments which may make the jury's task more difficult'. The Court of Appeal accepted that whilst the court was closed the trial had in effect halted for the jurors to look at exhibits, just as if they were studying documents or photographs in an ordinary criminal case:

> Exhibits must be produced and identified in open court; but when nothing more than looking at or reading them is required, this can be done anywhere which is convenient. In most cases the open courtroom itself will be as convenient as anywhere. It is for the judge to decide where, and under what conditions, jurors should look at or read exhibits. If he decides that they should do so out of court or in a closed courtroom, he is entitled to do so.[28]

It does not follow from *Waterfield* that a judge *must* exclude the public: the decision merely confirms that his doing so will not amount to an irregularity. In other cases judges have permitted 'as many members of the public as could be comfortably accommodated' to stay while allegedly obscene films are screened for the jury.[29] But whatever view a judge takes about members of the public, he should at least permit court reporters to remain throughout the exhibition. In *A. G.* v. *Independent Broadcasting Authority*, *exp. McWhirter* Lord Denning expressly invited the press to be present 'as representatives of the public' while the court viewed an allegedly indecent television documentary.[30]

The rationale for this distinction was explained by Lord Justice Lawton in *Waterfield*:

> . . . the public generally are interested in cases of this kind, and not for unworthy reasons. Concepts of sexual morality are changing. Whenever a jury in this class of case returns a verdict, whether of guilty or not guilty, intelligent readers of newspapers and weekly journals may want to know what kind of film was under consideration. Experience during the past two decades has shown that every acquittal tends to lead to the greater exposure to public gaze of what previous generations thought seemly only in private, if seemly anywhere. Members of the public have to depend on the press for information on which to base their opinions; but if allegedly indecent films are always shown in closed courtrooms the press cannot give the public the information which it may want and which is necessary for the formation of public opinion.

If the public learns through the press what kind of films some jurors are adjudging not to be indecent, it may say 'enough is enough'; but if it does not know, persons with a taste for pornography may suggest and convince some that obscurantist prosecuting authorities are trying to impose a form of film censorship which might have satisfied standards of sexual behaviour which have long been abandoned: a slide into public licentiousness may result. It follows, so it seems to us, that normally, when a film is being shown to a jury and the judge, in the exercise of his discretion, decides that it should be done in a closed courtroom or in a cinema, he should allow representatives of the press to be present. No harm can be done by doing so: some good may result.[31]

This judgment does not give *carte blanche* to lurid newspaper reports of obscenity trials. The privilege accorded to fair and accurate reporting of judicial proceedings remains subject to section 3 of the Law of Libel Amendment Act 1888, which removes that privilege in relation to 'the publication of any blasphemous or indecent matter'.

THE COURSE OF EVIDENCE

Early decisions on the admissibility of evidence under the 1959 Act gave both parties wide scope to canvass the merits and demerits of allegedly obscene books. In 1964 experts were permitted to testify that a book about drug-taking would not deprave or corrupt readers,[32] and in 1967 Sir Basil Blackwell and the Reverend David Sheppard were allowed to confess, somewhat improbably, that *Last Exit to Brooklyn* had tended to corrupt them.[33] In that year the high-watermark of admissibility was reached when the Divisional Court ruled that psychiatrists could explain the effect of particular articles on children, and might even be asked whether such an effect would indicate corruption.[34] This largesse was withdrawn by the Court of Appeal in the *Oz* case, and a restrictive trend continued throughout the 1970s, as courts attempted to curb the acquittal rate of pornographers who proclaimed the therapeutic value of their wares.[35] The present rules relating to admissibility of evidence of fact and opinion in obscenity trials may be stated as follows:

1 Factual evidence may be led about the circumstances in which the alleged offence was committed. This could include photographs of the premises, evidence of its nature, layout and location, details of any restrictions on sale, (e.g. to minors); and advertisements and shop-front display. All these matters are relevant to the jury's assessment of the likely readership. A defendant may testify about his distribution outlets, his organization and his instructions to staff,

and explain how the offending book came to be on his premises. He may call evidence of his good reputation as a respectable trader, and of the fact that he has received no complaints from members of the public prior to the police visit. If similar books and magazines were on the premises at the time of the police raid but were either not seized, or else returned by police or magistrates after seizure, these may be referred to and perhaps exhibited. Either side may also call evidence – even expert evidence – to interpret unfamiliar terms in the publication at issue. In *Shaw's* case, which involved 'contact advertisements', prostitutes were called to explain the meanings of abbreviations which stood for particular sexual deviations.[36]

2 Factual evidence as to the class of likely readers may be led by either side. 'In each case it has to be decided who these readers are, and so evidence is usually given as to the type of shop or place where the material is, and as to the type of customer who goes there.'[37] Police may report the results of observations kept on bookshops and cinema clubs to ascertain the sex, age and behaviour of prospective customers. The defendant may give evidence about the nature of his clientele, and explain any restrictions imposed by him on the sale of sexually explicit material. He may call a sample of customers or readers to the witness stand so the jury can see examples, in the flesh, of the sort of persons at risk.

3 No witness may be asked his or her opinion of obscenity, in general or in relation to particular articles. The views of police, defendants and witnesses on this issue are irrelevant, and will not be allowed to cloud a decision which must be made by the jury alone.[38] Usually, in the course of a raid, some views will be exchanged on the question, but they should be edited out of depositions before the trial begins.

4 An apparent exception to this rule occurs when an accused raises a defence under section 2 (5) of the Act, by seeking to prove that he had not examined the article, and had no reasonable cause to suspect that it was obscene. His failure to examine it necessarily means that his opinion about its legality is uninformed, and the jury must decide whether or not the opinion was reasonably reached on the facts available at the time. This defence is usually applicable only to printers, shop assistants and the like who have assisted the distribution of a book without ever having reason to

look at it, sometimes after assurances from clients or other employees that there is no cause for concern.

5 Another exception to the rule may arise in rare cases where 'the likely readers are a special class, such that the jury cannot be expected to understand the likely impact of the material upon its members without assistance. In such a case evidence from persons qualified by study or experience of that class may be admissible.'[39] The only recorded example of this exception involved a series of cards depicting scenes of violence, contained in chewing-gum wrappers designed to be swapped among young children. The prosecution was permitted to call psychiatric evidence of the tendency of these cards to encourage children to emulate the violence depicted.[40] It would seem to follow that in cases where 'the class of likely readers consisted of, or as to a significant number included, sexual abnormals or deviants', experts would be entitled to testify about the deleterious or therapeutic effects of the material on persons in that class.[41] The courts have not yet considered the scope of this exception.

6 On the issue of obscenity, no evidence may be called relating to the contents of other books or magazines in current circulation. The jury cannot be invited to acquit a defendant on the grounds that his publication is 'less obscene' than others which have not been prosecuted.[42] Counsel may refer to the contemporary climate of permissiveness, but actual comparisons are forbidden. Evidence of other literature *is* admissable, however, when a 'public good' defence is raised. Expert witnesses may refer to other publications in order to compare literary or scientific merits, or simply to demonstrate the contemporary climate of writing.[43]

7 On the issue of obscenity, the defendant's intentions are irrelevant whether he is author, publisher or bookseller. The question for the jury is the actual impact of the material, and not the impact desired by those responsible for placing it in circulation. Evidence of motive frequently creeps into obscenity trials: the prosecution may stress commercial gain, and the defendant may dilate upon his commitment to freedom of expression or sexual liberation. Intention is relevant, in a limited respect, to a section 2 (5) defence, because it must be proved that the accused could have no knowledge of any corrupting tendency. The purpose for which an article is written or published does become relevant if a 'public good' defence

is raised, because the jury must consider the author's intention as well as the literary style he has used to achieve it.[44]

8 The accused may raise a number of factual defences. He may deny, for example, that the article was ever in his possession, or maintain that he kept it for personal perusal only. His counsel may rely upon gaps in the prosecution evidence on these points, but normally the defendant will enter the witness box and back his story with sworn testimony. If a section 2 (5) defence is raised, the accused will be obliged to give evidence, because he bears the burden of establishing, on the balance of probabilities, that he did not examine the article and had no reason to suspect an infringement of the law.

9 The defendant is entitled to an acquittal if the jury is satisfied that notwithstanding the obscenity of an article, its publication is justified as being for the public good in the interests of 'science, literature, art or learning, or of other objects of general concern'. Once this defence is raised the merits may be canvassed by experts for either side, although the onus is on the accused to establish the defence on the balance of probabilities.[45] An 'object of general concern' is an accepted value served by the intrinsic merit of an article, and not by its possible effect upon readers. The jury must be convinced that the publication makes some objective contribution to a recognized field of culture or learning, which can be assessed irrespective of the persons to whom it happens to be distributed.[46]

Experts who testify persuant to section 4 (2) may not trespass on the jury province of deciding the question of obscenity under section 1. They must not be asked questions about the 'effect' of the article on readers, and their evidence should be confined to an assessment of its intrinsic merits. Nor should they be asked to attempt the equation of section 4 'good' with section 1 'obscenity': this balancing act must also be left to the jury alone.

10 The section 4 defence must be raised and proved through the testimony of experts received in the course of the defence case. The prosecution may seek to shake it merely by cross-examination: the jury is entitled to disregard defence experts without hearing contrary testimony.[47] Alternatively, the prosecution may apply, at the close of the defence case, to call experts in rebuttal. In *R.* v. *Calder & Boyars* the Court of Appeal approved the trial judge's ruling that defence experts should be heard first:

Normally the crown cannot know in advance upon which of the many grounds referred to in section 4 the defendant intends to rely. If it were always for the crown to begin on this issue, there would be many cases in which ordinary caution would require a great deal of time and money to be spent in adducing evidence to meet a case which it turns out the defendants never intended to make. No doubt circumstances vary, and the judge has a discretion in the matter.[48]

This ruling gives the crown the advantage of having the 'last word' on section 4. Where the defence has notified the prosecution beforehand that a section 4 defence is to be raised on a specific ground, prosecution experts may be required to testify at the outset, rather than with the benefit of hindsight of the defence case.

At the close of evidence, the prosecution and then the defence make closing speeches and the judge sums up before the jury retires to consider its verdict. Neither counsel nor judge may themselves 'give evidence', but a good deal of extraneous comment inevitably creeps into forensic arguments over obscenity. Although evidence of the 'therapeutic' value of sexual material cannot be adduced, counsel may in his final speech 'canvass the supposed benefits of publication but not, of course, by reference to any expert opinion on the subject'.[49] Judge and counsel may take 'judicial notice' of the fact that standards change over time, and refer to current and historical examples of social change. Jurors must come to a decision based upon their own common sense and knowledge of the world, and perhaps the very evidence rigidly excluded from presentation or examination in court is in fact discussed and debated, unscientifically and anecdotally, in the jury room.

THE JURY DECISION

The jury decision is the pivot of the legal censorship process, and may have far reaching social importance: the acquittal of *Lady Chatterley's Lover*, for example, marked a turning point in the fight for literary freedom. But what special qualities fit a jury for the censorship decision? Judges maintain that 'current standards are in the keeping of juries who can be trusted to maintain the corporate good sense of the community and to discern attacks or values that must be preserved'. The difficulty with this argument is that there is no guarantee that a small and random sample will reflect real community consensus, and it is debateable whether it should ever be asked to do so. On the one hand, the jury is expected to function as the 'microcosm of democratic society'. On the other, 'the jury should be invited, where appropriate, to remember that they live in a plural society, with a tradition of tolerance towards minorities, and that this atmosphere of tolerance is itself part of public decency'.[50] A jury which reflects the view of the majority by condemning a book will necessarily ignore the rights of the minority who wish to read it. Any standard set in an obscenity case will hinge upon the moral outlook of a minimum of ten arbitrarily selected jurors, who may not be prepared to tolerate the alternative views either of dissenting jurors or of groups not represented on the panel. Some safeguard for minorities might be achieved by a requirement of unanimity in obscenity cases, which are characterized by long retirements, hung juries and majority decisions. In the *Oz* case, the only juror aged under thirty-five chose to dissent, and two jurors stood out against the conviction of *Gay News* for blasphemy. In these cases the jury may well have acted as a microcosm of social conflict, but the majority verdicts amounted to a refusal to tolerate minority viewpoints. The 'majority verdict' device was hastily introduced in 1966 as a safeguard against attempts which had been made by professional criminals to threaten and bribe individual jurors in trials involving allegations of violent crime.[51] This rationale does not of course apply to laws which are predicated upon a consensus of social conscience: in such cases, there is much to be said for Sir James Stephen's view that, 'to be able to punish, the moral majority must be overwhelming'.[52]

Since serious criminal consequences hang so precariously on the luck of the jury ballot, there is obviously need for research into the ways in which juries go about formulating their verdicts. But investigation of jury deliberations is frowned upon by the Lord Chancellor's department, evidently afraid that any revelations of slap-dash consideration or irrelevant argumentation might discredit the jury system as a rational method of proof. The Lord Chancellor's department takes its fears to extremes in an explanatory leaflet issued to each juror which asserts that, 'It must be remembered that what is said in the jury room should not be disclosed to any outside person, even after the trial is concluded. All these things are necessary to ensure that the very grave task of deciding whether a person is guilty or not guilty of a criminal offence is not only discharged with absolute fairness, but also without any suspicion of bias.'[53] If justice is *not* done, it will at least *appear* to have been done. Obscenity jurors sometimes exempt themselves from this official conspiracy of silence which is, after all, just another form of censorship. At the *Lady Chatterley* trial, for example, they let it be known that the 'public good' defence carried the day: 'There never was the smallest likelihood that they would agree on a verdict of "guilty", and almost certain, on the word of more than one of them, that at the very start they were nine to three for an acquittal (meaning that the majority thought the prosecution a mistaken one anyway). They remained thus divided until the last day, when the dissentient three, who thought the book obscene and felt that that was enough, were reminded by the others that they had to decide whether it was nevertheless redeemed by its literary excellence. On this they may have felt themselves to be outmatched by the thirty-five experts, some of whom they had seen on television: and they earned themselves niches in literary history by giving way.'[54]

Another breach in the embargo, made after the *Oz* conviction, suggests that the jury verdict in that case may have been reached upon irrelevant and improper grounds. Discovery of the breach was itself remarkable enough: the junior defence counsel happened to patronize the same hairdresser as the jury foreman, and learnt from this source that the foreman and his colleagues whiled away their time in the jury room reading back issues of *Oz*. It is settled law that a defendant must not be found guilty because the jury disapproves of his general publishing activities: only the article being prosecuted – *Oz 28* – should have been considered. Investigations were made, and the foreman admitted in a letter to the DPP that other editions of *Oz* had been scrutinized: 'I thought they (the *Oz* editors) had had a fair trial and had been warned frequently about publishing, particularly as I had seen the previous issues as these were available in the jury room.' In other words, the conviction may have been motivated at least in part by an adverse opinion of earlier editions, which had not been the subject of any evidence or argument. It is also interesting to note the emphasis that the foreman placed on police cautions given to the defendants in relation to the earlier editions. Evidence of these cautions was strictly inadmissible, and they had not been mentioned at all by the prosecution. They were introduced by the defence at the insistence of the editors themselves as examples of continual police harassment of the underground press. The defendants miscalculated the jury reaction: what for their own peers would have been cogent proof of victimization, appeared to their middle-aged jury to be wilful disobedience of friendly police counsel. The Court of Appeal refused to speculate on the mystery of how the *Oz* back-issues came to be left in the jury room, on the hallowed legal principle that 'what passes in a jury room during the discussion by the jury of their verdict should be confidential'.[55]

An important development in breaking down the inscrutability of jury verdicts was made in the *Nasty Tales* trial, when editor Mick Farren, during his evidence, invited jurors to question him. Jurors have always had the right to address questions to the witness through the judge, although they are rarely reminded of it. The *Nasty Tales* jury jumped at the opportunity, and asked a number of questions in the form of notes handed up for the judge to read out. Interestingly enough, the first thing they wanted to know was the defendants' motive – a matter which is irrelevant in law, although obviously of concern to common sense. The next question was: 'Is the freeing of the sexual imagination and its communication an essential part of your idea of an open and healthy society?' Farren replied:

I do believe that the communication of one's fantasies is very important to the health of any society. Communication is all important for any kind of society which is aiming towards the happiness and well-being of its population. A lack of communication can only produce, in my opinion, fear and isolation. Lack of communication in the field of sex is what our society is suffering from. Otherwise there would be no dirty bookshops. We are not pornographers. We are using an unconventional medium to make very serious points about the health of our society.

Another question indicated criticism of the DPP's decision to charge the editors of the magazine, rather than the careless shopkeeper who had sold it to an eight-year-old child and thereby provoked complaint from an angry parent.

After the 'not guilty' majority verdict one juror was quoted in *The Times* as saying that he thought the charge was ridiculous from the beginning: 'I did not think we should have to give a verdict on the basis of Edwardian morals.' Outside the court, jurors told Farren that nine of them had been in favour of acquittal from their first reading of the magazine: they took the view that nobody should tell them what they could read, and had sat through the trial in a state of boredom, exacerbated by the constant defence assumption that they were hostile to the magazine. The three dissenters, unlike their counterparts in the *Lady Chatterley* trial, had not been swayed by arguments of literary merit. However, after four hours of stonewalling, one of the three remembered a dinner date, and fearing that he would remain locked up until an agreement was reached, threw in his lot with the libertarians, enabling a ten-to-two majority acquittal.

The role of the jury in deciding the issue of obscenity is rarely challenged, because a random sampling is at least more representative of public opinion than magistrates, judges or experts, but some disquiet has been voiced over the capacity of ordinary jurors to pass the sort of literary or artistic judgments required by the statute. They must first decide the question of obscenity, and only if they are sure that the article does tend to corrupt should they go on to consider the public good defence, and then proceed to the balancing act wherein 'corruption' is 'weighed' against 'merit'. There have been suggestions that special juries should be empanelled to decide 'public good' issues,[56] but Parliament has never been willing to delegate decisions about individual liberty to panels of 'experts', and special juries, however much they might more accurately represent the views of the reading public, have fallen out of favour in the pursuit of egalitarian ideals. The only satisfactory brake within the present system upon prosecutions of meritorious material lies in the DPP's discretion to evaluate literary opinion before launching a prosecution.

Another imponderable influence upon the jury is the impact of the judge's summing-up. The controversial nature of obscenity cases makes it difficult for the fairest referee to restrain expressions of personal prejudice. In ordinary criminal cases judges are permitted to comment in strong terms on the credibility of witnesses and the merits of defences.[57] Opinions from men experienced in sifting truth within the trial process may help jurors to assess the facts. But in cases which depend upon value-judgments, judicial comments can be tendentious, and detract from the principle that the morality of the man in the jury-box must govern the decision. Judicial prejudices may well misfire if they are expressed intemperately, but authoritative moral pronouncements may condition the jury response. Some judges find it difficult to comprehend how sexually explicit material can be defended at all – the convictions of *Last Exit to Brooklyn* and *Oz* were both quashed on appeal because trial judges had misunderstood the case for the defence. Judges can be particularly insensitive when confronted with youthful rebels, as the summing-up in the trial of *Nasty Tales* demonstrated:

> It may have surprised you that anyone could come forward to tell you that anything in this magazine has literary or artistic merit, but the world is full of surprises and it happened ... you may think it would have been more for the public good if *Nasty Tales* was designed to make the hippies come to terms with *us* and understand what is wrong with *them*.

The Times reported that these remarks drew 'gasps from the public gallery, which was crowded with young people'.[58] Recently the High

Court has become more diffident about assuming the role of an oracle of popular standards. In 1977 the Court of Appeal admitted that 'judges were not in a position to decide if the climate of opinion had changed. Their background and life made it impossible for them to know what went on all over the country, in factories and offices.'[59] If sex magazines are being handed around in factories and offices, judges would be among the last to know. But jurors drawn from those factories and offices would appreciate any change in the climate of opinion, and this may explain their acquittal of material which judges have thought irredeemably obscene.

Judicial scepticism about expert evidence may also intrude upon jury assessment. Mr Justice Byrne wearily lamented that

As we all know, in these days the world seems to be full of experts. There is not a subject you can think of where there is not to be found an expert who will be able, or says he will be able, to deal with the situation; but our criminal law in this country is based upon the view that a jury takes of the facts and not upon the view that experts may have.[60]

Denigration of the expert was a factor in the *Oz* verdict, according to Jonathan Dimbleby:

The judge's summing-up was stunning. Suddenly the defence witnesses became 'so-called defence experts, some of whom, members of the jury, you may think reached the position where they either had to admit they were wrong or tell a lie'. If *Oz* was a window on the hippy world – 'well, windows sometimes need cleaning, don't they?' As he finished with a witness, he would toss his copy of *Oz* disdainfully down on to the table, and with it, one felt, the case for the defence. It was a distressing and perhaps crucial exercise. For after constant 'exposure to' (a favourite expression of the prosecutor's) 'fucking in the street' 'masturbation' 'deviation' 'lesbianism' 'corruption' and 'cannabis', this middle-aged group of British householders – the jury – was asked quite simply to 'set a standard'. What an invitation.[61]

The Court of Appeal was inclined to agree that 'the judge was biased against experts as a group and was inclined to make little of their evidence whenever he got the chance to do so'.[62]

In some American systems of trial, judges merely direct juries on the applicable law, and do not venture 'assistance' upon the evidence or the merits. There is merit in the suggestion that summings-up in obscenity cases should be confined to an exposition of the law, because judges cannot venture comments on the facts without expressing personal opinions on the very questions which should be left for the jury alone to decide.

SENTENCING POLICY

Most crimes have a 'tariff', a generally accepted penalty for an average offence in each particular category, adjusted in appropriate cases to reflect aggravating or mitigating factors. Sentences for obscenity tend to reflect the personal opinion of the trial judge, expressed within a range of three years imprisonment and by an unlimited power to fine. The Court of Appeal, in two decades of reviewing obscenity sentences passed under the 1959 legislation, has failed to lay down workable guidelines for judges, so that the consequences of a conviction are almost as unpredictable as police action in the first place. The passing of sentence upon a pornographer is sometimes an occasion for moral satisfaction and public denunciation of vice. In 1974 one trial judge, jailing a pornographer named Collingbourne, hailed the conviction as

a clarion call for reticence and privacy in matters of personal sexual behaviour. These verdicts in my judgment strikingly condemn the claim that a commercial enterprise of this large nature is acceptable to this society and further, in my judgment, the shrill petulant protest of licentious libertines has been resoundingly rejected.

Collingbourne is a loathsome lecher: I do not punish him for that, but that is the mainspring which drove him to this enterprise. In my judgment he is depravity and corruption incarnate, exploiting the weakness of others for money and leading his associates astray and, indeed, corrupting them, and conspiring with distributors. Such conduct demands a prison sentence. The sentence of the court, in effect, is five years' imprisonment.[63]

The following year another trial judge took an entirely different approach to a defendant convicted of selling similar material:

I feel this case may have done good, not only to you but to the public in this area, because the jury have drawn a clear line between what is permissible in this sort of material and what is not. So far as you are concerned, you cannot be under any illusions as to what you can legitimately sell and what you must avoid selling ... on each of the sixteen counts I shall impose a fine of £10 making a total of £160.[64]

These cases stand at the extremes of a sentencing pattern beset by conflict and confusion. A study of all obscenity cases prosecuted in 1970 revealed that of eighty-eight cases prosecuted by the police, sixty-seven resulted in fines (ranging upwards from £5) and ten in sentences of imprisonment varying from eight months to two years.

Cases prosecuted by the Director of Public Prosecutions in 1970 had the following results:[65]

Class of offender	Number convicted	Imprisoned	Fined	Range of fine
Distributor with previous obscenity convictions	10	4	6	£10–200
Distributor with no previous obscenity convictions	32	1	31	£25–200
Person with private pornography collection, published for friends, workmates, etc	20	4	16	£10–100

These wide variations in penalties reflect the diversity in outlook of different magistrates and judges. Even in the same court consistency is hard to find: at Bow Street one Soho bookseller, who had been conditionally discharged a few months previously for the same offence, was fined £10 for possessing a vast array of obscene films, books, photographs and slides. A Soho neighbour with no previous convictions and a much smaller stock of obscene books was sentenced to four months imprisonment shortly afterwards.

In 1971, sentencing policy in obscenity cases was considered by the Lord Chief Justice when he presided over the *Oz* appeal. The tribulations of the three *Oz* editors had provoked intense public debate over the appropriateness of prison haircuts, remands for psychiatric reports, and sentences of imprisonment. Although the convictions were quashed, Lord Widgery warned:

to send a man to prison for offences in this classification has been a relatively unusual thing in the past. However, those of us who sit regularly in this court are only too familiar with the fact that, when a particular offence becomes prevalent and a wave of it appears, the only course which can be taken is to increase the sentences in order to adjust for the increase in the incidence of the offence.... We would therefore like to make it quite clear in general terms that any idea that an offence of obscenity does not merit a prison sentence should be eradicated. There will be many cases in future in which a prison sentence is appropriate if the court imposing the sentence thinks fit, and any general impression to the contrary should not be retained.[66]

The pornographic wave descried by the Court of Appeal in 1971 has not receded, despite deterrent sentences. The following year the

Court of Appeal advocated heavy fines, noting that the pittances exacted by magistrates 'are obviously no deterrent. They are a mere trifle compared to the profits.'[67] The pornographer, like the punter, paid his money and took his chance. A Soho shop assistant earning £50 per week was jailed for eighteen months; a 'porn king' caught with eighteen tons of hardcore worth £500,000 received a £50,000 fine.

From this confusing picture no sentencing principle could emerge, and the Court of Appeal admitted as much in *R. v. Angel*, a 1974 case involving the publisher of a 'contact' magazine:

> Counsel for the defendant took us painstakingly through the details of the comparable offences for which other accused persons received but suspended sentences or fines or both. It is in this court almost impossible to compare the different cases without the full detail of each case.... We can only look at the matter broadly and make the best comparison we can between the various cases. On the basis of that comparison, some of the other offences for which suspended sentences or fines or both were imposed seem to us at least arguably to have been worse than the offences committed by the defendant. The defendant has no previous convictions. He has a job now open to him. He has a good work record. In these circumstances and not without further reluctance, for in truth this is a nauseating story, we shall substitute like sentences suspended for two years from today. If the defendant offends in these or in any other respects during the next two years he can expect neither mercy nor leniency on any future occasion.[68]

In the absence of any guidance from the Court of Appeal as to which obscenity cases merit a custodial sentence, variations have persisted between jurisdictions and between judges. In 1977 a bookseller in Plymouth was jailed for one year for selling pornographic American novellas; two weeks later a bookseller in Liverpool was fined £150 for selling similar titles, obtained from the same source. The particular form of disposal – fine, suspended sentence, or custody – will depend upon the personal outlook of the particular trial judge, although the severity of that penalty may in turn be influenced by the following factors:

1 Genuine test-case prosecutions of reputable publishers for books which are of 'borderline' obscenity will be treated leniently. The publishers of *Last Exit to Brooklyn* were fined £100, and Mr Richard Handyside was fined £50 for *The Little Red Schoolbook*.

2 The judge's 'gut reaction' to the subject-matter of the material will act as an aggravating or mitigating factor. Material involving

children, animals, sado-masochism or incest is usually placed at the top of the scale.

3 A defendant who pleads 'guilty' will be given credit for saving court time, public expense, and jury sensitivities.

4 A defendant who has given up his former trade, and is no longer associated with pornography, is entitled to a sentencing discount.[69]

5 Punishment will escalate for subsequent offences.

6 If the defendant is close to the source of supply, in the sense of either producing it himself, organizing its distribution, or putting it directly into the hands of the public by owning a bookshop, he will be more severely dealt with than employees or authors. Profiteering from pornography is a graver offence than dispensing it for a fixed wage.

7 A penalty may be reduced, as it was in *Angel*, to avoid disparity with other obscenity sentences. The judge may give some effect to the argument that, at a time when almost every brand of sexual material has been acquitted by some jury or other, the defendant should not be penalized too severely for blundering across a legal line of uncertain location.

8 Convicted defendants may be further penalized by orders to contribute to their own, or to the prosecutor's, costs. Even successful defendants are sometimes made to suffer in respect of their costs by judges who disagree with jury acquittal, although such action runs counter to the spirit of the 1973 practice direction which provides that costs should normally be awarded to successful defendants.[71]

The upsurge in obscenity offences in England since Scandinavian countries legalized pornography is reflected in sentencing homilies as a 'wave' threatening to 'engulf' society. It can be eradicated, so the metaphor continues, by 'closing the floodgates' and imprisoning pornographers. A deterrent sentencing policy may have worked when public opinion was universally on the side of repression and the closest legal market-place was located at Port Said. Now that sex has become the stock-in-trade of the advertising agencies and daily newspapers, and pornography of the hardest core is obtainable for the price of a cross-channel ferry ticket, the judge who imposes a custodial sentence may appear more like King Canute than the boy with his finger in the dyke. Shortly after the Lord Chief Justice advocated jail sentences for obscenity offences, the Commissioner of Police, Sir Robert Mark, entered a notable dissent:

> Our experience with pornography shows that some activities, even if most people think them undesirable or offensive, cannot, in practice, be stopped. The most one can hope for is to regulate the way in which they are carried on. Gambling, brothel-keeping, unconventional sexual practices, are all in this category. There is no certainty that very severe penalties would suppress them. The demand will always be there. A more likely effect is that they would be driven underground, raising the cost to the consumer and the profit to those willing to take the risks. The incentive to oppose or corrupt the police would be greatly increased. Prohibition in the United States, which created a climate in which gangsters could thrive, is surely the classic example of a self-defeating attempt to eradicate the ineradicable.[72]

TRIALS ON TRIAL

In orthodox criminal trials the burden of proof rests throughout upon the prosecution: the Crown must demonstrate beyond reasonable doubt that it was the defendant who performed certain actions which indisputably constitute the crime charged. At an obscenity trial there is rarely any contest about the only *fact* the prosecution has to prove – whether the defendant published the article in question. The only matter in dispute is whether the article is likely to corrupt its readers, and prosecution arguments assume that depiction of deviant activity will encourage reader emulation. The defence has a complicated task to rebut this assumption: it must first establish just what effect perception of the sexual material would have on the minds and behaviour of the likely readership. What would drawings and articles make readers think, and would their thoughts issue in action of any kind? Once this effect is established, the defence has then to argue the second limb of its case, that the assumed effect is not harmful, at least in the sense of being an example of moral corruption. The jury might conclude that a particular picture would predispose certain classes of reader to masturbate, or participate in oral-genital intercourse, so the defence must maintain that masturbation and oral-genital contacts are not of themselves harmful or immoral. The first proposition is a question of fact: 'What is the causal connection between reading about sex and indulging in certain thoughts and behaviour?' The second is a matter of opinion, a value judgment which will be answered in different ways by different tribunals. 'Is it morally corrupt to engage in oral intercourse?', a question which a jury is obliged to answer if it is satisfied that an article about the subject will encourage readers to experiment, cannot be resolved except by resort to personal codes of morality. In the absence of expert guidance, obscenity verdicts are matters of faith rather than foresight.

The practice of law is dependent upon the use of verbal skills and of certain logical patterns of thinking associated with reliance on language. But the deeply emotional, often intuitive issues of sexual morality involved in obscenity trials cannot be handled by legal language or by conventional legal analysis. 'Moral corruption' cannot be described, in the sense that murder or theft can be described, in a general definition which will give a litmus result – positive or negative – when applied to any factual situation. The law against theft, expressed in the words 'it is an offence to take property belonging to others', has an indisputable central meaning: it can be matched with the statement (a verbal projection of facts evidenced by witnesses or uncovered by cross-examination) that 'John Smith took the television set belonging to Peter Jones', to form the syllogistic conclusion 'John Smith has committed an offence'. But when the major premise is 'it is an offence to deprave and corrupt' the verbal projection 'John Smith has published homosexual contact advertisements' requires the jury to supply a further value-loaded premise of its own making before John Smith can be convicted of obscenity. Obscenity laws are directives to judges and juries to make their own law, to supply some verbal denotation of the phrase 'a tendency to deprave and corrupt', before matching that unwritten law – the law of their own particular sexual morality – with the defendant's conduct.

Obscenity trials reflect the inability of traditional modes of criminal adjudication to comprehend the issues which can arise in the decision to censor. Criminal law has developed as a method for obtaining the truth in a world of fingerprints, alibis, police informers, blood stains, and the dog that doesn't bark in the night. These are facts able to be tested: the evidence can be weighed, the credibility of witnesses can be shaken by confrontation. The machinery of the criminal law is geared to adjudicate disputes about *facts*. Obscenity cases call for decision, not about truth or falsity, but about which of two plausible opinions is to be preferred.

The device of the criminal trial transforms the question of whether and to what extent a publication should be censored into a forensic struggle to brand its publisher a felon. The juror is ordered not to discuss a verdict with his colleagues until the conclusion of the judge's summing-up. He is called upon to answer questions of enormous psychological complexity and is locked up and told he will not be released until a verdict is reached. At no stage has he been able to question witnesses, except in the limited manner employed at the *Nasty Tales* trial, or discuss the material with its publisher. He is deprived of any opportunity to explain or qualify his decision, and is thrown back in the final analysis on his own prejudices. Suppose he disapproves of only one small item, and wants to warn the defendant not to publish that sort of material again. 'Not guilty' hardly carries this message, but 'guilty' might send the publisher to jail, a remedy he may feel to be too drastic to punish one small error of taste. Yet the criminal process offers no alternatives. Criminal trials are not only irrational *methods* of censorship, they require censorship decisions to be made in an artificial and emotion-laden atmosphere. The prison officers who flank the defendant in the dock and escort him to and from the cells, the excessive formality of legal etiquette and jargon, the regimentation by court officials, are all unnecessary distractions. Some jurors may react by straining to acquit, to save a sad or sympathetic defendant from the risk of prison for publishing material which in any other circumstances they would not hesitate to destroy. Other jurors may feel obliged to adopt a more authoritarian attitude than they would in a normal setting, for reasons explained by Germaine Greer:

> It is not as if the jury is encouraged to assess the situation in terms of their own behaviour; rather they accept the solemnity of a new position in the community. A juror is no longer the man who says 'fuck' with his workmates and is rather a dab hand at telling hair-raisingly dirty jokes. He is now a juror sitting up in his best suit in a court of law. Instead of the standards relating to his own way of life, he adopts the standard of another, imaginary way of life. The first time he hears the word 'fuck' in the courtroom he may actually wince.

Perhaps the most noticeable difference between an obscenity trial and the rational appraisal of a sex publication is the absence of laughter in the courtroom. During the *Oz* trial spectators were constantly ejected from the public gallery for laughing, and the judge issued daily warnings that his courtroom was not a theatre for public entertainment. But when extracts from the trial transcript were performed by the Royal Shakespeare Company on a West End stage, the reaction of most members of the audience was to roar with laughter. 'It is a legal comedy better than any Beachcomber ever invented,' chuckled *The Times* theatre critic. 'Laughter came in gales,' observed the *Daily Telegraph*. 'A delightful ding-dong in the liveliest tradition of courtroom comedy. Most of the fun derived from the incongruous spectacle of a pompous judge and pompous prosecutor being confronted by the struggle to define obscenity and the aims of the "alternative society".'[73] Yet the same 'delightful ding-dong', a few months before, had put the defendants' freedom at stake. It can hardly be in the interests of a rational system of justice, let alone the dignity of or respect for the law, that criminal proceedings should be permitted which, when transposed word-for-word to a less repressive setting, provoke an audience to gales of laughter.

Obscenity trials tend to be counter-productive. Their immediate and most tangible result is enormous publicity for the article prosecuted. No advertising campaign can match an Old Bailey prosecution. The circulation of *Inside Linda Lovelace*, for example, jumped from 20,000 to 600,000 after its much-publicized acquittal, while *Lady Chatterley* has sold over four million copies. A prosecution which fails is doomed by the force of its own logic to become a source of more depravity and corruption than the reprieved book could ever have achieved of its own or its publishers' momentum. It is also arguable that the *Oz*, *I.T.*, *Nasty Tales* and *Little Red Schoolbook* trials were counter-productive in that they exacerbated tension between the establishment and minority groups. This kind of generalization is difficult to prove, but the angry young men and women who danced around a burning effigy of Judge Argyle in front of the Old Bailey did not lack sympathizers throughout the country. In similar vein the prosecution of *Gay News* for blasphemy was perceived, rightly or wrongly, as a crusade against homosexuals. The rough-and-tumble of courtroom rhetoric provides ample scope for defendants in obscenity cases to suggest that they are on trial for opinions held, rather than for the manner in which these opinions have been expressed.

Despite these drawbacks, is there an acceptable alternative to a trial jury as the ultimate arbiter of freedom of expression? The paternalistic imprimatur of a censorship board would merely offer a narrower and more predictable set of prejudices unless its role were confined to classification rather than suppression. A satisfactory measure of decriminalization and delegalization would be attainable with an administrative licensing system, modelled on gaming legislation, which could at least control the dissemination of pornography. An administrative procedure which preserved the power to ban books, however, would require an appeal mechanism, and the obscenity trial, with all its faults, at least ensures that the final decision to censor is made openly, after public debate, by a tribunal more likely to be a touchstone of common sense and common morality than any group of experts or administrators. The obscenity trial is an inefficacious and embarrassing method of censorship largely because it is a criminal procedure, conducted in criminal courts and carrying criminal consequences. The threat of imprisonment is only appropriate for those who deliberately flout clear law, and engage in criminal conduct verifiable as an issue of fact, such as selling restricted material without a licence, or to children, or by public display or unsolicited mailings. A jury can only deliberate rationally over more general censorship decisions once the shadow cast by prison gates is dissolved.

6

Experts and the public good

THE MARCH OF SCIENCE

The common law assumed that erotic writing had a baneful influence on the mind. The effect of 'lascivious metres to whose venom sound the open ear of youth doth always listen' was necessarily to corrupt and deprave. Although an intention to corrupt morality was alleged in obscene libel indictments, that tendency was always to be found in the publication itself if it went beyond the bounds of decency by suggesting 'to the minds of the young of either sex, or even to persons of more advanced years, thoughts of a most impure and libidinous character'.[1] Expert evidence was unnecessary; the tribunal could simply look at the material and see whether it made immoral suggestions – if it did, it was *ipso facto* obscene. It was inconceivable that the promulgation of immorality could be other than corrupting – that notion was a contradiction in terms. In a few instances involving sex education books, doctors were permitted to testify about the propriety and clinical effectiveness of proffered advice, but before the publication of the Kinsey report in 1948 there was no scientific basis for any argument that sexual arousal might be good in itself, and such an argument was not in fact mounted in an English court until 1971. Nor did it matter, on the common law approach, that the erotic material might have literary or artistic merit. Logically, the more skilful the writing, the more it was likely to affect its readers. 'Obscene classics,' Judge Frank pointed out, 'just because of their greater artistry and charm, will presumably have far greater influence on readers than dull inartistic writings.'[2] This consequence of the obscene libel law proved less palatable than the basic taboo on sexual arousal, and powerful arguments were soon deduced for distinguishing between good and bad obscenity. Mr Justice Stephen first formulated a 'public good' defence in his *Digest of Criminal Law*, and in 1912 George Santayana gave it a philosophical justification: 'Lascivious ... works when beauty has touched them, cease to give out what is wilful and disquieting in their subject and become altogether intellectual and sublime. There is a high breathlessness about beauty that cancels lust.'[3]

The cancellation of lust was only apparent, however, to those whose eyes could behold beauty, and this was not a qualification for the stipendiary magistry. Although there were exceptions, most courts declined the assistance of literary and artistic experts, much to the displeasure of the cultural establishment, whose efforts finally secured in the 1959 Act the statutory admission of expert evidence pursuant to a 'public good' defence. The sponsors of the new legislation assumed that sexual arousal was of itself dangerous and potentially corrupting: the risk was only worth taking in the pursuit of civilizing values like art, literature, science and learning. Pornography, which deliberately and solely titillated sexual appetites, would remain irredeemably obscene. Educational works and literature which employed 'erotic realism' to explore human relationships might be justifiable if experts could establish a cultural significance which would outweigh any tendency to corrupt. Titillation and aesthetic merit were metaphorically placed in alternating scales of justice, and the weight of scholarship was permitted to tip the balance.

These comfortable assumptions of the 1950s were built into the Act with legislative language so mobile in meaning that it soon permitted arguments which were the very antithesis of those assumptions. Erotic writing was thought to deprave and corrupt. Denmark legalized erotic writing, but the rate of sex crime, instead of spiralling, fell dramatically. In America, some scientific studies of the impact of erotica suggested beneficial rather than harmful effects on the mind. The common law assumption that sexual arousal necessarily entailed corruption could no longer be maintained with absolute confidence. If these advances of science were propounded before juries, by qualified and sincere experts, the 1959 Act might produce consequences which would have surprised its sponsors. These consequences would not always militate in favour of acquittal. In 1959 'obscenity' was confined to 'sex': it was not applied to depictions of violence, dangerous drugs, or racial intolerance. But other scientific studies soon suggested that media preoccupation with violence could corrupt both by desensitization and by provoking aggressive impulses. If that evidence was placed before a jury by psychologists and psychiatrists, convictions might be obtained in cases which would hitherto have been laughed out of court. Science was giving new meaning to the concept of corruption, and the framers of the 1959 legislation, in their wisdom or in their recklessness, had provided a formula elastic enough to encompass these changes. Moreover, the infant science of sociology was producing data about sexual behaviour which placed 'community standards' in a new perspective. Sexual deviations once thought highly depraved were apparently widely practised at all levels of society. A tolerance of homosexuality was emerging which would have appalled the prosecutors of *The Well of Loneliness*. The 'public good' defence specifically permitted expert evidence, not merely of literature and learning, but about 'other objects of general concern'. At first blush, the psychiatric health of the community seemed such an object, and if hard-core pornography had a therapeutic effect by acting as a 'safety valve' for potential sex offenders, its publication would be justifiable under section 4.

Much of the expert evidence advanced under the 1959 Act was unscientific and irrelevant, but it was ultimately excluded because the courts feared it was too persuasive. At first, the rules were permissively applied, and in 1967 pyschiatrists were permitted to testify for the prosecution that scenes of violence would have a harmful effect on young children. But when the *Oz* defence, four years later, made similar use of psychiatric evidence to challenge the claim that sexual references would have a harmful effect on teenagers, the Court of Appeal ruled it inadmissible. The following year the same type of evidence was again advanced, but this time by way of the 'public good' defence. Over the next four years doctors, psychiatrists and psychologists testified that sex magazines had a therapeutic effect on those who sought them out, so that publication was justified in the interests of mental health and hygiene. Even when these opinions were contested by prosecution experts they were blamed for producing acquittals, and a good deal of partisan obloquy was directed against a 'circus' of defence experts whose travelling shows brought permissiveness to the provinces. If obscenity trials appeared to be a circus, the performance of experts who used pornography to tame wild libidos was perhaps less miraculous than the jury's balancing act on the metaphysical tight-rope between corruption and public good. The curtain was rung down by the House of Lords in *DPP* v. *Jordan*, in a decision which construed 'other objects of general concern' to mean the values inherent in obscene material, rather than the benefits which might incidentally accrue by its therapeutic impact on certain readers.[4] The ruling in *Jordan* may have little effect on conviction rates, but it has shortened the length of many obscenity trials and reduced media interest in their results.

INADMISSIBLE EVIDENCE

Relatively little research has been done in England on the effect of erotic publications, so those psychiatrists and psychologists called to testify to the 'public good' of obscene articles in the pre-*Jordan* years proffered evidence from their own consulting-room experiences. The first to offer empirical insight was Dr Eustace Chesser, the veteran psychiatrist who had defended his own work, *Love Without Fear*, at the Old Bailey in 1941. In 1972 in *R. v. Gold* he affirmed that publication of several 'soft porn' magazines was for the public good:

It is my considered opinion that the free dissemination of such magazines is in the public interest, because they help to lower the threshold at which guilt and shame attach to natural sexual expression and cause unnecessary psychological problems. These magazines contain sensible articles about sex practices which, although widespread in modern society, differ from the 'missionary position' approved by tradition. Oral and anal intercourse, masturbation, and the use of mechanical stimulation, are all incidents of human sexuality which, when practised in an honest and affectionate relationship, can enrich and satisfy. Yet it has been my experience in my consulting work that many people who engage in these practices become disturbed by the guilt and shame which tradition attaches to them.

In my opinion the publication of magazines which openly and intelligently discuss such subjects will have an overall therapeutic effect on the very large – in the case of masturbation and fantasy, at least, overwhelmingly large – proportions of the population who do engage in such practices. They contribute to a saner and more healthy approach to sex. Conversely, to stamp them out because they refer to these practices will have a correspondingly harmful effect, by reinforcing outmoded taboos which, in modern society, are psychologically damaging.

Chesser's evidence assisted an acquittal in *Gold*, but Scotland Yard kept the exhibits and showed them to the Court of Appeal the following year, to demonstrate the difficulty of obtaining obscenity convictions. The court pronounced them 'extremely obscene' and lamented that the wide scope of 'other objects of general concern' had entitled them to an expert defence.[5] Lord Denning alliteratively asserted that pornography is powerful propaganda for perversions, and there is no doubt that its frequent discovery in the libraries of sex criminals has convinced many lawyers and policemen that erotica triggers sex crimes. But evidence for an alternative hypothesis – that pornography provides, at least for a time, a harmless fantasy outlet used as a substitute for criminal conduct – accumulated rapidly between 1967 and 1973, largely as a result of the Danish government's decision to remove most restrictions on distribution of erotic material to adults. It had acted on a report from the Danish Forensic Medicine Council, which included the finding that 'it is commonly known in medical science that sexual leanings are fixed at an early age, probably around five or six years old, and are in any case completely established by the end of puberty. It is therefore hardly likely that the reading of 'obscene' writings or the sight of films etc. will change the sexual leanings of an adult person.' If that view were mistaken, legalization would have coincided with a significant increase in deviant behaviour. On the contrary, the rate of serious crimes of sexual violence showed no tendency to increase, while the incidence of other sex-related offences fell significantly. Dr Berl Kutchinsky, of the Copenhagen Institute of Criminal Science, concluded that availability of pornography was a direct cause for this decrease, and he postulated a 'safety valve' theory: pornography provides a fantasy release for sexually disturbed individuals, enabling them to slake their appetites by masturbation rather than inflicting unwelcome attentions upon women and children. Kutchinsky conceded that the drop in minor sexual offences, such as exhibitionism, might be explained by concomitant changes in public perception of sex crime and a greater reluctance to complain to police, but the startling diminution in the serious offence of child molestation could not be explained other than by the appearance of a legal 'safety valve'.[6] Kutchinsky appeared on several occasions as a defence expert in British obscenity trials, and he drew attention to the fact that production and home consumption of pornography in Denmark declined rapidly after an initial upsurge: popular interest was based on curiosity rather than genuine need, and a satiation point was quickly reached. Fears about the corruption of public morality, as distinct from individual depravity, were, he claimed, unfounded.

In 1969 an Arts Council working party with a distinctly liberal membership concluded that there was 'a complete absence of evidence to suggest that sex in the arts, even when aphrodisiac in intention, has criminal or anti-social repercussions'. It endorsed the testimony of several leading psychiatrists to the effect that persons are not encouraged, merely by reading, to engage in sexual perversions which they might otherwise never have thought of. Dr Anthony Storr explained:

In my view, disturbances of sexuality of this kind have their origin in early childhood and are the result of the family environment to which the individual was exposed during his first five or six years. It is therefore highly unlikely that a book will have the effect of making somebody perverse who is not so already. My own view is that people who are afflicted with sexual perversions go out and find the literature which fits in with their own particular predilection. In other words, literature is secondary to the presence of perversion and does not induce or cause it.[7]

These assumptions were challenged by a committee headed by Lord Longford, which was motivated by an avowed opposition to the spread of sexual explicitness. The Report's recommendations for tougher legal sanctions against obscenity were undermined by its own survey of scientific literature, conducted by Maurice Yaffé, who gave some credence to the findings that pornography had little effect on individual sexual habits and could not be confidently isolated as a causal factor in sex crime.[8] Yaffé's own work at London hospitals subsequently strengthened his views, and juries doubtless found it ironic to see Lord Longford's own expert entering the lists as an advocate for pornographic publications at a number of pre-*Jordan* obscenity trials. A study of offences committed in Britain between 1949 and 1976 suggests that the 'boom years' for sex crime were in the fifties and early sixties; the availability of sexually explicit materials coincided with a deceleration in the incidence of sexual offences.[9] Although pornography causes great offence and embarrassment, on the present evidence it cannot confidently be held responsible for initiating anti-social behaviour in those not already so disposed.[10]

In 1970 the American Presidential Commission on Obscenity and Pornography reported that the studies they had sponsored 'failed to establish a meaningful causal relationship or even significant correlation between exposure to erotica and immediate or delayed anti-social behaviour among adults'.[11] The Commission, which comprised seventeen sociologists, psychiatrists, criminologists and clergymen, sat for two years, expending over two million dollars on original research and on public hearings and opinion polls. Its central recommendation, based upon a somewhat partisan evaluation of this evidence, was that all legislation prohibiting the sale, exhibition or distribution of sexual materials to consenting adults should be repealed. Established patterns of sexual behaviour, it concluded, are too stable to be altered significantly by erotica. In 1973 a major American study of sex offenders, involving comparisons with law-abiding consumers of erotica, strongly supported the majority conclusions of the Presidential Commission.[12] Pornography, it found, did not incite criminal or anti-social acts, but rather the reverse. Greater and earlier exposure to erotica was educational, and lessened the development of deviant attitudes and behaviour in some readers. For potential rapists, it served as a means of warding-off disturbing impulses, and as a substitute for sexual engagement, delaying or dissipating the drive towards an act of violence. For the adolescent, it satisfied sexual curiosity without distorting personal standards or values, which were moulded by real people in his environment rather than by sexual stimuli. For the adult, erotica increased sexual interest and impulse, but only for a short time – there was no evidence of long-term preoccupation with pornographic images or themes, and the experience in some cases 'enhanced marital communication'. Another major American study of rape offenders found no evidence that erotic materials contributed to their crimes, although alcohol played a significant part in over sixty per cent of the cases.[13]

Dissenting voices point out that sex research is still in its infancy, and the conclusions drawn from American and Scandinavian studies must be regarded as preliminary at best. Even if pornography has an educative or therapeutic function for some persons, it is likely to have a debilitating effect upon others. Most of the early American studies involved co-operative college students, rather than persons who would be most at risk from the dissemination of obscenity. At least one study of sex criminals lends support to the theory that early exposure to pornography may be causally related to adult deviance.[14] The Danish statistics ignore demographic factors and attitudinal changes which may have contributed to lowering the rate of crime, and take no account of the psychological consequences for those actually enmeshed in the production of pornography. Dr John Court, a psychiatrist appearing as a crown witness, claimed that the increase in circulation of pornography in many Western countries has in fact coincided with a rise in reported sex crimes.[15] To the extent that pornography is a symbolic representation of infantile sexual and sadistic desires, obsessional reading could interfere with normal development and contribute to morbid fixation and regression, which may in turn affect the development of moral attitudes and character. It could inflame, or at least reinforce, existing sadistic or anti-social desires, and regular consumption may habituate a reader to a mental state of sexual callousness. Brands of obscene literature which carry messages of hate or degradation of women are unsuitable as source material for healthy sexual fantasy. The psychoanalyst Robert Stoller argues that many readers are attracted to pornography by a subconscious desire to harm, which is fed by images which are full of hostility and neurosis.[16]

The range of these arguments highlights the present state of uncertainty about the overall effects of pornography on readers. It cannot be disputed that erotica has effects, but these will vary according to the psychological make-up of the consumer. Each case depends on its facts, and the risk in disseminating some articles would doubtless be greater than that attaching to others. The jury's task is to weigh the risks in relation to each individual article, and the present state of scientific knowledge cannot supply any conclusive answers. Every experiment, in field and laboratory, conducted to date is open to some methodological criticism, and conclusions can generally be explained by alternative hypotheses. For example, it is all very well for researchers to announce confidently that 'exposure to erotica enhances marital communication' – until subsequent researchers suggest that the marital communication was enhanced, not by exposure to the erotica, but by jolly domestic discussions about how to fill in the forms supplied by the original researchers after each 'exposure'. Researchers, like everyone else in this field, generally produce the conclusions which most closely conform with their own personal prejudices and reactions. Some studies have found a clear correlation between personal reaction to pornography and the attitude taken to censorship: those who repress their own instincts are keenest to deny temptation to others. As Eysenck and Nias conclude, 'People who almost decided to live in glass houses may be the ones who are most prone to throw stones.'[17]

In the courtroom, whenever the defence led evidence that erotic arousal was in the interests of the health and happiness of a section of the community it was always open to the prosecution to rebut the claims of defence experts with the testimony of psychiatrists whose patients had suffered from the availability of pornography. These competing claims could be tested by cross-examination, and acquittal was by no means a regular reaction to expert testimony. In 1975 several juries were unable to agree, even after hearing Dr Kutchinsky explain, with the use of graphs, the benefits derived by Danes from the legalization of pornography. In 1976 one jury convicted, after hearing Dr John Court expound his views about the danger of an increase in sex crimes. Sometimes the expert testimony did seem to assist juries in making intelligible distinctions. In *R. v. Ransom*, a distinguished Crown psychiatrist conceded that of the thirty publications at issue, those which dealt with straightforward heterosexual or homosexual themes were innocuous by comparison with others which dwelt upon sexual perversions. The jury accepted his opinion, and acquitted those magazines and films which related to 'acceptable' (including oral and anal) sex between consenting partners, but brought down 'guilty' verdicts in respect of those publications which treated of incest, bestiality or sado-masochism.[18] These decisions demonstrate that 'defence experts' were not primarily responsible for acquittals in obscenity cases, although that impression was fostered by sensational press accounts of their testimony. Nonetheless, the Court of Appeal's concern about the scope of 'other objects of general concern' was widely shared, because it seemed to offer an escape to the very genre of literature – pornography – which Parliament had sought by the Obscene Publications Act to suppress.

This paradox was resolved in 1976 by the House of Lords decision in *Jordan* that 'other objects of general concern' was a phrase which did not relate to the effect of an article, but was solely applicable to its intrinsic merit.[19] The decision arose from the conviction of a Swansea bookseller, who had stocked a wide range of hard-core pornography. A professor of psychology with a lifetime's experience in marriage-guidance counselling and treatment of sexual offenders opined that publication would contribute to the psychological health of the community by releasing emotional and psychological tensions, reducing mental ill-health, and reducing the incidence of anti-social behaviour and sexual offences. The House of Lords ruled that the health of a section of the community is not an 'object of general concern' for the purpose of section 4, so that evidence of therapeutic value was inadmissible. Henceforth, publishers who seek to bring the therapeutic benefit of their wares to the attention of a British jury have no alternative but to print such evidence in the article itself.

THE OBSCENITY ISSUE

In ordinary criminal trials expert opinion is regularly received to interpret proven facts, to explain custom and usage and to theorize about the mental state of the accused. The law recognizes that jurors are not properly equipped to draw inferences about matters which call for specialist skill or knowledge, and permits assistance from those qualified to give it. The line is drawn, however, if experts seek to prejudge the ultimate issue which a jury must decide. Scientific opinion may invite an inference of guilt or innocence, but it must never be permitted to transform trial by jury into trial by experts. The jury has the final responsibility for reaching a verdict which represents ordinary common sense, and that decision, while it may be assisted, cannot be dictated by specialist knowledge:

... An expert's opinion is admissible to furnish the court with scientific information which is likely to be outside the experience and knowledge of a judge or jury. If on the proven facts a judge or jury can form their own conclusions without help, then the opinion of an expert is unnecessary. In such a case if it is given dressed up in scientific jargon it may make judgment more difficult. The fact that an expert witness has impressive scientific qualifications does not by that fact alone make his opinion on matters of human nature and behaviour within the limits of normality any more helpful than that of the jurors themselves; but there is a danger that they may think it does.[20]

Under the present obscenity law the mysteries of moral corruption are left in the lap of the jury, beyond the help of experts. To determine whether a particular publication tends to deprave and corrupt, the jury should logically ask two separate questions:

1 What effect, if any, will it tend to have on its potential readers?

2 Can this effect properly be described as moral corruption?

The first question is one of fact, the second necessitates a value judgment. An answer to the factual question might be predicted by a psychiatrist who had studied the behaviour of groups subjected to similar materials. The second question can only be answered objectively in the sense that a sociologist, on the basis of cross-sectional value studies could say that the given effect would be described as 'corrupt' by the moral standards of a certain proportion, or by certain classes, of the community. English judges, unlike some of their Commonwealth counterparts, have set their faces against reception of evidence in either category.

(a) Evidence of effect on the mind

In a 1954 case Lord Goddard, speaking for the Court of Criminal Appeal, categorically denied that the *Hicklin* test allowed scope for expert witnesses.[21] The Obscene Publications Act made specific provision for such evidence where it related to the literary or artistic merit of the article in question, but made no mention of expert evidence directed to the likely effects of the article on a particular readership. In *Transport Publishing Co.* v. *Literature Board of Review* the Australian High Court has held that such evidence may be received if it is confined to the effect of erotic material on particular groups of readers, but cannot be given as regards effect on the 'average reader' or the community as a whole:

On the question of the tendency of the literature to deprave or corrupt any such persons important distinctions must be observed. For the question necessarily has two aspects, or falls into two parts. One is the content and nature of the literature and the other concerns the characteristics of the persons themselves. With reference to the second of these it may be said at once that ordinary human nature, that of people at large, is not a subject of proof by evidence, whether supposedly expert or not. But particular descriptions of persons may conceivably form the subject of study and of special knowledge. This may be because they are abnormal in mentality or abnormal in behaviour as a result of circumstances peculiar to their history or situation.... But, before opinion evidence may be given upon the characteristics, responses, or behaviour of any special category of persons, it must be shown that they form a subject of special study or knowledge and only the opinions of one qualified by special training or experience may be received....[22]

This view was accepted by the Divisional Court in *DPP* v. *A.&B.C. Chewing Gum Ltd.*, where testimony by child psychiatrists concerning harmful effects of the bubble-gum cards on young children was held admissible. Lord Parker CJ explained:

There were two matters really for consideration. What sort of effect would these cards singly or together have upon children, and no doubt children of different ages; what would it lead them to do? Secondly, was what they were led to do a sign of corruption or depravity? As it seems to me, it would be perfectly proper to call a psychiatrist and to ask him in the first instance what his experience, if any, with children was, and to say what the effect on the minds of children of different groups would be if certain types of photographs or pictures were put before them, and indeed, having got his general evidence, to put one or more of the cards in question to him and say what would their effect be upon the child. For myself, I think it would be wrong to ask the direct question as to whether any particular cards tended to corrupt or deprave, because that final stage was a matter which was entirely for the justices.... When you are dealing here with children of different age groups and children from five upwards, any jury and any justices need all the help they can get, information which they may not have, as to the effect on different children....[23]

After the *Chewing Gum* case ruling, it seemed that psychologists and psychiatrists who were experts on the behavioural motivations of particular groups within the community could give evidence about the likely effect of the material on the minds and conduct of the group they had studied, in cases where the prosecution alleged that the material was distributed to that group. But they could not be asked whether the outlook and behaviour resulting among members of the group from reading the material was 'depraved' or 'corrupt'. This was a question for the jury alone. Both the *Transport Publishing* and the *Chewing Gum* cases involved the introduction of psychiatric opinion on behalf of the prosecution to identify readers at risk, and it was accepted that evidence of harm, while it could not be decisive, would nonetheless assist the administration of the law.

Lord Parker's encouragement to bring science to bear on obscenity was short-lived. In *R. v. Calder & Boyars* the Court of Appeal noted that the *A.&B.C. Chewing Gum* rule applied only 'in very special circumstances' which did not exist where the article in question was on sale to all members of the public.[24] In *Anderson's case*, where psychologists and sociologists had opined that a 'schoolkids *Oz*' would not harm those young persons whom the prosecution claimed would purchase it, the Court of Appeal effectively confined the *Chewing Gum* case to its own special facts:

> That case in our judgment should be regarded as highly exceptional and confined to its own circumstances, namely a case where the alleged obscene matter was directed at very young children, and was of itself of a somewhat unusual kind. In the ordinary run-of-the-mill cases in the future the issue 'obscene or no' must be tried by the jury without the assistance of expert evidence....[25]

It is not entirely clear just how far the *Chewing Gum* case still stretches. The House of Lords considered it inconclusively in *DPP* v. *Jordan*. Viscount Dilhorne doubted whether it had been correctly decided, because 'If an article is not manifestly obscene as tending to deprave and corrupt, it seems to me somewhat odd that a person should be liable to conviction for publishing obscene matter if the evidence of experts in psychiatry is required to establish its obscenity.'[26] But Lord Wilberforce, who gave the leading judgment, conceded that the *Chewing Gum* case might retain some evidential flavour:

> there may be an exception in a case where the likely readers are a special class, such that a jury cannot be expected to understand the likely impact

of the material upon its members without assistance. In such a case evidence from persons qualified by study or experience of that class may be admissible.[27]

He defined the 'special class' to include 'sexual abnormals or deviants', and emphasized that the expert evidence tendered in *Jordan* was inadmissible under section 1 because the shop was a *normal* newsagency, the pornography was bought by *ordinary* members of the public, and the articles were not priced in a way which might suggest they were *specialized* publications. If it had been sold only to persons with sexual abnormalities, expert evidence might have been admissible on the obscenity issue to explain its impact upon readers of that class. But how specialized must the class be to warrant the reception of expert testimony? Very young children, or very rare sexual deviants, would seem to qualify, but it is uncertain whether the exception would extend to larger groups such as homosexuals.[28]

(b) *Evidence of community standards*

The decisions in the *Chewing Gum* and *Transport Publishing* cases rested upon the theory that an ordinary jury cannot be expected to fathom deep questions of psychology without expert assistance. The rules of evidence were complied with by permitting experts to describe the likely effect of publication, while the jury was left to decide the ultimate issue of whether such an effect could be indicative of corruption. The rejection of this approach was justified not only on the ground that a jury of ordinary people could appreciate the effect of a particular publication on the minds of ordinary readers, but also because the function of a jury at an obscenity trial is in any event to reflect in its decision the normal standards of the community, which exist quite independently of the preponderance of psychiatric evidence. The fallacy in the latter argument is that section 1 of the Obscene Publications Act makes no reference to community standards, and a jury is logically entitled to say that deeply offensive publications which traduce those standards may nonetheless carry no real danger of corrupting readers' minds. To say that juries act as custodians of moral standards is to confuse the role of a jury in cases brought under the 1959 Act with its function in cases of indecency or conspiracy at common law, where the issue is whether recognized standards of propriety have been infringed. Laws against indecency necessitate the identification and application of community standards, but these standards are irrelevant to the issue of whether a publication might corrupt the mind. This distinction was very carefully drawn by Mr Justice Stable in his *Philanderer* direction:

> During the closing speech for the prosecution it seemed to me that there was, if I may say so without offence, a certain confusion of thought. It was suggested that you are, by what you decide today, to determine whether books like this will or will not be published in the future. May I venture to say that your task is nothing of the kind. We are not sitting here as judges of taste. We are not here to say whether we like a book of that kind. We are not here to say whether we think it would be a good thing if books like that were never written. You are here trying a criminal charge. In a criminal court you cannot find a verdict of 'Guilty' against the accused unless, on the evidence that you have heard, you are fully satisfied that the charge against the accused person has been proved.[29]

In strict legal theory, an obscenity jury cannot be a mechanism for enforcing the aesthetic taste or moral judgment of the ordinary man. This function can only be performed where the offence requires the Crown to prove a breach of standards of propriety or of public morality. Confusion between these two distinct categories of offence has been produced when dicta from conspiracy and indecency cases is cited with approval in the different context of obscenity. The most potent of these dicta has been a passage in the speech of Lord Morris of Borth y Gest in *Shaw* (a case of conspiracy to corrupt public morals):

> Even if accepted public standards may to some extent vary from generation to generation, current standards are in keeping of juries, who can be trusted to maintain the corporate good sense of the community and to discern effects upon values which must be preserved.[30]

In conspiracy and indecency cases, the jury's perception of community standards must decide whether an offence has been committed and an expert opinion would trespass upon that issue. Jurors 'do not need assistance; they are themselves, so to speak, the custodians of the standards for the time being'.[31] But in obscenity cases, community standards cannot be decisive: they merely form part of the background to the decision.

If community standards were relevant in obscenity cases, a sociologist or scientific researcher who had made a special study of the incidence in the community of the sexual behaviour described in a publication could assist the jury with evidence of his findings. If the behaviour was common to a significant group in the community, and accepted by the standards of that group, this evidence would be useful in considering whether the behaviour was 'corrupt', but would not usurp the jury function because it would remain theoretically open for them to decide that the significant group – even if it was a majority – had itself been corrupted. Evidence of this kind has been admitted and even welcomed by Canadian courts as an antidote to the prejudices of the tribunal. Justice Bora Laskin has observed:

> It is important in this branch of the law that judges, especially when trying cases without a jury, and magistrates should be exposed to the persuasion of evidence and extrinsic materials to counter-balance the ineradicable subjective factor residing in the application of any legal standard of obscenity, however objective it purports to be.[32]

Even the Gallup poll may have a part to play in establishing the prevailing Canadian mores:

> ... it would seem to me that, when it becomes necessary to determine the true nature of community opinion and to find a single normative standard, the court should not be denied the benefit of evidence, scientifically obtained in accordance with accepted sampling procedure, by those who are expert in the field of opinion research. Such evidence can properly be accorded the status of expert testimony. The state of mind or attitude of a community is as much a fact as the state of one's health; it would seem therefore as proper to admit the opinion of experts on the one subject as on the other.[33]

The Canadian approach accepts that 'community standards' may be ascertained with a sufficient degree of scientific objectivity to rectify distorted perceptions of individual judges and jurors. Opinion polls are admitted to show the basis upon which an expert has formed his conclusions, but difficulty has been experienced with the methodological weakness of many surveys which have been tendered in evidence. The 'community' whose standards are relevant must be the entire population, and not those which dominate a particular locality or class. The Canadian courts have warned that 'the findings of a poll can be deceptively simple and frequently misleading ... such evidence must, therefore, if it is to be admitted, be received with caution and carefully evaluated before weight is given to it.'[34] The courts have insisted upon three safeguards:

1 It must be conducted by an expert in the science of opinion research, who should himself be called to explain his methods of sampling.

2 The sample must be scientifically selected so that the opinions constitute a prototype of the opinions of Canadian people, rather than a mirror of the views of unrepresentative or parochial groups.

3 The questions asked must not be 'loaded' towards any particular
conclusion, and they must be relevant to, but not determinative
of, the issue before the jury. If the case involves the alleged obscenity
of a film depicting nudity, the jury would be assisted in its
assessment of community standards of tolerance by a poll which
asked questions of a factual nature such as 'have you seen nudity
in other movies, and if so, how often?' But questions of the sort
'do you regard nudity as obscene?' would be inadmissible hearsay
evidence of opinion necessarily prejudging the ultimate issue.[35]

Although opinion research evidence of the sort permitted by
these Canadian decisions has never been tendered in an English
court, rejection would almost certainly follow from the application
of existing embargoes on expert testimony in obscenity cases.

The rule that English juries cannot be informed by experts of either
the probable effect of a publication on the minds of likely readers, or
the public acceptability of the behaviour it describes, has been justified by a judicial genuflection to the common sense of the ordinary
man and an assumption that this common sense will always be reflected by ten out of twelve jurors, so long as they are not 'diverted
... by the irrelevant opinions of experts'.[36] But why should common
sense be so precarious a commodity that it is apt to dissolve at the
wave of a doctorate? If obscenity juries are paragons of good sense
they can be trusted, with the help of competent cross-examination,
to reject half-baked theorizing. If they are not, then they need expert
assistance to predict effect on the mind and to provide information
about current community standards of behaviour and moral values.

The case for experts was stated by Lord Parker in the *Chewing Gum*
case:

> I cannot help feeling that with the advance of science more and more in-
> roads have been made into the old common law principles. Those who prac-
> tise in the criminal courts see every day cases of experts being called on the
> question of diminished responsibility, and although technically the final
> question, 'Do you think he was suffering from diminished responsibility?' is
> strictly inadmissible, it is allowed time and again without any objection. No
> doubt when dealing with the effect of certain things on the mind science may
> still be less exact than evidence as to what effect some particular thing will
> have on the body, but that, it seems to me, is purely a question of weight.[37]

This argument has never been answered on its merits, and the Court
of Appeal in *Anderson's* case was not unaware of its force: 'We are
not oblivious of the fact that some people, perhaps many people, will

think a jury, unassisted by experts, a very unsatisfactory tribunal to decide such a matter. Those who feel like that must campaign elsewhere for a change of law.'[38] This comment has particular irony because the court in *Anderson* reversed the *Oz* conviction on the ground that the 'aversion theory' was not properly explained to the jury by the trial judge. Yet at the trial that theory had been elaborated by psychologists with experience of aversion therapy, the likes of whom the court were proposing to exclude from future obscenity trials. The aversion defence may have little impact in the absence of experts to give examples from their own research. In 1978 the Court of Appeal again emphasized that the aversion defence 'had to be mentioned in the summing-up because the idea might never occur to some jurors unless they had it pointed out to them'.[39] Yet defence counsel's final speech is hardly a satisfactory time or place for 'pointing out' a psychological theory about human behaviour to jurors who may never previously have considered it. The rule that no opinion evidence is permitted touching the very issue the court has to decide is nowadays more honoured in the breach than in the observance, and is not infringed by asking an expert to describe objectively a mental or behavioural response, without inviting him to classify it in moral terms as 'corrupt'.

The 'ultimate issue' rule in English law has been heavily criticized. Wigmore condemned it as 'a rare bit of empty rhetoric', impractical and misconceived, and lacking any justification in principle.[40] Sir Rupert Cross has warned that 'the exclusion of opinion evidence can easily become something of a fetish.'[41] Experts who are cross-examined, and whose testimony is followed by counsel's speeches and an authoritative judicial summing-up, are never in a meaningful position to 'usurp' the jury function, especially since jurors are invariably told 'This is a trial by jury, not by experts', and 'You are the final judge of all issues of fact'. To say that 'obscenity' is a matter of common sense on which experts have nothing to contribute, but that 'public good' is a matter of expertise on which the experts *do* have something to say, seems contradictory. The science of opinion research may be in its infancy, but it usually offers a more convincing cross-section than a sample of twelve.

The decision to exclude experts' testimony on obscenity issues would be more compelling had it been justified on the basis that much of the proffered testimony amounted to inconclusive hearsay evidence. References to 'ultimate issues' and jury capabilities are technical ploys which have precluded proper analysis of the weight and the relevance of opinions based on Danish and American studies of different people and different literature. The rationale of exclusion in *Jordan* was that expert evidence might legitimize the very class of literature – pornography – that the legislature in 1959 wished to suppress. The courts might have achieved a more satisfactory result by distinguishing between the expert who examines the publication at issue and gives a reasoned opinion as to its effect, based on his own consulting experience, and a witness who merely purports to 'apply' a foreign study he has read about to a class of literature which may have a content and effect never considered in the studies quoted. General conclusions about the effects of erotica in different societies cannot properly form the basis of a defence to a specific charge of obscenity. English judges might have done better to follow their Canadian brethren in controlling expert testimony by a stringent insistence that witnesses put forward as experts have suitable qualifications and personal knowledge of the facts on which their views are based. Quality control, rather than blanket exclusion, would be a more satisfactory option at a time when scientific research is being undertaken to provide answers, or at least empirical data on which to base answers, to questions of community standards and individual responses to erotic materials. The misfortune of *Jordan* is that it precludes prosecution testimony to the harmful effect of violence and sadism, at a time when this evidence is rapidly accumulating. Unless courts become more receptive to Lord Dunedin's exhortation that they are bound to follow, as far as they can, the discoveries of science and the results of experience, the law will be ridiculed for battling against speculative evils while the real obscenity goes unprosecuted.[42]

THE 'PUBLIC GOOD' DEFENCE

The motivation behind reform of the common law of obscene libel was to protect worthy literature from censorship. The framers of the 1959 Act sought a formula which would distinguish between literature and pornography, between defensible obscenity and the irredeemably obscene. The literary lobbyists suggested two tests, which were in reality the perception of literary merit from two different angles. The first looked at the dominant effect of the work as a whole: if it were elevating or enlightening, then the impact of isolated obscenity would be cancelled out by the overall value of the work. This result could equally be achieved by a direct assessment of literary or artistic merit inherent in the publication. These two tests were different sides of the same coin: obviously any expert evaluation of merit would take into account the overall impact of the publication at issue. The only reason for a distinction between the two tests was a defensive reaction by the reformers to a series of adverse judicial rulings on the common law of obscene libel. These rulings implied that literary merit was irrelevant, but they took two forms; permission for the prosecution to rely upon 'purple passages' lifted out of their context, and an exclusion of literary experts. The Society of Authors, chief protagonist of obscenity law reform, sought to reverse both these tendencies by providing a new concept of legal obscenity. Its draft bill, introduced by Mr Roy Jenkins under the House of Commons ten minute rule, defined 'obscenity' as a legal classification imposed by a jury after weighing four factors:

In deciding ... whether any matter is or is not obscene, the court shall have regard to the following considerations:
(a) whether the general character and dominant effect of the matter alleged to be obscene is corrupting;
(b) evidence, if any, as to the literary or artistic merit, or the medical, legal, political, religious or scientific character or importance of the matter; and for this purpose expert opinion shall be admissible as evidence;
(c) evidence, if any, as to the persons to or among whom the said matter was or was intended, or was likely to be distributed or circulated ...;
(d) evidence, if any, that the said matter had had a corrupting effect.[43]

In retrospect, there seems a great deal of wisdom in this approach, which was after all settled by lawyers who knew something about literature. The characterization 'obscene' was simply a label imposed by the court after weighing four factors which took into account the merits and demerits of the overall impact of the article in the circumstances of its publication.

When the House of Commons Select Committee reported on obscenity law reform in 1958, its recommendations were encapsulated in a Bill which followed the suggestion of the Society of Authors in making merit a factor in the issue of obscenity:

For the purposes of this Act, any publication shall be deemed to be obscene if its effect as a whole is such as to tend to deprave and corrupt persons to or among whom it was likely to be distributed, circulated, sold, offered for sale, or let on hire:
Provided that in deciding whether or not the publication is obscene the court shall take into consideration any evidence proffered, whether by the defence or by the prosecution, as to the literary, artistic, scientific or other merits of the said publication.[44]

162 EXPERTS AND THE PUBLIC GOOD

Extraneous concepts of 'public good' and 'balancing acts' were nowhere apparent. These emerged for the first time in a government initiative during the committee stage of the Bill. Suddenly, 'merit' was hived off from 'obscenity'. The parliamentary draftsmen produced a new formula: obscenity was defined in section 1 as a tendency to deprave and corrupt likely readers, and questions of merit were to be considered, under a separate clause, if and only if the article was found as a fact to have a corrupting effect. Section 4 of the Act was worded:

> (1) A person shall not be convicted of an offence against section 2 of this Act ... if it is proved that publication of the article in question is justified as being for the public good on the grounds that it is in the interests of science, literature, art or learning, or of other objects of general concern.
>
> (2) It is hereby declared that the opinions of experts as to the literary, artistic, scientific or other merits of an article may be admitted in any proceedings under this Act either to establish or negative the said ground.

The Government's decision to split the issue into separate parts – in effect, to provide two different ways of assessing guilt or innocence in relation to the one offence – was seen by some commentators as an example of its 'blatant hostility' to obscenity law reform.[45] A less sinister explanation is the influence of precedent on minds trained to law rather than aesthetics. The idea of a 'public good' justification was drawn from a suggestion made in the nineteenth century by Mr Justice Stephen in his *Digest of Criminal Law*:

> A person is justified in exhibiting disgusting objects, or publishing obscene books, papers, writing, prints, pictures, drawings, or other representations, if their exhibition or publication is for the public good, as being necessary or advantageous to religion or morality, to the administration of justice, the pursuit of science, literature or art, or other objects of general interest.[46]

This suggestion was made when 'obscenity' was assumed from any writing about sex which was shocking or disgusting. Stephen lived in an age when these reactions were aroused by almost any public reference to sex, and so the most logical way of mitigating the rigour of the law in favour of literary classics was to provide that 'disgusting' passages could be justified by the public good which was served by their overall merit. This approach was no longer valid when 'obscenity' was statutorily defined in terms of harmful effect rather than textual coarseness. However distinguished its judicial pedigree, the formula had no place in an Act which shifted the emphasis from disgusting words and phrases to the effect of the whole text on the mind. The lateness of its adoption during the Bill's passage through Parliament obscured a warp which legal ingenuity subsequently failed to disentangle.

During the legislative gestation of section 1 a carefully elaborated concept of obscenity was wrecked by a misguided affection for a nineteenth-century formula. The new section 1 was an abortion: it contained one aspect of aesthetic value (the dominant effect on likely readers) but not the other (the intrinsic merit). The value of a work was to be considered from two perspectives, at two artificially but rigidly separated stages, and courts were debarred from assessing merit when deciding an article's effect on its likely readers. Instead of one clause enabling a court to weigh all aspects of the publication in one decision, the two-tier approach set up an illogical and unworkable dichotomy between 'obscenity' and 'artistic merit'. The first stage defined obscenity by reference to the dominant effect of actual publication on the minds of likely readers, and the second required a balance of that supposedly harmful effect against the intrinsic merit of the work, irrespective of the circumstances of publication. A book's contribution to literature was not a factor in assessing its obscenity, but rather a 'justification' for the publication of a provenly obscene book. The result was a half-baked decision on 'obscenity' under section 1, and then a half-baked decision on 'public good' under section 4, followed by acute judicial indigestion as both commodities were swallowed at once. The rigid distinction between 'section 2 effect' and 'section 4 intrinsic merit' committed the law to an intellectual confusion which contributed more than anything else to its uncertain and unacceptable operation for the next two decades. It first became apparent in the summing up in *R.* v. *Penguin Books*:

> There are two limbs in this case, and they cannot be dealt with both at once.... If you are not satisfied that the book is obscene ... that is an end of the case; you acquit. But if, on the other hand, you are satisfied that the book is an obscene book, then you must go on to consider this further question ...: have the defendants established the probability that the merits of the book as a novel are so high that they outbalance the obscenity, so that its publication is for the public good?[47]

The two-stage approach and the 'balancing act' were endorsed in *R.* v. *Calder & Boyars*, a decision which was firmly approved by a majority of the House of Lords in *DPP* v. *Jordan*. Lord Salmon even described it as 'extremely sensible', although it might more accurately be described as a worthy judicial attempt to make at least verbal sense out of legislative nonsense:

> ... judges have rightly, in my view, directed juries to consider first whether they are satisfied beyond reasonable doubt that the article complained of was published by the accused and is obscene within the meaning of section 2 (1). If they are not so satisfied, that is an end of the matter and they must return a verdict of 'not guilty'. If, however, they are satisfied that the article was published by the accused and is obscene they should then go on and consider whether on a balance of probabilities, the defence of public good under section 4 (1) (if relied on by the accused) has been made out.[48]

The 'balancing act' described in *Calder & Boyars* takes the following form:

> The jury must consider on the one hand the number of readers they believe would tend to be depraved and corrupted by the book, the strength of the tendency to deprave and corrupt, and the nature of the depravity and corruption; on the other hand, they should assess the strength of the literary, sociological or ethical merit they believe the book to possess. They should then weigh up all these factors and decide whether on balance the publication is proved to be justified as being for the public good.[49]

Unfortunately, 'corruption' and 'literary, sociological or ethical merit' do not admit of meaningful comparison, and the balancing act is a logical nonsense. 'Depravity and corruption', a predicted change for the worse in the characters of a significant number of readers, cannot be quantified, and even if it could, its quantity could not meaningfully be compared with literary ability, or scientific value. The legislative formula requires the measurement of an effect against an intrinsic merit, ignoring the fact that publications have merit precisely *because* of their effect. A meritorious article will elevate the mind, and a harmful article will debase the mind: but a book's effect, whether elevating or corrupting, depends on its literary style, and conversely its merits as literature must be assessed, at least in part, on the feelings it engenders in the minds and emotions of its readers. No book exists in a vacuum: one of the merits of *Oliver Twist* was to awaken the public conscience, and the value and purpose of Greek tragedy was to purge an audience with pity and terror.[50] Nor is it logically possible to 'weigh' such disparate concepts as 'corruption' and 'literary merit'. An Arts Council enquiry wondered whether an ounce of depravity-spreading was more or less potent than an ounce of artistic merit, and concluded that criminal sanctions should not hang in the balance with such metaphysics.[51] Even if the jury manages to find a common measure, the outcome may well be foreclosed against the defendant by the jury's reluctance to find that it could *ever* be in the public interest to spread depravity. 'The publication of this book is for the public good, although it will deprave and corrupt a significant number of its readers' is a verdict any jury would be reluctant to deliver.

Jurors will of course hear the 'public good' evidence before retiring, and it may be impossible for them to compartmentalize their mental approach to the two issues as rigidly as the law requires. Expert evidence may spill over and affect their minds on the obscenity issue. No matter how clearly the judge differentiates the two questions, a jury may amalgamate them into the single issue of whether the article is fit for public consumption. In *Calder & Boyars* the Court of Appeal recognized that it would not be easy for laymen to understand the distinction between an issue which the prosecution must prove beyond reasonable doubt, and another issue which must be proved by the defence 'on the balance of probabilities'.

> The defence of public good under section 4 does ... require to be carefully explained to the jury. The jury may have great difficulty in reconciling that section with section 1 and section 2 of the Act of 1959. ... The jury may not understand how it is possible that if a book has such a tendency it can be justified on any ground as being for the public good. ...[52]

No matter how careful the explanation, the issues will inevitably be blurred in the jury room. As one obscenity trial observer has remarked, 'a jury who could sit for the best part of a fortnight maintaining at all times such a rigid compartmentalization in their own minds would deserve an award for productive schizophrenia'.[53]

Section 4 does offer a measure of protection to literature precisely *because* expert testimony spills over to influence the obscenity decision. Despite the most stringent judicial safeguards, experts who claim that publication of the article is for the public interest will inevitably impinge in their answers on matters relevant to the question of whether it will corrupt its readers. Thus when the Bishop of Woolwich testified to the ethical merits of *Lady Chatterley's Lover* – its 'positive effect on human relations and affirmation of Christian values' – he was in effect asserting that the book would not deprave and corrupt.[54] At the trial of *The Mouth and Oral Sex* medical practitioners, social workers and sociologists testified to the widespread community acceptance of the allegedly corrupt behaviour the book was allegedly encouraging, and asserted its educative value for sexually curious or inadequate persons.[55] At both trials the defence shaped its section 4 evidence into a claim, not merely that the book had merit, but that the merit was of a kind which elevated or enlightened its readers – an argument which is in reality a very strong claim that the book does not deprave and corrupt, rather than a defence that its public importance outweighs its corruption. The rule that section 4 evidence must not trespass upon section 1 issues is unrealistic and unenforceable. The *Last Exit* verdict was overturned because the judge 'threw (the jury) in at the deep end of section 4 and left them to sink or swim in its dark waters'.[56] It may be doubted whether juries have derived much benefit from the rescue operation attempted by the courts.

The 'balancing act' between section 1 obscenity and section 4 public good involves an attempt to measure immeasurables. Earlier drafts of the Act obviated the problem by adopting a definition which permitted aesthetic merit to be considered as part and parcel of the obscenity decision. Another approach, which at one period worked with reasonable success in America, is to bar obscenity proceedings against any work which can be proven to have some cultural value, irrespective of any tendency it might have to disgust or deprave. This offers a much more reliable protection to serious works than the precarious balance of sections 1 and 4. In *Memoirs* v. *Massachusetts*, Supreme Court Justices Brennan, Warren and Fortas decided that the three defining characteristics of an obscene publication were (1) an appeal to prurient interest, (2) offensiveness to the community, *and* (3) the absence of any redeeming social value. The fact that distinguished experts had testified to the literary and historical merit of *Fanny Hill* was sufficient proof that it possessed a modicum of social value, and therefore fell outside the definition of 'obscene'.[57] Adopting this approach to the scheme of the English legislation, section 4 might be converted into a 'plea in bar', whereby a publisher would be entitled to have proceedings terminated before the jury considered arguments about obscenity if it could be proved, as a preliminary issue, that publication served the interests of literature or learning. Attempts to read this approach into the existing statutory wording of section 4 have failed,[58] but it could be secured by a minimal legislative adjustment. Judges (or perhaps special juries) would be obliged to halt obscenity trials if it appeared at a preliminary hearing that the preponderance of evidence established that a work possessed some social value. Publishers in any doubt could assess their prospects by obtaining expert opinion prior to publication, and the avowed aim of the 1959 Act, 'the protection of literature', would be substantially achieved.

THE SCOPE OF SECTION 4

The defendant to an obscenity charge 'shall not be convicted' (despite the fact that he has been found to have published an obscene article) if 'publication of the article in question is justified as being for the public good. . . .' The ground upon which the defence may be made out is that publication, in the case of books and magazines, is 'in the interests of science, literature, art or learning, or of other objects of general concern'. The ground for exculpating plays and films is somewhat narrower: they must be 'in the interests of drama, opera, ballet or any other art, or of literature or learning'. Section 3 (1) of the Theatres Act 1968, the counterpart of section 4, was drafted in more restricted terms because the inclusion of 'science' and 'other objects of general concern' was thought irrelevant to the protection of quality theatre: plays which could not be justified by reference to dramatic art or learning were unlikely to be redeemed by any other feature. The 1977 Criminal Law Act, which extended obscenity legislation to the cinema, adopted the Theatres Act formulation in preference to section 4 because the Law Commission thought that 'there is a genuine parallel to be drawn between conditions in which the great majority of films will be seen by viewers and the performance before an audience of a play'. The Commission made its recommendation in the belief that, 'on a fair construction of the word "learning" . . . it is probable that everything that ought to be covered in a defence applying to films would in fact be adequately covered'.[59] At first the 'public good' defence was given the broad ambit which the legislative language seemed to require, although more recent decisions have narrowly construed its 'objects' in order to limit the scope of expert testimony. The prevailing literal construction of section 4 and its theatrical and cinematic equivalents requires separate elucidation of the words and phrases which appear in the statutes.

'Publication'

The defendant must prove that '*publication* of the article in question is justified as being for the public good on the ground that it is in the interests of science, etc.' Does 'publication' refer to the limited publication proved pursuant to section 1, or does it mean publication to the world at large? Is the 'it' which 'is in the interests of science etc.', the publication, or the article in question? The section is ambiguous, even though the interpretation of 'publication' may in some cases be crucial. Suppose the 'publication' which must be justified is the defendant's act of publishing a book in the limited circumstances proved by police evidence under section 1. The book may have literary value, but the defendant may not have published it to those persons who would benefit. 'Publication' of *Lady Chatterley's Lover* by a man who read it to a schoolgirl with the object of corrupting her would not, on this interpretation, be justified by the book's literary value, because this was minimal in the circumstances in which it was actually published. The argument for relating the 'publication' in section 4 to the 'publication' proved under section 1 draws strength from the legal presumption that a word used in an Act of Parliament should bear the same meaning wherever it appears in the Act, and from the statement in section 1 (3) of the Act that the meaning given there to 'publish' is given 'for the purposes of this Act'.[60]

The scheme of the Act is not to declare material obscene *per se*, but to enable a jury to look at the circumstances of publication and then to ask, in balancing section 1 against section 4, 'Has the publication, in its context, more merit than demerit?' If the jury must balance obscenity against merit, the task is slightly easier if both scales relate to the same act of publication, rather than a specific act (section 1) balanced against publication to the world at large (section 4). If 'publication' in section 4 refers to the 'publication' under section 1, the defendant's task of justification might be made more difficult, because an expert opinion of the intrinsic merits of the article would have to be related to the circumstances in which the defendant disseminated it.[61] When the publishers of *Fanny Hill* were obliged to defend copies of the book seized from a Soho bookshop, expert testimony was undermined by the prosecution insistence that the customers who frequented that bookshop were unlikely to be interested in good literature.[62]

The decision of the House of Lords in *Jordan*, although it does not specifically cover the point, favours the view that 'publication' in section 4 means 'publication to the world at large'. Moreover section 4 (2) refers to expert evidence of the 'merits of an article', which suggests that such testimony must relate to the value of general publication, rather than publication to a restricted class. On this interpretation a defendant may exculpate himself under section 4 no matter how far his purpose was removed from the advancement of culture or learning, because the intrinsic merits of the material exist irrespective of whether they are in fact served by the circumstances of publication. For Lord Justice Bridge, 'The question to be asked is "what are the merits of the article *per se*?" and not "what are the possible results of its dissemination?'' Thus a painting may be lewd but its artistry of such a high order as to transcend or redeem the objectionable character of the subject matter; so also a book may be salacious and yet possess such style and quality as to make it of value as literature.'[63] Lord Wilberforce endorsed this approach:

> The section is dealing with a different range, or dimension, of considerations from that with which section 1 is concerned. It is not raising over again the issue of 'deprave or corrupt' versus 'innocuousness' or 'benefit' in relation to likely readers, which is the essence of the earlier section. It assumes that, apart from what section 4 itself may do, that issue would be resolved in favour of 'deprave and corrupt' and having assumed that, it allows a contention to be made and evidence to be given that publication of the material is, on specified grounds, for the public good.[64]

Although the point is still open, it would seem to follow from the reasoning in *Jordan* that the 'publication' referred to in section 4 (1) is publication to the world in general, and that expert testimony under section 4 (2) should not relate the merits of the article to the actual circumstances in which it saw the light of day.

'*Article*'

Under the 'item by item' test adopted in relation to magazines, a work may be adjudged obscene if one particular item is likely to have a corrupting effect on the minds of potential readers.[65] This test results from the statutory wording of section 1, which defines obscenity by reference to the effect either of an article taken as a whole, 'or (where the article comprises two or more distinct items) the effect of any one of its items....' Section 4 makes no reference to this distinction between 'articles' and 'items'; it entitles a defendant to raise the 'public good' issue in relation to 'the merits of an article'. 'Article' here refers to the work as a whole, so that where an article (such as a magazine) comprises separate items, its publication may be justified by the merits of 'items' other than those which the jury finds to be obscene. A magazine with obscene pictures may therefore be redeemed by the literary or journalistic quality of its other contents.

'*In the interests of*'

The exculpatory grounds set out in section 4 (1) might have been expressed in terms of 'merit', but public good is not served by merit alone. An article may be 'in the interests of' literature and learning without being either literary or learned. Section 4 (1) looks to the advancement of cultural and intellectual values, and the expert opinion as to the 'merits of an article' must be able to relate to the broader question of 'the interests of' art and science. A publication of obscene primitive art may lack objective merit, but nonetheless may be defended on the grounds of its contribution to art history. (The DPP once considered a complaint about the ancient drainage ditch at Cerne Abbas, which forms the outline of a giant with a truly giant-size erection. In the interests of history, and the interests of the local tourist trade, he declined the request to allow grass to grow strategically over the offending area.)

The *Oz* editors contended that although their Schoolkids Issue had no particular literary or artistic brilliance, its publication was 'in the interests of' literature and art because it gave creative youngsters the opportunity to display their potential talents in a national magazine. The end product was 'in the interests' of sociology, not because of any profundity in its contents, but because sociologists were interested in the results of the experiment of giving schoolchildren an uncensored forum to air their grievances.

'Science', 'art', 'literature' and 'learning'

The jury must decide as an issue of fact whether and to what extent obscene material serves the interests of any of these 'intellectual or aesthetic values'. In *Attorney General's Reference* (No. 3 of 1977) the Court of Appeal construed 'learning' to mean 'the product of scholarship . . . something whose inherent excellence is gained by the work of a scholar'.[66] It follows that a publication cannot be defended under section 4 because of its value as a teaching aid, since this would require assessment of its effect upon readers' minds. A sex education booklet is not defensible because it provides good sex education, but if research has gone into its compilation, then no matter how ineffectual or misguided as an instructional aid it possesses some inherent worth as 'a product of scholarship'. This result is hardly rational, but it represents a logical extension of the quest for intrinsic merit. The most simple and straightforward instructional aids are valued precisely because they are comprehensible to people with little or no formal education; in the absence of scholarly footnotes, they may not be considered 'in the interests of learning'.

'Learning' overlaps with 'science', which is defined in most dictionaries as 'knowledge acquired by study'. A publication may possess scientific interest if it adds to the existing body of knowledge or if it presents known facts in a systematic way. Recent legislation defines 'science' to include the social sciences and medical research, and works with serious psychiatric, psychological or sociological interest would qualify for a 'public good' defence. Studies of human sexual behaviour might contribute to scientific knowledge, although it is doubtful whether pornographic fantasies, unless genuine and collected for a serious sociological purpose, could legitimately be defended.

'Literature' is widely defined as 'any printed matter', and the courts have been prepared to award copyright protection to the most pedestrian writing.[67] In the context of section 4, however, experts would be required to find some excellence of style or presentation to redeem the assumed tendency to corrupt. Excellence of prose style is not the only criterion for literary judgments, however, and books may be defended on the strength of wit, suspense, clarity, bombast or research if these qualities distinguish them in a particular genre of literature or in a particular period of literary history. Similarly, 'art' comprehends the application of skill to any aesthetic subject, and is not conventionally confined to the reproduction of beautiful images. In a different context, Lord Reid has warned against the application of orthodox or elite artistic standards:

> It is, I think, of importance that the maker or designer of a thing should have intended that it should have an artistic appeal, but I would not regard that as either necessary or conclusive. If any substantial section of the public genuinely admires and values a thing for its appearance, and gets pleasure or satisfaction, whether emotional or intellectual, from looking at it, I would accept that it is artistic, although others may think it meaningless or common or vulgar.[68]

In both the *Oz* and *Nasty Tales* cases underground comics were accepted as 'art' for the purposes of a section 4 defence. One expert, the painter Felix Topolski, reminded the court that 'unexpected elements, when brought together, produce the art of creation . . . I think one should accept that any visual performance executed in earnest is a branch of artistic creation.'[69]

In 1975 the New Zealand courts held that drawings of toilet fittings were artistic works – a conclusion the surrealist school would never have doubted.[70]

'Other objects of general concern'

In *DPP* v. *Jordan* the House of Lords ruled that the psychiatric health of the community allegedly served by 'therapeutic' pornography was not an 'object of general concern' for the purposes of section 4. Their Lordships declined to elucidate the phrase, beyond affirming that it had a 'mobile' meaning which changed in content as society changes, and that

(a) It referred to objects of general concern similar to those aesthetic and intellectual values specifically enumerated in section 4.

(b) It could not comprehend any object which was served by direct impact of publication on the mind of likely readers.

(c) It related to 'inherent personal values of a less transient character assumed, optimistically perhaps, to be of general concern'.[71]

There are many objects which survive these three tests. Among the 'objects of general concern' advanced on behalf of *Lady Chatterley's Lover* were its ethical and Christian merits: 'I suppose the section is sufficiently elastic to say that such evidence is admissible,' remarked the judge, as he permitted the Bishop of Woolwich to testify to the book's contribution to human relations and to Christian judgments and values.[72] Other witnesses testified to its educational and sociological merits, and the editor of *Harper's Bazaar* was called as an expert on 'popular literature'. In *R.* v. *Calder & Boyars* the Court of Appeal conceded that 'sociological or ethical merit' might be canvassed.[73] Other objects of general concern which have been relied upon at obscenity trials include journalism, humour, politics, philosophy, history, education and entertainment.

THE NATURE OF EXPERT EVIDENCE

It is impossible to assess the merit of literature or art without considering its emotional impact, without appreciating its creator's purpose and without understanding its historical context. Expert testimony is not confined to a consideration of content alone, but may explore the ways in which intellectual and aesthetic values could be served or diminished by publication. The general rules, largely settled by Mr Justice Byrne in *R.* v. *Penguin Books*, include:

1 The intention of an author or publisher is relevant to a section 4 defence. 'The jury must have regard to what the author was trying to do, what his message may have been, and what his general scope was.'[74]

2 The author's general reputation and his place in the history of literature may be discussed. Otherwise, as Gerald Gardiner QC pointed out, 'if my clients were to publish tomorrow Chaucer's *Canterbury Tales* one couldn't call evidence as to who Chaucer was. I suppose if some members of the jury were not familiar with his book

they might think that, somewhere in London, this Mr Chaucer was publishing some pretty odd stuff.'[75]

3 Other books may be considered, either by way of comparison of their literary quality with the book at issue, or to establish the contemporary climate of literature.[76] It is not permissible to suggest that other books are 'more obscene', although experts may be invited to compare the value of an expurgated edition with the merit of the uncensored text.

4 An expert must not express any opinion as to whether the value of a work outweighs its tendency to deprave and corrupt. The 'balancing act' is for the jury alone to perform. Thus the Bishop of Woolwich, who testified that *Lady Chatterley's Lover* served Christian values, could not be asked whether it was a book which all Christians should read, because his answer might have implied the opinion that its ethical merits outweighed its obscenity.[77]

5 Experts may be asked questions about the class of persons who would be attracted to the publication and the way in which they would appreciate or interpret its language or style. The rule in *Jordan* cannot strictly be applied to criticisms of art or poetry, where merit may be judged by the skill with which an appeal is made to the senses.

6 The court has a discretion to disallow testimony if it is satisfied that a witness is not an expert in any relevant field. Otherwise, the extent of experts' qualifications go to the weight which the jury is entitled to place on his or her testimony. The last witness called for *Lady Chatterley* was a twenty-one-year-old Oxford graduate with a second class honours degree in literature who had commenced her first novel.

7 The defendant carries the burden of proving public good on the balance of probabilities. Even if the prosecution calls no experts in rebuttal the tribunal is entitled to decide that the public good derived from publication is insufficient to outweigh the public danger of widespread corruption.[78]

8 There is no limit to the number of expert witnesses who may be called by either side. Thirty-five extolled *Lady Chatterley's Lover*, and seventeen entered the lists on behalf of *Oz*. In Canada, not more than five experts may be tendered by either side without leave of the court.[79] In England, the limit is reached in practice at the point when counsel feels that repetition will bore or antagonize the jury.

7
Laws against rudery

THE CONCEPT OF INDECENCY

Society has an interest in protecting its members from having offensive sexual material thrust before them against their wishes. This interest is not concerned with the moral fibre of the community, but rather with the right of an individual to choose to avoid material which offends his sexual modesty. Prohibition of public displays which seriously discomfort a significant section of the community, and measures to prevent unsought intrusions of erotica into private homes by exploitation of the postal services, require a more stringent legal test than the concept of obscenity. These measures are not concerned with the danger of corruption, but with the outrage to public susceptibilities occasioned by unlooked-for confrontations with lurid displays of sexual activity. The distinction between immorality and indecency was recognized in Roman times: the function of the Censor, who protected public morals, was strictly divorced from that of the Aedile, who was concerned with maintaining decency and order.[1] 'Obscenity' is punished because it promotes harm, 'indecency' because it is a public nuisance, an unnecessary affront to people's sense of aesthetic propriety. Obscenity laws infringe individual freedom by protecting people from themselves, but indecency laws protect the freedom of individuals to venture out in public without suffering shock:

the law relating to indecency is not a law which impinges upon the liberty of the individual but rather is one which protects that liberty. A man in whom indecency raises feelings of outrage, affront, anger, shame, or even discomfort is entitled to be protected in his freedom and to be unmolested not only in his person but in his feelings. It is true that in that protection the liberty of others is limited, but this is natural in a society – a man is only entitled to liberty of action so far as his liberty of action does not harm others. The law relating to indecency is not concerned with the individual's morals but with his liberty to live free from interference by the presentation before him of what offends him, what is indecent to him as a member of the community.[2]

That, at least, is the theory, and it finds a measure of support in those statutes which prohibit offensive public displays (the Vagrancy Acts and the Indecent Advertisements Act), offensive words uttered in public places (Town Police Clauses Acts), and offensive mailings of sexual literature (the Post Office Act and the Unsolicited Goods and Services Act). But in all this legislation choice of the word 'indecent' as the test of criminality, unaccompanied by any additional requirement of 'grossness' or 'public outrage', prohibits dissemination of harmless rudery in circumstances where no offence is occasioned. 'Indecency' offences lack provisions for jury trial, or evaluation of a work 'as a whole', or for the defence of 'public good'. These omissions may be justifiable so long as charges are only levelled against people who have deliberately provoked public outrage, but the history of their use demonstrates that prosecuting authorities incline to take advantage of them as an easy option for cases which should properly be prosecuted under the Obscene Publications Act. This trend has not been universally deplored: in *R.* v. *G.L.C.*, *ex parte Blackburn* Lord Denning enthused:

The proof of the pudding is in the eating. The Customs authorities and Post Office apply the simple test: 'Is this indecent?' They have no difficulty in condemning millions of magazines on that account, without their decisions being questioned. But when jurors are asked to apply the test: 'Does this tend to deprave or corrupt?', they have been known to allow the most indecent articles to get into circulation.[3]

Customs and Post Office decisions are not questioned because victims are usually advised not to indulge in vain attempts to convince a bench of lay justices that anything pertaining to sex is not 'indecent'. The test may be simple, in the sense that it usually leads to a conviction, but it has produced the anomaly that a book which is 'indecent' but not 'obscene' may legally be sold over every counter in the country, while if it is discovered in Her Majesty's mails or amongst the luggage of a returning traveller, a criminal offence has been committed. In the *GLC* case, Lord Justice Bridge was markedly less optimistic: 'I don't know how many people today would accept as an appropriate test of criminality what is "shocking, disgusting and revolting".'[4] Sir Robert Megarry warns that in a statute which 'contains a word as subjective and emotional in its contents as "indecency" there can be little of that precision which is so desirable in criminal law'.[5] This view was shared by Mr Roy Jenkins, who announced in 1974 his Government's abandonment of an Indecent Displays Bill promoted by the previous administration because 'the term "indecency" has no meaningful definition and should not be part of any criminal statute'.[6]

However meaningless the word 'indecent' may be in real life, it does occur in numerous criminal statutes, and the courts have ventured several broad definitions. In *R. v. Stanley* Lord Parker decided that it encompassed sexual material which a tribunal found to be embarrassing, or in poor taste. 'Indecency' was 'something that offends the ordinary modesty of the average man ... offending against recognized standards of propriety at the lower end of the scale.'[7] In *Knuller* v. *DPP* Lord Reid added: 'Indecency is not confined to sexual indecency; indeed it is difficult to find any limit short of saying that it includes anything which an ordinary decent man or woman would find to be shocking, disgusting or revolting.'[8] In other words 'indecent' in law is that which marginally shocks ordinary modesty. It is a standard so vague and arbitrary that no citizen can know, at least before a court has found him guilty, whether or not he has committed an offence.

'Indecent' is a word of 'common import', and 'Anyone called upon to consider the question whether a particular article offends against one or other of the provisions has before him not necessarily an easy, but a simply expressed task....'[9] Notwithstanding such judicial optimism, there is no measure of agreement about whether this simple and common word pertains to anything other than sex. It is usually used to denote sexual immodesty, which would exclude some publications which fall within the narrower statutory definition of 'obscene'. On the other hand, descriptions of drug-taking or brutal violence might be perceived as breaches of recognized standards of propriety, along with the expression of extreme social, political or religious viewpoints. Violence coupled with eroticism, such as sado-masochism and flagellation, is clearly within the definition,[10] but full-blooded accounts of straightforward torture and massacre, however horrifying, might escape. What has to be applied is the word 'indecent' in its ordinary linguistic use, and not judicial glosses about 'recognized standards' or 'anything which shocks or revolts' in *their* ordinary meanings. However much the public finds violence disgusting, or contrary to prevailing standards, its depiction cannot be classed as 'indecent' unless a court is prepared to apply that label outside a sexual context. In one nineteenth-century case the public display of a picture of a diseased body, 'so disgusting that it is calculated to turn the stomach', was held to be a common-law nuisance, although the court stressed that it could not be considered indecent or immoral.[11] On the other hand, judges have despaired of finding any limit to the meaning of the word[12] and the Home Office is confident that it would include 'the depiction of other kinds of violence, such as the deliberate infliction of torture, which affronted normal conventions'.[13] In law, as in life, indecency is in the eye of the beholder.

What 'offends the ordinary modesty of the average man' is decided in most cases by what offends the extraordinarily prudish modesty of the average magistrate. In those rare cases which are tried on indictment there is very little guidance which can or should be given to a jury which is presumed to act as the custodian of recognized standards of decency. 'You look at it for what it is and you judge what it is. You say to yourselves then: What are the standards of propriety recognized today by ordinary people like us twelve people?'[14] This amounts to asking 'Do you like it or not?' – and in 1973 anything pertaining to sex seemed to attract official dislike. The DPP launched a prosecution against an 'indecent' questionnaire devised by a leading sociologist as part of his research into sexual behaviour, which had been sent to those readers of the magazine *Forum* who had volunteered to answer. The alleged indecency consisted in asking whether the interviewees had experienced anal intercourse or bestiality. The Inner London Crown Court decided that vibrators and dildos were 'indecent articles', despite medical testimony to their therapeutic use, and Customs confiscated as an 'indecent import' a sex education booklet published by the Unitarian Church which had been ordered by the education department of the BBC. The Court of Appeal branded indecent the following scenes in a television documentary about the American artist Andy Warhol:

A FAT GIRL, stripping to the waist, daubing her breasts with paint and then painting a canvas with them. She also throws paint down a lavatory pan to form weird patterns. This one she calls Flush Art.

A discussion between a young girl and a man dressed as a Hell's Angel on how they can have sex. She says she will only do it at 60 m.p.h. on his motor cycle.[15]

But then, America is another country, with liberal judges like William O. Douglas, who world-wearily remarked in the same year:

> People are offended by many offerings made by merchants in this area. They are also offended by political pronouncements, sociological themes, and by stories of official misconduct. The list of activities and publications and pronouncements that offend someone is endless. Life in this crowded modern technological world creates many offensive statements and many offensive deeds.... There are regimes in the world where ideas 'offensive' to the majority (or at least to those who control the majority) are suppressed. There life proceeds at a monotonous speed. Most of us would find that world offensive. One of the most offensive experiences in my life was a visit to a nation where bookstalls were filled only with books on mathematics and books on religion.[16]

Books on art continued to provide an offensive experience for British customs officials. In 1976 they seized an edition of the work of Thomas Rowlandson RA, impervious to the fact that the originals were hanging decently in the George IV collection at Windsor Castle. The Arts Council might plead that 'to shock has always been one of the beneficent social functions of art, an inevitable by-product of the fresh vision which characterizes a good artist and which helps to protect society from inertia and paralysis',[17] but Her Majesty's Commissioners of Customs and Excise were using the indecency laws to maintain a *cordon sanitaire* against the shock of artistic indelicacy.

Most statutes which prohibit indecency also prohibit obscenity: the two concepts are generally expressed as alternatives by the phrase 'indecent or obscene'. The word 'obscene' when used outside the 1959 Act may mean simply 'filthy, disgusting, revolting, loathsome or lewd', but it is in any event a stronger epithet than 'indecent'.[18] The two words convey the same idea, in the sense that both denote an infringement of recognized standards of propriety, 'indecent being at the lower end of the scale and obscene at the upper end of the scale'.[19] The distinction is usually explained to juries with the help of an example devised by a Scottish judge in 1931:

> I do not think that the two words 'indecent' and 'obscene' are synonymous. The one may shade into the other, but there is a difference of meaning. It is easier to illustrate than define, and I illustrate thus. For a male bather to enter the water nude in the presence of ladies would be indecent, but it would not necessarily be obscene. But if he directed the attention of a lady to a certain member of his body his conduct would certainly be obscene. The matter might perhaps be roughly expressed thus in the ascending scale: Posi-

tive–Immodest, Comparative–Indecent, Superlative–Obscene. These, however, are not rigid categories. The same conduct which in certain circumstances may merit only the milder description, may in other circumstances
deserve a harder one. 'Indecent' is a milder term than 'obscene'. . . .[20]

The problem with this example is that, although it shows the difference in degree between the two concepts, it muddles the distinction
between an indecent act and the *depiction* (which may not be indecent)
of that same act. The nakedness of a bather might be indecent in the
flesh, on a crowded beach, but nakedness itself does not make post-
cards of the Sistine Chapel or the picture parade in the *Sun* incapable
of being sent through the post. The confusion which comes from
applying examples from life to comparisons with art is evident in this
extract from the cross-examination of *Oz* editor Jim Anderson about
his decision to publish a cartoon by the French humourist Siné. The
cartoon depicted a woman urinating on a phallic-shaped potted
plant, and was doubtless intended as a crude caricature of the feminist
position. It was alleged to be an example of the sort of indecency which
was unlawful when despatched by post.

PROSECUTOR: Do you find anything indecent?

ANDERSON: Yes, I find lots of things indecent.

PROSECUTOR: Just name one ... you said many things, name just one.

ANDERSON: Well, if somebody urinated in front of me I might find it indecent.

PROSECUTOR: Well, what happens to you each time you leave a public house
after a drink and you go to the urinal attached to the public house? Is
that being indecent?

ANDERSON: No, not at all. But to urinate in the courtroom is a different matter.

PROSECUTOR: But is it because you were once a barrister that you find it
indecent for somebody to pass water in the courtroom?

ANDERSON: No. It's just that it's the wrong place for passing water.

PROSECUTOR: Please turn to page 28. See – there's a lady passing water.
Since you've chosen the example of a man passing water as being something
typically indecent, do ladies fall into the same class?

ANDERSON: The action depicted is a very difficult thing for a lady. This is
a satirical drawing by a very famous cartoonist. I don't see how you can
draw any parallel.

PROSECUTOR: Well, is it indecent?

ANDERSON: Not in the least.

PROSECUTOR: Well, why is it then that the lady who appears to be watering
her cactus is doing it with her own urine and the cactus is not a real cactus
but is one of your phallic symbols, because the cactus is drawn in the shape

of the erect male penis? I would ask you again, do you consider it an indecent drawing?

ANDERSON: No, I don't. I consider it very humorous. Quite savage in its context.

PROSECUTOR: I agree it's savage. It's savagely indecent.

ANDERSON: Not at all. It's a valid artistic expression. It's very typical of Mr Siné's drawings.

The saga of Art and Life continued in the closing addresses. For the prosecution, the indecency of the act was enhanced by its reduction to a publishable form:

It is interesting to see how the minds of the accused men react to questions as to what is, and what is not, indecent. Remember Mr Anderson coming up with the suggestion that if someone urinated in front of him in the courtroom that would be indecent. And I respectfully agree with him. If somebody did urinate in front of a crowd of people, so that some of them were offended and disgusted that *would* be indecent. Members of the jury, it is as simple as that. It is the fact that the lady urinates on the cactus, the fact that it happens where people can see it which makes it indecent.

Co-editor Richard Neville sought to make the obvious rebuttal:

A man actually urinating in court is indecent, we all agree on that. But a drawing of a man urinating in court need not be indecent. A drawing doesn't smell, doesn't trickle over the exhibits, doesn't wet the lawyers' shoes and splash over the court papers and make the ushers work overtime to clean it up. This is what makes urination in court indecent and offensive. Yet the prosecution have time and again failed to make the elementary distinction between portraying an indecent action and the indecent action itself. They seem to think we are actually in the firing line of the cactus waterer.

But Judge Argyle, in explaining that concept of indecency to jury, returned to the 1931 example, with an athletic twist:

Indecent means 'unbecoming' and 'immodest' in my dictionary, and indecent is at the bottom end of the scale. We have had a number of examples given in this court of what indecency is, but I think that the original illustration given by counsel for the prosecution was the most helpful. If you are on the beach with your children and a woman takes off her clothes, that is indecent in this country. We just don't do that sort of thing in this country. Or let us say you were attending an athletic or sporting event and the athletes, beautiful physiques though they may have, have not got clothing which fits properly, and as they perform you see their private parts. This is indecent.

The House of Lords has recently emphasized that minimum standards of decency change over time, and that 'public decency must be viewed as a whole; and the jury should be invited, where appropriate, to remember that they live in a plural society, with a tradition of tolerance towards minorities'.[21] This consideration assumes importance in these cases where the allegedly offensive article is destined for a restricted group whose right to receive material of minority interest may overcome the adverse reaction of jurors who do not share the same proclivities. But although juries may be reminded rhetorically about climates which change and minorities which must be tolerated, they must not hear expert evidence on these subjects. None of the 'indecency' statutes contains the equivalent of a 'public good' defence, and the Court of Appeal ruled in *R.* v. *Stamford* that a defendant who sent homosexual magazines by post could not call evidence about current social attitudes on the subject.[22] A 'community standard' is something which emerges from the consensus reached in a jury deliberation: it is neither a fact capable of proof nor an idea which can be canvassed by experts.

Where the question of indecency turns on the circumstances or meaning of a publication, however, some assistance may be provided. In *Abrahams* v. *Cavey*, anti-Vietnam protestors had interrupted a televised church service held during a Labour Party conference. The argument that their 'indecent' interventions were in accord with the spirit of Christianity was supported by an expert witness, the Reverend Lord Soper, who testified that robust disputation in church was in the tradition of the Methodist religion, and had in this case been properly provoked by the political nature of the occasion.[23] In other cases, expert opinion has been introduced as testimony of fact, to explain the reputation of authors and artists and to provide general information about the work at issue. In 1977 Customs officers seized a number of books about classic art edited by international experts, despite the fact that many of the original pictures had been displayed at public galleries in England. Art critics testified to the standing of the editors and the artists, and gave details of a recent exhibition of some of the offending works at the Victoria and Albert Museum.[24] In the same year a professor of English literature traced for a court the etymology of the word 'bollocks', from the literal meaning of 'testicles' which appeared in early editions of the bible (the King James edition replaced it by 'stones'), to its modern colloquial meaning of 'rubbish' or 'nonsense'. The promoters of a record album entitled *Never Mind the Bollocks, Here's the Sex Pistols* were cleared of a charge under the Indecent Advertisements Act, thereby relieving some future court from considering the proposed alternative title, *Never Mind the Stones, Here's the Sex Pistols*.

Indecency offences are viewed as a class of public nuisance, and do not attract heavy sentences. Most are triable only in magistrates' courts, although postal offences carry a maximum sentence of twelve months if tried on indictment, and serious smuggling offences may attract two years imprisonment. Sentencing policy draws a distinction between the graver offence of obscenity (involving an element of corruption) and indecency (a contravention of standards of taste) on the basis of Lord Parker's dictum in *Stanley*. Normally, where a statute prohibits 'obscene or indecent' articles, the prosecution will charge only indecency, which is easier to prove but by the same token must attract a lighter sentence. The principle was explained by the Court of Appeal in *R. v. Waterfield*:

> There must be some scaling-down where the allegation is not of obscene articles but of indecent articles. . . . If what was alleged against this appellant were merely an affront to morality he ought not to be dealt with as severely as if he had been charged with evading the prohibition against articles which were likely to deprave or corrupt . . . the case should be approached on the basis of public annoyance or nuisance.[25]

There is a danger that trial judges will be tempted to aggrandize their role into one of moral guardianship when punishing nuisance offenders. Sentencing a first offender to prison for sending indecent brochures by post, one judge declared:

> I see very little difference between conduct such as smuggling drugs, which injures the health of the nation physically and morally, and conduct such as the offence to which you have pleaded guilty, which must injure the health of the nation in a moral sense. . . . Speaking for myself I cannot contemplate that this offence should not attract a custodial sentence.

Speaking for the Court of Appeal, Lord Justice Bridge saw 'by no stretch of the imagination' any comparison between importing heroin and posting lewdly-worded leaflets. The sentence was 'erroneous in principle and manifestly excessive' and was reduced to a fine of £100.[26]

RELATIVE INDECENCY

The idea of an 'indecent action' presents no problem in sexual offences, because the quality of indecency is readily inferred from the defendant's motive of sexual gratification. An indecent assault must be 'accompanied with circumstances of indecency on the part of the accused'.[27] The intention and the setting are of paramount importance: physical contact is unobjectionable in a doctor's surgery but criminal if unsolicited on the Central line. The most difficult question in the law relating to indecent publications is whether the circumstances of publication may be taken into account in deciding whether the quality of indecency inheres to a particular book or photograph. Is the test objective, in the sense that a tribunal must consider whether text or presentation is shocking or disgusting in itself, or does the yardstick of 'recognized standards of propriety' permit consideration of the context and circumstances in which the matter is exhibited? A photograph of the vagina will traduce recognized standards if displayed outside a cinema or sent unsolicited to an unsuspecting member of the public, but not if shown to medical students at a hospital lecture or sent by post from one gynaecologist to another. The obscenity law adopts a relative test, in that no publication is 'obscene *per se*': that quality is deduced from the circumstances of publication and the effect on likely readers. But in determining whether an article sent by post is 'indecent', the courts have imposed an objective criterion, so that the character of the addressee and the purpose of the mailing are irrelevant. The distinction between 'obscenity' in the 1959 Act and 'indecency' in the Post Office Act was strikingly illustrated in 1964 by the trials of photographer Jean Straker, who was acquitted of an obscenity charge over his sale of some artistic nude studies. But when he sent the same pictures by post, to persons interested in photographic art who had requested and paid for them, the Lord Chief Justice upheld his Post Office Act conviction:

It is an attractive point put by Mr Straker ... that just as obscenity must be tested by the effect on the people to whom it may be published, so must questions of indecency relate to the people to whom they are published. Mr Straker prides himself on being very careful in his distribution, as he puts it, in only sending photographs to people who, he is quite satisfied, will not find them indecent. It is, as I said, an attractive way of saying it, but unfortunately the Post Office Act of 1953 does not so provide.[28]

This decision was reinforced by the Court of Appeal in *R. v. Stamford*, in excluding evidence from recipients as to their reaction on opening mail and discovering allegedly indecent material: 'the test of indecency was objective, and the character of the addressee immaterial'.[29]

Finally, in the 1975 case of *Kosmos Publications Ltd* v. *DPP*, the Divisional Court decided that all the circumstances of mailing were irrelevant to the question of indecency.[30] A publishing company had dispatched by post a number of magazines to one of its own employees, for the purposes of his job as a sales representative. The DPP conceded that none of the magazines could be regarded as obscene, and all were on open sale. The court decided that standards of decency were objective and evidence about the circumstances and purpose of the mailing was rightly excluded: 'indecency' must be discerned by looking at the article itself, and nothing else. It followed that an offence might be committed for the most laudable purpose, as when a concerned member of the public posted an indecent article to the DPP with a request for legal action. Spouses who exchanged frank love-letters, and publishers of magazines on open sale who send copies under plain wrapper to subscribers, all in theory offend against the 'objective' standard of postal indecency, and it might still in theory be an offence to mail a copy of *Lady Chatterley's Lover*. The Divisional Court's refuge against such consequences was reliance upon official discretion: the DPP would not prosecute, and even if he did, the courts could impose a low penalty. This answer would not have satisfied Lord Reid. Criticizing the vague and possibly absurd applications of indecency laws in *Knuller*, he remarked that 'a bad law is not defensible on the ground that it will be judiciously administered'.[31]

The idea that 'indecency' is an objective quality, discoverable by examination as if it were a mineral, may be confined to prosecutions under the Post Office Act. In cases under other statutes, courts have been prepared to accept that the context of publication may blunt the offensiveness of particular words or phrases. The case of *Wiggins* v. *Field* arose from a public reading of Allen Ginsberg's poem 'America', including the line, 'Go fuck yourself with your atom bomb.' The reader was charged with using 'indecent language' in contravention of a local bye-law, but the Divisional Court said that the case ought never to have been brought. 'Whether a word or phrase was capable of being treated as indecent language depended on all the circumstances of the case, the occasion, when, how and in the course of what it was spoken and perhaps to a certain extent what the intention was.'[32] It decided that in the work of a recognized poet, read without any intention of causing offence, the word 'fuck' could not be characterized as 'indecent'. The same robust attitude was expressed by the court in quashing a doctor's conviction for using indecent language when he described workmen as 'a pair of stupid bastards' for making a noise outside his surgery. 'It is quite impossible to say that the word in this context was indecent.'[33] But just as context may render rude words inoffensive, so it may make respectable words indecent. In 1966 a group of anti-Vietnam protestors interrupted a church lesson read by the Foreign Secretary. In *Abrahams* v. *Cavey* the Divisional Court upheld their conviction for 'indecent behaviour' contrary to an ecclesiastical statute, on the grounds that the outburst was unseemly because a church service was in progress. The defence argued that 'indecency' was a constant factor which had to be considered *per se*: words which were not of themselves indecent ('Oh you hypocrites, how can you use the words of God to justify your policies?') were not made indecent by the place or context in which they were uttered. The court rejected this submission, and held that the circumstances made all the difference: 'It is clear that an act done in a church during divine service might be highly indecent and improper, which would not be so at another time.'[34]

Speech alleged to be 'insulting' must be considered in context in Public Order Act prosecutions. A speaker must take his audience as he finds it, and Mr Colin Jordan's pronouncement that 'Hitler was right', however palatable to fellow fascists, was 'insulting' when declaimed at a public rally in the presence of hostile Jews and communists.[35] In *Cozens* v. *Brutus* the House of Lords ruled that, 'It is for the tribunal which decides the case to consider, not as law but as fact, whether in the whole circumstances the words of the statute do or do not, as a matter of ordinary usage of the English language, cover or apply to the facts which have been proved.'[36]

An allied, but similarly unresolved, problem is whether 'indecency' must be gathered from the overall tone and presentation of an article, or whether isolated offensive parts will suffice. The Obscene Publications Act requires a work to be judged 'as a whole' unless it comprises separate items, but there is no authoritative judicial guidance on whether the same approach is permissible for testing indecency. That this question may assume crucial importance is illustrated by *A.G. ex rel McWhirter* v. *IBA*.

The Independent Broadcasting Authority, required by statute to ensure so far as possible that television programmes do not include anything which 'offends against good taste or decency', defended its decision to screen tasteless scenes in a programme about avant-garde film-maker Andy Warhol on the ground that the film 'taken as a whole' was not offensive. Individual scenes must be related to the overall theme, and

A film of a tea party with a bishop and a nun using a four-letter word three times, apparently as part of their normal conversation, may be grossly offensive; but it may be wholly inoffensive if the same word were used three times in a programme about Army training . . . it is idle to suppose that there is an absolute standard of what is decent or indecent.[37]

The Court of Appeal agreed that the film 'taken as a whole' was not offensive, although about ten per cent of it depicted 'indecent incidents'. Lord Justice Lawton suggested that context was a relevant factor:

> A possible appreciation of the programme could be that it was an attempt to give the television-viewing public an opportunity of seeing something of, and understanding what, in modern idiom, has come to be called a 'sick society'. If this was the intention the distasteful and indecent incidents become relevant. It would be no answer to a charge of disregarding the Television Act 1964 for the Authority to say that their motives in broadcasting indecent matter were worthy; but whether an incident is indecent must depend upon all the circumstances, including the context in which the alleged indecent matter occurs.[38]

Whether circumstances and overall impact are relevant to consideration of indecency will depend upon judicial construction of the statute containing the prohibition. In a Post Office Act prosecution the purpose of mailing the article could not be considered, and it is uncertain whether it could be viewed 'as a whole'. In *Wiggins* v. *Field*, the Divisional Court said that both approaches were proper in applying a local ordinance against 'indecent language'. In prosecutions at common law for the offence of 'outraging public decency', it seems that isolated 'purple passages' will render the entire article indecent. 'If there were in any book, new or old, a few pages or even a few sentences which any jury could find to be outrageously indecent, those who took part in its publication or sale would risk conviction.'[39] In 1975, distributors of *More About the Language of Love* were convicted at common law for an outrage to public decency occasioned by one-tenth of the film's contents.

The uncertainty in English law over whether an allegedly indecent article must be viewed as a whole, and whether it may be considered in the circumstances of its publication, has been resolved in other jurisdictions in favour of asking whether 'ordinary decent people' would be horrified, not at the publication itself, but by the circumstances in which it is exposed. The High Court of Australia has ruled that:

> In relation to indecency ... it is an act in its setting and circumstances which constitutes the offence. To publish or exhibit a particular picture or print might amount to a publication of indecent matter in one set of circumstances although in other circumstances this would not be so. When it is said that a print or picture is indecent because it is 'an affront to modesty' what is meant is that it is of such a character that its publication in the way alleged is an affront to modesty.... The publication is to be considered as a whole,

its several parts in the context of the whole. When the question is whether there has been a publication of indecent matter, the goodness of part does not necessarily redeem the whole. It is the whole that is on trial in the whole circumstances of its publication. If the Gospels were printed with indecent pictures interleaved the indecency would be the greater.[40]

This approach is much more realistic than a dogged insistence that 'indecency' is some objectively ascertainable quality inherently present or absent in a particular article. In America, Customs prohibitions are dependent upon the purpose and character of the importer. The Kinsey Research Institute was entitled to import Scandinavian pornography for research purposes, although the same articles would have been prohibited had a bookseller sought to introduce them for general sale.[41] This approach is consonant with the purposes of indecency offences: as the Court of Justiciary in Scotland has pointed out, 'the mischief resides not so much in the book or picture *per se* as in the use to which it is put . . . what is in a real case a local public nuisance.'[42]

POSTAL REGULATIONS

It is obviously convenient for those who wish to obtain non-obscene erotica to mail-order their requirements, using the anonymity of the postal service and so avoiding embarrassment to themselves or others. There are drawbacks, however, which have been thought to justify the tougher standard of 'indecency' for material despatched by post. The availability of mail-order erotica encourages practical jokesters to fill in the coupons in the names of friends or enemies whom they know will be embarrassed when salacious material arrives on their doorstep, and avaricious publishers may exploit the postal service by indiscriminate and unsolicited mailings of lurid advertisements. Unsolicited porn-in-the-post may not be the most serious permissive phenomenon – it has inspired the long-running West End comedy *No Sex Please, We're British* – but there can be no doubt about public attitudes towards commercial use of the mails to intrude offensive material into private homes. The Younger Committee on Privacy reported that unsolicited advertisements for sexual literature were an intrusion on home life which aroused considerable concern: sixty-seven per cent of a large public sample regarded it as an invasion of their privacy. Although thirty-four per cent maintained indifference at the prospect of puffs for sex technique manuals arriving through their letter box, twenty-one per cent admitted that they would be 'a bit' annoyed and forty-six per cent would be 'very' annoyed.[43] A poll taken in 1973 showed a heavy preponderance of opinion in favour of continued legal prohibitions on unsolicited salacity.[44] Even in America, home of the hard-sell, postal authorities in 1968 received 450,000 complaints from citizens who had been subjected to offensive and unsolicited mailings.[45]

The difficulty with existing legal controls in England is that they are ill-defined, they penalize mailings which cause no offence, and they are inapt to catch some genuine cases of public nuisance.

Section 11 of the 1953 Post Office Act provides that:

A person shall not send or attempt to send or procure to be sent a postal packet which (a) save as the authority (i.e. the Post Office) may either generally or in any particular case allow, encloses any explosive, dangerous, noxious or deleterious substance, any filth, any sharp instrument not properly protected, any noxious living creature, or any creature, article or thing whatsoever which is likely to injure either other postal packets in course of conveyance or a person engaged in the business of the authority; or (b) encloses any indecent or obscene print, painting, photograph, lithograph, engraving, cinematograph film, book, and written communication, or any indecent or obscene article whether similar to the above or not; or (c) has on the packet, or on the cover thereof, any words, marks or designs which are grossly offensive or of an indecent or obscene character.

The purpose of section 11 is evidently to protect members of the postal services from exposure to articles which might prove dangerous in transit. The physical or moral welfare of the recipient is not mentioned: the offence is committed whether or not the packet arrives at its destination. Sections 53 and 58 of the Act make it a criminal offence for Post Office employees to open postal packets, so it is difficult to understand how they could be 'injured' unless the indecency appeared on an envelope, or unless the package was so poorly fastened that it broke open in transit, spilling offensive contents over the sorting-room floor. Nevertheless, the courts have given a wide interpretation to section 11: the definition of 'indecency' would include most sexual material, irrespective of the circumstances of posting or the character of the addressee. Most importantly, the Act applies irrespective of whether the indecent article has been solicited. Any 'adult' magazine with a subscription list may be prosecuted, and cases have been brought over mailings to recipients who have actively sought the material and have paid for it beforehand – often by postal order. Public support for postal prohibitions has been expressed only in relation to *unsolicited* publications: there can be no breach of privacy by supply under plain wrapper in response to a genuine request. Moreover, there is no public good defence, and evidence of the effect of the material on its recipient is rigidly excluded. Nor is it a defence that the material was only posted to adults who had sought it or who would not be embarrassed by receiving it: the test is the modesty of the *average* man.

The rule that 'indecency' is much less serious than 'obscenity' produces the bizarre result that a publication which would bring a blush to many cheeks without depraving or corrupting any other part of the person can be sold over any counter in the country, but the moment it is concealed in an envelope and despatched via Her Majesty's Mails a criminal offence is committed. Thus section 11 may be deployed for purposes of censorship rather than to curb public nuisance. Most magazines build up a subscription list, and their publishers could be successfully prosecuted under section 11 without the benefit of a 'public good' defence. In 1972 a publisher of 'indecent' homosexual magazines was refused permission to call expert evidence which would have been admissible pursuant to section 4 of the Obscene Publications Act, and in 1974 a record promoter was unable to invoke the musical merit of an album with indecent lyrics. This latter case illustrates the extent to which section 11 prosecutions can be divorced from their original purpose of protecting Post Office workers, who would hardly have access to a gramophone in the course of their duties. A possible remedy for attempts to use section 11 to circumvent the Obscene Publications Act lies in section 75 of the Post Office Act, which empowers a court to stop section 11 proceedings if it appears that the offence charged is also punishable at common law or under some other Act, and to direct that a more appropriate charge be preferred.

The defendant to a section 11 charge had no right to insist that the matter go for jury trial. The James Committee on the Distribution of Criminal Business unequivocally recommended that section 11 offences should be tried on indictment if the defendant so wished,[46] and this result has been achieved by the provisions of the 1977 Criminal Law Act. An election for jury trial probably increases the defendant's chances of acquittal, at the risk of increasing the sentencing maximum from £1,000 to a possible term of twelve months' imprisonment.

Section 66 of the Post Office Act makes it an offence to 'send any message by telephone which is grossly offensive or of an indecent, obscene or menacing character'. The section might in theory extend to the erotic importunings of loving couples, although its purpose is obviously to protect subscribers from annoyance. It is doubtful whether this offence is appropriate to catch one breed of telephonic nuisance, the 'heavy breather'. Exhalation of breath, however erotic or menacing, may not amount to a 'message'.

Unsolicited brochures may give offence by referring to sexual matters in language which lacks the element of vulgarity or explicitness required for an 'indecency' conviction. Under section 11, the circumstances of posting are irrelevant: one leaflet advertising *A Manual of Sexual Technique* was not in itself indecent, although public outrage followed when it was sent to schoolchildren and nuns. This in turn provoked a back-bench amendment to the 1971 Unsolicited Goods and Services Act by the addition of section 4:

> A person shall be guilty of an offence if he sends or causes to be sent to another person any book, magazine or leaflet (or advertising material for any such publication) which he knows or ought reasonably to know is unsolicited and which describes or illustrates human sexual techniques.

The section was a panic measure, introduced against government advice, and the authorities very soon had difficulty with the meaning of 'human sexual technique'. Did this include an article on abortion or gynaecology? A magazine piece on teenage dating? An advertisement for family planning clinics? The clause as originally drafted proscribed 'sexual techniques', the word 'human' being added at the insistence of the Ministry of Agriculture to protect its flow of breeding information to farmers. There was another ambiguity – was it essential for the 'book, magazine or leaflet' *itself* to describe human sexual techniques, or did the words in parentheses make it an offence for a leaflet couched in the chastest prose to advertise a book about such techniques? The Divisional Court opted for the latter interpretation in *DPP* v. *Beate Uhse (UK) Ltd.*, where the offending letter announced the firm's catalogue of books dealing with human sexuality, without actually describing or illustrating either the catalogue or the books listed in it. The Court ruled:

> It is clearly within the mischief of this legislation that there should be a prohibition of advertising material of that kind, even though the advertising material does not of itself contain illustrations or descriptions of human sexual techniques.[47]

In two respects this Act is preferable to section 11: it penalizes only unsolicited mailings, and imposes a graduated scale of maximum fines, which increases for subsequent offences.

Neither section 11 nor section 4 is apt to punish one common mail-order practice which involves the fraudulent exploitation of sexual curiosity. Provocative brochures, purportedly emanating from Scandinavian businesses with London box offices, promise a pornucopia of delights to those stupid or desperate enough to send money orders. In return, the 'punter' will receive material more tepid than that openly displayed at his local newsagency. In one case a firm advertised a magazine entitled *Women and Animals*, which purportedly displayed the intimate performances of horses and dogs with humans of the opposite sex. Those who subscribed received photographs of stately equestriennes and ladies taking their dogs for walks. The Obscene Publications Squad, which had launched an investigation, declined to prosecute, although the advertisement was a blatant breach of the Trade Descriptions Act.

The gulling of prurient-minded people is a constant theme in classical and Restoration comedy, but perhaps it is time that law displayed a little tenderness for the weak and curious, and provided some means for parting confidence tricksters from their considerable profits. Section 11 of the Post Office Act permits mail-order houses to provoke desire, but then it takes away the performance. Victims are understandably reluctant to complain, because they would be obliged to confess to the offence of 'procuring' an indecent postal packet – albeit one which turned out to be offensively decent. So long as section 11 remains, the dishonest advertiser can enter the pious defence that his customers cannot expect him to break the law. The 1968 Trade Descriptions Act makes it an offence to apply false or misleading descriptions of quantity or composition to advertised goods, and would directly cover cases in which material advertised as pornography is in fact the mildest form of pin-up magazine. The DPP has never seen fit to use the Trade Descriptions Act in this context, with the result that these rackets have thrived, and misleading advertisements may be found in most 'adult' magazines. If the purpose of obscenity laws is to protect the weak and the credulous, it is only reasonable that the safeguard should extend to their pocket-book as well as to their moral values.

The public nuisance caused when insensitive publishers use postmen as unwitting door-to-door salesmen is not satisfactorily prohibited by the Post Office Act or the Unsolicited Goods and Services Act. The simplest reform would be to abolish section 4 and amend section 11 so that financial penalties are increased and it covers mailings which the sender knows are both unsolicited and likely to cause gross offence to recipients. A step in this direction was attempted by the Home Office in its 1973 Indecent Displays Bill, which provided heavier penalties for any person who

sends or delivers to another any articles which he knows or ought reasonably to know to be unsolicited and which either
    (a) consists of or contains any indecent matter, or
    (b) advertises any article in a way likely to be taken as indicating that the article consists of or contains indecent matter

Poor drafting drew strong criticism of subsection (b). The mere use of the word 'sex' in a book title in advertising circulars or publishers' lists might 'be taken as indicating that the article contains indecent matter'. In theory at least, it would have been dangerous to despatch an unsolicited advertisement for the Coronet Book entitled *Pornography – the Longford Report*, because unsuspecting purchasers could take that title to indicate that indecent matter lurked within. Nonetheless, this 1973 formula retains the support of some law reformers. In 1979 Parliament gave a second reading to an Indecent Displays (Control) Bill which contained a section couched in identical terms.

A more imaginative solution has been recommended by the Younger Committee on Privacy, namely legislation requiring that unsolicited sexual matter should be 'double enveloped', with the outside envelope bearing the legend 'unsolicited advertising matter'. 'The cardinal principle', it urged, 'should be that the recipient should have at the outset the choice between disposing of sealed matter unopened or investigating it further.'[48] In America, under the Federal Anti-Pandering Act, a recipient of unsolicited and sexually provocative advertisements is entitled to request the Postmaster-General to direct the offending publisher to remove his name from its mailing list. A criminal offence is only committed if a further mailing ensues in defiance of the order. The scheme has proved expensive to operate, and its protection is limited to subsequent mailings from one particular source. Some members of the Presidential Commission on Obscenity were driven to conclude that 'The assaults on individual privacy are so great in so many other areas of a citizen's life that the reception of unsolicited mail that can readily be thrown away can hardly be viewed as socially significant.'[49] Not, perhaps, in a nation abandoned to the techniques of hard-sell, but dismay at the prospect of porn in the family post requires some legal protection for the equanimity of British breakfast tables. The Canadian solution extends the obscenity law to cover transmission by post of any obscene article, and provides the Postmaster-General with a general power to deny service to any individual or company using the mails to facilitate a suspected criminal offence.[50]

CUSTOMS LEGISLATION

In 1976 114,000 books and magazines, 4,000 films and no less than 57,000 'indecent objects' were seized and destroyed by Customs officers, enforcing a prohibition on the importation into the United Kingdom of 'indecent or obscene prints, paintings, photographs, books, cards, lithographic or other engravings, or any other indecent or obscene articles'.

This ban, which was incongruously inserted in 1876 between the prohibitions on coffee and snuff in section 42 of the Customs Consolidation Act, was maintained when Parliament modernized and collated previous statutes in the Customs and Excise Act of 1952. Retention of the test of 'indecency' imposes a different standard for imported books and magazines to that which governs home-produced literature, and the result, if not the intention, has been to protect the British indecent publications industry from overseas competition. Imported publications which do not tend to deprave or corrupt and could not therefore be suppressed by internal controls may be destroyed at ports of entry if they shock or disgust Customs officials – men who are more experienced in financial than in moral evaluation. Section 42 has been interpreted as a catch-all provision, applying even to those articles whose indecency is not visible to the naked eye. In *Derrick* v. *Commissioners of Customs & Excise* the Divisional Court applied the prohibition to film transparencies and negatives, inoffensive enough on casual inspection until processing and projection made their indecency apparent.[51] The phrase 'any other indecent ... article' is not to be interpreted *ejusdem generis* with the preceding references to printed matter: it covers sex-toys, statues, ball-point pens, key rings, candles, chessmen, dildoes, inflatable rubber ladies, penis-shaped plastic mouth-organs and any other objects which the wit or perversity of man can make for indecent use.

Many of the problems with section 42 derive from the simple fact that 'indecency' is not a physical quality which inheres to written material or to physical objects in a way comparable to other excluded items. Prohibited properties of metals and drugs may be scientifically established, but 'indecency' is in the mind of the beholder, and is really a matter of opinion rather than a fact which can be established by evidence. The wide operation of section 42 is limited only by the common sense of Customs officials and the sheer impossibility of monitoring all publications brought in from abroad. On some occasions Customs officials in their attempts to abide by the letter of the law have only been held up to public ridicule. For example, in 1973 the BBC gave advance notice that it was importing the most scientifically-advanced sex education kit in the world, prepared under the auspices of the Unitarian Church by associates of Kinsey. These considerations were deemed irrelevant to the decision to confiscate, because the Customs Acts contained no saving clause for articles whose importation is justified in the public interest.[52] In 1964 Sir Dingle Foot QC bought a copy of *The Perfumed Garden* at a bookstall at Heathrow Airport prior to departure for an overseas conference. On his return, the book was confiscated on the grounds that he was seeking to bring an indecent article into the United Kingdom. In order to avoid similar embarrassments, the Customs Department in June 1978 warned its officers against prying into personal luggage. The directive reads:

Articles not to be detained: In no circumstances is a person to be asked if he has any indecent or obscene books, pictures or other articles, or to be questioned about the character of any book which is found in his possession.

With the exception of child pornography, officers are not to detain small quantities consisting of single copies of obscene or indecent books or other articles which have been imported in baggage, and which appear to be intended solely for:

(a) the passenger's or crew member's own personal use; or
(b) serious professional work by university staff, artists, students, etc.

In other words, the letter of the law is to be ignored in practice. Tourists are permitted to return with personal souvenirs of holidays in liberated climes, and Customs officers are henceforth to concentrate on commercial importations and child pornography.

In deference to the distinction between 'obscenity' and 'indecency', no notice is taken of obscenity trial acquittals. In 1976 a confidential reminder was sent from the General Customs Directorate to all officers:

In view of the wide publicity given to the recent acquittal of the British publication of *Inside Linda Lovelace* which had been prosecuted under the Obscene Publications Act, staff are reminded that departmental policy has not changed and that any commercial importations of this title should be detained and reported to branch GCC4B for appropriate action.[53]

In the same year Customs officials in both England and America were confronted with attempts to import the celebrated Japanese film *Empire of the Senses*. In both countries entry was permitted for one Film Festival screening (in Britain it won the British Film Institute Award) and the film was then ordered out of the country. In America, the courts held that this order violated the First Amendment of the Constitution: 'the federal Government has ample authority to proceed against obscenity without giving this kind of power to Customs officials'.[54] In Britain, legal action by the importer was defeated on the technical ground that Customs had declined to accept the duty which was payable on the film, and so were entitled to exclude it. The film was sent out of the country and then re-imported again under its original title *Ai No Corrida*. Customs raised no objection, accepted payment of the appropriate duty, and *Ai No Corrida* began a long run at a London film club, to considerable critical acclaim and no public complaint.

Customs officers who intercept articles considered indecent may proceed either by seeking forfeiture without criminal consequence to the importer, or by charging him with one of a variety of 'smuggling' offences in the 1952 Customs and Excise Act. A criminal charge will only be preferred where there is evidence of a positive intention to evade the prohibition on a large scale, so that cases other than commercial importation of hard-core pornography will normally proceed to a civil forfeiture hearing, either before local justices or before a High Court judge, sitting with or without a jury.[55] Whenever goods are seized the importer must be notified, and has one month to apprise the Commissioners of his intention to dispute their claim for forfeiture, otherwise the goods will be destroyed. In disputed cases the Commissioners must institute proceedings, unless they decide on reflection that the seizure was over-zealous, in which case they are empowered to release the goods subject to 'such conditions, if any, as they think proper'.[56] Conditions can only be imposed if the article has been seized at point of entry: an importer whose goods have cleared Customs and who has paid the appropriate duty cannot be subject to any restriction if Customs officers realize with hindsight that it was an indecent import.[57] The discretion to impose conditions must in any event be exercised reasonably and lawfully. If the purpose of the importation were relevant to assessing the 'indecency' of the import, a condition for restricted circulation might not be objectionable.

A prosecution for smuggling indecent articles may be brought within three years of the commission of the offence. The maximum penalty is two years' imprisonment, and a fine of either £100 or three times the value of the goods on the open market at the time of importation.[58] In *Byrne* v. *Low* the importer of a consignment of hard-core pornography valued at £2,335 was initially fined only £100 on the ingenious basis that there could be no 'open market' in illegal pornography. But the Divisional Court held that markets which were 'black' were nonetheless 'open' for the purposes of assessing penalty. The relevant price was that which a willing seller would accept from a willing buyer at the port of entry.[59] This approach suggests that the price must be calculated as a bulk purchase, and not by totting up the Soho-level price of each magazine.

Section 45 of the 1952 Customs and Excise Act penalizes the person who receives the goods at the port of entry, together with others who 'assist or are otherwise concerned in' the actual importation, provided that their actions are accompanied by an intention to evade the prohibition. Section 304 (a) casts the criminal net a good deal wider, by penalizing anyone who 'knowingly and with intent ... to evade any prohibition ... acquires possession of, or is in any way concerned in carrying, depositing, harbouring, keeping or concealing or in any manner dealing with' prohibited articles. This section catches those who subsequently handle indecent goods in the knowledge that they have been illegally imported. The fact that acquisition took place at some stage after the importation will be no defence if the accused knew at the time he handled the articles that they had been imported in breach of the prohibition on indecent articles.[60] Section 304(b) makes it an offence to be 'in any way knowingly concerned in any fraudulent evasion or attempt at evasion ...', whether the accused actually handles the goods or not. It covers those who make arrangements for smuggling, or who wittingly profit from the distribution of the smuggled goods, without ever coming into contact with them. The additional requirement of 'fraud' implies that knowledge of the importation must include the realization that it was accomplished by dishonest or deceitful methods (e.g. in secret compartments of lorries or by false declarations on Customs forms) rather than by oversight on the part of Customs officers. Although the word 'fraudulent' does not appear in sections 45 or 304 (a), it may be that the word 'knowingly' in those sections also implies an awareness of deception.[61] It is an offence to make an untrue statement to a Customs officer, but if 'borderline' articles are correctly described as 'books' or 'films' the onus will be on the Customs to inspect them for possible indecency. Officers generally work on the principle that you *can* judge a book by its cover, and their seizure record includes *Rape Around Our Coast* (a study of soil erosion) and *Fun in Bed* (a book of games for sick children).

A provision of the Customs and Excise Act which applies both to civil forefeiture proceedings and to criminal prosecutions shifts the burden of proof to the respondent/defendant on the issue of indecency. Section 290 (2) provides that

> Where in any proceedings relating to customs or excise any question arises ... as to whether or not ... (b) any goods or other things whatsoever are of the description of nature alleged in the information, writ or other process ... then, where those proceedings are brought by or against the Commissioners ... the burden of proof shall be upon the other party to the proceedings.

Section 42 uses 'indecent' along with other descriptions to denote the particular quality of a thing which makes it prohibited. Other qualities prohibited by the section, such as 'silver coin', 'metal' and 'hides, skin, horns, hoofs of cattle', are ascertainable by inspection or scientific examination, and it may not be unreasonable to relieve Customs of the burden of calling evidence to verify identification. In contrast to qualities which can be objectively established, 'indecency' depends for its ascertainment on the standards of propriety recognized by a particular tribunal. In no other statute where 'indecency' is the test of a criminal offence is the burden placed on the accused to negate its existence, and the courts have not fully considered the implications of this unique feature of the Customs legislation. In *Commissioners of Customs and Excise* v. *Paul Raymond Publications Ltd.*, Mr Justice Bristow was inclined to minimize its significance for civil forfeiture cases:

> The other element in the 1952 Act that has been referred to, and you may think when we come to the end of the day that it is really not very important, is that the burden of proof is on Paul Raymond to satisfy you, if you are in doubt, that on the balance of probabilities the thing is not indecent or obscene. But, Members of the Jury, when what you have to consider is simply one body, as I ventured to call it early on, there is not much room, you may think, for having to worry about burden of proof. There it is, you are the judges.[62]

The burden of proof may be important, however, in criminal prosecutions where the defendant argues that he did not 'intend to evade' the prohibition in section 42 of the Customs Consolidation Act because he honestly believed that the articles he was importing were not indecent. The effect of section 290 is to place the onus on the accused to lay an evidential foundation for this defence. In *R. v. Waterfield*, the Court of Appeal noted that the defendant had admitted organizing a smuggling operation in which pornography was transported from Copenhagen in Danish bacon lorries. On these facts, he

never laid any credible foundation for a defence of honest belief. He admitted in terms in the witness box that some of the films revolted him, without specifying how many; and all the circumstances of this case, with large quantities of films and magazines being introduced hidden away amongst sides of bacon, make it impossible to say that there were the beginnings of a defence that he honestly thought that a substantial proportion of these films were not indecent within the meaning of the Customs and Excise legislation.[63]

If an accused, or a respondent to a forfeiture summons, is entitled to 'lay a credible foundation,' either for the honesty of his mistaken belief (if he subsequently acknowledges that the material *is* indecent) or for a submission that the material is in fact unobjectionable, it may be that evidence can be called about the basis for his belief in its public acceptability.

An unresolved question is the extent to which use of section 42 to prevent and punish the importation of indecent articles from EEC countries is compatible with the Treaty of Rome. Article 9 of the European Economic Treaty prohibits any restriction on the free movement of goods between member states, and Article 30 outlaws 'quantitative restrictions on imports and all measures having equivalent effect as between member states'. Article 36 does permit restrictions on transit if they can be justified on grounds of 'public morality, public policy or public security', although these considerations will not save prohibitions or restrictions which effectively constitute 'a means of arbitrary discrimination or disguised restriction on trade between member states'. The prohibition on obscene articles might be justified in order to preserve morality and prevent threats to physical safety from those susceptible to depravity and corruption. But articles may be impounded as 'indecent' if they merely affront community standards 'at the lower end of the scale', and public morality is hardly put at risk by bad taste. If it were, it could only be because the articles were intended for distribution in a way which would cause public concern, and a blanket prohibition on 'indecency' might not take these circumstances into account. Public policy could not justify a discriminatory application of the section if magazines produced in Denmark or Holland were subjected to greater restrictions than those originating in other member countries, and nor could it excuse a prohibition which had the effect of protecting British publishers and manufacturers of 'indecent' articles, lawfully sold on the home market, from European competitors.

In *R.* v. *Henn* the Court of Appeal decided that the Treaty of Rome did not affect Customs action against bulk importation of hard-core pornography from member states. 'The plain purpose of article 36 was to preserve prohibitions which had the plain purpose of supporting public morality. A prohibition on the introduction of obscene literature could not be otherwise than a prohibition justified on the grounds of public morality and public policy'.[64] This must be so in relation to articles which tend to deprave and corrupt, and the obscene nature of the material in *Henn* precluded any argument that the Customs prohibition constituted 'a means of arbitrary discrimination or a disguised restriction on trade between member states'. The public morality clause might not avail Customs if articles identical to those impounded could lawfully be manufactured or sold within Britain – which would be so if they were indecent but not obscene. In such cases the Customs Act embargo on 'indecency' would only survive if it did not constitute a 'quantitative restriction or a measure having an equivalent effect'. In *Henn* the Court of Appeal was inclined to the view that the Customs prohibition was not concerned with quantities, but it conceded that a broader interpretation of 'quantitative' had been applied in other EEC cases. The EEC Treaty was written into English law by the European Communities Act of 1972: in so far as it conflicts with any prior English legislation, the latter is implicitly amended so that the conflict is settled in favour of the Treaty provisions. The Treaty may yet serve to protect from Customs seizure indecent articles of EEC origin which could be lawfully manufactured in Britain.

PUBLIC DISPLAY

The public exhibition of offensive pictures has long been a common-law nuisance, and a number of statutes passed in the nineteenth century specifically penalized indecent displays. The rationale is that 'reasonable people may venture out in public without the risk of outrage to certain minimum accepted standards of decency'.[65] But while the common law concerned itself with public 'outrage' – a strong word implying serious discomfort from the display of material 'calculated to turn the stomach' – the nineteenth-century statutes relied upon the milder notion of 'indecency', with less acceptable results when used in modern times against art galleries, VD clinics, and newspapers which advocate legitimate, albeit radical, political change. Even when these laws are activated to subdue genuine social mischiefs, their outdated penalties provide a poor deterrent against those who profit from public prurience – and, in any event, 'indecency' is too nice a word to incriminate delicately-phrased insults to women in modern advertising, or racist propaganda uncoloured by coarseness.

Section 4 of the 1824 Vagrancy Act punishes

> Every person wilfully exposing to view, in any street, road, highway, or public place, any obscene print, picture, or other indecent exhibition. . . .

An amendment in 1838 expanded the section to include indecent exhibitions

> exposed to public view in the window or other part of any shop or other building situate in any street, road, highway or public place. . . .

One hundred and fifty years after the Vagrancy Act became law, the Home Office was still uncertain on two fundamental points of construction: 'Does this extend to material exposed inside a building and not visible from the street? Does it make any difference whether the public have paid for admission or not?'[66] Decisions at magisterial level are conflicting: in 1966 the Director of Public Prosecutions obtained a conviction against an art gallery for an 'indecent display' of paintings which were not visible from the street, but in 1974 one director of private prosecutions, Mrs Mary Whitehouse, failed to convince a magistrate that a West End cinema screening an indecent film was a 'public place'. The only relevant difference is that entrance to a cinema is obtained by payment, and this fact may suffice to remove the element of 'public' access from the 'place' for the purposes of the Act. At common law, a 'place' is public if illegal activity therein is capable of being seen by more than one person.[67] But if 'public place' in the Vagrancy Act is construed *ejusdem generis* with 'street road highway', section 4 would be limited to exhibitions which are actually visible to users of public thoroughfares because they are displayed in the window 'or other part' of a building abutting the highway. The phrase 'other part' would mean 'any other part of the shop which is visible from the highway': if an indecent exhibition were displayed on a counter so that it could be seen by passers-by through an open door the offence would be committed, but not if it were displayed on a shelf so as to be visible only after entry into the premises. The essence of the offence is prevention of shock to people venturing out in public, and this limiting construction would provide them with adequate protection. But if the phrase 'or other part' were given its full implication, 'public place' would include the interior of every building which abuts a public street. In this event, the Vagrancy Act would extend to all shops and art exhibitions open to the general public, although there would remain an uncertain point at which entry restrictions, such as ticket prices or admission by invitations only, would be deemed to remove the description 'public' from the class of potential entrants. It is regrettable that these ambiguities were not removed from the Vagrancy Act in 1959, when the Street Offences legislation exhaustively defined the phrase 'street or public place'. The mischief produced by indecent displays is akin to that caused by indecent solicitations: both cause offence when 'projected to somebody walking in the street'.[68]

The Vagrancy Act prohibition on indecent display overlaps with local legislation and byelaws. In London, section 54 (12) of the Metropolitan Police Act 1839 makes it an offence to use, or exhibit to public view, 'any profane indecent or obscene' language or article, 'to the annoyance of the inhabitants or passengers'.[69] In 1970 the DPP prosecuted the London Art Gallery for exhibiting the indecent art of John Lennon 'to the annoyance of passengers', but the magistrate ruled that this requirement of the charge excluded exhibitions not visible to the by-passing public: 'As I understand the word "passenger", it means someone on the move, but people who enter the gallery are not "passengers"; they then finish for the time being "passaging".'[70]

Outside London, section 28 of the Town Police Clauses Act 1847 catches

> Every person who publicly offers for sale or distribution, or exhibits to public view, any profane, indecent or obscene book, paper, print, drawing, painting or representation, or who sings any profane or obscene song or ballad, or uses any profane or obscene language to the annoyance of residents or passengers.[71]

Many local byelaws additionally prohibit 'riotous violent or indecent behaviour', and this formula is used in section 2 of the Ecclesiastical

Courts Jurisdiction Act in relation to any place of religious worship, church or graveyard. The term 'indecency' in these statutes involves an element of disorderliness: in the ecclesiastical context the Divisional Court has indicated that the words from the genus of creating a disturbance in a sacred place, and as such could include mockery or disrespect for the dead.[72]

This concatenation of Acts and byelaws, grafted on to the common law against outraging public decency, provides unnecessarily repetitive protection against public nuisances. Usually invoked against offensive behaviour, such as 'flashing' or public urination, they are also apt to cover any form of publication. They have been used to harass street-sellers of the radical political magazine *Black Dwarf*, and to contain a recent vogue in tasteless teeshirts. Time and place will figure in police activity, if not in the definition of 'indecent': in 1976 a man was arrested at the statue of Eros for wearing a teeshirt depicting 'two naked but limp cowboys standing forlornly outside a dance hall' after public concern had been aroused by a television documentary about boy prostitutes in Piccadilly Circus.[73] Lord Justice Lawton has warned that section 4 of the Vagrancy Act could be used against television retailers whose shop window set display was tuned to a channel transmitting an indecent scene.[74]

The Indecent Advertisements Act of 1889 provides an additional remedy against anyone who

affixes to or inscribes on any house, building, wall, hoarding, gate, fence, pillar, post, board, tree, or any other thing whatsoever so as to be visible to a person being in or passing along any street, public highway, or footpath and whoever affixes to or inscribes on any public urinal, or delivers or attempts to deliver or exhibits to any inhabitant or to any person being in or passing along any street, public highway, or footpath, or throws down in the area of any house, or exhibits to public view in the window of any house or shop, any picture of printed or written matter which is of an indecent or obscene nature.

The Act provides no 'public good' defence, so public health and safety bodies are obliged to tread warily. Advertisements for family planning require a restraint which is not imposed on the purveyors of cigarettes or alcohol. There have even been demands for prosecution of the Water Board for a poster on the theme 'Save Water – Shower with a Friend'. Section 5 of the Act specifically deems any advertisement indecent if it relates to 'syphilis, gonorrhoea, nervous debility or other complaint or infirmity arising from or relating to sexual intercourse'. In theory this covers a wide range of pharmaceutical advertising, and if pregnancy is an 'infirmity arising from sexual intercourse', the proprietors of 'Mothercare' shops might look to their window displays. Advertisements for VD treatments are punished more severely by section 2 of the Venereal Diseases Act 1917, which provides that

A person shall not by any advertisement or any public notice or announcement treat or offer to treat any person for venereal disease, or prescribe or offer to prescribe any remedy therefor, or offer to give any advice in connection with the treatment therefor.

These antiquated prohibitions severely hampered an anti-VD campaign launched by the Health Education Council, until both acts were amended to exclude advertisements published for a local or public authority and approved by the Secretary of State. That they still handicap the fight against the most infectious disease in Britain was proved by the prosecution of a London student newspaper in 1970 for publishing this advertisement:

Give us your headaches – abortion, adoption, contraception, drugs, educational problems, homosexuality, lesbianism, marriage, pregnancy testing, psychiatric help, venereal disease. The Advisory Centre has given free help to hundreds of young people. If you (or any of your friends) need help, ring *Student* magazine and ask for the Advisory Centre.

The director of the Student Advisory Centre was Mr Richard Branson, the grandson of a High Court judge and son of a Metropolitan magistrate. He was convicted of an offence against the 1889 Act, although the 'advice' he was offering was merely the address of the nearest hospital VD clinic. The magistrate rejected a charge under the 1917 Act on the basis that it only applies to offers of unqualified treatment – a sensible enough ruling, but one which is not in accordance with the absolute terms of the section. Mr Branson grew up to become the owner of a chain of record stores which was prosecuted under the 1889 Act for its display of a 'punk rock' album entitled *Never mind the Bollocks, Here's the Sex Pistols*. He had greater success as a commercial exploiter of vulgarity than as an idealistic public benefactor – this time he was acquitted in widely publicized proceedings which greatly boosted sales.

The melange of outdated public indecency offences requires urgent reform, if only to tailor penalties to the outsize pockets of modern advertisers. The most recent initiative, a private member's bill which had a second reading in January 1979, threatened up to two years' imprisonment for indecent displays – a punishment which seems far too draconian to redress an error of taste. In 1973 the Government

came under heavy back-bench pressure to contain such public manifestations of the permissive society as fleshy advertisements outside
'X' certificate cinemas, and the air-brush nudity of covers of magazines openly displayed in suburban newsagencies. The Indecent Displays Bill, which fell with the dissolution of Parliament the following
year, remains of some historical interest as an exercise in bad drafts-
manship and counter-productive law reform. It retained the meaningless term 'indecent' as the test for imposition of increased criminal
sanctions, and publishers were obliged to avoid titles, covers or publicity which might 'be taken as indicating that the article contains
indecent matter'. This would only have increased the risk of offence,
by encouraging deceptive titles and advertising, which would not
forewarn book buyers of any indecent content.

Indecency could, however, be displayed in a place to which the
public had access if they were required to make a payment which
'is or includes payment for the display'. In consequence, bookshops,
newsagents, private art galleries and sex shops would have had to provide a special room for the display of any indecent wares, and charge
an entry fee for customers who wished to inspect them. This might
have facilitated the spread of 'hard-core' pornography: once an ordinary newsagent set up a 'back room', he would be tempted to stock
it with more than merely 'indecent' books and magazines, and the
unintended result of the Bill would have brought Soho to the
suburbs.[75]

One novel clause provided that

If any person produces *by any means* of sound reproduction or amplification
indecent sounds (whether or not consisting of words) which are audible in
a place to which the public have or are permitted to have access, whether
on payment or otherwise, he shall be guilty of an offence.

If the human vocal cords are one 'means of amplification' or 'reproduction', then hecklers at political meetings who blew raspberries
would commit a criminal offence. Similarly, those unfortunates who
break wind loudly in public places could have found themselves in
serious trouble – particularly if a constable had exercised his power
under another section of the Bill to 'seize any article which he has
reasonable cause to believe to have been used in the commission of
an offence. . . .'

In many European and American cities a reasonable solution to
the public nuisance provoked by offensive exhibitions has been found
in zoning legislation. Particular streets of major cities have been desig-

nated areas where erotic material may be sold or exhibited, such areas being located well away from shopping precincts, residential and industrial zones, schools, churches and public institutions. Indecency is 'contained' within one definable vicinity, so that its promotion may be effectively policed and no offence given to unsuspecting members of the public. Overt displays within the designated area are further restricted by specific anatomical prohibitions. This dual approach is exemplified in a zoning ordinance passed by the City Council of Houston, Texas, in 1977, which prohibits the operation of 'adult commercial establishments' in specified areas:

(A) It shall be unlawful for any person to operate or cause to be operated an adult commercial establishment within two thousand (2000) feet of a church, school or other educational or charitable institution.

(1) An 'adult commercial establishment' means any business or enterprise having as a substantial or significant portion of its stock-in-trade or activity the sale, distribution, lending, rental, exhibition, or other viewing of material depicting sexual conduct or specified anatomical areas for consideration;

(a) 'Material' means a book, magazine, newspaper, or other printed or written material; a picture, drawing, motion picture, or other pictorial representation; a play, dance, or performance; a statue or other figure; a recording, transcription, or mechanical, chemical, or electrical reproduction; or other article, equipment, or machine.

(b) 'Sexual conduct' means:

(i) any contact between any part of the genitals of one person and the mouth or anus of another person;
(ii) any contact between the female sex organ and the male sex organ;
(iii) any contact between a person's mouth or genitals and the anus or genitals of an animal or fowl;
(iv) patently offensive representations of masturbation or excretory functions.

(c) 'Specified anatomical areas' means:
(i) less than completely and opaquely covered (a) human genitals, pubic region, (b) buttock, and (c) female breast below a point immediately above the top of the areola; and,
(ii) human male genitals in a discernibly turgid state; even if completely and opaquely covered.

(B) For the purposes of this section, measurements shall be made in a straight line, without regard to intervening structures or objects, from the nearest portion of the building or structure used as a part of the premises of an adult commercial establishment to the nearest property line of a church, school or other educational or charitable institution.[76]

The citizens of Houston at least know where they stand – or can find out with the help of a surveyor and a medical dictionary.

THE MYTH OF RECOGNIZED STANDARDS

Indecency, as a word of 'common import', is assumed to have an ascertainable meaning in law. Jurors and justices who use it as part of their everyday language are trusted to know it when they see it, just as they are relied upon to identify dishonesty and negligence. In cases of doubt, they are provided with a judicial yardstick – 'recognized standards of propriety' – which is assumed to be verifiable, if only because the 'standards' are described as having been 'recognized'. But by whom, and for what purpose? Killing is improper, but not in self-defence; rape is deplored but seduction may be glamorized; drugs are dangerous in the palm of a dealer but not in the hands of a skilled physician. A law which makes careful distinctions in every other criminal area abandons 'indecent articles' to the aesthetic taste of random tribunals, reposing blind faith in subjective responses and mythical absolutes. Scientific surveys, parliamentary debates and jury verdicts demonstrate no measure of consensus either about community standards or the sort of material which infringes them. Laws against 'indecency' merely fudge the issue of exactly what is unfit for public view or inclusion in postal packets or importation into Britain.

It is sometimes urged that 'indecent' is an easier standard for jurors to apply than the test of 'obscenity'. Lord Denning believes that it offers no difficulty at all: 'they know it when they see it'.[77] But opinion polls suggest that the word 'indecent' has little objective meaning in the English language. In 1973 a representative sample of 953 adults throughout Great Britain was asked for views on the decency of three pictures: a photograph of Rodin's sculpture *The Kiss*; a drawing by costume designer Leon Bakst of a reclining nude who sported a tuft of pubic hair; and the front cover of *Men Only*. Regional and social differences emerged. Scotsmen were most inclined to brand the pictures 'indecent', followed by the Welsh (a finding which provokes the thought that devolution may bring a return to 'Merrie England'). There was no national community consensus in the reactions: one person in three knew that the Bakst nude was indecent when they saw it, the others, when they saw the same picture, knew that it was not. Those who branded the Bakst 'indecent' frequently explained that they simply 'didn't like it', which confirms that 'indecency' provokes judgments founded on personal taste and temperament rather than any objective consideration of an article's tendency to corrupt. A jury accurately reflecting community consensus on the Bakst drawing would be divided thirty per cent for conviction, thirty-six per cent for acquittal, with twenty-six per cent inclined to think that it was 'not really indecent', but who might be prepared to find that it offended 'at the lower end of the scale'. The *Men Only* cover produced similar dissension: twenty-eight per cent thought it indecent, twenty-seven per cent 'not really indecent' and thirty-seven per cent 'not indecent at all'. A strong majority verdict was entered in favour of Rodin, with only seven per cent disagreement. The survey also demonstrated that standards of propriety appear very different when perceived through youthful eyes. Of the interviewees aged between fifteen and twenty-four, only eleven per cent voted the Bakst 'indecent', and eighteen per cent gave a like verdict to *Men Only*. Interviewees in the more judicial age group over sixty-five found both pictures 'indecent' by majorities of fifty-seven per cent and fifty-one per cent respectively. 'Recognized standards of propriety' simply do not exist if differing ages and classes of the community recognize different standards.[78]

In 1974, a Home Office working party on the Vagrancy laws reported that 'police receive surprisingly few complaints from the public'. In 1972, the year before the Government discovered a pressing need for a new Indecent Displays Bill, only thirty-four prosecutions were brought under the Vagrancy Act and eighteen under the Indecent Advertisements Act.[79] That this absence of public complaint may simply be due to an absence of public offence was suggested by the 1973 Opinion Research Centre poll, which found that seventy-one per cent of its representative sample had never been seriously upset by an indecent exhibition.

The survey suggests that many people apply the term 'indecent' to incidents perceived as 'rude' or 'sexy', but which do not in fact seriously upset them. If this is the case, then the judicial interpretation of the word as denoting material which ordinary people find 'shocking disgusting and revolting' does not strictly accord with common usage.

If the general public has become more enured to indecency, their parliamentary representatives are still against it in principle, and the

Indecent Displays Bill received all-party support on its second reading. But closer scrutiny in committee convinced erstwhile supporters that it pivoted upon a meaningless concept. One MP explained how a nude pin-up on page 3 of the *Sun* had divided the House:

> I tried that picture out on a test sample of my colleagues around a table in the Tea Room and found there was a wide variety of views about whether it was indecent ... if there is one thing which has caused offence widely it is the very fact that the *Sun* has chosen to expand its circulation by going in for nude pictures. It has caused a grave offence to a lot of decent people and it would not surprise me if someone did not decide to make a test case of it in order to stop the *Sun* and similar newspapers doing just that.[80]

There was further confusion over whether 'indecency' would extend to road safety films deliberately designed to shock, or to news pictures of naked and starving victims of the Ethiopian famine. One MP pointed out that 'to many people of the Catholic faith who hold their faith strongly, a contraceptive is an indecent article. To many other people it is no more nor less than part of modern living.'[81] MPs inconclusively debated whether sexual appliances, pub strip shows, rude jokes told by Max Miller and *Playboy* gatefolds fell below recognized standards, and whether 'raspberries' blown at Speakers' Corner would constitute 'indecent sounds'. In 1974 the Labour Government, which had previously supported the Bill, refused to reintroduce it, on the ground that 'the term indecency has no meaningful definition and should not be part of any criminal statute'.

'The difference between pornography and art', insisted Kurt Vonnegut's Senator Rosewater, 'is bodily hair.' It is time that Parliament eschewed the weak, buck-passing test of 'indecency', and actually specified the kind of material deemed unfit for unpremeditated human gaze. The issue is really one of securing a pleasant environment, and should be regarded more as a matter of civic planning to prevent aesthetic offence than as a moral lapse fit for redress by fines or jail sentences. The offence should be confined to displays in roads and pedestrian thoroughfares, and the ban should relate only to items clearly visible from such vantages. There must be a particularization of the nature of the displays to be prohibited, and of the circumstances in which the prohibition is to operate. Any legislative provision would ideally elaborate in detail the kind of material prohibited, providing a list which could be renewed by the Home Secretary every few years, considering representations from advertisers and members of the public in the light of the shifting limits of community tolerance. It

is not beyond the wit or resources of the Home Office to ascertain
public feelings: in 1973 the *Sunday Times* commissioned the major research study which destroyed the assumptions of the Indecent Displays Bill. Asked 'What would you personally regard as indecent if
it were on display in a public place?' respondents listed:

	%
Nakedness	24
Suggestive nude poses	21
Female breasts	6
Nipples	6
Sex organs	18
Pubic hair	9
Sexual intercourse	48
Scenes of violence	4
Cruelty or brutality	2
Bad language	1
Homosexuality	1

If the question were rephrased, to begin 'What would seriously discomfort you. . . .', some indication of the real range of public concern
(which might include cruelty and violence) would be elicited. Society
is justified in outlawing pandarers who seek to maximize profits by
aggressively salacious advertising, but it should do so in terms which
do not fudge the issue or resort to prudish circumlocution.

8

The common law

WILLIAM PENN: I desire you would let me know by what law it is you prose-
cute me, and upon what law you ground my indictment.
THE RECORDER OF LONDON: Upon the common law.
WILLIAM PENN: Where is that common law?
RECORDER: You must not think that I am able to run up so many years,
and over so many adjudged cases, which we call common law, to answer
your curiosity.
PENN: This answer I am sure is very short of my question, for if it be common,
it should not be so hard to produce.
RECORDER: You are an impertinent fellow, will you teach the court what
Law is? It's *lex non scripta*, that which many have studied thirty or forty years
to know, and would you have me to tell you in a moment?

The Trial of Penn and Mead, Old Bailey, 1670

Laws are of two different kinds, statute law and common law. Statutes
are Acts of Parliament, laws passed by elected representatives which
have merely to be interpreted and applied by the courts. Common
law, on the other hand, is the body of doctrine built up by court decisions over the centuries – 'judge-made law' as opposed to laws which
originate in the democratic process. Judges are no longer entitled to
'make' new law, but they may 'declare' what the common law has
always been, and 'adapt' it to meet new situations. Elastic common
laws against immorality have been declared and adopted by modern
judges to punish conduct which they dislike but which Parliament
had declined to make specifically illegal.

Judges in past centuries developed the common law in a social context where any speech or writing against the established order was
perceived as a threat to the peace. Their responsibility, as the 'most

godly, honourable, wise and learned persons in the land,'[1] was to maintain the equanimity of a morally homogeneous society, and they claimed a residual power to superintend behaviour by punishing any action which outraged the moral feelings of right minded members of society, i.e. themselves. Today, democracy demands that criminal laws should originate in the legislature rather than in the antipathies of the judiciary, and a society which claims to tolerate the views of minorities cannot entertain a jurisprudence which makes popular indignation at dissent from social or political norms a yardstick for imposing criminal sanctions. But the trend towards overt sexual permissiveness in the 1960s provided the stimulus for a re-assertion of legal powers to punish sexual conduct which the judiciary found immoral, disgusting and barely comprehensible. Common law offences of corrupting public morals and outraging public decency were pressed into service against the 'underground press' and other newspapers which carried personal contact advertisements. The offence of 'keeping a disorderly house', a relic of eighteenth-century attempts to curtail cock-fighting and bear-baiting, was refurbished by the Court of Appeal in 1961 'as a deterrent to others who may be minded to exploit what is said to be a current craze for strip-tease'.[2] In 1977 the obsolete offence of blasphemous libel was reincarnated to threaten writers and publishers who deal indecently with sacred subjects. The ambit of the common law is as obscure and as uncertain for modern publishers as it seemed to William Penn in 1670.

CONSPIRACY TO CORRUPT PUBLIC MORALS

The crime of conspiracy entered English law in the Middle Ages in the form of a carefully defined statutory device to punish those who falsely accused their neighbours. An individual who had been indicted on false information, tried, and acquitted, was entitled to sue his accusor for damages, issuing a 'writ of conspiracy'. At first conspiracy was a civil remedy, similar to redress by a modern action for malicious prosecution. In the fourteenth century it became a criminal offence as well, punishable by 'villainous judgment' – the conspirator forfeited his rights as a citizen, had his house and goods seized and his trees cut down.[3] The modern law of conspiracy dates from 1611, when the Star Chamber decided that it was conspiracy to agree to make a false accusation,[4] even if the accusation itself was laughed out of court, and nobody was harmed. In 1616, the Star Chamber extended the meaning of conspiracy from agreements to give false information to any agreement to commit any crime at all, by resolving that 'to this court of King's Bench belongs authority, not only to correct errors in judicial proceedings, but other errors and misdemeanors extrajudicial, tending to the breach of the peace, or oppression of the subjects, or to the raising of faction, controversy, debate, or to any matter of misgovernment'.[5] The borders of the new crime of criminal conspiracy were vague, proof was readily available by way of guilt by association, and punishment was unlimited. In the reign of Charles II the king's judges assumed jurisdiction over disorderly conduct, which had previously been tried by ecclesiastical courts. Their first victim was the drunken poet Sir Charles Sedley (see page 21), whose demand for benefit of clergy was rejected by the king's judges in 1663, on the grounds that 'this court is the custodian of the morals of all the king's subjects, and it is high time to punish such profane conduct'.[6]

R. v. *Sedley*, in historical perspective, shows that the doctrine that British judges have inherent power to punish whatever they or their juries think is subversive of public morality, whether or not Parliament has legislated against it, was a device used to facilitate the punishment of miscreants who would otherwise have escaped by seeking the kinder mercies of the ecclesiastical court. In 1727 this jurisdictional theory was adopted to create the common-law offence of obscene libel, when Edward Curl published a book which tended to 'weaken the bonds of civil society, virtue and morality'. Religion was part of the common law, and morality was a fundamental part of religion, *ergo* 'whatever strikes against morality must for the same reason be an offence against the common law'.[7]

There were some eighteenth-century suggestions that the residual power to punish immorality extended further than obscene libel whenever a conspiracy was involved. In 1763 Sir Francis Delaval was charged with conspiring to debauch an eighteen-year-old girl apprenticed to him for music lessons. Her former teacher (who had assigned her articles of apprenticeship to Sir Francis) and the solicitor who had drawn them up were charged as co-conspirators. To the familiar argument that such moral lapses were cognizable only in ecclesiastical courts, Lord Mansfield replied that:

> This Court is the *custos morum* of the people, and has the superintendency of offences *contra bonos mores*, and upon this ground both Sir Charles Sedley and Curl, who had been guilty of offences against good manners, were prosecuted here.[8]

In 1774, while holding that a wager laid on the result of an appeal to the House of Lords was not contrary to 'good manners or policy' Lord Mansfield repeated that, 'Whatever is against good morality and decency, the principles of our law prohibit and the King's Court as the general censor and guardian of the public morals is bound to restrain and punish.'[9]

These were the precedents relied upon by the House of Lords judges in 1961, in the case of *Shaw* v. *DPP*, for arrogating to themselves the right 'to guard the moral welfare of the state against attacks which may be more insidious because they are novel and unprepared for'.[10] The occasion for this announcement by Viscount Simonds was the publication of *The Ladies Directory*, a 'who's who' of London prostitutes. The idea was certainly not novel – the magazine was a pallid imitation of the *Exact description of the most celebrated Ladies of Pleasure* published in the eighteenth century. Nor was it unprepared for. On the contrary, the use of contact advertisements was foreseen by the Wolfenden Report, which had warned that call-girls would ply their trade through small contact advertisements in tobacconists' windows and in newspapers, but argued that this was an acceptable price to pay for the removal of public offence from street level.[11] When Parliament debated the 1959 Street Offences Act, speakers in both Houses anticipated advertisements by prostitutes, using the euphemisms of 'masseuses', 'models' and 'companions'. In the House of Lords the subject was mentioned by several speakers in the course of the debate. Although Hansard records that Viscount Simonds was present on that occasion and voted, two years later he mistakenly assumed, in his speech in *Shaw*, that Parliament had not foreseen the danger:

> When Lord Mansfield, speaking long after the Star Chamber had been abolished, said that the Court of King's Bench was the *custos morum* of the people and had the superintendency of offences *contra bonos mores*, he was asserting, as I now assert, that there is in that court a residual power, where no statute has yet intervened to supersede the common law, to superintend those offences which are prejudicial to the public welfare. Such occasions will be rare, for Parliament has not been slow to legislate when attention has been sufficiently aroused. But gaps remain and will always remain, since no one can foresee every way in which the wickedness of man may disrupt the order of society.[12]

The *Ladies Directory* was a trade journal for prostitutes, listing their pseudonyms, addresses and telephone numbers, the services they were prepared to offer and the prices they charged. The DPP was in some doubt as to whether its publisher was guilty of living off immoral earnings, since only part of his income derived from advertising revenue,

and it was not certain that the advertisements were obscene, because
they were not couched in erotic language, and any corruption which
they facilitated would result from a conscious act of choice on the
part of the reader. Shaw was, however, charged with both offences
(which were, in the event, successful) and also with conspiring with
prostitutes:

to induce readers to resort to the said advertisers for the purpose of fornication
and of taking part in or witnessing other disgusting and immoral acts and
exhibitions, with intent thereby to debauch the morals as well of youth as
of divers other liege subjects of Our Lady the Queen and to raise and create
in their minds inordinate and lustful desires.

The Court of Appeal affirmed his conviction on the ground that there
was a substantive common-law offence of 'conduct calculated to corrupt public morals', hence any agreement to this end would amount
to an ordinary conspiracy to commit a crime. The House of Lords
eschewed this simple solution in favour of a general discretion to prosecute the perpetrator of any immoral (as distinct from criminal) conduct which injures the public, under the all-purpose rubric of 'conspiracy to corrupt public morals'. Any publication which might 'lead
astray morally' could be made the subject-matter of prosecution,
whether or not it fell within the statutory definition of obscenity, so
long as more than one person was involved in the decision to publish.

The decision in *Shaw's case* offends against the legal principle of
nullum crimen sine lege by permitting the courts to incriminate in retrospect actions which seemed to be legal, if morally dubious, at the time
they were committed. Lord Reid, in his notable dissent, protested that:

the law will be whatever any jury may happen to think it ought to be, and
this branch of the law will have lost all the certainty which we rightly prize
in other branches of our law.[13]

The majority in *Shaw* met this objection by an appeal to the infalli-
bility of the British system of trial by jury. Twelve good men and true
were as capable of perceiving a derogation from essential moral standards as they were of judging breaches in standards of care in civil
actions for negligence. Lord Morris thought that moral standards
were crystal clear: 'there are certain manifestations of conduct ...
which all well-disposed persons will stigmatize and condemn as
deserving of punishment'.[14] Lord Hodson reasoned that:

In the field of public morals it will thus be the morality of the man in the
jury box that will determine the fate of the accused, but this should hardly

disturb the equanimity of anyone brought up in the traditions of our common law.[15]

What lawyers concerned with the future of the common law found disturbing, however, was that they were unable to advise publishers whether an agreement to encourage adultery might now be a criminal offence, since in *Shaw*, Lord Hodson did 'not see any reason why a conspiracy to encourage fornication and adultery should be regarded as outside the ambit of a conspiracy to corrupt public morals'.[16] In *R. v. Knuller*, decided a decade later, Lord Morris expressed a similar view:

if by agreement it was arranged to insert advertisements by married people, proclaiming themselves to be such and to be desirous of meeting someone of the opposite sex with a view to clandestine sexual association, would it be a justification to say that adultery is not of itself a criminal offence?[17]

But in a case decided only one year after *Knuller*, Lord Cross confidently asserted that 'no one could seriously suggest' that an agreement to commit adultery could amount to a criminal conspiracy.[18] If House of Lords judges could not agree on such a basic question, there seemed little prospect that the morality of the man in the jury box would provide a consistent answer.

Although the *Shaw* decision was widely and bitterly criticized,[19] between 1964 and 1966 the Director of Public Prosecutions had managed to secure the conviction of 120 persons for conspiring to subvert the nation's morals.[20] Some of his victims were 'blue movie' moguls whose activities at the time fell outside the scope of the Obscene Publications Act, but others were sellers of erotic literature who had also been charged under that Act. In one remarkable case in 1967, the defendants were found guilty of conspiring to corrupt public morals by 'producing and offering for sale certain whips, leg irons, wrist irons, arm restrictors, belts, straps, chains, gags, hoods, masks, head harnesses, chastity belts, restrictive equipment and other articles, rubber and leather garments . . .'[21] The high-watermark of 'swinging London' was undoubtedly reached when men were convicted at the Old Bailey of conspiring to sell chastity belts.

By 1970, the only thing that was swinging was the pendulum of the DPP, who now launched a conspiracy campaign against the underground press. *I. T. (International Times)* was the first casualty, when its editors were convicted for publishing a 'Gentlemen's Directory' among their classified advertisements. The prosecution evidence established that these advertisements were answered by homosexuals, either by direct contact with the advertisers or through a box number service provided by the magazine. The advertisements appeared in a column headed 'Males', which carried the warning that 'it is illegal for minors to place ads in this classification, or for advertisers to seek to contact minors (under 21)'. The advertisements were of the sort:

Alert young designer, 30, seeks warm, friendly pretty boy under 23, who needs regular sex, reliability and beautiful surroundings. If the cap fits and you need a friend, write.

Good-looking boy, 23, desperately wants pretty younger boyfriend. All photos, letters answered.

Male (32) seeks younger male for genuine friend. Versatile/passive phase. Looks immaterial, but must be virile, quiet disposition. I have own house, would suit working boy, of boyish nature, for weekends or share house together.

In *Shaw* the Law Lords had condemned advertising for partners to share abnormal sex, even when the practice was not illegal and was to be performed in private. When homosexuality between consenting male adults was legalized, 'Would it not be an offence if, even without obscenity, such practices were publicly advocated and encouraged by pamphlets and advertisement?', Viscount Simonds had asked, rhetorically and prophetically.[22] The editors of *I. T.* had not studied Viscount Simonds' *obiter dicta* with sufficient care.[23] Counsel for *I.T.* argued that the advertisements were permissible since the passing of the 1967 Sexual Offences Act, which had decriminalized buggery and gross indecency between consenting male adults. They were merely public invitations to do in private actions which were now within the law. But the House of Lords held that conspiracy to corrupt public morals may be committed whether the actions advertised are legal or not, so long as, in the jury's opinion, the encouragement of them strikes at the nation's moral fibre. A jury was entitled to decide that an agreement to insert advertisements in a magazine for the purpose of facilitating homosexual relationships subverted the moral standards it wished to enforce. *I. T.* was fined £1000 and its editors sentenced to eighteen months imprisonment, suspended for two years.

Knuller provided an opportunity for the House of Lords to reconsider its decision in *Shaw*. Lord Diplock urged reversal: the crime of conspiracy to corrupt public morals, he argued at length, did not exist. 'The vice of *Shaw's case* was that it opened a wide field of uncertainty as to what other conduct was also criminal ... it would seem that any conduct of any kind which conflicts with widely held prejudices as to what is immoral and indecent, at any rate if at least two persons are in any way concerned with it, may *ex post facto* be held to have been a crime.'[24] But Lord Reid, who had expressed an identical view in his dissent in *Shaw*, now turned this uncertainty argument on its head. Since 1961 it had been certain, as a result of *Shaw*, that this form of conspiracy existed, and many prosecutions had been brought in the intervening years. The offence did not exist until it was created by *Shaw*, but 'however wrong or anomalous the decision may be it must stand and apply to cases reasonably analogous unless or until it is altered by Parliament'.[25] Lord Morris reaffirmed his faith in the ability of an English jury to discern attacks on essential moral standards. Lord Simon, who as Solicitor-General had argued the Crown case in *Shaw*, was the only judge to face up to the full implications of the uncertainty argument. He maintained that the degree of legal certainty demanded by critics of the *Shaw* decision 'cannot be vouch-safed by a system of law such as ours which depends in so many of its rules on the finding by a tribunal of fact whether the conduct in question viewed as a whole has reached a certain standard or degree – frequently the standard of the reasonable man'.[26] He cited in support of this thesis a number of examples drawn from the civil law, which are not analogous with criminal offences because infringements of civil standards of reasonableness entail compensation, and not punishment. He also relied upon cases of criminal negligence, such as motor manslaughter, which pivot upon standards of reason-ableness. But any uncertainty in such cases results not from the standard itself, which is clear, but from its *application* by a particular tribunal. The objection to 'conspiracy to corrupt public morals' is that the test of liability is ambiguous and hypothetical, unlike the yardstick of guilt for motor manslaughter, which requires negligence to the degree of 'disregard for the life and safety of others'.[27] Even the test of obscenity, which requires a tendency to deprave and corrupt a significant proportion of likely readers, is more comprehensible than a formula which requires a jury to consider whether a magazine tends to 'debauch and corrupt the morals as well of youth as of divers other liege subjects of our Lady the Queen'.

The House of Lords in *Knuller* did respond to the criticisms of *Shaw* by clarifying the ingredients of the offence of conspiracy to corrupt public morals in a number of ways which limit its future application:

1 The defendant must *intend* to corrupt public morals in the manner

alleged in the indictment. The prosecution had to prove that the editors of *I. T.* inserted the advertisements with shared intention to debauch and corrupt the morals of their readers by encouraging them to indulge in homosexual conduct.[28] In this respect, at least, the conspiracy charge is harder for the prosecution to prove than an obscenity offence, in which the defendant's intention is irrelevant.[29]

2 The jury must be told that 'corrupt' is a strong word. It implies a much more potent influence than merely 'leading astray morally', which was the definition approved in *Shaw*. The jury must keep current standards in mind,[30] and not be given 'too gentle a paraphrase or explanation' of the formula.[31] 'The words "corrupt public morals" suggest conduct which a jury might find to be destructive of the very fabric of society.'[32]

3 The essence of the offence was not the publication of a magazine, but the use of that publication to procure the advancement of conduct which the jury considered corrupt. The corruption in *Knuller* did not arise from obscenity, but from 'the whole apparatus of liaison organized by the appellants'.[33] The jury may have decided that the only objectionable advertisements were those which might attract under-age youths, as distinct from practising adult homosexuals, when published in a magazine bought by thousands of young persons.

4 The charge does not invite 'a general tangling with codes of morality'.[34] The courts possess no residual power to create new offences, despite Viscount Simonds' dicta to the contrary in *Shaw*. The conspiracy charge should only be applied to 'reasonably analogous' new circumstances.[35]

5 Dicta in *Shaw* to the effect that homosexual contact advertising, or any other sort of encouragement to homosexuality, would amount to a corruption of public morality are not statements of law. In every case it is for the jury to decide, as an issue of fact, whether the conduct alleged amounts to public corruption.[36]

6 Prosecutions for conspiracy should not be brought against publishers who would, if charged under the Obscene Publications Act, be entitled to raise a 'public good' defence. An undertaking to this effect was given to Parliament by the Law Officers in 1964, and it should be honoured by the legal profession.[37] Lord Diplock thought that the undertaking had been breached by the way the case against *I. T.* had been presented to the jury.

7 It may be that publications which could be justified as being for the public good could not in any event form the subject matter of a conspiracy to corrupt public morals. Expert evidence may be admissible to show that an agreement conduced to public good rather than harm.[38]

8 Evidence of the effect of a publication on its readers, which is strictly inadmissible on an obscenity charge, may be introduced at a conspiracy trial by either party. Police had gathered evidence of the effect of *I. T.* advertisements on readers who had responded to them, and the prosecution justified the decision to proceed by way of conspiracy rather than obscenity on the ground that this evidence would not otherwise have been admissible.[39]

The 'conspiracy to corrupt' charge has been used sparingly since the decision in *Knuller*. The *Oz* editors were acquitted of the offence because the jury was not satisfied that they intended to corrupt their readers.[40] *Oz* carried advertisements which catered to a wide variety of sexual fetishes, and provided the same 'box number' services as *I. T.* Experts testified that this 'apparatus of liaison' provided a social service for sexual minorities, and the prosecution was unable to show that any reader had suffered by taking advantage of the facility. In 1973 a Portsmouth jury was unable to agree about a publication similar to the *Ladies Directory*, despite evidence that it had attracted a response from public-schoolboys in search of prostitutes. In 1975 the DPP eschewed the charge entirely in an indictment against *Gay Circle*, a publication consisting entirely of homosexual contact advertisements.[41] The editor was charged instead with conspiracy to procure acts of gross indecency with under-aged males (contrary to section 13 of the 1956 Sexual Offences Act and section 4 (3) of the Sexual Offences Act 1967) and to procure acts of buggery (contrary to section 4 (1) of the 1967 Act) – charges which could equally have been preferred against *I. T.*[42] However it is doubtful whether mere publication of straightforward contact advertisements would carry sufficient element of persuasion to amount to 'procuration': in such cases the initiative to partake in sexual activity does not come from the editor, but from the reader who voluntarily chooses to respond.[43]

In 1973 the 'conspiracy to corrupt public morals' charge was given a new dimension by the indictment in *R.* v. *Brooks*, which charged heroin peddlers with conspiring 'to corrupt the morals of such persons as might consume heroin by procuring quantities of heroin and supplying the same to members of the public in and in the vicinity

of Gerard Street, London W. 1'.[44] The crime had hitherto been confined to persons who publicly cater for minority sexual tastes in ways
which might not be caught by existing legislation. *R.* v. *Brooks* was
clearly an attempt to do for public morals what the 1965 case of *Calder*
v. *Powell* did within the context of the Obscene Publications Act –
namely to justify the classification of drug-taking as an *immoral*
activity, quite apart from its illegality.[45] Movements to legalize cannabis, or agreements to publish the work of writers who treat drug-
taking sympathetically, might be indictable under the broad arc of
conspiracy to corrupt public morals.

Prostitution, homosexuality, and wife-swapping are all practices
which are legal when performed by consenting adults. Judges have
nevertheless decided that it is against public policy to promote them.
There is a material difference, it is said, between merely exempting
certain conduct from criminal penalties, and making it lawful in the full
sense. The problem is first to isolate those types of non-criminal conduct which are 'not lawful in the full sense' (the list is apparently
never closed, for 'who can foretell the ways in which the wickedness
of man may disrupt society?'), and, secondly, to decide whether publications which deal with such conduct amount to a 'promotion'. Does
an advertisement for a Gay Liberation Front Meeting 'promote'
homosexuality? It is open under the present law for a jury to say that
it does, and therefore that it constitutes a threat to public morals.
The crime of conspiracy to corrupt public morals was expressly preserved by section 5 (3) of the 1977 Criminal Law Act, but the failure
of Parliament to provide any legislative guidance in this difficult area
allows prosecuting authorities a potentially wide discretion to harass
and embarrass sexual minorities.

OUTRAGING PUBLIC DECENCY

The residual power of the courts to fashion new common-law crimes
as a means of enforcing 'good manners and decency' was not used
against offensive publications after 1727, when the crime of obscene
libel was created to deal specifically with immoral books and pamphlets. The common-law offence of outraging public decency was confined to indecent exposure of the person (exhibitionism,[46] sexual
intercourse in public,[47] and nude bathing[48]) and encouragements to
women to take up prostitution.[49] Non-sexual acts which 'outraged
decency' by 'revolting nature' included disinterring a corpse,[50] exhibiting deformed children,[51] and selling a wife.[52] The only reported

cases before 1960 which involved any form of publication were *R.
v. Grey*, where a herbalist displayed a disgusting picture of a man
covered in sores in his shop window,[53] and *R. v. Saunders*, when touts
for an indecent exhibition used crude language in public to encourage
entry to their booth on Epsom Downs.[54] These cases hinged on public
nuisance rather than publication, which was always charged as
obscene libel.

The 1959 Obscene Publications Act abolished the offence of
obscene libel, and prosecutors were forced to rely upon other 'un-
ravished remnants of the common law' to punish publishers whose
products offended but did not corrupt. The first extension of the
offence of exposing an indecent exhibition to public view occurred
when a count of 'conspiracy to outrage public decency' was added to
the indictment in *Knuller*. The prosecution argued that the crime was
committed when the editors agreed to distribute by public sale a newspaper with outrageously indecent contents, even though the alleged
indecency was confined to a column of classified advertisements on
an inside page. By a bare majority the House of Lords confirmed the
existence both of the substantive offence of 'outraging public decency'
and of a conspiracy to commit it, although the editors' conviction
on this count was overturned because the trial judge had not adequately explained the ingredients of the offence in his summing up.
Features of the offence were said to be:

1 The indecency alleged need not be immediately visible on the
   cover of the article. All that is required is public sale of books or
   magazines which contain grossly indecent inside pages.[55]

2 The contents relied upon must be so lewd, disgusting and offensive
   that the sense of decency of members of the public would be
   outraged by seeing or reading them.[56] 'Outrage', like 'corrupt', is
   a strong word, and goes considerably beyond offending the susceptibilities of, or even shocking, reasonable people. The jury must be
   told to apply modern standards, and 'to remember that they live
   in a plural society, with a tradition of tolerance towards minorities,
   and that this atmosphere of toleration is itself part of public
   decency'.[57]

3 The requirement of outraging *public* feelings must be related to that
   section of the public likely to frequent the place where the publication is sold. In this respect 'public decency' must be distinguished
   from 'public morals': the latter refers to standards accepted by the

general public, and upheld by all law abiding citizens. But 'public decency' refers to the feelings of that section of the general public likely to be exposed to the offending material. The prospect of outrage must be related to the time and place of the exhibition, and a different test would apply to publications of restricted availability.[58]

4 Although the offending content need not be visible to passers-by, the indecency must in some way be projected so as to have an impact in public. There must be some invitation, express or implied, to penetrate the cover and partake of the offensive display.[59] If the defendants had hired touts, or advertised the indecency of their product, or made reference on the cover of a book or magazine to indecent matter within, they would presumably have satisfied this requirement.

5 The offence is objective, in the sense that the motive of the publisher is irrelevant. The prosecution must prove that the defendant was aware of the offending contents, and knew that the article would be placed on public sale. If its contents can rationally be regarded as outrageously indecent he is liable to conviction, even if he did not intend to cause offence.[60]

6 Protection for genuine works of art and literature is provided by the Law Officers' undertaking that conspiracy will not be charged so as to circumvent the statutory defence of 'public good' in the Obscene Publications Act. The spirit and intendment of this assurance applies to the offence of conspiracy to outrage public decency as well as to the offence of conspiracy to corrupt public morals.[61]

The history of obscenity legislation since 1959 has been marked by one consistent theme, a steadfast refusal to allow conviction of editors and publishers whose work had not spread moral corruption. The *Oz* conviction was overturned precisely because the trial judge had sought to introduce the notions of 'outrage' and 'disgust' into the definition of obscenity. This whole philosophy may now be subverted by charging a common-law offence which catches publications which merely shock some members of the public, without posing any danger to their mind or morals. The Law Officers' undertaking cannot bind a private prosecutor, and in any event would apply only to those publications which prosecuting authorities deem to be meritorious. The offence would apply to television and radio programmes, although its application to films and theatre has been removed by statute.[62]

In *Knuller*, Lord Reid warned that the new offence could chill reputable publishing:

> If there were in any book, new or old, a few pages or even a few sentences which any jury could find to be outrageously indecent, those who took part in its publication and sale would risk conviction. I can see no way of denying to juries the free hand which *Shaw's* case gives them in cases of conspiracy to corrupt public morals.... Notoriously many old works, commonly regarded as classics of the highest merit, contain passages which many jurymen might regard as outrageously indecent. It has been generally supposed that the days of bowdlerizing the classics were long past, but the introduction of this new crime might make publishers of such works think twice. It may be said that no prosecution would ever be brought except in a very bad case. But I have expressed on previous occasions my opinion that a bad law is not defensible on the ground that it will be judiciously administered. To recognize this new crime would go contrary to the whole trend of public policy followed by Parliament in recent times.[63]

Parliament expressly preserved conspiracy to outrage public decency in the Criminal Law Act of 1977, although no further prosecution has been brought since *I. T.* – an indication that the offence serves no real purpose. Lord Simon defended its judicial creation on the grounds that reasonable people should be able to venture out in public without suffering outrage, but this protection is specifically provided by the Vagrancy and Indecent Advertisement Acts. Even assuming that minimum standards are generally recognizable, the common law goes far beyond the legal limit necessary to safeguard them. Timid maiden aunts are hardly deterred from venturing out-of-doors by fear of sighting a classified column buried in an underground newspaper, the appreciation of which requires close scrutiny of small type on an inside page. A law which penalizes publication of matter which might outrage members of a particular jury, even when tucked away in a minority publication likely to be purchased only by persons who would *not* be offended, is a wholly unnecessary restriction on free speech.

KEEPING A DISORDERLY HOUSE

The judicial widening of 'conspiracy' to punish modern manifestations of permissive mores has encouraged the revival of other relics of the common law. The offence of 'keeping a disorderly house' was created in the eighteenth century to 'correct as far as may be the habit of idleness which is become too general over the whole kingdom, and is productive of much mischief' because of 'the multitude of places of entertainment for the lower sort of people ... (who) are thereby tempted to spend their small substance in riotous pleasure'.[64] The earliest reported case concerned a premises where 'certain evil and ill-disposed persons ... came there to be and remain ... fighting of cocks, boxing, playing at cudgels and misbehaving themselves ... to the great damage and common nuisance of all'[65]. The crime was created by the courts in order to control entertainments which got out of hand and created a public nuisance, and it was used in the nineteenth century against unlicensed dance halls and notorious brothels. In the 1961 case of *R.* v. *Quinn & Bloom* it was refurbished by the Court of Appeal to punish over-enthusiastic strip-tease performances. In a decision heavily influenced by the 'residual power' theory in *Shaw*, which was to be rejected a decade later in *Knuller*, the Court propounded the following definition:

A disorderly house is a house conducted contrary to law and good order in that matters are performed or exhibited of such a character that their performance or exhibition in a place of common resort (a) amounts to an outrage of public decency or (b) tends to corrupt or deprave or (c) is otherwise calculated to injure the public interest so as to call for condemnation and punishment.[66]

The offence of keeping a disorderly house was abolished in respect of gaming clubs and theatres in 1968, and film shows were exempted by the Criminal Law Act of 1977. It is still applicable to places of refreshment or entertainment which feature live performances with sexual overtones, if these presentations do not involve the acting of a dramatic role so as to amount to a 'play' for the purposes of the Theatres Act. The offence in practice covers those strip clubs, discotheques, massage parlours, sauna baths, pub shows and variety performances which feature acts which outrage public decency. The two alternative tests provided by subsections (b) and (c) of the *Quinn & Bloom* definition are seldom relied upon: the test of outrage to public decency is wider than, and must necessarily include, any proven element of depravity or corruption, and the test of whether the conduct is 'calculated to injure the public interest so as to call for condemnation and punishment' is inconsistent with the decision in *Knuller* that the courts no longer have any residual power to punish immoral conduct which does not fall within established statutory or common-law prohibitions. Lord Simon in *Knuller* described keeping a disorderly house as an example of conduct which outrages public decency, and in both offences the jury must be directed that 'outrage' is a very strong word, going beyond offending the susceptibilities of, or even shocking, reasonable people.[67] Other ingredients of the disorderly house offence are:

1 There must be an element of persistency about the use of premises for indecent performances. Evidence that outrageous routines crept into a long-running variety show on only one or two nights will not suffice.[68] There must also be evidence of persistent indecency throughout the course of the performance. In *Quinn & Bloom*, eight of the seventeen items on the programme caused offence. In one 1976 prosecution, *R.* v. *Cinecentre Limited*, Mr Justice Bush directed the jury to 'look at the films as a whole. You look for an element of persistency. You do not condemn the defendants if there is only one film or only one isolated incident which you regard as outraging public decency.'[69]

2 The premises must be a 'place of common resort', and it is for the jury to decide, on the facts of each case, whether there has been 'an element of keeping open house'.[70] An entrance fee would not exclude the offence, but a jury might find that a well-regulated club, which had proper procedures for vetting all prospective members, could not be characterized as an 'open house'. In prosecutions of cinema clubs prior to the 1977 Criminal Law Act the Crown claimed that membership regulations were mere shams, and plain-clothes policemen invariably testified that they were permitted to enter either immediately or after a derisorily short 'waiting time'.

3 Although the disorderly house offence, as its name implies, was created by the courts to punish encouragement to unruly behaviour by 'lewd and immoral persons' at places of public entertainment, the prosecution is not required to show that any disorder broke out among spectators. In *Quinn & Bloom* the Court of Appeal upheld convictions in a case where members of a strip club were said to be respectable persons who behaved with propriety during the performance. However any evidence of misbehaviour triggered by on-stage indecency is admissible to show that the performance was 'calculated to stir the emotions of the audience'.[71]

4 The nature of a live performance will have to be imagined by the

jury from verbal evidence of police observations and the recollections of defence witnesses. No 'public good' defence may be
advanced, and in *Quinn & Bloom* the Court of Appeal ruled that
a filmed reconstruction of a strip-tease act was inadmissible as evidence of what happened on the dates set out in the indictment.
There was no guarantee that the filmed performance would coincide, motion for motion, with the live show, because 'some of the
movements in the film (for instance that of a snake used in one
scene) could not be said with any certainty to be the same movements as were made at the material time'.[72] English law offers no
solution to the problem which bedevilled the American satirist
Lenny Bruce, who complained that he was never convicted for his
own night-club routine, he was always blamed for bad imitations
of his act performed by policemen on witness stands.

5 Consistent with Lord Simon's definition of 'outraging public
decency' in *Knuller*, and with Lord Reid's references to 'open and
notorious lewdness' in the context of disorderly house offences in
Shaw, it would seem that the indecent performance 'must at least
in some way be so projected as to have an impact in public'.[73] Newspaper advertisements for strip shows, or posters indicating the
risqué nature of live performances, would presumably fulfil this
condition.

6 Recent cases suggest that the 'public' which must be protected from
having its sense of decency outraged is not the general public, but
those of its members who are likely to frequent the premises alleged
to constitute the disorderly house. In *Knuller*, Lord Simon emphasized that in this class of offence 'public' refers to the place in which
the offence is committed. This is borne out ... by what is presumably the purpose of the legal rule – namely, that reasonable people
may venture out in public without the risk of outrage to certain
minimum accepted standards of decency.'[74]

In the *Cinecentre* case, Mr Justice Bush directed the jury to

ask yourselves having regard to (1) the place in and the circumstances under
which the films were shown, and (2) the quality of people who were likely
to attend the performances, was there an outrage of public decency? In
respect of (2) that is an outrage to those who are likely to go to see the
performances ... a film shown in one place – for example a church fete
– might outrage public decency, whereas shown in another place it might
not.[75]

It follows from this dicta that the jury should not consider the impact that the performance might have on ordinary members of the public, but must concentrate on any outrage to the feelings of those members of the community who would be likely to watch the performance. The logical difficulty with this approach is that strip shows, massage parlours and the like usually attract persons who enjoy indecent behaviour, and who would only be 'outraged' if the performance did not live up to their expectations. On the other hand, if a rigidly objective test of community standards were to apply, club shows would be artificially judged by the susceptibilities of persons who would never choose to see them. This dilemma could be resolved by implementation of the Law Commission's recommendation that the test of obscenity should replace that of outraging decency as the criterion of criminality for live entertainment.

7 The prosecution must prove that each defendant 'kept' the premises, within the meaning of section 8 of the 1751 Disorderly Houses Act. This ancient legislation recites that:

> Whereas, by reason of the many subtle and crafty contrivances of persons keeping bawdy-houses, gaming-houses, or other disorderly houses, it is difficult to prove who is the real owner or keeper thereof, by which means many notorious offenders have escaped punishment: be it enacted by the authority aforesaid, that any person who shall at any time hereafter appear, act, or behave him or herself as master or mistress, or as the person having the care, government, or management of any bawdy-house, gaming-house or other disorderly house, shall be deemed and taken to be the keeper thereof, and shall be liable to be prosecuted and punished as such, notwithstanding he or she shall not in fact be the real owner or keeper thereof.

Neither performers nor members of the audience have the 'care government or management' of the house. Brothel-keeping cases suggest that landlords also fall outside the prohibition, even though they collect rent in full awareness that their premises are continually used for immoral purposes.[76] In 1964 it was held that 'management' implies the taking of an active or controlling part in the business, 'something a cut above purely menial or routine duties, such as cleaning the stairs or answering the door'.[77] In *Jacobs v. Bryor*, the choreographer and musical director of a dance hall conceded to be a disorderly house were acquitted on a direction that the jury 'are to be satisfied that the defendants appeared, not only as managers of their respective departments, but as masters or managers of the house'.[78] Mere employees, such as waiters, projectionists and doormen, cannot be convicted in the absence of evidence that they played some proprietorial role in the establishment. Those who perform the indecent acts, or who tout for custom, are immune from the 'disorderly house' charge, although they may be prosecuted for the offence of outraging public decency by participating in, or aiding and abetting, an indecent exhibition.

There is no limit to the financial or custodial penalties which a court may impose upon those guilty of keeping a disorderly house, although recent cases have stressed the principle that an affront to public decency must be treated less severely than conduct which corrupts morals. Where sexual acts are merely simulated by performers, the courts will generally impose a fine tailored to the profits of the enterprise: in *R. v. Quinn & Bloom* Paul Raymond was fined £5,000. A prison sentence may be appropriate where sexual intercourse takes place, especially as a result of invitations to members of the audience. The severest sentence for running a disorderly house – thirty months imprisonment and a fine of £1,000 – was imposed on the organiser of 'heterosexual, homosexual, bestial, sadistic and necrophilial performances'. The Court of Appeal dismissed his appeal against imprisonment, adding tersely that it was 'not a moment too long'. Other matters which aggravate the offence are pressure on performers to behave indecently, encouragement of audience participation, disorderliness and public nuisance, and the presence in the audience of children or persons who had not been led to expect erotic entertainment. In *R. v. Farmer* the Court of Appeal substituted a fine of £1,000 for a jail sentence which had been imposed on a publican who hosted over-enthusiastic lunch-time strip shows:

This kind of case is beginning to come before the courts in many parts of the country and it is the experience of this court that they vary very greatly in character. Sometimes adolescent girls are involved. Very occasionally animal acts are involved. In those sort of cases there is clearly a corrupting element. Also on occasions the kind of exhibition is a real outrage to public decency. That is a factor which has to be taken into consideration. But the court has thought it necessary to analyse the facts of this case carefully. First of all it has looked to see who these so-called striptease artists were. They certainly were not young girls. They perhaps could be described – I hope not unfairly – as middle-aged strippers nearing retirement age. The police estimated the age of one as forty or thereabouts, and the age of the other as about thirty-five. There cannot have been much of a corrupting element about asking them to perform in this public house in the middle of the day. Secondly the evidence was to the effect that there were no youngsters in the bar, no-one under the age of eighteen. If men go along in the middle of the day and spend their money watching this kind of entertainment it really is quite unrealistic to think of them as being corrupted by it. If there is any corruption about the matter, they are well on the way to corruption in paying their 50p. There was no evidence that there was any disorder. Sometimes on these occasions as a result of a combination of erotic excitement and drink disorder does break out. That was not this case. Although the activities of these two striptease artists were crude and to most people distasteful, it was not so crude and so distasteful that this court can say that there was an outrage to public decency. There was an affront to public decency, but not much more than that.[80]

THE CASE AGAINST CONSPIRACY

The chief requirement of the rule of law is certainty: no citizen should be declared a criminal unless he has broken a specific rule established before he offended against it. But the crimes of conspiracy to corrupt morals and outrage decency are so uncertain that judges and prosecuting authorities act as pile-drivers, staking out the bounds of criminality from case to case. Conspiracy charges may catch activities which are outside both the criminal and the civil law, as a result of their use 'to guard the moral welfare of the state against attacks which may be the more insidious because they are novel and unprepared for', by punishing conduct which jurors dislike but which Parliament has not seen fit to make illegal. For the Law Commission,

> It seems to us not merely desirable but obligatory that legal rules imposing serious criminal sanctions should be stated with the maximum clarity which the imperfect medium of language can attain. The offence of conspiring to do an unlawful act offends against that precept in two ways. First, it is impossible in some cases even to state the rules relating to the object of criminal agreements, except in terms which are at best tautologous and unenlightening. Secondly, in those cases where at least a statement of the offence is possible, that statement covers such a wide range of conduct that it is impossible to decide whether an offence has been committed or not.[81]

The law against corrupting public morals is predicated upon the hypothesis that there is one all-embracing moral code to which all classes of the community subscribe – a notion which sociologists have demonstrated to be wishful thinking. Moreover, this assumed moral consensus is further assumed by the conspiracy law to be so vulnerable that a single publication is capable of jeopardizing it. It is not illegal to take advantage of a prostitute's services, but to facilitate this, to help shortcut the sordid and possibly dangerous process of tramping red light districts by publishing a prostitute's telephone number, may be a serious crime. By allowing juries in effect to make law by deciding what constitutes a corruption of public morality, while at the same time recognizing that standards change over time and one jury's nightmare may be another jury's bedtime reading, the criminal law is thrown into an unacceptable state of uncertainty: a man who publishes contact advertisements does not know, until twelve arbitrarily chosen people return with their verdict, whether he has done a public service or a grave criminal wrong. Retrospective legislation in criminal matters is abhorred in legal philosophy because of its unfairness: it is thought to be almost a defining characteristic of 'law' that it be understandable and acceptable in advance, so that citizens can order their conduct to avoid transgressions. But 'conspiracy to corrupt public morals' is such a vague and dragnet charge that it is impossible to predict the scope of the law's operation before a jury returns its verdict.

These objections apply even more strongly to the new head of conspiracy discovered by the prosecutors of *I. T.* – conspiracy to outrage public decency. The ambit of this charge is alarming: it need not be confined to sexual matters, but could provide a potent weapon against the expression of unpopular (and therefore outrageous) ideas. Films portraying violence or sex, articles advocating abolition of the monarchy, legalization of LSD or euthanasia, or indeed photographs of war atrocities, could all be said to 'outrage public decency' by disgusting and offending an ordinary viewer. The majority of judges in *Shaw* and *Knuller* were complacent about the operation of the law because of their unbounded confidence that juries will administer it reasonably. But there have no doubt been juries assembled whose personnel could be convinced by a skilful prosecutor that computer dating programmes, sex education, communist propaganda, and advertisements for VD clinics are all harbingers of moral decadence.

In *Shaw's* case Lord Reid protested that the legislation of morality is a matter for politicians, and 'where Parliament fears to tread it is not for the courts to rush in'. This accords with the democratic political theory that government depends on the consent of the governed, and obedience is owed to laws passed or approved by a majority of elected representatives. In the seventeenth century, when these common-law offences were created, Parliament met infrequently and was in any case subservient to the sovereign. It was convenient that the King's Judges should have the power to develop the criminal law on a case-by-case basis, punishing new forms of public nuisance as they arose. But the subsequent development of the law-making role of Parliament, to the point reached today where it meets with sufficient regularity to legislate against any undesirable conduct, makes it unnecessary for judges to wield a power to make new criminal laws, or to stretch existing laws to cover novel situations. While politicians are drawn from all strata of society, and are despatched to Westminster as representatives with a mandate to legislate, judges live socially isolated lives and may desire to enforce moral values at odds with those held by many classes within the community. Moreover, laws which originate in Parliament are subjected to scrutiny by expert draftsmen and lawyers, parliamentary debate and amendment, submissions from interested bodies, public criticism and publicity which warns potential offenders of the penalty in store. Developments in the common law are noted only in dusty volumes of law reports quite inaccessible to the general public, and require extrapolation from discursive and sometimes contradictory speeches in cases like *Shaw* and *Knuller*.

In the sphere of morals, the development of the common law may cloak judicial impatience, even disagreement, with legislative liberality. In 1972, for example, the *Longford Report* urged the adoption of a law which would punish the publication of material whose effect 'is to outrage contemporary standards of decency or humanity accepted by the public at large'. This recommendation aroused widespread controversy, and the then Home Secretary expressly rejected it. But that same year, unobtrusively and entirely without public comment, three House of Lords judges decided that since the common law already contained the power to punish outrages to contemporary standards of decency, there was nothing to stop the DPP indicting publishers for conspiracy to produce books or magazines which are merely offensive or embarrassing. Parliament has not yet prohibited the publication of prostitutes' telephone numbers, or forbidden adult homosexuals to advertise for partners. The illegality of these practices has been decreed by retrospective approval of prosecutions undertaken by the DPP against activities which are stigmatized as 'more insidious' because Parliament has never thought of passing a law against them – the very reason why they should not have been prosecuted in the first place.

Common-law conspiracy charges carry a number of tactical advantages unavailable to the prosecution in proceedings brought under the Obscene Publications Act. In law, 'conspiracy' is merely an agreement, and not necessarily a legally binding or even a serious agreement. 'A nod or a wink may amount to a conspiracy,' juries are usually told. All the prosecution has to prove is that the defendants made an agreement to publish: if the jury decides that what they agreed to publish is immoral or outrageous, then a 'guilty' verdict should follow. Agreements to advertise the services of prostitutes or to facilitate homosexual get-togethers are serious crimes if a particular jury finds prostitution or homosexuality grossly offensive. It is irrelevant that no member of the public has in fact been corrupted or outraged, so long as the jury is satisfied that an agreement was made. In 1964 the Solicitor-General gave a categorical assurance to the House of Commons that conspiracy proceedings would never be used 'so as to attempt to evade the statutory defence of public good',[82] but the prosecution of *I. T.* for conspiracy rather than obscenity in 1970 did exactly that, by denying the editors the opportunity of justifying their advertisements.

When a defendant is charged only with an offence against the 1959 Obscene Publications Act his intention in publishing the material is irrelevant. But where a conspiracy to corrupt morals charge is added to an obscenity indictment, as it was in *Shaw* and the *Oz* case, the prosecution can blacken a defendant's character and arouse jury prejudice against him with evidence which would otherwise be inadmissible on the obscenity charge. Thus the *Oz* editors were kept in the witness box for days, and cross-examined about their views on group sex, permissiveness, drugs and other issues on which their opinions might have been too libertarian for the jury to stomach. A conspiracy count can put the whole life-style of the accused on trial: he can be convicted for what he is and for what he believes, and not just for what people do after reading something he once published. The addition of the conspiracy count turned the *Oz* proceedings into a political trial: the prosecution pilloried the ideas and the 'dangerous doctrines' of the defendants and their associates:

These accused men agreed to publish a magazine which would carry, as it had carried before, the banner of the alternative society. Look at that magazine and ask yourselves: 'What alternatives are there?' Dropping out of society. Expecting the state to provide, and by the state I mean nothing more than you and me – those of us who don't mind working, who think it's right to work, those of us whom advocates of the alternative society might describe as 'those foolish enough to work.' ...

You won't, I know, members of the jury, be too ready to sneer at accepted values as some of the witnesses in this case have done.... Right at the outset, you were told that *Oz* was undesirable from the family point of view. Members of the jury, that's a consideration for you to think about, because it is not right to be too ready to sneer at accepted values and to destroy everything we believed until now....[83]

It was once the proud boast of English law that 'the thought of man cannot be tried, for the devil himself knoweth not the thought of man'. The Star Chamber put paid to that when it fashioned the modern theory of conspiracy to mean in law merely an agreement. Once the mental act of agreement, the meeting of two or more minds, was made a crime, then men's thoughts could be put on trial, and their guilt could be deduced from their political opinions, their life-style, even their bedtime reading. Where a conspiracy charge is added to an obscenity indictment, there is a danger that even if acquitted of the conspiracy, some of the mud thrown pursuant to it will stick, and the jury, prejudiced against the defendants by what they have heard of their life-styles and beliefs, will be satisfied with less than conclusive proof before returning a 'guilty' verdict on the obscenity charge.

REFORM AND THE LAW COMMISSION

The common-law offences of holding an indecent exhibition, keeping a disorderly house, conspiring to corrupt public morals and outraging public decency have been criticized as being irrational in theory, undemocratic in origin, uncertain in scope, and unfair in operation. They owe their revival in part to a refusal to accept the 1959 legislative reforms embodied in the Obscene Publications Act and the Street Offences Act, and to the desire to punish manifestations of the permissive society which Parliament has not seen fit specifically to prohibit. Their use has in some respects been circumscribed: by the Law Officers' undertaking in 1964 that they would not be charged so as to deprive publishers of a 'public good' defence, and by their abolition in relation to theatrical performances (Theatres Act 1968) and film shows (Criminal Law Act 1977). In 1977 Parliament specifically preserved conspiracies to corrupt morals and outrage decency, despite no less than three exhaustive reports by the Law Commission which have urged their abolition, on the ground that

A law of conspiracy extending beyond the ambit of conspiracy to commit

234 THE COMMON LAW

crimes has, in our view, no place in a comprehensively planned criminal code.... It may be true that there is a danger of cases in which justice is apparently evaded. We regard this as an inevitable and acceptable price to pay in order to avoid the creation of oppressive 'catch all' offences. If there are to be such offences, we believe that their creation is a matter for Parliament....[84]

After surveying all the cases brought at common law since 1959, the Commission concluded that outright abolition of these offences would not preclude prosecuting authorities from proceeding in proper cases, once the Obscene Publications Act is extended to cover live performances.

Advertising for sex

The Law Commission takes the view that contact advertisements in the form of newspaper classifieds and display cards in kiosk windows are an acceptable price for 'driving the prostitute from the street'. Equally it must be in the public interest for adult homosexuals to make contact through advertisements rather than by sordid meetings in public parks and toilets, and for other sexual minorities to identify possible mates and shortcut the uncertainties and agonies of the social process. So long as the advertisements are decently worded, and do not involve invitations to illegal acts or the exploitation of children, it is difficult to maintain that they create a social mischief appropriate for redress by the criminal law. Individuals more interested in love than money should be entitled to advertise for partners with sexual proclivities similar to their own. Although the contacts which result may not often lead to happy long-term relationships, this must be in part the responsibility of a society which forces such people to meet in this way. It is no business of the law to seek to enforce profundity in human relationships.

The common law has occasionally been used against vendors of sexual accoutrements, and against street touts who solicit custom for obscene exhibitions. In neither case did the Law Commission recommend new legislation to fill any gap left by the abolition of common-law offences. 'Touting' is an act of assistance which can be prosecuted on the basis of criminal complicity, and requires no separate legal prohibition. Most instruments sold to enhance sexual pleasure have everyday uses. Any law which prohibited the sale of rubber, plastic and leather garments, exotic underwear, belts, straps, chains, hoods, surgical appliances, vibrators, unguents and other impedimenta of sexual fantasists would impinge upon the legitimate activities of pharmacies, boutiques, hospitals and hardware stores.

Live entertainment

The one area where legislation has not yet superseded the common law relates to live performances which fall outside the definition of 'play' or 'ballet' in section 18 of the 1968 Theatres Act. The Act applies the test of obscenity to 'any dramatic piece ... in which the whole or a major proportion ... involves the playing of a role'. This formula excludes most variety shows, strip-tease acts, stand-up comedians, tribal dancing and other forms of popular entertainment, which fall to be judged by the broader common-law standard of 'outraging public decency', unmitigated by any public good defence. There is no requirement that such entertainments be considered as a whole, or in relation to their actual impact upon the audience. Managers and licensees of premises where 'indecent' performances recur may be charged with 'keeping a disorderly house', while performers and producers are vulnerable to indictment for participating in outrageously indecent exhibitions. Clearly there is need for some legal regulation of this class of entertainmment, but it is anomalous that an identical act should be judged by a more stringent test when presented in a working man's club than when incorporated into a piece of West End theatre. Performances involving satire, comedy or modern dance routines are denied a legitimate claim to artistic merit, and are subjected to the standards of people who would not normally choose such forms of entertainment. The problem with 'live shows' is that they may go beyond simulation and titillation, and offer an opportunity for audience members to participate in sexual acts on stage – an invitation which would, if anything, tend to corrupt rather than provoke outrage to the sense of decency of those who, by seeking out such occasions, might be said to have little sense of decency at all.

The Law Commission, in recommending abolition of all common-law offences relating to morals and decency, accepts that live shows are one form of entertainment which require statutory regulation.[85] It suggests an extension of the Obscene Publications Act to punish those who present, organize or participate in any obscene live performance or display, subject to a defence of 'public good' if the entertainment is 'in the interests of drama, opera, ballet or any other art, or of literature or learning'.

This defence, lifted uncritically from the Theatres Act, focuses too narrowly upon conventional arts. Live entertainment often has a social or political dimension which deserves protection just as much as classic artistry. Police persecutions of Lenny Bruce ignored the social justification of his monologues which redeemed their overt crudity. One purpose of satire is to expose corruption, often by means of outrageous example, and any 'public good' defence should permit the advancement of such an aim. A good deal of 'vulgar' comedy has an entertainment value which should equally be reflected in any defence applicable to variety performances, otherwise the court-room appearances of Max Miller and his ilk may go unappreciated. Some modern dance routines possess an artistic merit which cannot be expressed in conventional balletic terms. The value of new and startling forms of artistry should at least be arguable in court, otherwise the law will discriminate against the avant-garde in a way which may in retrospect appear philistine.

BLASPHEMOUS LIBEL

Indecent descriptions applied to sacred subjects may amount to the recently revived crime of blasphemy, which evolved by the same process as the punishment of immorality, namely the assumption by the King's Courts in the seventeenth century of jurisdiction over ecclesiastical offences, in the interests of maintaining public order. Blasphemy began its legal life as a particular form of sedition. In 1617 Nicholas Atwood was fined for sneering at Anglican preachers, thereby attacking both the king and the law – the king in his capacity as head of the Church, and the law which had by this time established Anglicanism as the only official religion.[86] The offence of publishing a blasphemous libel was created by the courts in 1677 in order to punish John Taylor for denouncing orthodox religion as a cheat, Taylor being a madman who described Christ as a whoremaster, while claiming to be His younger brother. The House of Lords committed him to the keeper of Bedlam, with directions that he should be cured by a treatment of bread, water and bodily correction. His dementia persisted, so the Chief Justice recommended cure by common-law indictment, because 'many of the said words tend immediately to the Destruction of all Religion and Government'.[87] At the ensuing trial Taylor retained sufficient of his faculties to argue that his words had been misunderstood, but Lord Chief Justice Hale was unimpressed, for a crime against religion was a crime against the State, and

... to say, Religion is a Cheat, is to dissolve all those Obligations whereby the Civil societies are preserved, ... Christianity is a parcel of the laws of England and therefore to reproach the Christian religion is to speak in subversion of the law.[88]

Taylor was set in the pillory, wearing a placard inscribed 'For blasphemous words and tending to the subversion of all Government'.

Until the Darwinian revolution in the latter part of the nineteenth century, the offence was regularly used to punish attacks upon articles of Anglican belief, on the principle that strange gods might subvert familiar government. Even after religious toleration, the law protected only Anglican sensibilities. In 1838 Baron Alderson ruled that:

If this is only a libel on the whole Roman Catholic Church generally, the defendant is entitled to be acquitted. A person may, without being liable to prosecution for it, attack Judaism or Mahometanism; or even any sect of the Christian religion, save the established religion of the country.[89]

At the beginning of the nineteenth century the evangelical fervour of the Vice Society coincided with fear of French revolutionary atheism, to produce a rash of prosecutions against freethinkers and publishers of the works of Thomas Paine.[90] Blasphemy was irreverence, irrespective of motive: in 1840 the Attorney-General secured the conviction of a bookseller named Hetherington for publishing an attack on the violence and obscenity of the Old Testament, 'careless of the effect it might have on the morals of the unthinking working class'.[91] If workers needed protection against the unexpurgated Old Testament it seemed only fair that literary salons should be protected from the heretical imaginings of great poets, so Hetherington emerged from prison to secure the conviction of a respected bookseller for selling copies of Shelley's *Queen Mab*.[92] The stringency of the blasphemy law became an embarrassment to the Government: in 1851 the Law Officers reluctantly advised the Home Office that John Stuart Mill was liable to prosecution for expressing mildly agnostic views in a public lecture, although 'we should in this case consider it highly inexpedient for the Government to institute any such proceedings'.[93] The fear that agnosticism was the harbinger of revolution had subsided, but a confident and stable society still harboured a law which threatened to jail an increasing number of distinguished freethinkers.

Churchmen had begun to doubt the wisdom of enforced piety: Bishop Jeremy Taylor argued that

> You may as well cure the colic by brushing the man's clothes, or fill his belly by a syllogism, as prosecute him for blasphemy. The blasphemer may be provoked into confidence and vexed into resoluteness. So, instead of erecting a trophy to God, you build a monument to the Devil.

As the theory of evolution gained increasing acceptance, lawyers came to agree with Lord Macaulay: 'It is monstrous to see any judge try a man for blasphemy under the present law. Every man ought to be at liberty to discuss the evidences of religion.'[94] Judges had made the law, and in the nineteenth century it was the judges who changed the law to serve different social conditions. They altered the gist of the offence from an attack upon the Christian faith to the mode of expressing that attack. Christianity might be challenged, but only by moderate and respectful language. Religious beliefs might be examined 'in a sober and temperate and decent style ... but (not) if the tone and spirit is that of offence and insult and ridicule, which ... cannot truly be called an appeal to the judgment, but an appeal to the wild and improper feelings of the human mind, more particularly in the younger part of the community'.[95] In 1883, a new definition was spelled out by Lord Chief Justice Coleridge in his direction to the jury in *R* v. *Ramsay & Foote*:

> the mere denial of the truth of Christianity is not enough to constitute the offence of blasphemy.... A wilful intention to pervert, insult and mislead others by means of licentious and contumelious abuse applied to sacred subjects, or by wilful misrepresentation or wilful sophistry calculated to mislead the ignorant and unwary is the criterion and test of guilt.... If the decencies of controversy are observed, even the fundamentals of religion may be attacked without the attackers being guilty of blasphemous libel.[96]

This direction was adopted by trial judges, and in 1917 it received the imprimatur of the House of Lords in *Bowman* v. *Secular Society*. In that case the court rejected the argument that a trust for the propagation of anti-Christian doctrines was illegal, dismissing as rhetoric Hale's statement in *Taylor* that, 'Christianity is a parcel of the laws of England.' The court did not specifically consider whether 'wilful intention' was a necessary ingredient of the offence, but all five Law Lords stressed that the rationale of the law was maintenance of public order. Lord Parker, for example, was of the opinion that 'to constitute blasphemy at common law there must be such an element of vilification, ridicule or irreverence as would be likely to exasperate the feelings of others and so lead to a breach of the peace'.[97] The only reported prosecution during the next sixty years was that of *R. v. Gott*, the case of an incorrigible nuisance who distributed crude lampoons on the life of Christ in the public street. In 1922 the Court of Appeal upheld Gott's conviction, because his actions were calculated to outrage the feelings of Christian sympathizers, and might well have provoked a breach of the peace.[98] By 1949 Lord Denning could boast, 'We have attained to as high, if not a higher degree of religious freedom than any other country. . . . The reason for this (blasphemy) law was because it was thought that a denial of Christianity was liable to shake the fabric of society, which was itself founded on the Christian religion. There is no such danger to society now and the offence of blasphemy is a dead letter.'[99]

In 1977 it rose from the dead to protect the sensitivities of believers in an age of sexual tolerance. Eroticism in religious contexts had been a stock in trade of pornographers since 1650, and the crime of obscene libel was created in 1727 to deal with just such a work – Edmund Curl's *Venus in the Cloister*. Until 1959 publications which coupled indecency with sacred subjects were prosecuted as obscene libels, on the theory that 'if the Gospels were interleaved with indecent pictures, the indecency would be all the greater'.[100] Such works did not attack the tenets of Christianity, nor were they intended to insult believers or likely to provoke a breach of the peace. The third phase of the law of blasphemy, ushered in by the Court of Appeal judgment in *R. v. Lemon and Gay News* in 1978, was marked by the shedding of any requirement of an 'attack' on Christianity, and any need to prove wilful intention or a probable breach of the peace. This last requirement was effectively removed as an essential ingredient for criminal libel by *R. v. Wicks* in 1936;[101] applied to blasphemous libel, it meant that publication need only cause resentment to Christian sympathizers. There can be no doubt of the extent or genuineness of such resentment: in 1976 the Home Office received 10,000 letters of alarm at the very idea of a pornographic film about the life of Christ. The possibility, however remote, that the producer of such a film might be acquitted of an obscenity charge revived interest in the law of blasphemy. Some months before, *Gay News* had unobtrusively published a poem about a homosexual's conversion to Christianity, which metaphorically attributed homosexual acts to Jesus Christ. Professor James Kirkup intended to celebrate the universality of God's love; in so doing he referred explicitly to acts of sodomy and fellatio. Although publication excited no immediate concern, six months later leave was obtained for a private prosecution against both editor and publishing company for the offence of blasphemous libel, in that they 'unlawfully and wickedly published or caused to be published in a newspaper called *Gay News No. 96* a blasphemous libel concerning the Christian religion, namely an obscene poem and illustration vilifying Christ in his life and in his crucifixion'.

After the *Gay News* case, it appears that the law of blasphemy no longer relates to attacks on, or criticisms of, Christian doctrine, but is concerned solely with indecent or offensive treatment of subjects sacred to Christian sympathizers. Blasphemy is no longer a crime of disbelief: it may be committed with the profoundest religious intentions if Christian sentiment is expressed in an eccentric or shocking manner. The offence now relates to outrageously indecent or irreverent comments about God, holy personages, or articles of Anglican faith. The defendant's published words must speak for themselves, since he will not be permitted to testify as to his reasons for publishing them. Once publication has been proved, the only question remaining for the jury is 'whether the dividing line ... between moderate and reasoned criticism on the one hand and immoderate or offensive treatment of Christianity or sacred subjects on the other, has been crossed'.[102] Although dicta in *Ramsay & Foote* and subsequent cases refer to 'a wilful intention to insult and attack', the courts returned in 1978 to the strict liability imposed on John Taylor, whose attempts to explain away the obvious meaning of his remarks had been disallowed by Lord Hale. If it was blasphemy to describe Christ as a whoremaster in 1677, it was blasphemy to depict Him as a practising homosexual three hundred years later. Between the ravings of a lunatic from Bedlam and the measured metaphors of a professor of poetry, the literal-minded law allowed no distinctions.

Any speech or writing about the Christian religion which vilifies, insults, or brings into ridicule or contempt any sacred doctrine or personage may amount to a blasphemy. The gist of the crime is an insulting style or manner of expression, apt to cause resentment among Christians and their sympathizers. The jury must decide issues of interpretation unassisted by experts, whether literary or theological. The common law contains no 'public good' defence, so publishers charged with blasphemy cannot justify their works by reference to literary, sociological or even theological merit. Evidence of the place and circumstances of publication, however, would be relevant to the likelihood of public outrage,[103] and evidence as to the character of the readership would be admissible on the issue of whether resentment was likely to be aroused.[104]

The prosecution must lead prima facie evidence that the accused was responsible for the blasphemous publication. The defendant may exculpate himself by proving that the decision to publish was made without his knowledge and without his negligence. This defence is provided by section 7 of the Libel Act 1843, which places the onus on the defendant 'to prove that such publication was made without his authority, consent or knowledge, and that the said publication did not arise from want of due care or caution on his part'. Section 7 will normally protect newspaper proprietors who entrust questions of taste to editorial discretion,[105] although it would also avail an editor who was absent at the time of publication, or had himself delegated responsibility for content to the editors of particular sections or pages.

Newspaper prosecutions must be commenced by leave of a High Court judge under section 8 of the Law of Libel Amendment Act 1888. A 'newspaper' is defined by the Newspaper Libel and Registration Act 1881 as any paper 'containing public news, intelligence, or occurrences, or any remarks or observations therein', published periodically at intervals not exceeding twenty-six days. The satirical fortnightly *Private Eye* is a 'newspaper', although monthly periodicals would fall just outside the definition, and their editors may be summoned and committed for trial by magistrates in the normal course. One limitation on the initiation of proceedings is the requirement that the prosecutor must establish a weighty case. In the 1976 case of *Goldsmith* v. *Pressdram Ltd* Mr Justice Wien considered that he should be satisfied of three matters before exercising his discretion to order the prosecution of an editor for libel:

(a) There must be a prima facie case so clear as to be 'beyond argument'.

(b) The libel must be very serious before the criminal law should be invoked. A relevant, but not exclusive, factor in assessing its gravity would be that a breach of the peace might be occasioned by further publication.

(c) The public interest must require the institution of criminal proceedings.[106]

These principles, enunciated in a case concerning criminal libel, are applicable to proceedings for blasphemous libel under the 1888 Act. They should also be applied by magistrates in deciding whether to issue summonses or commit for trial, otherwise it could be anomalously easier to proceed against blasphemies in books and speech than those printed in newspapers.

The law of blasphemy punishes a particular kind of obscenity, in a way which circumvents all the reforms of the 1959 Act. Modern blasphemy is no more than old obscene libel in the context of religious subjects. The test is indecency rather than a tendency to corrupt; the work need not be considered as a whole, nor in relation to likely readers; and there is no 'public good' defence. The *Gay News* decision extends the bounds of criminality to serious literature, which is endangered whenever it couples sex with religion, irrespective of the pureness of its purpose. Shelley and Byron may rest in peace, but the erotic affirmations of faith by St John of the Cross may require reconsideration. Writers and artists must be extra-sensitive in dealing with Christian themes, lest their work satisfy one of the tests propounded to the jury by the trial judge in *Gay News*:

> Do you think God would like to be recognized in the context of this poem?
> Did it shock you when you first read it?
> Would you be proud or ashamed to have written it?
> Could you read it aloud to an audience of fellow-Christians without blushing?
> Is the poem obscene?
> Could it hurt, shock, offend or appal anyone who read it?

These tests of criminality are not really appropriate to modern conditions. The law should, and does, punish those who deliberately insult the deepest feelings of citizens, particularly in circumstances where public discord may be provoked. The existing range of statutory protection is more than adequate to curb public nuisances of this sort, for example:

(a) Customs legislation prohibits the importation of indecent articles, and would apply to any book or film about the sexuality of Christ or other religious figures.

(b) The Obscene Publications Act, Theatres Act and Criminal Law Act permit prosecution of any pornographic treatment of religious subjects by way of drama, film, speech or writing.

(c) The Post Office Act and the Unsolicited Goods and Services Act ensure that gratuitous offence is not occasioned by the mailing of blasphemy (in 1977 a successful prosecution was brought against a secularist who sent a copy of the *Gay News* poem through the post).

(d) Section 5 of the Public Order Act 1936 outlaws the public dissemination of any 'abusive or insulting' writing in circumstances which endanger the peace.

(e) The Metropolitan Police Act and the Town Police Clauses Act prohibit both 'indecency' and 'profanity' in public places. 'Profanity' is a wider concept than blasphemy, and includes any disrespectful or irreverent treatment of a sacred subject.

(f) The Ecclesiastical Courts Jurisdiction Act prohibits any 'riotous violent or indecent behaviour' in churches or other places of worship.

This web of statutes sufficiently penalizes any blasphemy which is apt to produce genuine public offence. The common law survived the abolition in 1967 of all the old blasphemy statutes and persists to provide preferential treatment for Anglicans in a multi-racial, multi-religious and increasingly secular society. Its discriminatory protection is incompatible with Article 9 of the European Convention on Human Rights, which upholds 'freedom of thought, conscience and religion', and Article 14, which outlaws discrimination on grounds of race or religion. The sensitivities of Anglicans are no more, and no less, deserving of protection than those of Jews, Roman Catholics, Buddhists, Muslims and humanists. A law which holds a publisher strictly liable for any statement which would shock the Christian on the Clapham omnibus seems inappropriate to an age in which the creeds of passengers to Clapham, if they have any, are many and various.

9

Censorship in the media

If Poets and Players are to be restrained, let them be restrained as other Subjects are, by the known Laws of their Country; if they offend, let them be tried as every Englishman ought to be, by God and their Country. Do not let us subject them to the arbitrary Will and Pleasure of any one Man. A Power lodged in the Hands of one single Man, to judge and determine, without any Limitation, without any Control or Appeal, is a sort of Power unknown to our Laws, inconsistent with our Constitution. It is a higher, a more absolute Power than we trust even to the King himself; and therefore I must think, we ought not to vest any such Power in his Majesty's Lord Chamberlain.

(Earl of Chesterfield, speech on a Bill to License Dramatic Performances, House of Lords, 1 June 1737.)

Those who publish books may only be damned after presentation of an argued case to a public tribunal, whose application of recognized legal standards is both visible and appealable. Those who work in the medium of film, however, are additionally constrained by institutional systems of censorship which operate prior to publication, conducted by reference to standards more stringent than those applied by law, and providing no mechanism for publicity or appeal. Television and radio are strictly controlled by internal policies which operate more represssively than the common law to which the media is in theory subject. Institutional censorship invariably imposes more stringent standards than either common or statute law, so that freedom of expression in the media lags demonstrably behind the literary frontiers established by jury verdicts in obscenity trials.

The purpose of pre-censorship is protection from law: it affords insurance to promoters, securing investments against legal suppression, at the expense of the work of creative artists. Courtroom battles for literary freedom have been fought by publisher and author standing together against the official custodians of morality, but where pre-censorship operates these ranks are broken as creator fights against promoter, and the artistic interest in preserving a work intact is sub-ordinated to the commercial interest in avoiding the cost and in-convenience of possible legal action. The most determined champions of prior restraint have been societies of theatre managers, independent television companies and the film industry, all craving protection from an obscenity law which book publishers must endure with forti-tude. Censorship bodies – the Lord Chamberlain, the Independent Broadcasting Authority and the British Board of Film Censors – have operated to keep them out of trouble by excising sexual indelicacy and, occasionally, suppressing political comment embarrassing to those in authority. Television companies, required to remove from the screen whatever might prove 'offensive to public feeling', are prone to assume that the public will be offended by criticism of those they have elected to power, or of institutions which act in the name of the public. The catch-cry of 'political censorship' cannot fairly be raised against a legal process which reserves the final decision to a random jury, but it is apt to describe a system by which government appointees arbitrate over 'good taste' and 'public offence' behind closed doors.

Discriminatory and extra-legal controls over stage and screen have traditionally been justified on the ground that life-like presentations carry a more immediate impact than the written word. In 1909 a Parliamentary Committee on stage censorship assumed that

> Ideas or situations which when described on a printed page may work little mischief, when represented through the human personality of actors may have a more powerful and deleterious effect. The existence of an audience, moved by the same emotions, its members conscious of one another's presence, intensifies the influence of what is done or spoken on the stage.[1]

This argument was convincingly directed against a common law more concerned with literal indecency than emotional impact. The 1959 Obscene Publications Act shifted the focus to effect on the mind of the beholder, so that atmosphere and emotional influence became highly relevant to the assessment of the strength of any tendency to deprave and corrupt. The impact of stage and cinema presentations was particularly appropriate for the new test. In 1968 the Lord Chamberlain's censorship was abolished, and in 1977 common-law prohibitions on 'gross indecency' were lifted from the cinema, although restrictions could still be imposed by the British Board of Film Censors and local authorities. A much heavier extra-legal censorship operates for television, justified on the grounds that the medium has attracted, and in some cases addicted, a captive family audience unwilling to 'switch off'. Broadcasters do possess some power to alter moral and political perceptions, and a law designed to deal with individual acts of outrage is powerless to combat the dripping, undermining effect of conditioning which persists night after night. Subtle problems of emphasis and direction cannot be resolved by recourse to blunt criminal law, but require some institutional supervision. These considerations produce the overall principle that artistic freedom in the media is inversely limited by the size of the potential audience: the greater the number of viewers, the less they are permitted to view.

THE THEATRE

Theatre censorship was originally imposed to curb opposition to the Reformation. In 1543, four years after Henry VIII closed the monasteries, an 'Act for the advancement of true religion' directed that 'plays ... and other fantasies' which 'meddle with the interpretations of scripture' should be 'abolished, extinguished and forbidden'. In 1551 fear of sedition as well as heresy prompted a royal proclamation that no play was to be performed without a licence from the Master of the Revels, an officer of the Lord Chamberlain. At first, the royal licence afforded protection from puritan hostility: theatre was an aristocratic entertainment, and so long as no insult was offered to Church or State, dramatic invention was unrestrained. Shakespeare was patronized by the Lord Chamberlain – his sexual candour and bawdy caused no contemporary offence because his political themes did not challenge the existing social order – and bawdy Restoration drama pandered to the tastes of the King and his court clique. It was a Prime Minister who first invoked considerations of decency and good manners as an excuse for protecting his own dignity. In 1737 Sir Robert Walpole, goaded beyond endurance by caricatures of himself in the plays of Henry Fielding, introduced legislation empowering the Lord Chamberlain to close down theatres and imprison actors as 'rogues or vagabonds' for uttering any unlicensed speech or gesture. The Act was passed despite the Earl of Chesterfield's ringing opposition, and thereafter political satire was banned or heavily censored for 'immorality'. The first victim of the Lord Chamberlain was, predictably, Henry Fielding, who stopped writing plays after a series of licence refusals and turned his talents to the novel. As late as 1965, a stage version of *Tom Jones* could not be performed with bedroom scenes.[2]

After 1737 English drama was emasculated in the interests of political or moral orthodoxy, and even performances of existing masterpieces were subject to control. *King Lear* was banned during the reign of George III, lest its depiction of royal derangement might catch the conscience of the King. In 1843 a new Theatres Act was passed to consolidate the Lord Chamberlain's power to prohibit the performance of any stage play, or any scene of any stage play, for as long as he thought necessary, 'whenever he shall be of opinion that it is fitting for the preservation of good manners, decorum or of the public peace so to do'. Repressive licensing was in some measure responsible for the sterility of British drama in the nineteenth century. *La Dame aux Camélias* and Oscar Wilde's *Salome* were refused licences, although operatic versions – *La Traviata* and Richard Strauss's *Salome* – could be sung in a foreign language. In 1892 the Lord Chamberlain's Examiner of Plays informed a Parliamentary Committee that his prohibition on the performance of Ibsen's plays was justified in 'the permanent interests of the stage'. He explained:

I have studied Ibsen's plays pretty carefully, and all the characters ... appear to me to be morally deranged. All the heroines are dissatisfied spinsters who look on marriage as a monopoly, or dissatisfied married women in a chronic state of rebellion against not only the condition which nature has imposed on their sex, but against all the duties and objectives of mothers and wives; and as for the men, they are all rascals or imbeciles.

Many serious writers eschewed the drama, and those few who persisted suffered intolerable restrictions. *Mrs Warren's Profession* was banned from 1894 to 1925, as were a number of other ventures into social realism by Shaw and Harley Granville Barker. Not even Gilbert and Sullivan was sacred: in 1907 licences for all performances of *The Mikado* were withdrawn for one year to avoid offence to a visiting Japanese prince. In 1909, in response to complaints from Shaw, Granville Barker, Barrie, Galsworthy, Gilbert and other literary figures, a Joint Parliamentary Committee was set up to investigate theatre censorship. Reform was strongly opposed by theatre managements, who cared less for the future of drama than for their own immunity from prosecution afforded by the Lord Chancellor's licence. The Committee recommended a compromise: licensing should continue as an option for managerial security, but it should be lawful to produce an unlicensed play, subject to the prospect of an injunction or criminal prosecution by the Attorney-General in the event of blasphemy or indecency. This recommendation was never implemented, although the Committee did lay down guidelines for stage censorship which persisted until the 1968 Theatres Act. Plays were to be licensed unless reasonably held

    (a) to be indecent;
    (b) to contain offensive personalities;
    (c) to represent on the stage in an invidious manner a living person or a person recently dead;
    (d) to do violence to the sentiment of religious reverence;
    (e) to be calculated to conduce to crime or vice;
    (f) to be calculated to impair relations with a foreign power; or
    (g) to be calculated to cause a breach of the peace.

The Lord Chamberlain operated a broad definition of 'indecency', and excised all vernacular references to intercourse, genitalia, birth control and venereal disease. In 1930 he settled rules for stage dress (or undress):

A. Actresses in movement must not wear less than briefs and an opaque controlling brassiere.
B. Actresses may pose completely nude provided:
The pose is motionless and expressionless.
The pose is artistic and something rather more than a mere display of nakedness.
The lighting must be subdued.[3]

For many years the Lord Chamberlain maintained an absolute ban on all references to homosexuality, and casualties included Lillian Hellman's *The Children's Hour*, Sartre's *Vicious Circle*, Arthur Miller's *A View from the Bridge* and Robert Anderson's *Tea and Sympathy*. In 1946, and again in 1951, he secretly consulted 'a wide circle of persons prominent in clerical, legal, scholastic, medical, governmental, judicial and artistic circles' on the merits of lifting the prohibition, but they decided it should stay. In 1958 he indicated that serious plays on homosexual themes would at last be considered for licensing, but only if homosexual characters were essential to the plot, and the play was not written to propagandize for changes in the law. 'Embraces or practical demonstrations of love between homosexuals will not be allowed.'[4] Notwithstanding this cautious advance, he refused to license John Osborne's *A Patriot for Me*, which won the 1965 Evening Standard Drama Award when presented as a 'club' performance. The following year he ordered the deletion of an E.E. Cummings poem 'I Sing of Olaf' from a presentation by the Royal Shakespeare Company, although it had been broadcast on radio and television without complaint. The offending lines were published in permanent form in the theatre programme, and the Company complained:

> We must point out the oddity of having two retired Army colonels and a professional civil servant as arbiters of public taste in an art form which they clearly neither like nor understand . . . we find it difficult to communicate with minds which can laugh urbanely in the privacy of their offices at the obscene implications which they detect, and then insist that these passages should be cut in order to 'protect' the 'public'.[5]

The Lord Chamberlain's office had always been eager to censor any lines which might impair relations with friendly foreign powers. Irreverent references to fascist dictators were suppressed throughout the thirties and plays sympathetic to communism were banned. Attacks on Nazism were not allowed, and as late as 1939 a revue song was banned on account of its opening line: 'Even Hitler had a mother.' This obsessive deference to heads of state extended in the sixties to satires on the Kennedy family, and to aspersions on long-deceased relatives of royalty – in 1960 Sadler's Wells Opera were forced to rewrite the libretto of Edward German's *Merrie England* to remove scenes where Elizabeth I conspired to poison a rival. The Lord Chamberlain refused permission for the RSC to perform Rolf Hochuth's *The Representative* unless a Vatican apologia was printed in the programme, and declined to license *The Trial of J.Robert Oppenheimer*, a documentary critique of McCarthyism. Commercial managements accepted political discipline without demur, but state-subsidized companies had no profits at stake, and the RSC launched an all-out attack after the Lord Chamberlain objected to *US* on the grounds that it was 'beastly, anti-American, and left-wing'.

Political censorship was only tolerable so long as unlicensed plays and satires could be performed at theatre clubs to avant-garde audiences. This device was declared unlawful in 1966, when the Royal Court Theatre was convicted of an offence under the 1843 Act for a club performance of Edward Bond's *Saved*. It followed from this decision that no word could be uttered on any stage without the Lord Chamberlain's prior approval, and even ad-libbing by an actor who had forgotten his lines was technically an offence.

In 1966 the Joint Committee on Theatre Censorship commenced its deliberations. Dramatists, state theatre companies and drama critics overwhelmingly demanded abolition of the Lord Chamberlain's powers, but West End theatre managers lobbied to retain their 'father confessor' who dispensed the indulgence of 'total security in relation to substantial investments'.[6] Lord Cobbold, the incumbent Lord Chamberlain, was content to be divested of the censor's mantle because his position as senior courtier to the Queen had associated the monarch too closely with criticism of his decisions. But he argued that *somebody* had to protect the royal family, heads of foreign states, and the sensitivities of theatre-going families:

> I am only thinking of making life more pleasant. It can be an awful nuisance if one takes one's family or friends to a play that simply turns out to give offence to them. I am merely thinking of providing a service to playgoers which might be good for the theatre.

The Joint Committee rejected his paternalism, and was satisfied that pre-censorship provided a service neither to playgoers nor to dramatic art:

> Attendance at a theatre is a voluntary act, usually decided upon after more conscious thought than going to the cinema or turning on the television ... it is better that an individual should have the right to decide, with full knowledge, what sort of play he wishes to see than that some central authority should attempt to lay down what is suitable for the 'average person'.[7]

Its report recommended repeal of the 1843 Act, and new legislation subjecting the theatre to control by the law of obscenity. All political censorship should cease, together with special protection for the Church, the royal family or foreign heads of state over and above the common law of blasphemy, sedition and libel. Legislation should, however, echo the Race Relations and Public Order Acts by prohibiting any performance designed to stir up racial hatred or calculated to provoke breaches of the peace.

The Joint Committee's recommendations were embodied, almost without exception, in the 1968 Theatres Act. The 1843 Act was repealed, and the test of obscenity installed as the sole basis for theatre censorship:

> a performance of a play shall be deemed to be obscene if, taken as a whole, its effect was such as to tend to deprave and corrupt persons who were likely, having regard to all relevant circumstances, to attend it.

Decisions on the interpretation of section 1 of the Obscene Publications Act now apply with equal force to stage plays, with the exception of the 'item by item' test: all performances, even of revues comprising separate sketches, will not infringe the law by reason only of one salacious scene, unless it is sufficiently dominant or memorable to colour the entire presentation. Obscenity is defined by reference to the circumstances of the staging and to its impact upon an audience more readily ascertainable than the readership for books on general sale. A more stringent test would apply to West End theatres, trading for tourists and coach parties, than to 'fringe' theatres or clubs with self-selecting patronage. The Act applies to 'plays', defined as

(a) any dramatic piece, whether involving improvisation or not, which is given wholly or in part by one or more persons actually present and performing and in which the whole or a major proportion of what is done by the person or persons performing, whether by way of speech, singing or acting, involves the playing of a role; and

(b) any ballet given wholly or in part by one or more persons actually present or performing, whether or not it falls within paragraph (a) of this definition.

Reference to 'improvization' includes ad-libbing and extempore performances, although the requirement of role-play excludes the stand-up comedian, unless his routine consists of playing different characters in a series of sketches. It would exclude some variety performances, although music-hall numbers usually require melodramatic characterizations which arguably involve the 'playing of a role'. 'Ballet' is broadly defined in the Oxford Dictionary as the 'combined performance of professional dancers on the stage', and subsection (6) expressly excludes the requirement of role-play. It may therefore be more embracing than the 1843 Act, which applied only to dancing which was set within some dramatic framework.

In *Wigan* v. *Strange* the High Court held that whether a 'ballet *divertissement*' constituted 'an entertainment of the stage' under the 1843 Act was a finely balanced question of fact:

A great number of females, it seems, dressed in theatrical costume, descend upon a stage and perform a sort of warlike dance: then comes a *danseuse* of a superior order, who performs a *pas seul*. If this had been all nobody would have called the performance a stage play. But the magistrate adds that the entrance of the *première danseuse* was preceded by something approaching to pantomimic action. The thing so described certainly approaches very nearly to a dramatic performance: and it is extremely difficult to tell where the line is to be drawn.[8]

The Law Commission doubted whether displays of tribal dancing

could be classed as 'ballet', and ballroom or discotheque performances, even by professional troupes of dancers, would fall outside the
definition.[9]

The Act applies to every 'public performance', defined to include
any performance 'which the public or any section thereof are permitted to attend, whether on payment or otherwise', and any performance held in a 'public place' within the meaning of the Public
Order Act 1936, namely

any highway, public park or garden, any sea beach, and any public bridge,
road, lane, footway, square, court, alley or passage, whether a thoroughfare
or not; and includes any open space to which, for the time being, the public
are permitted to have access, whether on payment or otherwise.[10]

This would cover street theatre, open-air drama and 'end of the pier'
shows. It would also include performances in restaurants,[11] public
houses,[12] buses and railway carriages,[13] and possibly boats on public
hire.[14] But the Act does not apply to any performance 'given on a
domestic occasion in a private dwelling', or to a performance 'given
solely or primarily' for the purposes of rehearsal, or for the making
of a cinema or television film or a radio broadcast.[15] Whether the
occasion was 'domestic' or whether the performance was 'primarily'
for rehearsal or recording purposes are questions of fact for the jury.
Public 'previews' of a play prior to its opening night would not be
characterized as exempted rehearsals if the tickets were issued to the
general public, albeit at a reduced rate. Similarly, out of town 'try-
outs' could not be classed as 'rehearsals', although they are designed
to test audience reaction and frequently occasion script changes prior
to the West End run. A performance staged primarily for the purposes
of recording, filming or broadcasting is exempt from the operation
of the Act, even where a large audience is invited to supply appropriate applause. Outrages to public decency which take place at
rehearsals and filmed performances could still be prosecuted at common law, however.[16]

The Joint Committee identified five matters of particular significance for the application of criminal law to live theatre:

(a) The prevention of frivolous prosecutions
Section 8, following the Committee's recommendation, makes prosecution dependent upon consent of the Attorney-General. The Committee feared 'a wide discrepancy of views among the judges' if leave

to prosecute were made contingent upon an application to a judge in chambers.[17] The Solicitor-General, Sir Dingle Foot QC, maintained that the decision to prosecute a theatre would involve a major question of public policy, and the Attorney's grant or refusal of a fiat should be subject to public scrutiny by questions in the House. Obscenity was an area where 'difficulties of definition are such that the letter of the law becomes substantially wider than the spirit. In these cases, particularly those which may attract vexatious prosecutors, the Attorney's fiat is required by statute in order to ensure that the letter and spirit of the law remain reasonably close together'.[18]

(b) The right of trial by jury

Section 2 (2) bestows a right to elect jury trial, at the risk of a substantially increased penalty in the event of conviction. This right is also provided, with similar consequences, to those charged with inciting racial hatred (section 5) or provoking a breach of the peace (section 6).

(c) The admissibility of expert evidence

The Joint Committee recommended that 'every effort should be made to see that the trial takes place in circumstances that are likely to secure a proper evaluation of all the issues at stake, including the artistic and literary questions involved'.[19] A 'public good' defence contained in section 3 admits expert evidence to justify stage performances which are 'in the interests of drama, opera, ballet or any other art, or of literature or learning'. The 'merit' to which experts must testify is not of the play itself, but of 'the giving of the performance in question', so that pedestrian writing may be redeemed by the excellence of acting, direction or choreography. Experts who have not witnessed the performance may nonetheless testify to its dramatic, literary or educative value by reference to the script, which under section 9 'shall be admissable as evidence of what was performed and of the manner in which the performance ... was given'.

(d) The effective treatment of obscene plays

The Joint Committee was disinclined to have a controversial play closed down before its alleged obscenity could be tested in the courts. An injunction pending trial would 'introduce a new and undesirable feature into the criminal law',[20] and any extension of search and seizure powers 'would in fact mean vesting the police with a power of state censorship'.[21] The Committee was mindful of the distinction made by the literary manager of the National Theatre:

> When you stop a theatre production you are destroying something which is probably irreparable and cannot be put together again. If you stop the distribution of a book, you are simply imposing a temporary halt on a process. Therefore the stage production needs, and I think deserves, greater safeguards in this respect than a book does.[22]

The best deterrent against repetition by a promoter charged with obscenity would be the prospect of a heavy penalty, 'since each further performance would be an aggravation of his offence in the eyes of the court in the event of his conviction'.[23] The penalty provided by the Act is a maximum of three years' imprisonment and/or an unlimited fine, and the Court of Appeal has approved sentences of fifteen months' imprisonment for organizers of obscene performances who procured the participation of 'quite young girls' with the motive of 'seeing how far they could go and making money from as filthy a performance as they could put on'.[24] Heavy penalties are also attached to the offences of inciting racial hatred (up to three years' imprisonment, and a maximum fine of £1,000) and provoking a breach of the peace (twelve months' imprisonment and a £500 fine; anomalously a heavier fine of £1,000 may be imposed after summary conviction).[25] All offences may be tried summarily, with the consent of the accused, in which case the custodial penalty is limited to six months.

Police have no power to close down the performances, or to seize programmes, scripts or items of stage property unless they feature writing or representations which contravene the Obscene Publications Act. Their power is limited solely to attendance, and is enforceable by warrant, issued under section 15 by a justice who is given reasonable grounds to suspect that the performance will infringe the Act.

(e) The uniform application of the law
Theatre managers were particularly concerned lest abolition of the Lord Chamberlain's censorship would encourage local authorities to impose censorship conditions on licensees of theatres. This fear was removed by section 1 of the Act, which abolishes the power of licensing authorities to impose any restriction 'as to the nature of the plays which may be performed under the licence or as to the manner of

performing plays thereunder'. Licence conditions may only impose restrictions necessary 'in the interests of physical safety or health', or to regulate exhibitions by hypnotists. The GLC maintains that licence conditions which regulate front-of-house displays are still valid, because restrictions on publicity do not affect the nature of plays or the manner of their performance. In 1978 the owners of the Windmill Theatre were fined for failure to remove a poster which had offended the GLC licensing committee.

Section 2 (4) of the Act sweeps away prosecutions at common law or under the Vagrancy Act in respect of theatrical performances, with the consequence that the only criminal laws which remain applicable, apart from offences created by the Act, are blasphemy, sedition and criminal libel.

Liability for prosecution
The Act applies to any person who, whether for gain or not, 'presented or directed' an obscene performance. In *R.* v. *Brownson* the defendants 'presented' and 'directed' by their actions in commissioning the script, engaging the cast, directing rehearsals, organizing the performances, managing the premises and promoting the production.[26] Although rehearsals themselves fall outside the scope of the Act, a director will be liable for scenes prepared under his instruction after opening night, even though his association with the production may have ended. Section 18 (2) provides that 'a person shall be taken to have directed a performance of a play given under his direction notwithstanding that he was not present during the performance'. A director is not responsible, however, for obscenity introduced after his departure: the Act applies to 'an obscene performance', and imposes liability only on those who have 'presented or directed *that* performance'. Promoters, on the other hand, may be vicariously liable for obscenity inserted without their knowledge if the play is presented under their auspices. The wording of section 2 (2) suggests strict liability, and in *Grade* v. *DPP*, a case under the 1843 Act, it was held that a promoter 'presented' a play with unlicensed dialogue, although the offending words had been inserted without his knowledge and without any negligence on his part.[27] Producers who act in a personal capacity are more vulnerable than those who operate through a corporate structure: section 16 imposes liability only on company officers who act knowingly or negligently. Actors will not be liable for any offence arising from participation in an obscene performance unless the obscenity arises from their own deviation from the script, whereupon

they become the 'director' of their own unrehearsed obscenity. Section 18 (2) provides

(a) a person shall not be treated as presenting a performance of a play by reason only of his taking part therein as a performer

(b) a person taking part as a performer in a performance of a play directed by another person shall be treated as a person who directed the performance if without reasonable excuse he performs otherwise than in accordance with that person's direction.

What constitutes 'reasonable excuse' is a question of fact, and actors unable to control themselves in shows requiring simulated sex acts might perhaps plead automation or provocation. Actors' Equity now insists that theatre managements give written notice of any scenes of nudity or sexual simulation prior to the contract of engagement.[28]

The Theatres Act makes no reference to the liability of dramatists. An obscene playscript would constitute an 'article' within the meaning of section 1 (2) of the Obscene Publications Act.[29] A dramatist 'publishes' a playscript by giving it to a producer, but it does not become an *'obscene* article' unless it is likely to deprave the people who read it, i.e. members of the theatre company, and not the theatre audience, which does not see 'the article' (i.e. the script itself) but the play, which is not an 'article', nor is it 'published' to them by the dramatist. Prosecution under the Obscene Publications Act would therefore be unlikely to succeed, and an author cannot normally be said to 'present or direct' a performance which is contrary to the Theatres Act. It follows that dramatists are only liable if their script incites blatant obscenity, or if they assist in some other way to mount a performance calculated to deprave or corrupt.

Evidence

Section 10 empowers senior police officers to order the presenter or director of a play to produce a copy of the script on which the performance is based. 'Script' is defined in section 9 (2) as the text of any play, together with stage directions for its performance. This script becomes admissible as evidence both of what was performed and of the manner in which the performance was given, thereby ensuring that courts are not obliged to rely upon police recollections of dialogue and action. Neither the effect nor the merit of drama can be fully appreciated from textual study, but there is an evidential obstacle to restaging the performance for court proceedings. In *R.* v. *Quinn & Bloom* the Court of Appeal rejected a film of a strip-tease performance taken three months after the date of the offence, because there

was no guarantee that the reconstruction exactly mirrored the performance on the date charged in the indictment.[30] *Quinn's case* was
a disorderly house charge which carried no 'public good' defence, and
it may be that the rule would be relaxed in a Theatres Act prosecution
if the defence of 'dramatic merit' were invoked. Comparative evidence has been admitted under section 4 of the Obscene Publications
Act,[31] and reconstructions of accidents for the benefit of the jury are
common in civil cases.[32] A re-staged performance might be inadmissible on the question of obscenity on the occasion charged, but it
would be highly relevant to a jury's assessment of theatrical merit.

Other offences

Section 5 of the Theatres Act makes it an offence to present or direct
a play with the intention of stirring up hatred against any section
of the public 'distinguished by colour, race, or ethnic or national origins'. The play must involve the use of 'threatening, abusive or insulting words', and the performance must, taken as a whole, be likely
to provoke racial hatred. The equivalent provision in the 1965 Race
Relations Act was amended in 1976 to remove the requirement of
intention, but section 5 was not affected. It is difficult to envisage
a successful case being brought against a stage play, although racist
lampoons performed as part of a rabble-rousing political platform
might provoke prosecution.

Section 6 makes it an offence to present plays involving the use
of threatening, abusive or insulting words or behaviour which are
either intended, or if taken as a whole are likely, to occasion a breach
of the peace. Section 6 is wider than Section 5: if an intention to provoke can be proved, it does not matter that no disorder broke out;
alternatively, if a danger to public order was reasonably apprehended, the intention of the promoter is irrelevant. Presenters and
directors must take their audiences as they find them: if the theatre
is open to the public, they take the risk that persons unduly sensitive
to the theme will attend.[33]

THE CINEMA

Film censorship operates at four different levels. The distributors of
feature films risk prosecution for obscenity at the instance of the Director of Public Prosecutions; exhibitors may be refused a licence to show
particular films by district councils; the British Board of Film Censors
may insist upon cuts before certifying a film's fitness for the public

screen, or for certain age groups; and customs authorities are empowered to refuse entry to any foreign film classified as 'indecent'. Neither theatre promoters nor book publishers suffer institutional restrictions imposed by trade censors or local councillors, and the standards of acceptability endorsed by those bodies are such that cinema censorship is more pervasive, and more arbitrary, than the limitations imposed on other forms of artistic expression. The cutting-room counsels of the BBFC avowedly err on the side of caution, in an effort to protect the established film industry from criticism as well as from prosecution. Most district councils devote a good deal of public time and money to reviewing films already certified by the Board, so that controversial releases are banned in some districts and licensed in others, sometimes only a short bus-ride away. Local film censorship is either delegated to magistrates or entrusted to standing committees: some district councils rely upon their Fire Brigade committees to extinguish any flames of passion which may have escaped the BBFC hose, while one Cornish borough solemnly bans films despite the fact that there are no cinemas within its jurisdiction. The protective axis of the BBFC and the local authorities operates haphazardly and somewhat pointlessly now that determined exhibitors may escape it altogether by the device of the 'cinema club'. In 1977 the Obscene Publications Act was extended to cover all film exhibitions – a reform which called into question the continued operation of extra-legal film censorship.

The first public film exhibition was held in 1896. Early film was printed on a nitrate base which flared easily on the application of heat, and public concern was initially directed at the fire hazards of the new entertainment. The Home Office responded to demands to secure the safety of cinemas by the 1909 Cinematograph Act, which provided that

A county council may grant licences to such persons as they think fit to use the premises ... on such terms and conditions and under such restrictions as ... the council may by the respective licences determine.

This Act was directed at safety, not censorship, and the ensuing Home Office regulations were concerned only with fire danger. Local councils, however, soon became concerned with the moral as well as the physical well-being of cinema audiences, and in 1911 the Divisional Court upheld a condition prohibiting Sunday film shows. The 1909 Act was 'intended to confer on the County Council a discretion as to the conditions which they will impose, so long as these conditions are not unreasonable'.[34] This ruling opened the door to local authority censorship, and the London County Council made its licences 'subject to no picture or film being shown which the council may disapprove'. The first banned film, a newsreel of an American prize fight, earned a disapproval 'not unconnected with the fact that it showed a negro defeating a white man'.[35] The film industry took fright at the prospect that distribution might be subjected to the whims of different local councils, and a consensus emerged that 'it would be far better for the trade to censor its own productions than to see all films at the mercy of an arbitrary authority'.[36]

In 1912 the Cinematographic Exhibitors Association announced the formation of the British Board of Film Censors, whose duty 'would be to induce confidence in the minds of the licensing authorities, and of those who have in their charge the moral welfare of the community generally'.[37] A former Examiner of Plays for the Lord Chamberlain was appointed as Secretary, and the film industry lobbied to give the Board an exclusive statutory position. But some local councils hesitated to relinquish their new powers of censorship, and in 1917 the Home Office encouraged the use of these powers independently of the BBFC by recommending 'model licensing conditions' which included the requirement that

No film shall be shown which is likely to be injurious to morality, or to encourage or incite to crime, or to lead to disorder, or to be offensive to public feeling, or which contains any offensive representation of living persons.

The industry, despairing of government support for the BBFC, turned its attention to local authorities, and convinced some of them to replace the Home Office model with a condition that no film be shown 'which has not been certified for public exhibition by the British Board of Film Censors'. In 1921 the Divisional Court held that this was an improper delegation of council powers, which under section 5 of the 1909 Act could only be exercised by committees of the council or by justices sitting in petty sessions. Mr Justice Avory noted that the BBFC might grant or refuse certification 'for reasons which may be private or may be influenced by trade considerations'.[38] But in 1924 the BBFC received its judicial imprimatur in *Mills* v. *London County Council*, when the court upheld the validity of a condition that 'No cinematograph film ... which has not been passed for ... exhibition by the BBFC shall be exhibited without the express consent of the council.' So long as a council reserved the right to review BBFC decisions, it was entitled to make the grant of a cinema licence contingent upon the screening of certified films.[39] In 1976 *Mills* was approved by Lord Denning in *R. v. GLC ex parte Blackburn*:

> I do not think the county councils can delegate the whole of their responsibilities to the board but they can treat the board as an advisory body whose views they can accept or reject; provided that the final decision – aye or nay – rests with the county council.[40]

After *Mills* the BBFC, an unofficial body established by the film industry and financed through fees imposed on every film submitted for censorship, exercised a persuasive and in most cases determinative influence over the grant of local authority licenses. 'I freely admit that this is a curious arrangement,' conceded the Home Secretary (Mr Herbert Morrison) in 1942, 'but the British have a very great habit of making curious arrangements work very well, and this works. Frankly, I do not wish to be the minister who has to answer questions in the House as to whether particular films should or should not be censored.'[41]

Cinematograph Act 1952

The 'curious arrangement' did not work quite as well as Herbert Morrison claimed, and in 1952 it received a comprehensive parliamentary overhaul. The 1909 Act applied only to inflammable films, and new processing techniques had rendered most films non-inflammable. The BBFC was prone to regard the cinema as entertainment rather than education, and had a set policy of refusing 'propaganda' films, by which it meant films dealing with progressive subjects such as birth control and racial tolerance. *The Battleship Potemkin* and other classics had been refused certification and Russian films critical of Nazi antisemitism were turned down in the thirties after pressure from the Foreign Office. 'Workers' Film Societies' suffered political discrimination at the hands of some local councils, especially when they sought licences for Sunday exhibitions. When a film about Edith Cavell was banned lest it offend Germany, the London County Council refused to permit even a private screening for invited Members of Parliament. Exhibitors had no right of appeal against these arbitrary decisions. After the war there was growing concern about the effects of films on children, and a committee chaired by Professor K.C. Wheare proposed that local authorities, in consultation with the BBFC, should classify films which were unfit for children (the 'X' certificate) and advise on other categories such as 'family entertainment' or 'preferably for adults'.[42] The Cinematograph Act 1952 resolved these problems: it abolished the distinction between 'flammable' and 'inflammable' films; established a category of exhibition exempted from local authority censorship; provided a framework for appealing local authority decisions; and adopted many of the Wheare Committee recommendations in relation to the exhibition of films to children.

Exemptions
Section 5 of the 1952 Act exempts from licensing control

1 Cinematograph exhibitions to which the public are not admitted.

2 Cinematograph exhibitions to which the public are admitted without payment.

3 Exhibitions, whether with or without payment, given by an 'exempted organization', namely 'a society, institution, committee or other organization as respects which there is in force at the time of the exhibition in question a certificate of the Commissioners of Customs and Excise certifying that the Commissioners are satisfied that the organization is not conducted or established for profit'. Such exhibitions must not be held more than three times in any one week on the same premises.

Section 5 established a distinction between commercial shows, which must be licensed, and non-commercial shows by film societies, charities, and clubs, which are free from all local licensing requirements, although they remain subject to the criminal law. If such shows are held at a licensed cinema they will be covered by its safety regulations, but not by censorship conditions normally attached to the licence.

Appeals
Any person aggrieved by the refusal or revocation of a licence, or by any terms, conditions and restrictions on a licence, may appeal to a Crown Court judge (section 6). Although section 2 of the 1909 Act permits councils to grant licences 'to such persons as they think fit ... on such terms and conditions and under such restrictions as ... the council may by the respective licences determine', every council must observe the rules of natural justice and act reasonably in exercising its discretion. In 1977 a freshly elected Conservative majority of the Greater London Council determined to wage a 'clean-up' campaign by reducing the numbers of sex cinemas in Soho. The first licence which came up for renewal was refused by the committee chairman in fixed pursuance of the new policy, without giving consideration to the merits of the case. In *GLC* v. *Langian Ltd*, the

applicant successfully appealed.[43] The court described the Council's power to revoke an existing licence, with calamitous consequence to heavy investment in a cinema, as 'draconian', and one which should only be made after full investigation by all members of the relevant committee. Delegation of the power to a committee chairman was consequently invalid. So too was any decision influenced by information which had not been communicated to the licensee, or made without opportunity being afforded the licensee to oppose revocation. Although the court could not interfere with political policy decisions to limit the screening of explicit films, 'the court could and should intervene to ensure that the council acted fairly and that it paid due regard to conflicting interests'.[44] A condition requiring cinema proprietors to give prior notification to district councils of all proposed 'X' certificate films has been held unreasonable in several Crown Court cases, although conditions limiting the explicitness of front-of-house publicity have been upheld.[45] The Greater London Council has rules prohibiting the sale or display at or outside cinemas of any poster, photograph or programme deemed by the Council to be 'unsuitable for general exhibition', and persistent breaches of this rule would provide a ground for revocation of the cinema licence.[46]

Children
Section 3 of the Act imposes a duty on licensing authorities to place restrictions on the admission of children to cinemas which show works 'designated, by the licensing authority or such other body as may be specified in the licence, as works unsuitable for children'. The reference to 'such other body' was the first parliamentary acknowledgement of the BBFC, and the 1952 Act established its position, if not as a censorship body, at least as an authorized classification tribunal for films unsuitable for young people. Although local councils have increasingly disagreed with BBFC decisions to grant or withold certification for adult viewing, its other classification decisions have won general approval. The present classification, endorsed by all local councils in July 1970, is

> *Category 'U'*   Passed for general exhibition.
>
> *Category 'A'*   Passed for general exhibition but parents/ guardians are advised that the film contains material they might prefer children under fourteen years not to see.

Category '*AA*'   Passed as suitable only for exhibition to persons of fourteen years and over. When a programme includes an 'AA' film no persons under fourteen years can be admitted.

Category '*X*'   Passed as suitable only for exhibition to adults. When a programme includes an 'X' film no persons under eighteen years can be admitted.

The revival of the criminal law

In the 1970s the 'curious arrangement' between the BBFC and local councils became curiouser and curiouser. The common law was invoked for the first time against controversial films which slipped through the censorship net, with such unsatisfactory results that in 1977 the commercial cinema was brought within the scope of the Obscene Publications Act. In 1959 Parliament had deliberately excluded cinemas because they 'have in practice not been prosecuted in the past and ... are most unlikely, so far as can be contemplated, to be prosecuted in the future.'[47] The Government was satisfied with the control of local authorities and the BBFC, for reasons which the DPP had explained to the Select Committee on obscenity in 1957:

If I wished to prosecute a film – and it has been suggested on two occasions to me that certain films that had passed the British Board of Film Censors were obscene – my answer would be, as it was in those two cases, 'I shall have to put the British Board of Film Censors in the dock because they have aided and abetted the commission of that particular offence.' So that it inhibits me to that extent. As long as I rely on the judgment of the British Board of Film Censors as to the suitability, under the various categories, of films for public showing, which I do, I do not prosecute.[48]

In 1959 the Government could not foresee that serious rifts would develop between the BBFC and certain local authorities, or that assiduous private prosecutors would invoke the common law to challenge the decisions of both bodies. Such a prospect was unrealistic so long as the Board and the local councils imposed tests more restrictive than the common-law standard of 'gross offence' and 'outrage'. The model licensing rules drafted by the Home Office went further, by prohibiting the exhibition of films which would merely '... offend against good taste or decency'. Some authorities, however, rejected this repressive test in favour of the standard which applied to books and theatres, and in 1967 the Greater London Council agreed to license indecent films, so long as they did not tend to deprave and corrupt. The position was further confused by the fact that the BBFC applied its own tests, which were sometimes at variance with the Home Office model, the common law, and the standard of obscenity. It was less severe with major films than it was with B-grade money-spinners, and it denied certification alike to some harmless low-quality romps and to con-troversial works by avant-garde directors.[49]

The Board viewed its certificate as a badge of merit, but the merit was not always apparent to organizations concerned with the level of sex and violence in the cinema. They prevailed upon some local authorities to ban films like *Clockwork Orange*, which had obtained certification, and the BBFC was obliged to defend its decisions to local viewing committees. On the other hand, the Board denied certification to many films which were not obscene, some which were not outrageously indecent and a few which were not even offensive to public feeling. Its Secretary, aware of the unfairness and hardship to genuine film-makers that his decisions sometimes caused, encouraged and supported their applications to those local authorities which, like the GLC, had adopted the test of 'a tendency to deprave and corrupt', and were in consequence prepared to license films which had not been approved by the BBFC. The result was anarchy in the distribution of controversial works like *Ulysses*, *The Killing of Sister George* and *Straw Dogs*, which were banned by some councils but licensed by others. The BBFC lost credibility as a censorship authority: its time was increasingly spent in the anomalous tasks of justifying its grant of certification to the more cautious authorities, and encouraging liberal councils to permit the screening of meritorious films which it had denied an 'X' certificate.

This conflict and confusion over film censorship was increased by the activities of private prosecutors. In 1974 one vigilante launched an Obscene Publications Act prosecution against the distributors of *Last Tango in Paris*, but the Court of Appeal confirmed that the 1959 statutory definition of 'publication' did not include publication to a cinema audience. In 1975 the Director of Public Prosecutions broke his long-standing policy of non-intervention by a common-law prosecution of a film which had been licensed by the GLC. The exhibitors were convicted, because one eight-minute sequence transgressed the bounds of public decency. In *R*. v. *GLC ex parte Blackburn* the Court of Appeal declared that the GLC's licence conditions were *ultra vires*, because the test of obscenity might permit public exhibition of gross indecency, and no licensing authority could properly consent to breaches of the law. The court noted that no council was obliged to censor films, but if it chose to do so by imposing licensing conditions, those conditions would have to be at least as strict as the common law. Lord Denning warned that 'if [the GLC] continue with their present wrong test, and in consequence give their consent to films which are grossly indecent, they may be said to be aiding and abetting a criminal offence.'[50]

If licensing is an act of complicity, might the granting of an 'X' certificate also aid and abet the offence? The DPP had thought so in 1957, but in a private prosecution of the film *The Language of Love* in 1976 the Chief Metropolitan Magistrate refused to commit the President and Secretary of the BBFC for trial, on the ground that certification was not a legal mandate for exhibition but merely an expression of opinion.[51] However, the film's exhibitors were committed for trial at the Central Criminal Court charged at common law with 'showing an indecent exhibition'. The President of the Board appeared as a witness for the exhibitors and explained the Board's reasons for granting its certificate. After the jury acquitted, the judge decried the 'shocking and appalling' attempt to prosecute the Board, and criticized the 'sad state of affairs' which permitted 'misguided' private prosecutions.[52] The case brought an immediate and important reform: in 1977 Parliament amended the Obscene Publications Act to include feature films, and abolished the right of private prosecutors to appeal to juries against BBFC or local authority largesse.

The Criminal Law Act 1977

There were other reasons for the reform. In 1975 the GLC's viewing committee recommended abandonment of its power to censor films, and the decision in *R. v. GLC ex p. Blackburn* made it likely that many local councils would try to avoid liability for aiding and abetting a vague common-law crime.[53] Cinema clubs had mushroomed, exempt both from licensing requirements and from the Obscene Publications Acts, and undue expenditure of police time and money was required to collect evidence of 'persistency', necessary for prosecuting them as disorderly houses. The common law, fashioned before the invention of film, was neither fair to the defence nor effective for the police. In 1976 the Law Commission recommended that Obscene Publications Act control should be extended to cover all film shows, and this was achieved by section 53 of the Criminal Law Act which came into force on 1 December 1977. Section 53 (1) simply deletes from the definition of 'publishing' in section 1 (3) of the 1959 Act the proviso which formerly prevented 'anything done in the course of a cinematograph exhibition ...' from amounting to a 'publication' within the meaning of the Act.

Section 1 (1) of the Obscene Publications Act deems any 'article' obscene if it tends to deprave or corrupt persons likely to see or hear the matter contained or embodied in it. Section 1 (2) defines 'article' to include 'any film or other record of a picture or pictures', and section 1 (3), as amended by the 1977 Act, now reads:

(3) For the purposes of the Act.
... a person publishes an article who
(a) distributes, circulates, sells, lets on hire, gives, or lends it, or who offers it for sale or for letting on hire; or
(b) in the case of an article containing or embodying matter to be looked at or a record, shows, plays or projects it.

Provided that paragraph (b) of this subsection shall not apply to anything done in the course of television or sound broadcasting.

The amendment was supported by the BBFC and the film industry, conscious that the test of obscenity would provide more freedom for meritorious works than the common-law standard of 'outraging public decency'. The Law Commission rejected the alternative of giving the BBFC statutory censorship powers: this would be 'an unsatisfactory course having regard to the history of the body as an entirely voluntary one which acts essentially as an adviser to local authorities rather than as an official censor'.[54] It also rejected the argument that the medium of film required more stringent legal control than books or plays because camera techniques had greater impact and the cinema catered to a wider and more vulnerable audience. Such considerations were more relevant to the test of 'obscenity' than to any other suggested standard:

If a film is more immediate and vivid in conveying its message, and is thereby likely to affect its audience more readily than a book conveying the equivalent message by means of words, then it seems to us that this can only mean that the film will more readily be held obscene, if, indeed, it is harmful; its 'tendency to deprave and corrupt' will be greater than the book. In other words, the arguments advanced in relation to the immediacy of films and the techniques of trick-photography, close-ups and the like are essentially matters which it is relevant to consider as evidence of the tendency of a particular film to deprave and corrupt; they are irrelevant to the question whether films should be subject to a different test from other articles.[55]

One welcome result of the change is that films which dilate upon violence and torture will now fall squarely within the law, although the 'aversion' theory would apply to works which depict scenes of cruelty in order to condemn them, within an overall moral or political framework. Common-law charges relating to one such film, Pasolini's *Salo*, were dropped after the 1977 amendment, and the BBFC published its own verdict:

> In almost every case, the sexual and other horrors are presented either in long shot or offscreen, and there is no exploitative sensationalizing. We are meant to hate everything we see, and there is no overt gloating over the spectacle. This is a turn-off film and not a turn-on, and in that sense it is unlikely that it would be found obscene by British law, since the film is intended to cause aversion or revulsion rather than a tendency to imitate....[56]

Time, and possibly a jury, will tell; but the film's future exhibitors will be able to avail themselves of an aversion argument and a 'public good' defence. At least, by shifting the emphasis from public outrage to the danger of moral corruption, the 1977 reform will permit limited screening of artistic films which use explicit sex or violence to make a moral statement, while deferring the public distribution of amoral works which glamourize vice and crime.

Limitations on prosecution

The Criminal Law Act 1977 abolishes the common law, including the conspiracies to corrupt public morals and to outrage public decency, in relation to cinemas.[57] The consent of the Director of Public Prosecutions is required for any prosecution of feature films, defined as 'a moving picture film of a width of not less than sixteen millimetres', and no order may be made to forfeit such a film unless it was seized pursuant to a warrant applied for by the DPP.[58] The Law Commission recommended these restrictions on proceedings to ensure that uniform standards applied throughout the country, and to discourage vexatious or frivolous prosecutions.[59] These provisions protect the 1,300 licensed cinemas, and those film clubs and societies which show feature films, from arbitrary police harassment of the sort visited upon booksellers and newsagents. In relation to eight millimetre 'blue movies', however, police will enjoy the wide powers of search and seizure contained in the Obscene Publications Act, and will no longer be obliged to mount extensive observations previously necessary to collect evidence of disorderly house offences. In one respect the power to seize films is wider than the power to seize books. Mere possession of a book for personal gratification is not a criminal offence, but the Criminal Law Act permits proceedings against films which are kept for domestic viewing, even if the owner merely 'shows, plays or projects' them to himself, and police are entitled to confiscate personal eight millimetre film libraries. The Law Commission has recommended that domestic screenings ought not to attract criminal sanctions, even when friends are invited, unless children are present or a charge is made for the occasion.[60]

The 1959 Obscene Publications Act, as amended by the 1977 Criminal Law Act, exempts from liability 'anything done in the course of television or sound broadcasting'. Video cassettes may be fed along short cables to standard television sets, tuned to standard channels, which then decode and depict obscene images, and sometimes emit obscene sounds, for the patrons of Soho's more technologically-advanced clubs. If this process amounts to 'television' or to 'sound broadcasting', such publications would fall outside the Obscene Publications Act. In that case, their organizers would escape prosecution entirely, since section 53 (4) of the Criminal Law Act excludes liability at common law for any 'exhibition of moving pictures produced on a screen by means which include the projection of light'. Light waves occur in most video systems from the original scene to studio camera, and there is of course an emission of light from the screen of the cathode ray tube – but neither phenomenon could be described as the projection of light onto a screen. Further legislation may be required if the obscenity law is to keep abreast with developments in porno-electronics.

'Public good' defence

The 'public good' defence provided for films by section 53 (6) of the Criminal Law Act is narrower than that which applies to books and magazines, omitting the grounds of 'science' and 'other objects of general concern' in favour of those objects enumerated in the Theatres Act, namely the interests of 'drama, opera, ballet or any other art, or of literature or learning'. The Law Commission noted that 'films have themselves an archival and historical value as social records, as well as being used for industrial, educational, scientific and anthropological purposes', and assumed that these merits would be canvassed under the head of 'learning'. The decision in 1978 that 'learning' in the Obscene Publications Act means 'something whose inherent excellence is gained by the work of a scholar'[61] casts some doubt on this prediction, although it may be argued that cameramen who film contemporary horrors are providing evidence which will be 'in the interests of' present and future scholarship. Expert evidence is admissible, and if a certified film were prosecuted representatives of the

BBFC could expatiate on the merits of the work. Such testimony might in any event be acceptable as evidence of fact: the BBFC certificate, screened at the commencement, would comprise part of the 'article' on trial, and the jury would be entitled to an explanation of what it meant.

Section 53 of the Criminal Law Act is an 'interim provision',[62] but it does establish for the first time that film is not a medium which in principle requires a separate legal regime to that which governs the printed and spoken word, art, and theatre. Now that the law permits prosecution for obscenity of any film exhibition, local authorities and the BBFC devote their time and money to amateur duplication of a function entrusted to DPP professionals. District councils are not legally obliged to exercise censorship, and the 1977 reforms were designed to meet the prospect that some councils would abandon a task which makes them vulnerable to charges of criminal complicity in the event of misjudgment. The BBFC censorship of adult films is similarly self-imposed and equally dangerous, at least if the award of an 'X' certificate amounts to an act of aiding and abetting an obscenity offence. On the other hand, its classification function has earned widespread approval, and its record justifies a grant of legislative power to categorize films for youthful age-groups, perhaps backed by a tougher law against assisting or permitting young persons to enter an adult exhibition. Members of local licensing committees are not elected for their talents as film censors, and their interaction with the BBFC has produced a high level of inconsistency and idiosyncrasy. District councils are appropriate bodies for determining questions of cinema safety, location, and front-of-house displays, and the BBFC for classifying films for children. But the power to censor by license condition and 'X' certificates imposes unique and anomalous restraints, under which films complying with the law of the land are arbitrarily denied exhibition in certain districts of the land.

BROADCASTING

The audience for a programme may total millions: but people watch and listen in the family circle, in their homes, so that violations of the taboos of language and behaviour, which exist in every society, are witnessed by the whole family, parents, children and grandparents, in each other's presence. These violations are more deeply embarrassing and upsetting than if they had occurred in the privacy of a book, or in a club, cinema or theatre. People distinguish between one medium and another: they are willing to accept scenes of nudity and violence in a novel, to which they would object strongly on television, less strongly in the press, and hardly at all in the theatre. In the theatre, cinema or bookshop you pay and thereby choose to see or read what is there. In television you make no such choice; and it is not a rebuttal to say that the viewer can press the button and change the channel after he has been grossly offended. The viewer feels himself implicated in the offensive act. The airwaves, unlike the printing presses, are licensed by Parliament. If the BBC is at fault, the viewer feels that the society to which he belongs, and he himself paying his licence fee out of his own pocket, are both involved.

Annan Report[63]

The Obscene Publications Act does not apply to 'anything done in the course of television or sound broadcasting',[64] but broadcasters are subject to criminal liability at common law for grossly offensive presentations which either outrage public decency or corrupt public morals. Institutional censorship exercised by the British Broadcasting Corporation and the Independent Broadcasting Authority goes so far beyond the requirements of common law that no prosecution has ever been seriously mooted. The legal tests of 'outrage' and 'corruption' imply a much more serious impact than transitory shock or discomfort, permit consideration of the context and time of transmission, and fall to be judged according to the tradition of tolerating minority viewpoints in a plural society.[65] Broadcasting authorities, however, are obliged to ban any programme considered offensive or in bad taste. The statutory justification for this extensive censorship is found in section 4 (1) (a) of the Independent Broadcasting Authority Act 1973, which requires IBA members

to satisfy themselves that, so far as possible, nothing is included in the programme which offends against good taste or decency or is likely to encourage or incite to crime or to lead to disorder or to be offensive to public feeling. . . .

This duty was imposed on independent television at its inception in 1954, when commercial exploitation of the ether was untried and untrusted. But in 1964 the BBC undertook to bind itself to the same standard:

The Board accept that, so far as possible, the programmes for which they are responsible should not offend against good taste or decency, or be likely to encourage crime or disorder, or be offensive to public feeling. In judging what is suitable for inclusion in programmes they will pay special regard to the need to ensure that broadcasts designed to stimulate thought do not so far depart from their intention as to give general offence.[66]

In addition to the obligation to uphold good taste, both authorities must maintain a 'proper balance' in programme content, and ensure that 'due impartiality' is preserved in the treatment of controversial subjects and matters of current public policy.[67] The BBC undertaking is not legally enforceable, although the courts could force IBA members to perform their statutory duty, in the unlikely event that they either refused to 'satisfy themselves' of programme content, or in so doing had reached perverse decisions. In practice, broadcasting stays above the law by dint of self-censorship of unseemliness. The Annan Committee, noting the strong and persistent pressures upon programme makers to avoid all risk of offence, feared that the medium would become anodyne, and called upon broadcasters 'to show their audience what they believe to be the truth, even if the truth shocks'.[68] If the truth does shock, the broadcasting authorities may be in breach of their undertakings and their statutory duty.

From its inception in 1924 the BBC exercised its monopoly of the airwaves according to Lord Reith's stern demand for 'intellectual and ethical responsibility'. The first Organizer of Programmes explained

... what justification is there for dragging into prominence the seamy side of private life? Is anyone the better for it?

If broadcasting is to be a permanent asset to our national life, it must at all costs avoid offence in any shape or form to the widely varying susceptibilities of the vast public which it serves.[69]

Lord Reith's moral paternalism was reflected in programme output, and even extended to vetting the private lives of programme makers. One senior employee who was forced to leave because of his divorce later reflected:

I have often thought that if there had been a world shortage of celluloid, as there is a shortage of wireless channels, we might even now be suffering the soporific of a nationalized cinema, and pompous people would be justifying boredom by pointing out the values of a clean screen.[70]

In 1923 the Sykes Committee on Broadcasting rejected the idea of radio advertising, and thirty years later Lord Reith could describe the introduction of commercial television as 'a betrayal and a surrender ... somebody introduced smallpox, bubonic plague and the Black Death. Somebody is minded now to introduce sponsored broadcasting in this country.'[71]

That 'somebody' was a public which had long been feared to want what was not good for it, represented by a breed of new conservatives who championed free enterprises. Old conservatives and socialists made common cause against the encroachment of commerce. Lord Beveridge claimed that advertising would lower standards, and Lord Simon confessed to a 'sense of sacrilege' at the very prospect of an advertisement broadcast on the Sabbath. Their opposition was unsuccessful, but their concern about a possible lowering of standards caused the insertion in the Television Act 1954 of the injunction against transmitting anything 'which offends against good taste or decency, or is likely to be offensive to public feeling'. Commercial television had phenomenal success in attracting a public following and making money, but its 'lack of effective restraint' in advertising was sharply criticized by the 1962 Pilkington Report, and in consequence the third television channel was awarded to the BBC. It fell to the Corporation to provoke the first serious clash between creative broadcasting and public feeling: in the sixties, under the direction of Sir Hugh Greene, it embarked upon a series of *succès de scandal* which questioned and satirized conventional morality. Greene's philosophy was that

The BBC should encourage the examination of views and opinions in an atmosphere of healthy scepticism ... in its search for truth ... a broadcasting organization must recognize an obligation towards tolerance and towards the maximum liberty of expression ... (it) should not neglect to cultivate young writers who may by many be considered 'too advanced', even 'shocking' ... tolerance is the key – relevance to the audience and to the tide of opinion in society. Outrage is impermissable. Shock is not always so. Provocation may be healthy and indeed socially imperative.[72]

Greene's distinction was legally correct, in the sense that 'outrage', and not 'shock', was the standard for public exhibition laid down at common law. But 'shock' was exactly what the BBC had promised to eschew by its undertaking to accept the spirit of the Television Act injunction on bad taste and offensiveness. Mrs Mary Whitehouse, founder of the 'Clean Up TV Association' denounced Greene as the Goebbels of the permissive society:

... why did he, as head of the great and powerful BBC, not only allow, but strongly encourage, the late-night satirists to have their way in the early and middle sixties? Why did he encourage programmes which ridiculed and denigrated our political leaders, the Church, the family, authority in all its forms, which were often anti-British, blasphemous and obscene? Why did he give *carte blanche* to writers to create plays which undermined our accepted values and standards?[72]

By 1973 television had largely surrendered to the dictates of good

taste. The BBC's General Advisory Council issued a prepared statement on 'Taste and standards in BBC programmes' which retreated
from Greene's philosophy in favour of the 'middle ground', and
renounced those programmes which had implied 'a contempt for
earlier standards'. In the same year the IBA was criticized by three
Appeal Court judges for its decision to broadcast tasteless and offensive scenes in a programme about Andy Warhol: 'they should always
remember that there is a silent majority of good people who say little
but view a lot. Their feelings must be respected, as well as those of
the vociferous minority who, in the name of freedom, shout for ugliness in all its forms'.[74] Opinion polls suggested that it was the vociferous minority who were shouting for cleanliness – only fourteen per
cent of interviewees admitted to being upset by television drama[75]
– but the BBC suffered 'some loss of nerve' as a result of the criticism,
seeing itself as 'beleaguered, pressurized, lobbied and compelled to
lobby'.[76]

'Reference up'

BBC censorship operates by a process of 'reference up' the Corporation hierarchy. Any producer who foresees possible offence must alert
middle management, which may pass borderline cases to departmental heads, who may in turn consult the Managing Director or even
the Director-General. The Controller of Programmes has explained:

> The elimination or alteration of material considered unsuitable for public
> broadcasting is an integral part of a whole system of editorial control....
> Reference is obligatory in matters of serious dispute or matters of doubt, and
> the wrath of the Corporation in its varied manifestations is particularly re-
> served for those who fail to 'refer'.[77]

Internal directives are issued from time to time about programme
content, especially in relation to sex, violence, and drugs. The 'middle
ground' is occupied by avoiding extreme political views and ensuring
that controversial opinions are 'balanced' by the dispensation of conventional wisdom, either in the same programme or over a series. Censorship is slightly relaxed for Radio Three and Four:

> We assume Third Programme listeners are discerning and intelligent
> enough to make a conscious choice of what they listen to, and, if they find
> something not to their taste, that they are adult enough to recognize that
> tastes differ and that the programme has been broadcast because other adult
> minds believe in its quality.[78]

'Gratuitous' bad language or behaviour is 'eliminated' when not
essential to plot or purpose, and four-letter words chanted by football

crowds are solemnly edited out of *Match of the Day*, but the Corporation claims to strike the balance in favour of creative freedom where it is exercised for genuine or socially redeeming purposes. Broadcasters, it is said, know honesty and quality when they see it: 'Subjectively most people – and certainly most broadcasters – are well aware when a writer, in trying to convey his perception of the truth and reality, is being honest in conveying sex, violence and blasphemy.'[79] Some BBC censorship decisions have led to doubts about whether these platitudes are any more applicable to television executives than to policemen or judges. *Brimstone and Treacle*, a morality play by a renowned television dramatist about the dilemma of reconciling the existence of both God and evil, was vetoed at the highest level although it contained no single scene which was offensive or in poor taste. Nor was it blasphemous at common law, because it lacked any element of indecency or scurrility. But its anti-Christian overtones, and particularly its portrayal of the Devil doing good, would doubtless have provoked complaints. The Director of Programmes 'found the play brilliantly written and made', (at a public expenditure of £70,000) 'but nauseating'.[80] The Chairman of the BBC maintained that 'the play ... would outrage viewers in a way that was unjustifiable'.[81]

In 1978 the same executives banned *Scum*, a violent and disturbing play about conditions in a borstal, based on actual experience of both inmates and prison officers. This time the BBC deferred to the opinion of Home Office 'experts' invited to view the film prior to transmission. It was conceded that every incident had real-life parallels, but the dramatist was accused of distorting reality because they could not all have happened in the one borstal at the one time.[82] *Scum* did not purport to be a documentary, but some credulous viewers might have taken it seriously. The serious television dramatist who explores contemporary themes must pilot between the Scylla of fantasy and the Charybdis of boredom, because BBC executives are inclined to assume that truth is unexciting. A more sinister censorship of art in the interests of conventional politics was essayed by the Corporation in the same year when some controversial lines about justice in Northern Ireland appeared in a *Play for Today*. Instead of banning the play outright, the management re-wrote and re-recorded the offending text to delete the message and convolute the theme – without bothering to notify the author. The purpose of the manœuvre was defeated on the day of transmission when the press published the original text, juxtaposed with the sanitized version prepared by the Corporation, after the director and dramatist had publicly protested against 'this new and Orwellian form of political censorship'.

The Independent Broadcasting Authority

Censorship of independent television is even stricter than that at the BBC, because 'reference up' within the fourteen contracting companies is buttressed by constant intermeddling from the IBA. The incentive for internal restriction is the commercial danger of non-renewal of franchise if good taste is noticeably infringed, while the IBA interprets its duty under section 4 of the 1973 Act as requiring direct intervention to excise controversial parts of programmes prior to transmission. This interpretation of the Act was reinforced by the Court of Appeal decision in *AG ex p. McWhirter v. IBA*, which concerned a documentary about the life and work of Andy Warhol. Although senior IBA staff had ordered a number of deletions from the programme, it had not been personally vetted by the eighteen members of the Authority at the time transmission was injuncted by the court on the strength of sensational newspaper publicity. Subsequently it was viewed and approved by all IBA members, and the court declined to hold that their decision was unreasonable, although it sternly reminded them of their duty to ensure that *'nothing* is included' in any programme which offends good taste. 'These words', Lord Denning emphasized, 'show that the programme is to be judged, not as a whole, but in its several parts, piece by piece,' although the court did concede that each 'piece' could be judged according to the purpose and character of the whole programme.[83] It stressed the personal duty laid on each member by the legislation – a duty which could not be delegated, at least in controversial cases, to members of the IBA staff: 'If at any time credible evidence to the contrary effect to a staff report becomes available, they should look at the programme themselves and make up their own minds.'[84] Although the *McWhirter* decision to grant an injunction at the behest of a private individual has been disapproved by the House of Lords in *Gouriet* v. *Union of Post Office Workers,*[85] the court's remarks about the IBA's duty of pre-censorship remain valid, and the duty may still be enforced at the instance of the Attorney-General.

It is a duty which produces frequent and frequently resented censorship, as the Annan Committee discovered when it investigated and criticized the extent of IBA interference in editorial decisions.[86] Instead of a detached and supervisory role, the IBA has become deeply involved in the editorial and creative process, casting a blanket of pre-censorship over current affairs programmes like *This Week* in the interests of good taste and good politics. One programme on Bangladesh 'was discussed with IBA officers almost line by line'.[87] Thames Television staff publicly protested when *Sex in our Time*, a series which had been sold, shown and acclaimed as peak-time viewing in Australia, was vetoed in response, it was claimed, 'to pressure exerted at the highest level by the most senior individuals in the IBA ... In the process the board overrode the judgment of its director of programmes; neglected to consult the production team who made the programme; and has failed to state publicly and in detail why the British television audience should be denied the opportunity to watch the series.'[88] IBA intermeddling may amount to direct political censorship. A blatant example occurred in 1978, when a *This Week* programme about an Amnesty International Report on brutality by the Royal Ulster Constabulary was banned after representations from the Ulster Secretary and the RUC's Chief Constable.[89] The IBA justified its action in terms of its statutory obligation to ensure 'balance', but the programme included defenders of the RUC, and the BBC, which is bound by the same obligation, had no hesitation in screening it when Thames executives made a copy publicly available in protest. The Government has not interfered directly with controversial broadcasts since the time of the General Strike, but the fate of the 'Ulster' programme demonstrates how political censorship may be achieved through pressure on the IBA to exercise its broad statutory powers of achieving 'good taste', 'balance' or 'impartiality'.

The Annan Report deplored the fetters on initiative and imagination caused by IBA intermeddling with programmes prior to broadcast. It recommended that the Authority should intervene to preview programmes only when it had good reason to believe that its policy was being flouted. Post-censorship should replace pre-censorship: criticism of errors of taste should be made by privately communicating IBA views to the company concerned *after* the broadcast, while major errors of judgment should be publicly condemned and drawn an apology from the company responsible. The ultimate sanction – loss of franchise – would be sufficient to ensure that television companies do not repeatedly outrage public feeling. If the IBA is to be forced to explicate rather than expurgate, section 4 (1) (a) of the Independent Broadcasting Authority Act 1973, which places an onerous personal duty on members to censor piecemeal offensiveness, will require amendment.[90] The IBA recognized as much in its response to Annan's criticism. 'Under the IBA Act', it pointed out, 'the Authority has editorial responsibility for the content of its services. If its obligations are to stay unaltered, it must continue to fulfil them.'[91] The Government agreed with the IBA: its 1978 White Paper on Broadcasting rejected the Annan strictures, and displayed no inclination to amend the legislation.[92] There is every indication that the IBA relishes a continuing role as a political and moral censor. Its Director-General, Sir Brian Young, contemptuously dismissed criticism of the ban on the 'Ulster' programme with the observation: 'We are given teeth for biting, not for gnashing.' He sees the IBA as a 'thoughtful editor', vetting scripts, previewing programmes and acting as a jury empowered to 'blow the whistle' on behalf of the viewers.[93] He is legally entitled to his complacency: unlike jury verdicts, his decisions cannot be appealed.

Children and television

The most intractable problem in television scheduling is the possible impact on children of realistic violence. British television averages 2·2 violent incidents in each hour of transmission, predominantly in programmes imported from America.[94] Although research is inconclusive, there is some evidence that brutality associated with screen heroes may encourage youthful emulation, and that constant exposure to television violence may weaken moral inhibitions against resort to force as a means of solving problems.[95] The IBA has a statutory duty to avoid transmission of anything 'likely to encourage crime', and both broadcasting organizations have published censorship codes on violence, which are relaxed for adult viewing hours after the watershed time of 9 pm. The codes outlaw 'gratuitous' violence and close-up details of assaults and murders, and discourage the depiction of torture techniques capable of easy imitation. They accept the desirability of avoiding scenes which might cause viewers unnecessary anxiety or disturbance, a prospect thought more likely if violence occurs in realistic contemporary settings than in historical contexts or stylized settings.[96] But vigilance is circumscribed by viewing patterns: the arbitrary 9 pm deadline may cocoon very young children, but forty-eight per cent of those aged between fifteen and seventeen view until 11 pm or later, and despite the emphasis on 'parental guidance' seventy-nine per cent of families are said to exercise 'no control whatever' over the viewing habits of their younger members.[97] Concern about the largely uncontrolled and unpredictable effects of television violence is understandable in relation to glamourized popular serials and movies, but it has less relevance to contemporary documentary and current affairs coverage which may serve to arouse compassion for the injured and anger against the injurer. In 1978, children's least favourite programmes were news bulletins and documentaries.[98]

Advertising

Fears of advertising excesses were responsible for the original injunction on bad taste and offensiveness in commercial broadcasting, and the IBA vets both advertising copy and visual material before transmission to remove 'potentially offensive sexual overtones'.[99] In 1969 the *News of the World* was not permitted to announce over the airwaves its serialization of Christine Keeler's memoirs: the author's very name was deemed to be 'potentially offensive'. Censorship is rigid but conventional: sexist Vikings may conspire to rape the glamorous Saxon who has used the right brand of shampoo, so long as they do not have the bad taste to refer to any method of avoiding pregnancy. Although Australians find television advertising for contraceptives neither embarrassing nor in bad taste, the IBA has declared that they would be offensive to a large section of the British public, and the BBC refuses to point its sports cameras at racing cars sponsored by the London Rubber Company with the dirty word 'Durex' on their bonnet.[100] This attitude reflects an irresponsible double-standard: the media is prepared to promote promiscuity by snigger and insinuation, but it refuses to help minimize the casualties by screening Government-funded family-planning advice.

IBA rules-of-thumb enforce decorum in lingerie and body odour:

> Foundation garments: in the use of live models care should be taken to ensure that no embarrassment is caused by over-exposure of the body.
>
> Deodorants: shots of armpits or reference to 'sweat' or 'smell' should be avoided.

The Independent Broadcasting Authority Act lays down that

> No advertisement shall be permitted which is inserted by or on behalf of any body the objects whereof are wholly or mainly of a religious or political nature, and no advertisement shall be permitted which is directed towards any religious or political end or has any relation to any industrial dispute.[101]

The IBA has ingeniously interpreted this section as prohibiting advertisements for the *Morning Star*. Time for Party Political Broadcasts is agreed between a joint committee of broadcasters and party representatives, and by convention the major opposition party is ceded a right to reply to ministerial broadcasts of a contentious nature.[102] The law which governs electioneering, embodied in the Representation of the People Act, is silent on the subject of pre-election broadcasts. These are allocated on the basis of non-legal arrangements devised in secret by the Committee on Party Political Broadcasting, which comprises representatives from the BBC, ITV and the three major parties. It has functioned, at the insistence of the party whips, to impose maximum restraint on political analysis in the interests of propaganda: in recent elections it has banned audience participation and critical evaluation of policy, and permitted party officials to dictate their choice of spokesman. Before the 1974 elections it made an arbitrary decision that every party fielding fifty or more candidates should have an uninhibited slice of air-time: the Flat Earth Society and the Monty Python Appreciation Campaign could all qualify for a brief monopoly of the airwaves if they managed to stake the minimum number of deposits. This idiosyncratic arrangement is open-endedly exploitable, because broadcasting authorities have cravenly accepted that party political propaganda should not be diluted by contemporaneous criticism or confrontation. In 1978 the Anti-Nazi League was accused of supporting censorship when it sought to curtail a prospective pre-election broadcast by the National Front, but others have questioned whether any political party should be entitled to a free plug at public expense.

The Annan Report accepted that 'while broadcasting can bring in the best of all forms of entertainment to people in their homes, it also exposes them to the work of writers and producers who are exploring new modes of expression. Freedom for the creative artist is bound to mean that sometimes programmes will offend and outrage many people who see them.'[103] Present law and practice fetters the exploration of new modes of expression precisely because it prohibits 'outrage' by common law and 'offence' by the Independent Television Act and BBC undertakings. The shibboleth of 'family viewing' which justifies these strict standards will increasingly be challenged by technological and political changes. Cable television offers its subscribers a multiplicity of channel choice, and censorship has been relaxed in New York and Toronto to permit cable companies to cater for minority tastes. The Post Office has announced that 'Viewdata', its television service linked with a computerized store of information, will not conform to restrictions on 'good taste', but will instead offer a self-censorship system enabling sensitive customers to block out information about contraceptives, gambling or other unpalatable facts of life. The

Annan Report recommended the establishment of an Open Broadcasting Authority to operate a fourth channel, free from the blanket of 'good taste' which protects addicted viewers of mainstream networks. Subject only to the law of obscenity, 'some programmes which would not be acceptable or appropriate on the existing channels would find an outlet on the fourth channel'.[104] But the Open Broadcasting Authority will not be as open as Annan suggested : the Government has announced that although it will be relieved of the need to ensure balance, the new OBA will be bound by the same obligations of good taste, decency and impartiality which shackle existing broadcasting authorities.[105]

The extent of television censorship is presently justified by the narrowness of television choice, and the increased availability of specialized outlets should be accompanied by a relaxation of restrictions for specialized viewing. Censorship in broadcasting takes place by stealth : the process of 'reference up' never involves reference up to the viewing public in whose name artistry is circumscribed. Public broadcasting requires public accountability, by implementation of the Annan recommendation that decisions to censor, and the principles upon which they are made, should be open to scrutiny at regular public hearings.[106] Programme makers who are victims of television censorship should have an ultimate right of appeal to the other victims of television censorship – the viewing public.

The pornographic market-place

LEGAL TABOOS

The modern obscenity trial recalls medieval procedures designed to test allegations of witchcraft. Sexual corruption, like sorcery, arouses deep instinctive fears which defy rational explanation. Vice squads, like witch-hunters, cannot define their quarry but claim to know it when they see it. The accuracy of their identification receives endorsement in a ritual whose credibility hangs upon a belief in the method of trial – once by divine providence, now by the luck of the jury ballot. Because the obscene, like the supernatural, exists most clearly in the mind of the beholder, the targets for public purgation are generally chosen by those who possess both the eyes to see and the powers to prosecute. Recently they have shown a marked reluctance to indict reputable book publishers and occupants of the 'upper end' of the mass-circulation magazine market, concentrating instead on low-life characters who disseminate pornography through specialized bookshops and cinema clubs. If the obscenity law is designed to ensure that women are treated with a minimum of dignity in the public prints in the hope that this may lead to their more dignified treatment in private life, the DPP's narrow selection of defendants is unlikely to allow the law to have much impact on the tone of mainstream publications. In 1978 the subject-matter of most trials was trashy masturbation fodder surreptitiously sold to self-selecting adult males already familiar with the genre: the more potent, insinuatingly seductive 'glamour magazines' on mass sale went unprosecuted.

What class of writing is most at risk from an obscenity prosecution? In *R. v. Calder & Boyars* the Court of Appeal observed that corruption 'may take various forms. It may be to induce erotic desires of a heterosexual kind, or to promote homosexuality or other sexual perversions or drug-taking or brutal violence.'[1] Or, of course, it may not, depending on the moral outlook of the jury, which 'must set standards of what is acceptable, of what is for the public good in the age in which we live'.[2] To determine whether a publication tends to deprave and corrupt, the jury must first establish what effect, if any, it will have on potential readers, and then decide whether this effect can properly be described as moral corruption. Under the 1959 Act there can be no love which dares not speak its name: obscenity is made to depend upon whether it shouts or whispers, and to whom. The tone and the audience are all important, and the subject-matter of itself is irrelevant. This, at least, is the legal theory, but in practice decisions to prosecute are heavily influenced by the notion that certain subjects are taboo. The taboo derives from the feeling that certain aspects of private sexual behaviour are unseemly subjects for explicit public discussion, at least in non-academic or non-condemnatory contexts, and from the entrenched fear that people are moved to emulate conduct they are permitted to read or see. Although behaviour of the sort depicted in much heterosexual erotica is capable of practice within perfectly happy relationships, prosecutions still sometimes proceed on the assumption that the missionary position is a major clause in the marriage contract.

Despite the uncertainty of the law, there is some consistency in prosecution targets. Descriptions of sexual deviations are much more likely to be attacked than accounts of 'normal' heterosexual behaviour. In practice, prosecuting authorities ignore the message of an article, and concern themselves instead with the physical incidents photographed or described. A book describing deviant behaviour, even if written with compassion and understanding for the participants, will be charged with obscenity long before a book whose heterosexual heroes exhibit the most callous disregard for female integrity. Stories may degrade women, 'do dirt on sex', by depicting them as objects to be manipulated for fun and profit, but obscenity for most prosecutors hangs on simpler things, such as whether the penis is erect, whether a whip is in evidence, whether the lady in the picture is wearing a wedding ring or a dildo. DPP officials have their lines to draw, and they draw them fairly consistently at the male groin: nudity is now acceptable and even artistic, but to erect a penis is to provoke a prosecution. Ingenious publishers spend thousands of pounds to circumvent the DPP's rule-of-thumb over male organs – by floating them on water, tilting them over thighs, and in one case sending a naked skier over a ski-jump, so that his flaccid penis would flutter suggestively in the up-draught. Such pubic hairsplitting represents the sort of test which is workable in practice by government lawyers with heavy case-loads as they flip through piles of erotica submitted by provincial police forces for a decision on whether to prosecute. But legal convenience has led to a social double-standard: photographs in popular magazines of female arousal and even masturbation go unprosecuted, although exception is taken to rampant masculinity. Men, it seems, must be protected from being treated as sex objects.

Written and pictorial accounts of straightforward copulation may attract prosecution if they are detailed and explicit. In *Whyte's case*, the House of Lords held that the arousing of libidinous thoughts fell squarely within the mischief aimed at by the Act. Lord Denning has decried heterosexual pornography as 'powerful propaganda for promiscuity', and other writers have argued that the message of straightforward sexual explicitness 'degrades the human being, reduces him to the level of an animal'.[3] If explicit accounts of normal sexual behaviour put readers in a frame of mind to act out the conduct depicted, no harm would result if they did so within an existing sexual relationship. Only if they went further, or sought release from an un-willing partner, or made exorbitant demands on a spouse, would danger arise from this class of material. This sort of pornography is ideologically vapid: pictures of people engaged in sexual intercourse are not usually located inside or outside marriage, and there is no reason why a reader should not associate sexual arousal from porno-graphy with his attraction for someone whom he loves and respects. As Britain's most experienced divorce judge once remarked,

> No-one can sit here as long as I have sat without realizing that there is the greatest diversity of standards between one set of spouses and another as to what is or is not a normal standard of sexual intercourse. What will be regarded as grossly excessive demands by one wife (or by one husband as the case may be) will be regarded as quite normal and reasonable by another wife or husband. I go further. There are things outside what may be called normal sexual intercourse which will be regarded by one wife (or husband, as the case may be) as so revolting as to be unmentionable, whereas other couples will regard them as nothing more than natural, normal love-making.[4]

These considerations now seem to weigh with prosecuting authorities, and pictures of orthodox sexual activity, short of erection, penetration and ejaculation, are usually made the subject of forfeiture proceed-ings rather than criminal trials.

Sexual behaviour is explicitly and enthusiastically discussed in the advice columns of those monthly magazines which largely comprise readers' letters (of dubious originality), either describing particular sex techniques or seeking guidance in sexual life from the psychiatrists and doctors on the particular magazine's advisory panel. These professionals, with names which do not always grace the pages of the medical directory, also contribute feature articles on the more common fetishes, illustrated by an abundance of intimate case histories. Understandably, the Court of Appeal takes the view that much of this 'soft-core pornography' is not produced from a benevolent concern for sexual health and happiness, but as an ingenious way of profiting from sexual titillation disguised by a thin but socially acceptable veneer of pseudo-medical advice.[5] This is undoubtedly an accurate description of the motives of some publishers, but whether it constitutes the spreading of depravity is another question. It is often alleged by prosecutors that these magazines tend to deprave and corrupt by putting ideas into readers' heads, and by encouraging them to experiment with sex techniques they might otherwise never have considered. Juries, however, have generally agreed with defence experts who argued, at least before *Jordan's* case, that the presentation of accurate information and advice about sexual behaviour is for the public good.

The boom in sex journals does underline the need for some check that information published and advice given is both accurate and reliable, because articles which propagate erroneous information could produce anxiety and depression. It is anomalous that under the present obscenity laws fraudulent mis-statements of medical fact go unpunished, while sound advice by qualified medical practitioners may be made the subject of a prosecution if the correspondence to which it is addressed is published in intimate detail.

The most widespread form of foreplay to feature in major obscenity trials has been oral/genital sex. The Chief Justice remarked that one item in *Oz* magazine 'is a salaciously written account of the joys from the female aspect of an act of oral sexual intercourse. It deals with the matter in great detail. It emphasizes the pleasures which the writers say are to be found in this activity, and there is in it no suggestion anywhere which would imply that this was a wrong thing to do, or in any way to induce people not to do it. The importance of that last observation is that there could be nothing here, as far as we could see, on which an argument that this was aversive, as tending to induce people *not* to conduct the activity described, could be founded.'[6] But the likelihood of the item affecting any behavioural change was doubted at the trial by Professor Eysenck, who commented that, 'There is a lot of experimental evidence from studies in the United States that showing people films explicitly portraying oral sex in a favourable light does not, except in a small minority of cases, change their behaviour so that if they have not done so before, they will do so later. It just doesn't seem to happen, even after thirty hours of seeing films of that kind. I see nothing specifically harmful in oral sex. It's a habit that's perhaps less encouraged in this country than others because it used to be regarded as perverted, but it probably is so wide-spread now that it cannot be regarded as perverted in any meaningful sense.'[7]

The presiding judge seemed genuinely mystified by the whole subject. 'I wonder how many of you, ladies and gentlemen of the jury,' he sighed, 'had heard words like "cunnilingus" before you came into this courtroom?' He asked jazz singer and critic George Melly to explain, 'for those of us who did not have a classical educa-tion, what do you mean by the word "cunnilingus"?' Melly obliged with some definitions: ' "Sucking" or "blowing", your Lordship, or "going down", and if I remember "gobbling" is another alternative. Another expression used in my naval days, your Lordship, was "yodelling in the canyon".'

In 1971 Paul Ableman's sociological study *The Mouth and Oral Sex* was prosecuted on the grounds that Ableman encouraged the deviate practices he described by omitting to condemn them. 'Why is it im-portant to read about it now?', complained the judge. 'We have managed to get on for a couple of thousand years without it.' The jury acquitted after medical practitioners told the court that their patients would be helped by reading *The Mouth and Oral Sex*, a 'valuable source of enlightenment which would dispel much needless suffering from feelings of guilt and anxiety'. In 1953 Kinsey found oral sex in vogue among fifty per cent of mid-Western Americans, and leading British psychiatrists no longer classify the practice as 'deviant'.[8] The taboo once attached to oral sex now seems of less significance in obscenity trials. In 1976 a jury at the Central Criminal Court acquitted the publisher of *Inside Linda Lovelace* which described the pleasures of oral sex by salacious accounts of the writer's bizarre experi-ences and by detailed advice on technique.[9] Literary experts, doctors, psychologists, women journalists and even the Oxford Professor of Jurisprudence were called upon to testify to the book's interest and acceptability, and the national press kept the public well informed of the issues ('Oral Sex Unnatural, Says Judge', reported one *Guardian* headline). When a Liverpool stipendiary magistrate subsequently ordered the seizure from W.H. Smith & Son of Dr Alex Comfort's bestseller *The Joy of Sex*, which enthusiastically encourages oral love-play, the DPP intervened to halt the proceedings. But jury verdicts will not change entrenched views about 'proper' sexual behaviour. When informed in another case that oral sex was widely practised in Britain, the Liverpool stipendiary remarked with sadness, 'If that is really so, I am glad I do not have long to live.'[10]

Descriptions of anal intercourse cause more problems, and several recent obscenity prosecutions have hinged upon the illegality of heterosexual sodomy. The DPP's argument – that couples who indulge in the abominable crime of buggery are depraved and corrupt, and any written or visual encouragement is therefore obscene – was first formulated in the wake of the *Lady Chatterley's Lover* trial. For the prosecution, Mr Mervyn Griffith-Jones QC had read to the jury: 'It was a night of sensual passion, in which she was a little startled and almost unwilling: yet it pierced again with piercing thrills of sensuality, different, sharper, more terrible than the thrills of tenderness, but at that moment, more desirable. Though a little frightened, she let him have his way....' 'Not very easy, sometimes', he observed, 'to know what in fact he is driving at in that passage.' Warden Sparrow of All Souls College, Oxford, claimed to know precisely which passage was being driven at, and devoted an article in *Encounter* to demonstrate that had the jurors shared his knowledge, they would surely have convicted.[11]

In 1972 an Old Bailey jury rejected the allegation that a detailed description of anal intercourse published in the magazine *In Depth* would deprave and corrupt, after hearing three eminent psychiatrists testify that disseminating information about the practice was for the public good.[12] Despite the acquittal of *In Depth*, lawyers are reluctant to approve publications about anal intercourse, because they fear obscenity or incitement prosecutions. In 1972 the DPP tried to stop research into the subject by two highly-qualified social scientists, who had sent a questionnaire to readers of the magazine *Forum* who had already volunteered to answer it. The very question, 'Have you had anal intercourse?', was alleged to be indecent, and hence an affront to Her Majesty's Mails. The magazine's editors were acquitted of the charge, and the survey ultimately revealed that forty per cent of the 3,600-strong sample had engaged in anal intercourse. Nevertheless, two years later a High Court judge reminded an obscenity trial jury of

The unnatural and horrible offence of sodomy ... if you have but a passing acquaintance with the Bible, you will know what happened in Sodom when Jehovah called forth fire and brimstone to punish the inhabitants for their unnatural practices. It has always been in this country, and in every civilised country, a serious offence to commit sodomy, which is punishable by life imprisonment. It is as serious as committing manslaughter, or grievous bodily harm. So that you can be aware of the seriousness of the offence, it is right that you should know how the law classifies it.[13]

The law – or rather the judges who made the law – first classified heterosexual anal intercourse as a crime in 1718, a time when sexual superstition was so rife that bestiality was declared illegal because 'a great lady had committed buggery with a baboon and conceived by it'.[14] Section 12 (1) of the 1956 Sexual Offences Act echoes the ancient taboo: 'It is an offence for a person to commit buggery with another person or with an animal.' The 1967 homosexual reform enabled males over twenty-one to be lawfully penetrated, but consenting ladies and their lovers were left liable to life imprisonment. In 1971 the Court of Appeal approved an eighteen-month jail sentence on a man who had committed an act of consensual heterosexual buggery: although married men who returned home drunk might commit the crime with their wives by mistake, 'deliberate acts ought not to be encouraged'.[15] Whether the publication of hygiene information about an illegal but widespread practice among consenting adults amounts to 'encouragement' is a matter for the jury, which may be less impressed by the absolute terms of the Sexual Offences Act than by Dr Anthony Storr's view that 'the chief interest which attaches to both sodomy and bestiality is not the practice of those acts but the savage penalties which the law attaches to them. Man's cruelty to man is surely more remarkable and shocking a phenomenon than his various forms of sexual activity.'[16]

The 1967 Sexual Offences Act may have decriminalized adult homosexuality, but the courts have continued to make its practice as difficult as possible. In 1972 the House of Lords judges declared that the propagation of homosexuality was still contrary to public policy. Lord Reid drew a distinction between merely exempting certain criminal penalties and making it lawful in the full sense:

I find nothing in the Act to indicate that Parliament thought or intended to lay down that indulgence in these practices is not corrupting. I read the Act as saying that, even though it may be corrupting, if people choose to corrupt themselves in this way that is their affair and the law will not interfere. But no license is given to others to encourage the practice.[17]

Acting on this principle, the courts have declined to grant custody of children to homosexual partners in divorce cases,[18] and have been more readily disposed to find publications obscene for carrying non-condemnatory accounts of homosexual experience than for concentrating on the degrading sexist stereotypes offered by 'girlie magazines'. zines'.

Lesbianism has never been unlawful, although it has long been regarded as perverse. In 1936, declaring *The Well of Loneliness* obscene, the Chief Metropolitan Magistrate thought that lesbianism in the book was all the more appalling a threat because 'the result is described as giving these women extraordinary rest, contentment and pleasure; and not only that, but it is actually put forward that it improves their mental balance and capacity'. In 1971, the Chief Justice drew attention to the cover of *Oz* magazine, a picture by the French artist Raymond Bertrand depicting five nude women. 'It is extremely attractively drawn, and at first inspection, as one of the witnesses said, it appears to be a simple piece of artistic work. Closer inspection, however, shows that … a woman is wearing strapped to her thighs an artificial penis or dildo, as apparently it is called, and other pairs are indulging in what are clearly lesbian activities. Attention has not unnaturally been drawn to that as an example of material in this magazine which might deprave or corrupt.'[19]

Prosecutors argue that to publish non-condemnatory accounts of homosexual experience, or a drawing or story which shows homosexuality favourably, constitutes a promotion. The term 'promotion' as a description of the business of publishing alluring, or at least non-condemnatory, accounts of sexual adventures rest on the assumption that people tend to emulate the practices they read about. This ignores the ambivalent response to homosexual erotica of many who feel repelled from practices which are outside their own long-established proclivities. Much of the experimental evidence points to the unlikelihood of a deep-seated sexual orientation, fixed in childhood, being diverted by written material, particularly where the postulated change is traumatic, as in a shift from hetero to homosexuality. It has also been argued that although homosexual advertisements, books and films would not be wholly responsible for changing a reader's sexual disposition, nevertheless their public availability would create a permissive climate in which homosexuality would be tolerated as a 'normal' condition, and latent homosexuals, who now refrain from acting out their impulses for fear of social disapproval, would be encouraged to do so. The argument might be justified if latent homo-

sexuals were happier repressing their inclinations than incurring guilt
or stigma in acting them out, but the 'permissive' climate of opinion
purportedly created by the availability of homosexual books and advertisements might help serve to reduce the guilt and stigma to a point
where the change could acceptably be made.

The judicial characterization of homosexuality as 'corrupt' means
that publishers of 'contact advertisements' enabling homosexuals to
meet each other run the risk of prosecution for the crime of conspiracy
to corrupt public morals. But if these advertisements are not of themselves obscene or indecent, then it might be 'a positive advantage that
homosexuals should make contact this way rather than in public toilets and parks. The chance of doing so is likely in at least some cases
to lead to a stable partnership'.[20] The same argument would apply
to heterosexual contact advertisements. If a man wants carnal connection with a male or female prostitute, he can go to notorious districts in any English city, and after a short but probably embarrassing
time make the desired contact. If his penchant is for more bizarre
sexual practices, the time will not be quite so short, and the embarrassment may be considerable. If the relationship he seeks is not commercial at all but lasting and worthwhile, the social process is usually
much longer and less predictable. An obvious way to avoid the embarrassment and lengthy duration of a personal approach is to place an
advertisement for the type of partner required, or to contact an advertiser whose services seem to answer the particular need. That advertisements which enable prostitutes to make contact with clients without causing public offence serve a social purpose was recognized by
the Wolfenden Committee, which foresaw, as a consequence of street
offences legislation, 'an increase in small advertisements in shops or
local newspapers, offering the services of masseuses, models or companions', and remarked that 'this would be less injurious than the
presence of prostitutes in the streets'.[21] The classified advertisements
in *Oz* magazine were examples of a kind of personal advertising which
since the legislative acceptance of the Wolfenden Report had become
a regular feature of both underground newspapers and soft-core sex
magazines, and even infiltrated serious publications like *Tribune* and
The New Statesman. For the prosecution, the small ads were designed
to pander to the lusts of perverts and to enable sex deviants to get
more recruits. The defence maintained they were merely a charitable
service for lonely people, and their social benefit was supported by
psychiatrists, sociologists and even professors of philosophy. Professor
Richard Wolheim thought that 'they might do something to mitigate

the kind of loneliness and distress which many people suffer', while Mr George Melly put the argument movingly: 'People advertising for each other, like the bisexual young man of Central London, seem to me sad, in that most people can happily find their partner without consulting small ads. But if people can't, or are too shy, then as most people need some love or at any rate some sexuality in their lives, if they resort to this advertisement and find somebody, well, I hope they are happy with them.'[22]

The essence of pornography is its breach of social taboos. It works – for good or ill – by liberating its readers from social conventions and enabling them to apprehend a pleasure in sex which some are incapable of realizing in normal surroundings. Although its end is sexual arousal, a common device for achieving that end is to break down traditional barriers by an outrageous story-line, within which the reader's mind concentrates on more conventional titillation. Reality is suspended by iconoclasm, after which the erotica has its effect. This is the psychological function of frequent references to behaviour which most readers would never wish to emulate in real life – incest, bestiality, necrophilia, coprophilia, and so on. Another purpose of such references may be to pander to morbid curiosity: the same instinct which causes sightseers to flock to plane crashes prompts some people to pay money to watch women copulating with donkeys. Erotic arousal may be less of an enticement to this class of reader than sheer inquisitiveness, the quest for novelty shared by those who roll up to see a circus freak. This is a common, though hardly attractive, human trait, and most pornography which panders to it is destroyed without murmur, although the aversion defence would theoretically be available. An exception may be made for material of psychological interest (such as the work of de Sade) or of historical value – in 1971 Croydon magistrates declined to destroy an illustrated account of bestiality in ancient Rome, on the basis that it would be more likely to disgust than to deprave its readers. The real obscenity of bestiality pictures lies not in their effects on readers' minds, but in the circumstances surrounding their production. Procuring girls for intercourse with donkeys would seem to be an indefensible case of human exploitation, which could be prosecuted and punished under the Sexual Offences Act.[23]

In real life these deviations are usually the last resort of desperate sexuality. Kinsey found that bestiality was not unknown to eight per cent of his male interviewees (for the most part mentally retarded and/or from country homes) and to four per cent of his female sample, who admitted to erotic play with domestic pets. Bad shepherds are sometimes prosecuted in west-country courts, but their crimes are usually the product of loneliness and opportunity, rather than the availability of pornography on Exmoor. Incest is taken more seriously: well over 100 cases are prosecuted in England each year, and many thousands more go undetected. Breaches of this powerful moral and genetic taboo have been attributed to slum housing, bereavement, rejection by spouse, and subnormality. It may be doubted whether consumers of pornography take references to incest as more than a peg on which to hang an erotic story. Nonetheless, non-condemnatory accounts of the practice are frequently prosecuted, especially if they occur in letters to sex magazines which refrain from advising readers that the crime is punishable by up to seven years in prison. Bizarre strains of pornography depicting extreme sexual violence, simulated necrophilia, and human excretory functions do exist in Scandinavia and are sometimes imported into Britain, where its distributors are almost invariably convicted. Juries which are sometimes inclined to support freedom for voyeurs are less keen to promote freedom for ghouls.

The advent of photographic pornography has provoked demands for protection of those who may be prevailed upon to participate. 'Feelthy pictures' of the kind available in Port Said during the first World War are now the stock-in-trade of some suburban newsagents, and models find themselves confronted with demands which may range from nudity to masturbation and other sexual acts. In theory, models could be charged with 'aiding and abetting' the publication of obscenity, but they are usually perceived as more sinned against than sinning, so that charges of procuring obscene performances are normally confined to those primarily responsible for production and distribution.

This is a sensible and humane distinction: the *Longford Report* pointed out that

many of those taking part in theatrical, club, cinema or other productions, and 'modelling', do so for what they regard as compelling economic reasons. These are likely to be very real at a time when there is heavy unemployment in the theatrical and allied professions.[24]

Those who counsel and procure obscene performances may be prosecuted for complicity if photographs of these incidents are published in circumstances which contravene the Act, but their guilt will hinge, not on any question of whether they have exploited models at the time of recruitment, but on whether the photographic reproduction of the performance is likely to corrupt the morals of those who may ultimately view it. Adults who participate in modelling sessions out of free choice do not require the protection of the criminal law. The gap at present lies in the failure of the law to punish promoters who pressurize models to participate in sexual activities which may cause personal distress, but which do not result, because of careful editing, in a publication which would infringe the Obscene Publications Act.

POLITICS, DRUGS AND VIOLENCE

The underground press

Moral guardians of earlier centuries were concerned to prohibit serious works which challenged government or faith, rather than bawdiness or the arousing of sexual appetites. The operators of modern obscenity laws have promoted salacity to the top of their moral blacklist, but between 1969 and 1973 a new and political dimension was given to a law which was generally thought to guard more against the arousing of emotions than ideologies. During that period the apostles of radical change, and not the pedlars of masturbatory fantasies, were indicted as depravers and corrupters of British youth. This tendency reached its climax in 1971 with the Oz trial and the contemporaneous prosecution of The Little Red Schoolbook. Police harassment of the underground press convinced cultural radicals that their life-style was being put on trial. The Crown accused the Oz editors of 'relentlessly promoting certain elements of the new culture, namely dope, rock and roll, and fucking in the streets', and one police officer involved in the case admitted that his real objection to the defendants was that 'they attack society and try to change it'.[25] The motive which ran through all the underground press obscenity prosecutions was a determination to halt the spread of radical ideas amongst schoolchildren: both Schoolkids' Oz and The Little Red Schoolbook were more concerned to promote ideas for breaking down the authoritarian structure of schools than to arouse adolescent libidos. When The Little Red Schoolbook decision was confirmed on appeal, the court seemed as much concerned by the book's political bias as by its sexual content. The judge deplored the suggestion that children might organize demonstrations or strikes, and condemned the book as 'inimical to good teacher/child relationships ... subversive, not only to the authority but to the influence of the trust between children

and teachers . . . the influence of parents, the church, youth organizations and other adults with whom they come into casual contact will
be very seriously affected in the face of a very considerable portion
of the children who read this book'.[26]

The result of this courtroom confusion of sex, politics and life-style
as prosecution targets was to produce verdicts heavily dependent on
the character of the tribunal. Middle-aged, middle-class jurors
detested cultural patterns which they were incapable of sharing or
understanding, but long-haired and irreverent jurors, like the young
man who embraced the *Nasty Tales* editors after their acquittal, were
more prone to view the proceedings as a political trial, in which they
identified more closely with the beads and jeans in the dock than the
wigs and gowns ranged against them. The DPP sought to silence
Oz, I. T. and *Nasty Tales* by invoking a law which adopted as its
measure of guilt the degree of corruption of moral standards. But these
newspapers were accused of 'carrying the banner of the alternative
society' – and if those alternative values were shared by a significant
section of the population, then they should have been reflected in the
DPP's assessment of contemporary moral standards. The US
Supreme Court has often insisted that the First Amendment protects
publications which deal with ideas, reason and truth-seeking, but does
not protect prurient material belonging to the realm of passion,
desires, cravings and titillation. The latter is not classified as 'free
speech' for the purposes of constitutional protection. In Britain for
a brief period the DPP seemed to prosecute certain publications precisely *because* they expressed ideas: ideas which were associated with
a life-style at odds with conventional mores. The last underground
press trial resulted in an acquittal for the editors of *Nasty Tales* in 1973,
and the DPP took no action against a revised edition of *The Little
Red Schoolbook* in which the anti-authoritarian passages reappeared
in full. In 1976 the Government, in its successful submissions to the
European Court of Human Rights in the *Handyside* case, firmly dis-
avowed any intention of using the Obscene Publications Act to muzzle
the expression of anti-establishment views.

Drug-taking

There is no indication in the deliberations on the Report of the Parliamentary Select Committee, or in the debates which surrounded the
Obscene Publications Act, that 'obscenity' pertained to anything but
matters of sex. United States legislation and practice is so confined,
but in Britain the courts have interpreted the statutory definition of

'obscene' to encompass encouragements to take dangerous drugs and to engage in violence.

The first case to push the notion of 'obscenity' beyond the bounds of sex arose from forfeiture proceedings in 1965 against *Cain's Book*, a novel by Alex Trocchi which dealt with the life of a New York drug addict. In the ensuing Divisional Court case, *Calder* v. *Powell*, it was held to be

perfectly plain that depravity, and, indeed, obscenity (because obscenity is treated as a tendency to deprave) is quite apt to cover what was suggested by the prosecution in this case. This book – the less said about it the better – concerned the life, or imaginary life, of a junkie in New York, and the suggestion of the prosecution was that the book highlighted, as it were, the favourable effects of drug-taking and, so far from condemning it, advocated it, and that there was a real danger that those into whose hands the book came might be tempted at any rate to experiment with drugs and get the favourable sensations highlighted by the book. In my judgment there is no reason whatever to confine obscenity and depravity to sex, and there was ample evidence upon which the justices could hold that this book was obscene.'[27]

It is impossible to divorce the underground press obscenity prosecutions from their background in the mutual hostility between the police and the 'alternative society', engendered particularly by police drug raids and 'stop and search' activities. One of the most noticeable ways in which the underground press 'attacked society and tried to change it' was by condemning the legal prohibition of marijuana, and by providing information services for drug-takers. Many peculiarities in the trials derived from prosecution attempts to prove that drug-takers could be further corrupted by descriptions of the drug scene which lacked any overtones of moral condemnation. For *Oz* or *Nasty Tales* to deplore cannabis use would have been akin to *The Economist* calling for the end of capitalism. It is quite unrealistic to expect newspapers to do otherwise than accept the prevailing morality of their readers: to censure them is to lose them. Yet when a *Nasty Tales* editor, asked why his magazine did not condemn cannabis, admitted 'if we had discouraged drug-taking in the magazine, I don't think it would have been bought or appreciated by our readers', the judge invited the jury to regard this as an admission of guilt. He refused the editors costs for their successful defence, on the grounds that the magazine, 'quite apart from sex and violence, freely advocates drug-taking'.

The judicial classification of cannabis smoking as a 'depraved and corrupt' activity is hardly compatible with the 1969 Report of the Government Advisory Committee on Cannabis, which concluded, after a thorough review of the evidence, that 'the long term consumption of cannabis in moderate doses has no harmful effect'.[28] Moreover, there is no evidence that people are impelled to take drugs merely by reading about them. The problem of proving a causal connection between drug references in literature and a reader's decision to experiment parallels the problem of proving that erotica encourages people to sexual misbehaviour. Such studies as are available suggest that initiation into drug-taking stems from sub-cultural involvement, associations with groups which tolerate and use drugs freely, the availability of the drug in a particular locality, and so on. The fact that drug-taking *can* be a pleasurable experience is known by most persons in a position to obtain narcotics, who do not need magazines to remind them of the fact. Genuine attempts to advise against drug-taking will be ineffectual if they do not concede the pleasures as well as the pains. There is also the danger that a prohibition on 'highlighting favourable sensations' might impose a severe limitation on the serious novelist, although the favourable descriptions of opium-taking in *The Count of Monte Cristo*, and the apparently productive use of cocaine by Sherlock Holmes have never been thought to justify obscenity prosecutions. The use of dangerous drugs usually amounts to a criminal offence, and writers who deliberately and specifically incite such offences could be prosecuted, in appropriate cases, for complicity in any crime which directly resulted from their acts of encouragement. The extension of the obscenity formula to encompass truthful accounts of hallucinatory experiences is confusing in principle and unnecessary in practice.

Violence

Any material which combines violence with sexual explicitness is a candidate for prosecution. In *Shaw* v. *DPP* evidence which showed that a magazine advertised the services of prostitutes prepared to cane their clients ('corrective training' offered by ladies named 'Miss Whiplash') was thought by one Law Lord to be 'conclusive proof that the magazine spread moral corruption'.[29] Yet there are many gradations between a friendly slap and a stake through the heart, and most 'spanking' books and articles escape indictment. Not all masochist magazines permit application of the simple formula devised by one North London magistrate in 1974: 'If the models are spanked with their pants on, they are acceptable; if the pants are down, the pictures are obscene.' Many cheap American novellas describe sexual torture in lurid detail, and foreign magazines and films depict violence in the context of particular sexual fetishes. In 1975 the distributors of *Bondage Bizarre, Hogtie* and *Double Pain Date in the Tower of Terror* were prosecuted in three trials at the Central Criminal Court. On each occasion the jury failed to agree, after hearing expert evidence that pictures of sexual violence and extreme bondage could be therapeutic to readers possessed of such fetishes, enabling them to find fantasy release in masturbation rather than inflicting unwanted attentions upon unhappy partners. This class of evidence has subsequently been ruled inadmissible, leaving only an extended version of the aversion theory, and the argument that literature does not incite sex crimes, as a basis for defence.

Flagellation has become the hallmark of British pornography, and one observer has calculated that 'ninety per cent of pornographic books imported into England are sado-masochistic. Obviously the market is geared to the demand, and the demand is for sadistic sex. It is very likely that sexual caning, that insular preoccupation – the *vice anglais* – has been acquired through the method usually considered popular for the upbringing of youth.'[30] However unpleasant sexual sadism may appear when pictured or described, it is at least questionable whether those with a natural penchant for pain are depraved or corrupt. Psychologists are able to detect masochistic tendencies in most people and Dr Antony Storr explains that 'pornographic literature is full of fantasies of stern, authoritarian women beating or making slaves of men; such figures solve the masochist's problem of how to obtain sexual pleasure without feeling guilty about it, for they combine within themselves the erotic enticement of a mistress together with the authoritarian function of a parent. . . .'[31] Other psychiatrists regard this genre of pornography as the most dangerous of all, inculcating a taste for degradation and, where the fantasy victim is female, encouraging rape and sexual humiliation. In consequence, the distributors of extreme sadistic pornography are generally prosecuted under section 2 of the Act, while section 3 forfeiture orders are sought in respect of milder masochistic material.

More difficulty is experienced with the depiction of violence in non-sexual contexts. The Divisional Court in the *A. & B. C. Chewing Gum* case approved the prosecution of a manufacturer of children's swap-cards depicting scenes of battle, on the theory that they were capable of depraving young minds by provoking emulation of the violence portrayed.[32] In *R. v. Calder & Boyars* the Court of Appeal confirmed that the test of obscenity could encompass written advocacy of brutal violence.[33] The difficulty with these decisions is that they permit the conviction of publications which are not normally regarded as 'obscene', and which require expert evidence to establish the existence of their corrupting potential. The decision in *Jordan*, by excluding psychiatric evidence on the obscenity issue, has made prosecutions for violence devoid of sex virtually impossible except in cases where the publication is directed to very young children. The prevalence of violence in the mass media must raise serious doubts as to whether any one publication should be singled out for prosecution under an act designed to suppress pornography, and any writing which advocates specific acts of illegal violence could be prosecuted as an incitement to commit crime. Little popular fiction would remain if all scenes of brutality were prohibited. The present liberal platitude, 'I don't mind the sex, it's the violence', is difficult to translate into law, and might in any event lead to a degree of censorship unpalatable to its proponents. For example, in 1973 several British trial judges blamed the film *A Clockwork Orange* for inciting teenage muggings. They described it as 'a wicked film', presenting 'an unassailable argument for the return of censorship'. Anthony Burgess, who wrote the novel on which the film was based, has pointed out that the problem is much more complex:

A perverse nature can be stimulated by anything. Any book can be used as a pornographic instrument, even a great work of literature, if the mind that so uses it is off balance. I once found a small boy masturbating in the presence of the Victorian steel-engravings in a family Bible. Blood-drinking murderers have admitted to the stimulation of the sacrifices of the Mass. One multiple child-murderer in the United States was, on his own confession, haunted by the Abraham-Isaac episode in the Old Testament. Ban the Marquis de Sade and you will also have to ban the Bible. No more Academy nudes, no more stocking advertisements, no women (except if Islamically shrouded) in the streets of cities. No Hamlet, no Macbeth. There would then, because of the outlawing of the reasonable catharsis of art, be far more Moors Murders.[34]

Horror comics

In one respect the obscenity formula has been adapted to outlaw depictions of non-sexual violence which might prove harmful to children. In 1955 Parliament sought to prohibit the importation and sale of 'horror comics' which had been blamed by American psychiatrists for causing an upsurge in juvenile delinquency. The Children and Young Persons (Harmful Publications) Act was designed, in the words of the Solicitor-General, to prevent 'the kind of state of mind that might be induced in certain types of children by provoking a kind of morbid brooding or ghoulishness, or mental ill-health'.[35] It provided a maximum penalty of four months imprisonment, and a fine of £100, for the printing, publication or sale of

any book, magazine or other like work which is of a kind likely to fall into the hands of children or young persons and consists wholly or mainly of stories told in pictures (with or without the addition of written matter), being stories portraying
(a) the commission of crimes; or
(b) acts of violence or cruelty; or
(c) incidents of a repulsive or horrible nature;
in such a way that the work as a whole would tend to corrupt a child or young person into whose hands it might fall.

Although the measure was perceived as an urgent and important one at the time it was passed, there have been as yet no prosecutions. Criminal proceedings require the consent of the Attorney-General, although this safeguard does not apply to imported comics, which may be seized and forfeited at the instance of Customs officials. These Customs seizures operate upon conventional principles: comics depicting Green Berets bombing and bayoneting Vietnamese are routinely permitted entry, while American 'underground comics' which use Disneyesque caricatures to lampoon materialism and moral hypocrisy are regularly intercepted and destroyed. An internal Customs directive issued in June 1978 indicates that the following literature will henceforth be deemed to fall outside the prohibition:

(a) novels with horror themes in which any illustrations are merely secondary to the reading matter; or
(b) newspapers or ordinary children's 'comics' in which, say, a cartoon strip on a gangster theme is an incidental feature; or
(c) copies of works of art, such as *The Rake's Progress*, which may depict scenes of violence but would not be likely to be studied by children; or
(d) 'comics' devoted to 'wild western' or other adventure stories, unless they are clearly of a morbid or obnoxious character, so as to render them harmful to children.

The Customs and Excise Act 1952 operates to shift the burden of proof to the importer contesting the confiscation, although this is mitigated by the evidential exception to the ruling in *Jordan* which permits psychiatric testimony as to the likely effect of the comics on youthful readers. Expert advice is not taken by Customs officers before they decide to confiscate, and they have been criticized for seizing 'adult' comics, imported for sale to collectors, under legislation designed to protect children. In 1976 they prevailed upon Southampton magistrates to destroy *The Illustrated Tales of Edgar Allan Poe*, although the same bench ordered the release of *The Adventures of Conan the Barbarian* after evidence from a child psychiatrist that the Conan legend would be perceived as moral and romantic by children enured to the adventures of *Starsky and Hutch*.

THE PROTECTION OF CHILDREN

The law will always be jealous to protect children, and whatever may be a person's intentions, if he, in fact, acts in a way likely to harm children, he can only expect that a grave view will be taken of his actions.[36]

Undoubtedly the greatest concern over sexually explicit publications is manifested at the prospect of the involvement of young people, either as readers or as models. The *Hicklin* test concentrated upon an article's potential for arousing impure thoughts in the young of either sex, and this concern is preserved in the 1959 Act, by its reference to the circumstances of the publication and the likely readership. The test of obscenity varies with the class of persons likely to read the publication. Instead of imposing censorship at the point of distribution, by making the actual sale of erotic material to children a crime, it must be established that the material on trial is *aimed* at impressionable young people. The case of the chewing gum cards illustrates how material which could be considered harmless if sold to adults by inclusion in cigarette packets may be made the subject of obscenity proceedings if it is marketed especially for children. Even in cases concerned with 'adults only' publications the jury is entitled to consider the possibility that teenagers may obtain them from careless booksellers. The spending power of modern pocket-money encompasses most paperback publications, and the dangers of unrestricted circulation provides prosecuting counsel with a strong emotive argument. 'Ask yourselves the question,' posed Mr Mervyn Griffith-Jones to the *Lady Chatterley* jury, 'would you approve of your young sons, young daughters – because girls can read as well as boys – reading this book? Is it a book you would have lying around in your own house? Is it a book that you would even wish your wife or your servants to read?'[37] The unlikely prospect of lower-middle-class jurors agonizing over the moral welfare of their servants brought some refinement to this theme when it was adopted by Mr Brian Leary at the close of his final speech in the *Oz* trial: 'The final question which you may like to ask yourselves, members of the jury, when you go out to consider your verdict is not "Would I like *my* children to see it?", because your children come from very nice homes and have no doubt been well brought up. But ask yourselves "Would I like *my neighbour's children* to see this particular magazine?"'[38]

Little is known about the effects of erotica on young people, and there are strong ethical inhibitions against conducting the sort of research which has measured adult reactions. The American Presidential Commission found that sexual precocity was linked with deviant home backgrounds and deviant peer influences, although one of its studies warned that early and persistent exposure to pornography might be a causal factor in delinquency.[39] One group of eminent psychiatrists maintains that although the reading of pornography by children is not harmful if it is done within the context of societal disapproval, it may become morally damaging if that disapproval is withdrawn, e.g. by repeal of all laws against obscenity:

> Psychiatrists ... made a distinction between the reading of pornography, as unlikely to be *per se* harmful, and the permitting of the reading of pornography, which was conceived as potentially destructive. The child is protected in his reading of pornography by the knowledge that it is pornographic, i.e. disapproved. It is outside parental standards and not part of his identification process. To openly permit implies parental approval, and even suggests seductive encouragement. If this is so of parental approval, it is equally so of societal approval – another potent influence on the developing ego.[40]

A law which expressly prohibited the sale of erotic material to young persons would provide a far more effective measure of societal disapproval than the 1959 Act, which seeks to regulate general publishing activities rather than specific acts of distribution.

No mercy can be expected in the courts for those who involve young persons, even with their consent, in modelling sessions for sexually explicit photographs. Section 1 (1) of the Indecency with Children Act 1960 provides that

> Any person who commits an act of gross indecency with or towards a child under the age of fourteen, or who incites a child under that age to such an act with him or another, shall be liable on conviction on indictment to imprisonment. ...

This provision would cover most cases in which children are encouraged to pose for erotic pictures, although the requirement of some indecent action 'with or towards' the child may arguably exclude photographic sessions in which an individual child poses provocatively without any physical contact with, or direction from, the photographer or procurer. The Court of Appeal has suggested that this provision would cover 'an act . . . which takes place in an indecent situation', but it is doubtful whether the indecency of the situation alone would render indecent an innocent action 'with or towards' a child.[41] The statute does not apply to children aged fourteen to fifteen, although children of this age cannot in law consent to an 'indecent assault', and any indecent action towards them in the course of a modelling session would amount to an offence. But a photographer who merely touches child models to indicate a pose, and does not otherwise behave in an indecent or threatening manner, cannot be convicted of indecent assault, although he may be prosecuted under the catch-all offence of a conspiracy to corrupt public morals.[42]

The gap in statutory protection for children of fourteen and fifteen was closed in 1978 by the Protection of Children Act. The Law Commission had proposed a simple amendment to section 1 of the Indecency with Children Act, substituting 'under sixteen' for 'under fourteen', but the possibility of a general election and a scare campaign about 'child pornography' combined to produce a major legislative initiative against the distribution, as well as the manufacture, of indecent photographs of persons under sixteen. Section 1 of the Protection of Children Act makes it an offence, punishable summarily by six months imprisonment or a fine of £1,000, or on indictment by up to three years imprisonment and/or an unlimited financial penalty,

(a) to take, or permit to be taken, any indecent photograph of a child (meaning in this Act a person under the age of sixteen); or
(b) to distribute or show such indecent photographs; or
(c) to have in his possession such indecent photographs, with a view to their being distributed or shown by himself or others; or
(d) to publish or cause to be published any advertisement likely to be understood as conveying that the advertiser distributes or shows such indecent photographs, or intends to do so.

A defendant 'distributes' photographs within the meaning of this section if he merely shows them to another, without any desire for gain. 'Indecent photographs' include films, film negatives and any form of video recording. There is no defence to section 1 (a) other than that the photographs are not indecent, or if indecent do not depict persons under sixteen, or that the accused in any event played no part in their production. Section 1 (d) does not even require the photographs on offer to be themselves indecent – an advertiser is guilty if his wording is 'likely to be understood as conveying' a willingness to sell or show nude pictures of children within the prohibited age-group. If the charge is laid under section 1 (b) or (c), however, the distributor or exhibitor is entitled to an acquittal if he can establish on the balance of probabilities

(a) that he had a legitimate reason for distributing or showing the photographs or (as the case may be) having them in his possession; or
(b) that he had not himself seen the photographs and did not know, nor had any cause to suspect them to be indecent.

A further safeguard against ill-conceived prosecutions is the requirement that the DPP must consent to all criminal proceedings initiated under section 1, although the Act does permit any police officer to obtain a search warrant to seize photographs reasonably suspected of contravening the section, and to have them destroyed by magistrates in proceedings similar to the forfeiture process under section 3 of the Obscene Publications Act.

The Preamble to the Protection of Children Act proclaims that the measure purposes

to prevent the exploitation of children by making indecent photographs of them; and to penalize the distribution, showing and advertisement of such indecent photographs.

Section 1 (a) will deter photographers from requiring child models to pose indelicately. Psychological harm may be caused to youngsters encouraged by adults to strike sexual poses in circumstances which fall short of sexual assault, and there is evidence that children exploited in this way become vulnerable to further and more damaging enticements. The effect of sections 1 (b), (c) and (d) is more problematic. Some psychiatrists fear that a ban on the very possession of child pornography may actually increase the incidence of molestation, by removing the one safety-valve which inhibits paedophiles from acting out their sexual urges. Others have warned that outcry, publicity and police interviews are likely to be more emotionally damaging for children than the incident itself, and have urged that responsibility for investigating offences should belong to social service departments rather than police officers. During the House of Lords debates Lord Gardiner expressed some alarm at the hasty introduction of a measure which was wider than necessary to remedy an admitted defect in the law:

... there is good law reform and bad law reform. Bad law reform takes place when there is some article in a newspaper ... or some scare, as a result of which there is a demand for instantaneous legislation – and instantaneous legislation is almost invariably bad. I approach this Bill on the footing ... first, that there was no evidence whatever that there had been any current increase in pornographic photographs of children. And secondly, that if there were, then, with one small exception, the police had ample power to deal with them. There was really only one small exception which needed to be covered.[43]

Whether the Act amounts to 'bad law reform' will in practice depend on the DPP's selection of targets for prosecution. The former statutory safeguards will continue to be used, and it may be that the Protection of Children Act, like the horror comics legislation passed in similar circumstances in 1955, will serve as little more than a catharsis for the public feeling whipped up by well-intentioned press campaigns. It is possible, however, that the extension of the Act to distribution and advertising may have an unforeseen and chilling effect on sex education material, the treatment of paedophilia, and the screening or advertising of certain feature films, even if no prosecution would seriously be contemplated in the circumstances. Whether such consequences would arise depends upon a number of questions left unresolved by the drafting of the statute.

The courts have been unable to provide a meaningful definition of 'indecent', short of 'offending against recognized standards of propriety at the lower end of the scale' or 'shocking ordinary people'. Fears that the Act would extend to home movies and family-album snapshots of children frolicking naked were dismissed in the House of Lords debates by reference to *Commissioners of Customs & Excise* v. *Sun & Health Ltd*. The question in that case was whether *Boys are Boys Again*, a book comprising 122 photographs of naked boys, was an indecent import. Lord Justice Bridge accepted that the publication was not obscene, and would not infringe the standards of decency current in 1973, if it depicted naked children without sexual overtones. But he held that this publication, although borderline, lacked innocence:

... there is a photograph which has been published upside-down and the boys are standing on their hands, and it has been published in such a way as to suggest, at a casual glance at all events, that those two boys' penises are certainly erect ... it seems to me that (two other photographs) are about as provocative poses of the young body as could be imagined ... the conclusion that I reach is that if that book is looked at as a whole ... the very essence of the publication, the reason for publishing it, is to focus attention on the male genital organs. It is a series of photographs in the great majority of which the male genitalia, sometimes in close-up, are the focal point of the picture ... they aim to be interesting pictures of boys' penises....[44]

'That is exactly how I would expect the issue under the Bill to be decided,' said the Secretary of State for the Home Office. 'I think, frankly, that there is no danger that ordinary family snapshots, or legitimate sex education material, would be caught by the terms of the Bill.'[45] This may be an optimistic view of the authority of the *Sun and Health* case as a precedent for the interpretation of section 1 of the Act. The judgment is unreported, it concerned a blanket Customs prohibition and not a statute which is expressly directed against child photographs, and its purposive approach directly conflicts with binding Court of Appeal and Divisional Court rulings that 'indecency' is a legal concept which must be entirely divorced from circumstances, context or intention. During the Third Reading debate the Secretary of State repeated the mistaken Home Office view that '... the test of indecency already exists to separate photographs which are offensive from those which are innocent or which have been taken with a clinical rather than a prurient approach'.[46] But the cases of *Stamford*,[47] *Stanley*,[48] and *Kosmos Publications*[49] establish that the test of indecency is absolute. If the Home Office wished to make illegal only that class of indecency which is designed to appeal to prurient interests, it should have said so in the statute, rather than in Hansard.

Those who are charged under section 1 (b) or (c) with publishing or distributing indecent photographs of children are entitled to show that they acted for a 'legitimate reason'. The defence is new to the criminal law, and, in accordance with the rule in *Brutus* v. *Cozens* it will fall to be interpreted by magistrates and juries applying colloquial and common-sense conceptions of legitimacy.[50]

Lord Scarman, the only judge to participate in the Parliamentary debates on the Bill, explained:

> The phrase 'a legitimate reason' has a certain originality about it, and it is the originality about it which commends it to my mind.... There will be parents and others who have no lawful authority – if that phrase means anything in that context – to have in their possession indecent photographs, and yet they do have a legitimate reason – one need not speculate what it is – for having them.... when it is available it is a highly respectable and dignified defence, the sort of defence one would wish to take if one had in one's possession for legitimate reasons an indecent photograph.
>
> Do not be frightened of introducing new and original, but simple and

understandable, language into our statute law. Welcome the opportunity. Get away from the old, hackneyed phrases and use a phrase which means something to ordinary people, and bear in mind that this phrase, 'a legitimate reason' really embraces a question of fact on which courts and juries are well able to reach a sensible decision in determining the meaning.[51]

Among the reasons for possession of indecent photographs of children which the Government has conceded would be legitimate are included academic study and research, medical advice and 'the use of such material in psychiatric treatment'.[52] On the strength of these assurances the DPP will presumably permit psychiatrists to continue using 'child porn' in the treatment of paedophilia, for example in the course of aversion therapy or to provide a substitute focus for illegal sex-drives. If the courts construe 'indecent' as an objective quality inhering to a photograph irrespective of its context, the 'legitimate reason' defence will avail publishers of clinical or sex educational material in which photographs of children's genitals may have a proper place.

Section 7 (2) of the Act defines 'indecent photograph' to include 'an indecent photograph comprised in a film', while section 7 (3) provides:

> Photographs (including those comprised in a film) shall, if they show children and are indecent, be treated for all purposes of this Act as indecent photographs of children.

This section will complicate the task of local authorities and the British Board of Film Censors, when faced with feature films which include child actors in immodest or disgusting scenes. Such scenes are deemed, by section 7 (3), to constitute 'indecent photographs of a child', even if the child is not participating in, or even aware of, the indecency. A plot which calls for a child to discover parents making love will be difficult to film or to distribute without contravention of the Act. The artistic merit or overall purpose will not redeem an offending scene: *The Exorcist*, banned by the Marxist government of Tunisia on the ground that it was propaganda for Christianity, might infringe the Act because it depicts a thirteen-year-old actress mouthing obscenities and simulating masturbation. The Hollywood vogue for casting actors and actresses aged under sixteen in major 'adult' movies may curtail distribution in the United Kingdom.

Section 1 (d) affects film and magazine titles, and requires careful vetting of advertising copy. Even if the product itself does not infringe the Act, 'any advertisement likely to be understood as conveying that the advertiser distributes or shows indecent photographs' may be prosecuted, without the benefit of a 'legitimate reason' defence. Films with titles which include *Schoolgirl, Lolita, Baby*, or other words which evoke the thought of under-age sex will be difficult to publicize. In the week that the Act came into force one West End cinema pointedly changed the name of its current offering from *Schoolgirls* to *Eighteen-Year-Old Schoolgirls*.

Although most strains of erotica have been defended at one time or another in proceedings under the Obscene Publications Acts, child pornography was always an exception, and there is no record of any jury acquittal of this class of material. If charges against distributors are laid in the alternative under the 1959 Act and the Protection of Children Act, it is likely that defendants will plead guilty to the latter in order to receive lighter sentences, on the principle that 'indecency' is a less serious offence than contributing to the spread of corruption.

The future of obscenity

English obscenity law may be illogical in theory, uncertain in scope, and unworkable in operation, but few nations have discovered any satisfactory alternative. Some have replaced the jury by censorship boards representing 'the good and the wise', others have opted for administrative classification systems operated by public officials. These reforms have brought certainty at the expense of the fundamental liberty to publish and be damned. Several continental countries have achieved maximum freedom of expression coupled with minimum public offence by abolishing obscenity altogether and confining the grosser forms of pornography to specific zones of major cities, while maintaining laws against public display, exposure to non-consenting citizens and direct sales to minors. This solution is the most attractive, because it provides a measured endorsement of the values of both liberty and privacy. As a practical political proposition for Britain, however, it has the drawback of legitimizing, albeit on a restricted and controlled basis, material which powerful lobbies would regard as wholly unfit for publication in any form. They share the mistaken belief, still prevalent amongst would-be law reformers, that the problem is soluble by tinkering with the statutory definition of 'obscene'. Suggested definitions include: 'indecent', 'outraging the recognized standards of propriety', 'undue emphasis on sex', 'grossly affronting contemporary standards of decency', 'appealing to a lewd and filthy interest in sex', 'depicting sexually criminal acts', and 'outraging contemporary standards of decency and humanity accepted by the public at large'. Yet these generalized formulae are open to much the same criticisms as those levelled at 'a tendency to

deprave or corrupt'. All require the return of a value-judgment verdict, after forensic debates about morality and community standards.
Criminality still arbitrarily hinges upon the character of the tribunal
of fact: libertines will find pornography acceptable to the public at
large, while paternalists will classify D.H.Lawrence and James Joyce
as writers who appeal to lewd and filthy interests in sex. It will remain
impossible to predict the moral shockability of a particular jury called
upon to give content to vague notions of 'community standards' after
interminable arguments as to which affronts are 'gross' and when an
interest in sex becomes 'filthy'. The decision to enlist the criminal law
on behalf of a particular moral standpoint will devalue that law in
the eyes of those whose moral standards are simply different.

The lack of community consensus on whether and to what extent
sexual explicitness should be proscribed makes it unwise for the law
to adopt an entrenched position in favour of deploring or in favour
of ignoring. Major reform is overdue, but a partisan approach risks
disaffection and disrespect from one or other substantial section of
the community which the reformed law must serve. The problem of
obscenity is intractable, and does not by its very nature admit of a
legal solution which will satisfy everyone. The 'best' solution will be
a law which promotes least disrespect for those who will be obliged
to administer it – in other words, one which is clear, consistent and
above all workable.

The experience of legislatures and courts in North America provides a salutary lesson in the impossibility of controlling obscenity by
toying with generalized definitions. The Canadian criminal code,
adopted in 1959, deems a publication obscene if its dominant characteristic 'is the undue exploitation of sex, or of sex and any one or more
of the following subjects, namely, crime, horror, cruelty and violence...'. Many years and many conflicting decisions later, the
Canadian Law Reform Commission voiced a familiar complaint:

> The meaning of the Criminal Code definition of obscenity is obscure.
> Although the constituent elements of it are understood, it is not clear how
> the different elements relate to one another and the test is inconsistently
> applied in practice. When translated into operational terms, the test of
> obscenity, as interpreted by Canadian courts, appears to be little more than
> 'does the publication shock the judge'.[1]

Canadian courts have had no more success with the notions of community standards, artistic merit or seriousness of purpose. Juries have
been left to ponder equations of the sort:

Base purpose, lack of merit, and an offence against community standards count individually towards a finding of obscenity, while serious purpose, artistic merit, and a non-offence against community standards do not individually count away from a finding of obscenity, unless all three point away.

An even worse jurisprudential morass prevails in the United States, where the Supreme Court has experimented with a bewildering variety of definitions since it decided that the constitutional protection afforded to free speech did not extend to obscenity.[2] At first it was thought that pornography could not qualify as 'speech' because it expressed no ideas and served no social purpose, and States were permitted to outlaw only those publications which were proved to be 'utterly without redeeming social value'.[3] Experts quickly redeemed every kind of publication by discerning some iota of therapeutic or sociological value, and in 1973 a new conservative majority of Supreme Court justices settled a more rigorous tripartite test in the watershed case of *Miller* v. *California*:

The basic guidelines for the trier of fact must be: (a) whether 'the average person, applying contemporary community standards', would find that the work, taken as a whole, appeals to the prurient interest ...; (b) whether the work depicts or describes, in a patently offensive way, sexual conduct specifically defined by the applicable State law; and (c) whether the work, taken as a whole, lacks serious literary, artistic, political or scientific value.[4]

Instead of simplifying the law, these guidelines proved such a recipe for confusion that few obscenity convictions stood appellate review. Was the 'local community' a State, a judicial district, or a metropolitan area? Nationally-distributed films and magazines were found to offend some communities but not others, and federal prosecutors carefully selected small mid-West venues for attacking publications popular on the East and West coasts. In 1978 the Supreme Court held that children were not part of the community by whose standards an 'adults only' publication fell to be judged,[5] but it has yet to explain the yardstick by which material designed for and sold to minorities is to be assessed, or how an 'average person' can be identified in such heterogeneous communities as New York. Must material distributed to homosexuals be judged by the standards of the average homosexual, or, if the community comprises one-tenth homosexuals, by the standards of an 'average person' who is basically heterosexual but with a ten per cent leaning towards members of his own sex? Most

American states now prohibit the depiction of a specifically defined 'laundry list' of sexual conduct, including

(a) Patently offensive representations or descriptions of ultimate sexual acts, normal or perverted, actual or simulated;
(b) Patently offensive representations or descriptions of masturbatory or excretory functions, and lewd exhibition of the genitals.

Even this list is not conclusive, however, for the average community member who applies average community standards must still be satisfied beyond reasonable doubt that the representation is 'patently offensive'. And if the first two limbs of the *Miller* test are made out, the jury must still consider whether the patently offensive prurience is redeemed by its serious social or political value. Expert evidence is admissible on this limb, and many obscenity trials have lasted for several months while 'respected physicians, critics, social commentators' have agreed to disagree.

There is a real prospect that the Supreme Court will shortly abandon its endeavours to define the indefinable. The *Miller* decision was reached by the narrowest five to four majority, after the minority spokesman, Justice Brennan, had despaired that

... after fifteen years of experimentation and debate I am reluctantly forced to the conclusion that none of the available formulas, including the one announced today, can reduce the vagueness to a tolerable level while at the same time striking an acceptable balance between the protections of the First and Fourteenth Amendments, on the one hand, and on the other the asserted State interest in regulating the dissemination of certain sexually orientated materials. Any effort to draw a constitutionally acceptable boundary of State power must resort to such indefinite concepts as 'prurient interest', 'patent offensiveness', 'serious literary value', and the like. The meaning of these concepts necessarily varies with the experience, outlook, and even idiosyncrasies of the person defining them. Although we have assumed that obscenity does exist and that we 'know it when (we) see it', we are manifestly unable to describe it in advance, except by reference to concepts so elusive that they fail to distinguish clearly between protected and unprotected speech.[6]

Justice Stevens, who was appointed to the Supreme Court bench after the *Miller* decision, has now declared his support for the Brennan position. He maintains that '... criminal prosecutions are an unacceptable method of abating a public nuisance which is entitled to at least a modicum of First Amendment protection ... the line between communications which "offend" and those which do not is too blurred to identify criminal conduct.' Nor is he prepared to 'rely on either the average citizen's understanding of an amorphous community standard or on my fellow judge's appraisal of what has serious artistic merit, as a basis for deciding what one citizen may communicate to another by appropriate means'. He could not determine whether or not 'ugly pictures' had any beneficial value, but 'in the end, I believe we must rely on the capacity of the free market-place of ideas to distinguish that which is useful or beautiful from that which is ugly or worthless'.[7]

The Supreme Court majority, however censorious it may be considered in America, would nonetheless have struck down any obscenity test modelled on English legislation. In *Miller* the Chief Justice insisted that only 'works which depict or describe sexual conduct' could be prohibited, and that conduct 'must be specifically defined by State law'. Definitions couched in such imprecise words as 'indecency' or 'a tendency to deprave or corrupt' would be constitutionally unenforceable.

Other countries with less constitutional respect for free speech have elevated administrative censorship into blanket moral and political control. In South Africa and Eire, Censorship Boards save the State the expense and embarrassment of obscenity proceedings by imposing rigid and unappealable controls over unconventional publications. In New Zealand, however, a measure of openness and consistency has marked the operations of the Indecent Publications Tribunal, which is empowered, as an alternative to total prohibition, to classify 'indecent' reading matter as unsuitable for sale to persons under eighteen. Although material in this category may be publicly distributed and displayed, a criminal offence is committed by selling it to a minor. A ruling may be sought by publishers, police or Customs officers, and all parties are afforded an open hearing at which expert evidence, statements from readers and affidavits from authors are admissible. Indecency is statutorily defined as

... describing, depicting, expressing, or otherwise dealing with matters of sex, horror, crime, cruelty, or violence in a manner that is injurious to the public good.

and the Tribunal is required to consider, in applying the test,

(a) The dominant effect of the book or sound recording as a whole:
(b) The literary or artistic merit, or the medical, legal, political, social, or scientific character or importance of the book or sound recording:
(c) The persons, classes of persons, or age groups to or amongst whom the book or sound recording is or is intended or is likely to be published, heard, distributed, sold, exhibited, played, given, sent, or delivered:

(d) The price at which the book or sound recording sells or is intended to be sold:

(e) Whether any person is likely to be corrupted by reading the book or hearing the sound recording and whether other persons are likely to benefit therefrom:

(f) Whether the book or the sound recording displays an honest purpose and an honest thread of thought or whether its content is merely camouflage designed to render acceptable any indecent parts of the book or sound recording.

Notwithstanding the provisions of subsection (1) of this section, where the publication of any book or the distribution of any sound recording would be in the interests of art, literature, science or learning and would be for the public good the Tribunal shall not classify it as indecent.[8]

These factors seem to protect serious literature, although the Tribunal has declined to approve many popular English 'men's magazines', even for restricted sale, on the grounds that 'entertainment value' is not a consideration which can outweigh a finding of indecency. The few monthly magazines of this sort which are deemed acceptable are reviewed at two-yearly intervals, and a former 'clearance' may be revoked in the event of any marked deterioration in standards.

The New Zealand censorship model has worked in a more progressive fashion than its equivalents in South Africa and Eire, largely because of the provisions for public hearings and reception of expert evidence. There is no right of appeal to a jury, which might provide a more satisfactory touchstone of common sense and common standards than five political appointees, who comprised in 1976 a solicitor, a university chaplain, the editor of the New Zealand *Listener*, a headmistress and a Maori housewife. The few 'indecent' magazines and books classified for restricted sale are granted competition-free monopoly of the market: *Penthouse* and *Playboy* leisurely compete for the custom of curious New Zealanders denied access to *Mayfair* and *Men Only*.

The only common-law jurisdictions to have 'solved' the problem of censorship in a way which deserves emulation in England are the Australian States of South Australia and New South Wales, which have combined decriminalization with a liberal classification system. In 1974 they established Classification Boards, with powers to impose restrictions on public display, advertising and sale to minors. Existing obscenity statutes were abolished, and the criminal law was confined to punishment of those who deal with restricted publications inconsistently with the terms of the restriction, or who entice children to participate in indecent photographs. Politicians supported the change on civil libertarian principles:

[This] represents a withdrawal of government from this area, an abandonment by government for the main part of the idea that it is not the right of adults to decide what they will or will not read, and the substitution of a system of classifying material, which is a workable way of seeing that people are not subjected to offensive literature in which they are not interested. Even the most offensive, most outrageous pornography is not to be prohibited; but its distribution will be restricted to those who wish to read it, either by way of direct sale rather than general distribution, or subject to certain restrictions relating to the age of those to whom it may be sold. Printers and publishers will not be liable to prosecution.[9]

The strength of the classification system lies in the definitive control which may be imposed on the sale or display of erotic publications. For example, in 1975 the South Australian Classification Board issued the following regulations:

Unrestricted	Full male or female nudity (frontal or otherwise) and Shaven pubic region accepted Depictions showing labia majora are acceptable, except on front covers
Not available to minors	Explicit depictions of male or female nudes Labia minora displayed Males with erections Heterosexual intercourse without organs displayed in detail Masturbation of an obvious nature
Not to be available to minors, nor to be publicly displayed	Heterosexual intercourse with organs displayed in detail Male or female homosexual fondling of an erotic nature

Not to be available to minors nor to be displayed publicly, and to be sold only to adults making a direct request and delivered only to the purchaser personally making the request	Homosexual intercourse Fellatio Cunnilingus Buggery Bestiality Masochism
Not to be available to minors nor to be displayed publicly, and to be sold only to adults making a direct request, delivered only to the purchaser personally making that request, and not to be advertised	Sadism (*not* just bondage for its own sake) Paedophilia

A classification system which applies to written works as well as pictorial representations might be abused to shrink the free market-place of ideas by restricting publications of political or social significance to minimal outlets. But there is no reason why a version of the Australian system could not be introduced in England, modified if necessary in deference to those who demand a residual right to censor by providing the Classification Board with a power to ban, but subjecting its exercise to an appeal to an ordinary jury. New South Wales, before reform, had a common law of obscenity in similar terms to, and in the same state of disarray as, the 1959 Obscene Publications Act. Trials of *Oz* and other student newspapers generated heat and emotion, while several juries were deadlocked over whether *Portnoy's Complaint* tended to deprave and corrupt. The change-over to classification procedures forced obscenity into circumspect rather than illegal markets, with results which seem reasonably acceptable to the community. One commentator observes that

The visible consequence of the new legislative models has been that it is now possible for adult Australians to obtain access to a wide range of sexually explicit material through discreetly store-fronted 'adults only' or 'love art' shops and restricted areas of newsagents and bookshops (other than in Queensland) or through the mail. What cannot be publicly displayed or sold to those under eighteen years can still, in most cases, be privately distributed to willing adults.[10]

A similar position could be achieved in England by decriminalization and cautious integration of a classification system into a censorship framework which provided ultimate recourse to a jury. A large measure of liberty without total licence could be achieved by the following set of reforms:

1 Repeal of the 1959 Act, and a lifting of all restrictions on written descriptions of sexuality, drug-taking and violence. Authors could say what they like, in any language they choose, subject to the laws of incitement to, and complicity in, crime. Incitements to drug-taking, violence and sexual offences would be prosecuted and punished as such, while those who advertise sexual services could, in appropriate cases, be convicted of living off immoral earnings or procuring acts of gross indecency, without recourse to the common law.

2 Establishment of a Classification Board, to which publishers, police or Customs officials could submit pictorial matter explicitly depicting specified anatomical details in non-clinical contexts, or photographs of brutal violence. The Board would be empowered to either
   (a) license for general sale or
   (b) direct that sale take place only to persons over eighteen or
   (c) restrict circulation to licensed shops which exclude children and specialize in classified publications or
   (d) if satisfied that the article submitted would cause harm if sold in any manner whatsoever, prohibit it from distribution other than for purposes of justice, or medical or psychiatric use.

3 Institution of an appeal system whereby any determination by the Board to prohibit or restrict sale could be reversed by a jury, in a procedure which would not entail a criminal conviction. The question for trial would be whether the publication was manifestly unfit for distribution in the circumstances set out in the original application to the Board, which would be required to justify its decision to ban or restrict in those circumstances. Both the appellant and the Board should be entitled to call any relevant evidence of fact or opinion.

4 Enactment of a new criminal offence of disobeying a Board prohibition on sale, or sale to minors, or sale in unlicensed shops.

5 Replacement of existing Customs prohibitions with a provision requiring Customs officers to detain pictorial material falling

within the Board's current classification policy, and to submit it directly to the Board for classification or prohibition.

6 Maintenance of existing prohibitions on exploitation of under-age children and unsolicited mailing of erotica, with appropriate amendments to the Protection of Children Act (to exclude publication and advertisement, which would be dealt with by the Board) and the Post Office Act (so that section 11 applies only to *unsolicited* mailings).

7 Repeal of the Vagrancy, Indecent Advertisement and Town Clauses laws, and their replacement by a statutory power granted to the Board to regulate public display of sex and violence. A list of prohibitions, with details of the kind provided by the South Australian Classification Board, could be issued, and updated as time and circumstance required.

8 Statutory provision for the Board to license and to police a limited number of specialist shops in discreet city locations entitled to sell pictorial pornography deemed unfit for open sale to adults. The structure of the Gaming Board of Great Britain would provide an appropriate model for exercise of this power: the Classification Board would similarly appoint inspectors and initiate prosecutions whenever its rules were transgressed, and a volume of public complaint or evidence that a licence applicant was connected with organized (or disorganized) crime, would be grounds for refusal or revocation of a licence.

A classification system which operated in the above way would reduce the role of the criminal law from the only form of control to a subsidiary adjunct of a fair and open administrative control. Publishers of pictorial prurience who wished to contest a classification could do so, both at a hearing before the board and, if unsuccessful, by way of an appeal to a jury, whose verdict would provide an ultimate safeguard against a resurgence of puritan licensors. Distributors would only face prison if they knowingly disobeyed a classification or deliberately sought to evade the system, and trials (other than appeals from Board decisions) would be confined to issues of fact rather than matters of opinion. When this kind of decriminalization was mooted in Parliament during the 1964 debates over the right to jury trial in forfeiture proceedings, the Solicitor-General accepted that 'There is certainly no objection in principle to proceedings for forfeiture being tried by jury in courts of criminal jurisdiction. It would be an innovation, but that should not prevent it happening.'[11] The Classification Board could intercede with the publishing and distributing trades to find mutually agreeable methods of minimizing public offence: in New Zealand, for example, the Indecent Publications Tribunal has encouraged newsagents to place indecent magazines on high racks, out of the reach of young children. Licensed pornographers would be obliged to pay for legal protection: not by way of bribes to corrupt policemen, but on audited accounts assessed by the Inland Revenue and VAT inspectors. When the French Government legalized obscenity it exacted a special rate of tax. Without emulating France by placing a premium on pornography, doubtless licence fees could be fixed at a sufficiently high rate to pay for the operation of the Board and its inspectors.

For those who see censorship in absolute terms, as a reflection of society's lack of confidence in itself, these reforms will have scant appeal. Conversely, those who fear that tolerance of pornography will demean and diminish the quality of life in society may not be much impressed by a proposal to legalize the availability of sexually explicit materials for consenting adults. At least there can be no objection to licensing laws which prohibit profit-making enterprises from advertising sexual wares in a manner calculated to embarrass many citizens going about their ordinary business. Assaulting passers-by with gratuitous erotic appeals is an invasion of their privacy, quite apart from any insult to their taste, but it is a misuse of language to claim that sexually explicit material kept in a locked drawer in a private home, or on a shelf of a soberly-fronted sex shop, is an environmental threat. Sexually explicit literature may serve as a boon to the lonely, the ugly, the aged, those who are forced by circumstances or by personal unattractiveness to live without love and companionship. Some 'adult' magazines disseminate a rudimentary form of sex education, combating ignorance of the sexual act and increasing popular knowledge of the possibilities of sexual pleasure. A system of control which requires responsible management of bookshops and cinema clubs presenting a modest front to a public street far from schools, churches and council flats deserves a try, based on a law which echoes the sentiments of Mrs Patrick Campbell that 'It doesn't matter what you do in the bedroom as long as you don't do it in the street and frighten the horses.'

In sum, those social interests which require regulation of erotic material are ill-served by the present obscenity law. They can be more effectively safeguarded by its replacement with precisely defined statutory offences relating to erotic publications which, while not criminal in themselves, may be found so by the particular manner of their distribution (e.g. to children or by unsolicited mailings) or display (e.g. in such a way as to embarrass passers-by). The emphasis would thus be shifted from an emotional debate about the degree of sexual arousal produced by particular material (such arousal having in itself little proven danger in mind or morals), to the use made of the material in a limited and recognizable set of situations in which social danger, although still perhaps unproven, is demonstrably greater. The justification for censorship would then cease to be stated in scientifically untenable propositions about erotic materials causing crime, or overwhelming majorities loathing pornography, but would instead draw support from the desirability of furthering undisputed social interests, such as the protection of individual privacy against unsolicited mailings of offensive literature, or protection of children from potentially damaging materials until they are sufficiently mature to handle them.

A Classification Board offers the most workable form of control, but so long as it is thought desirable to keep a generalized law against publishing material which tends to corrupt, that corruption must be perceived in realistic and modern terms, and not encased in the superstitions of traditional taboos. Publishers placed at risk should be those who pander to sexist hypocrisy and discriminatory prejudice which demeans the dignity and threatens the happiness of any social, sexual or racial class. True perversion lies in convincing white school-children that they should loathe their coloured classmates, or in encouraging hatred of homosexuals, or in degrading women as sex objects. The *Hicklin* test may have been laid down in an age which was imperialist, chauvinist and intolerant of sexual abnormality, but its words are wide enough to encompass moral and political changes. The standards Britain once put up are now standards up with which its law should not put.

NOTES

CHAPTER I

1 See C.H. Rolph, *The Trial of Lady Chatterley* (Penguin Books 1961) and [1961] Crim. L.R. 176.
2 *John Calder (Publications) v. Powell* [1965] 1 All E.R. 159.
3 [1968] 1 Q.B. 159.
4 [1963] 1 Q.B. 163 at 168.
5 [1962] 1 All E.R. 748.
6 *R. v. Calder & Boyars Ltd.* [1969] 1 Q.B. 509.
7 *Shaw v. DPP* [1962] A.C. 220.
8 *R. v. Stanley* [1965] 2 Q.B. 327.
9 *Wiggins v. Field* (1968) 112 Sol. J. 656; [1968] Crim. L.R. 503.
10 *Report of the Commission on Obscenity and Pornography* (Bantam Books 1970).
11 *DPP v. Whyte* [1972] A.C. 849.
12 *DPP v. Jordan* [1976] A.C. 699.
13 Barry Cox, John Shirley and Martin Short, *The Fall of Scotland Yard* (Penguin 1977), p. 158.
14 *The Report of the Commissioner of Police for the Metropolis* (1974), HMSO, Cmnd 5638, p. 21.
15 *R. v. Anderson* [1972] 1 Q.B. 304.
16 Quoted C.H. Rolph, *Books in the Dock* (Andre Deutsch 1969), p. 46.
17 *R. v. Metropolitan Commissioner of Police, ex p. Blackburn* [1973] WLR 43, per Phillimore CJ, at p. 52.
18 'Mintel' survey, reported in *Campaign*, 21 January 1977.
19 Affidavit of Sir Robert Mark, quoted in *Blackburn's case*, supra note 17.
20 *Blackburn's case*, supra note 17, per Lord Denning, at p. 46.
21 *Pornography, The Longford Report* (Coronet Books 1972), p. 37.
22 Cox, Shirley and Short, *The Fall of Scotland Yard*, p. 160.
23 *Report of the US Commission on Obscenity*, above note 10, 'Adult Bookstore Patrons', p. 157.

24 *DPP* v. *Whyte* [1972] 3 All E.R. 12.

25 ibid, p. 26.

26 Mintel Survey, *Campaign*, 21 January 1977.

27 Michael Pye, 'View from the Stalls', *Sunday Times*, 28 September 1975.

28 See 'It's Not Easy to Shock the British', *Sunday Times*, 30 December 1973, reporting conclusions of a poll conducted by the Opinion Research Centre.

29 *Knuller* v. *DPP* [1973] A.C. 435, at p. 457, per Lord Reid.

30 ibid, at p. 489, per Lord Simon.

CHAPTER 2

1 Ezekiel 23: 14–17.

2 *The Republic* (Everyman Edition), p. 71. Cited by Norman St John Stevas, *Obscenity and the Law* (Secker & Warburg 1956), p. 3.

3 Modern magistrates were much less tolerant: between 1951 and 1954 eight different Benches decided that the book was obscene and ordered its destruction. *The Decameron* was finally cleared in 1954 by Quarter Sessions after an appeal from a destruction order made by justices in Swindon: see H. Montgomery Hyde, *A History of Pornography* (William Heinemann 1954), p. 71.

4 Charter of the Stationers' Company.

5 There is some mention in the records of the Stationers' Company of the refusal of licences on the grounds of 'lewdness', but this may be explained by other references to 'naughty papisticall books'. See St John Stevas, *Obscenity and the Law*, p. 7.

6 Stubbs, *A Motive to Good Works* (1593).

7 C.H. Rolph, *Books in the Dock*, p. 32.

8 In 1646 the licensors suppressed one book entitled *The Women's Parliament* because it 'tended to corrupt youth'. Record of Stationers' Company, V,1vi.

9 Milton, *Paradise Lost*, Book II, lines 598–99.

10 The standards of the times are exemplified by the fate of William Prynne, who published crusading tracts against profanities on stage (*Women Actors Notorious Whores*) in the course of which he insulted the Queen. For this offence he lost his ears, and when it was repeated the Star Chamber ordered the stumps of his ears cut off as well, and both sides of his face branded with the letters 'SL' (for 'seditious libeller'). Donald Thomas, *A Long Time Burning* (Praeger 1969), p. 30.

11 ibid, p. 31.

12 'The Licensing Act is condemned, not as a thing essentially evil, but on account of the petty grievances, the exactions, the jobs, the commercial restrictions, the domiciliary visits, which were incidental to it. It is pronounced mischievous because it enables the Company of Sta-

tioners to extort money from publishers, because it empowers the agents of the government to search houses under the authority of general warrants, because it confines the foreign book trade to the port of London; because it detains valuable packages of books at the Custom House till the pages are mildewed. The Commons complain that the amount of the fee which the licenser may demand is not fixed. They complain that it is made penal in an officer of the Customs to open a box of books from abroad, except in the presence of one of the censors of the press. How, it is very sensibly asked, is the officer to know that there are books in the box till he has opened it? Such were the arguments which did what Milton's *Areopagitica* had failed to do.' See Dicey, *An Introduction to the Study of the Law of the Constitution*, 10th edn (Macmillan 1961), p. 252, citing Macaulay, *History of England*, vol. iv (1858), p. 543.

13 David Foxon, *Libertine Literature in England, 1660–1745* (University Books, 1965), p. 48.

14 *The Diary of Samuel Pepys*, ed. H.H. Wheatley (London 1952), VII, pp. 261, 290–1.

15 In 1675 some gentlemen of All Souls clandestinely used the college press to reproduce some obscene pictures 'for the private use of themselves and their friends'. They were discovered, however, by the Dean, Dr John Fell, who destroyed the prints and threatened the gentlemen with expulsion. *Letters of Humphrey Prideaux to John Ellis* (ed. Maude Thompson, Camden Society, 1875), p. 30.

16 Anthony Wood, *Athenae Oxienses, 1813–20*, IV, p. 373. Another account describes his offence as 'throwing down bottles (pist in) among the people in Covent Garden'.

17 *R. v. Sedley* (1663) 1 Sid. 168.

18 *R. v. Read* (1708) 11 Mod. Rep. 142.

19 Amory, *Life of John Buncle* (1825), III, p. 262.

20 From the *Weekly Journal*, quoted by H. Montgomery Hyde, *A History of Pornography* (Heinemann 1964), p. 159.

21 *Curlicism Display'd*, summarized by Hyde, loc. cit., pp. 159–60.

22 For sedition, he was ordered to stand in the pillory for an hour. Such punishment could endanger the life of men like Curl, who had deadly enemies, but he was saved by the cunning of his trade. He printed a handbill falsely stating that his offence had been to vindicate the memory of the much-loved Queen Anne. This was distributed on the day of his appearance in the pillory, and had such an effect on the sentimental crowd that 'it would have been dangerous even to have *spoken* against him and when he was taken down out of the pillory, the mob carried him off, as it were in triumph, to a neighbouring tavern.' State Trials, XVII, p. 160.

23 *R. v. Curl* (1727) 2 Stra. 788; 1 Barn K.B. 29; 93 E.R. 849.

24 *R. v. Delaval* (1763) 3 Burr 1438.

25 See also *Jones* v. *Randall* (1774) 1 Cowp. 17; 98 E.R. 944.
26 *Shaw* v. *DPP* [1961] 2 All E.R. 446, at p. 452.
27 Letter to Lovel Stanhope, 13 November 1749, Foxon, *Libertine Literature*, pp. 53–5.
28 Macaulay, *History of England*, II, pp. 606–7.
29 *Edinburgh Review*, XXVI, January 1809.
30 Hyde, *History of Pornography*, p. 167.
31 The Society had turned to the courts to suppress this trade, the Secretary explained, because 'denunciations against offenders from a Court of the highest jurisdiction in the Kingdom, tend to infuse a greater degree of dread among persons prone to such offences'. Police Committee of the House of Commons, 1 May 1817.
32 Thomas, *A Long Time Burning*, p. 194.
33 'The Trial of William Benbow' (1822) reported in *Rambler magazine*, June and August 1822. Republished in the Appendix to Thomas, supra, p. 442.
34 The trial which had opened his Lordship's eyes was that of William Dugdale, an incorrigible Holywell Street pornographer, whom he jailed for twelve months. Hansard, April 1857, CXLV, p. 102.
35 *Thomson* v. *Chain Libraries Ltd.* [1954] 2 All E.R. 616.
36 John Roebuck MP, Hansard, 12 August 1857, CXLVII, p. 1475.
37 146 Hansard Parliamentary Debates (3rd Series 1857), pp. 327 *et seq.*
38 (1868) L.R. 3 Q.B. 360, at p. 371.
39 *The Times*, 19 June 1877.
40 The jury was permitted to hear expert evidence on the population problem, and Lord Cockburn was prompted to ask one witness 'Is there anything in it calculated to excite sensual or libidinous feelings?' But what was at stake was the book's effect on public morality: its scientific language and non-erotic effect were irrelevant.
41 'If the effect is as here described, the defendants, as they certainly published the book advisedly and intentionally and well aware of its character, must abide the result, however strange and anomalous it may seem that, while it is admitted that they were acting in the belief that they were doing what was right, they are to be held responsible; and it must be found against them that they published the book intending to corrupt and vitiate the morals of the people.' See St John Stevas, *Obscenity and the Law*, p. 73.
42 Norman St John Stevas, op. cit., p. 74.
43 *Memories & Reflections* (London 1928), I, p. 89.
44 *The Times*, 1 November 1888.
45 Rolph, *Books in the Dock*, p. 59.
46 *Literature at Nurse* (London 1885), quoted by St John Stevas, op. cit., p. 76.
47 *Society for the Suppression of Vice, Occasional Report and Appeal* (London 1868), p. 7.

48 *R.* v. *Thomson* (1900) 64 J.P. 456, quoted in Thomas, *A Long Time Burning*, p. 269.

49 *Report of the Joint Select Committee on Lotteries and Indecent Advertisements* (1908), HMSO 275.

50 *The Times*, 15 November 1915.

51 Augustus John and several professors of Art volunteered to testify, but an eighty-two-year-old magistrate ruled that 'It is utterly immaterial whether they are works of art ... the most splendidly painted picture in the universe might be obscene.' The defendants withdrew, and replaced the Lawrence show with an exhibition of *Art Forms in Nature taken from vegetable Growths*. St John Stevas, *Obscenity and the Law*, p. 105.

52 *Glyn* v. *Western Feature Film* [1916] 1 Ch. 261.

53 Alec Craig, *The Banned Books of England* (Allen & Unwin 1962), p. 80.

54 'The Battles of Dr Leavis', *Sunday Times*, 23 April 1978.

55 Vera Brittain, '*Radclyffe Hall – A case of Obscenity*' (*Femina*, 1968), pp. 91–2.

56 ibid, pp. 98–100.

57 ibid, pp. 129–30.

58 Oscar Wilde, *The Importance of Being Ernest*, Act II.

59 Craig, *Banned Books*, p. 95.

60 Rolph, *Books in the Dock*, p. 85.

61 St John Stevas, op. cit., p. 107.

62 (1932) Cr. App. Rep. 182 at 183–4.

63 P.R.O. Mepol 3/390, quoted in Thomas, *A Long Time Burning*, p. 303.

64 Bertrand Russell, *Marriage and Morals* (Allen & Unwin 1929), pp. 91–3.

65 Craig, *Banned Books*, pp. 99–105.

66 Geoffrey Robertson, 'Obscenity – A Jury Decides', *New Statesman*, 17 November 1972.

67 Alfred C. Kinsey, Wardell B. Pomeroy, and Clyde E. Martin, *Sexual Behaviour in the Human Male* (Saunders 1948).

68 'The Kinsey Report', *Partisan Review*, April 1948.

69 *R.* v. *Reiter* [1954] 2 Q.B. 16.

70 Rolph, *Books in the Dock*, p. 96.

71 *R.* v. *Martin Secker & Warburg* [1954] 1 W.L.R. 1138.

72 St John Stevas, op. cit., p. 116.

73 See, for example, Lord Goddard's ruling in *Paget Publications* v. *Watson* [1952] 1 All E.R. 1256, that it was sufficient if the cover of a book was held to be obscene, irrespective of its contents.

74 Minutes of Evidence taken before the Select Committee, 16 December 1958. House of Commons, p. 122.

75 ibid, p. 89.

76 *Roth* v. *US* (1957) 354 US 463; see particularly Mr Justice Brennan at p. 470.

77 *The Spectator*, 26 August 1961.

CHAPTER 3

1 *DPP* v. *Whyte* [1972] 3 All E.R. 12, at p. 19.
2 *R.* v. *Hicklin* (1868) L.R. 3 Q.B. 360, at p. 371.
3 *R.* v. *Martin Secker & Warburg Ltd, and others* [1952] 2 All E.R. 683, at p. 686.
4 Rolph, *Books in the Dock*, p. 63.
5 C.H. Rolph, *The Trial of Lady Chatterley* (Penguin 1961), p. 229.
6 ibid, p. 228.
7 ibid, pp. 229–30.
8 [1969] 1 Q.B. 151.
9 [1971] 3 All E.R. 1152.
10 [1969] 1 Q.B. 151, at p. 168.
11 [1971] 3 All E.R., at p. 1160.
12 *Knuller* v. *DPP* [1973] A.C. 435, at pp. 491–8.
13 ibid, p. 436 (h).
14 *DPP* v. *Whyte* [1972] 3 All E.R. 12.
15 ibid, p. 20
16 ibid, p. 23.
17 ibid, p. 26.
18 *Roth* v. *US* (1957) 237 Fd 796 (1957).
19 John Chandos, *To Deprave and Corrupt* (London 1962), p. 45.
20 *R.* v. *Commissioner of Police of the Metropolis, ex parte Blackburn* (1973) 2 W.L.R. 43, at p. 48.
21 Judge Woolsey, *US* v. *One Book Called 'Ulysses'*, 5 F Supp. 182 (SDNY 1933) affd. 72 F 2d 705 (1934–2nd Cir.).
22 Hansard, 23 May 1949.
23 *R.* v. *Calder & Boyars* [1969] 1 Q.B. 151, at pp. 169–70.
24 *R.* v. *Anderson* [1971] 3 All E.R. 1152, at p. 1160. See also *R.* v. *Henn & Darby* [1978] 1 W.L.R. 1031.
25 *Mishkin* v. *New York* 383 US 502 (1966) at p. 514, per Justice Brennan.
26 This distinction was explored at one stage in *R.* v. *Anderson*. See Tony Palmer, *The Trials of Oz* (Blond and Briggs 1971), p. 145.
27 *DPP* v. *Jordan* (1977) A.C. 699.
28 (1868) L.R. 3 Q.B. 360, at p. 371.
29 *R.* v. *Reiter* [1954] 2 Q.B. 16, at p. 19.
30 *R.* v *Martin Secker & Warburg* [1954] 2 All E.R. 683.
31 Rolph, *Lady Chatterley*, p. 228.
32 [1962] 1 W.L.R. 349, pp. 351–2.
33 *R.* v. *Clayton & Halsey* [1962] 1 Q.B. 163, at p. 168.
34 [1976] 2 All E.R. 753, at p. 758.
35 *DPP* v. *Whyte* [1972] 3 All E.R. 12, at p. 17.
36 op. cit., p. 19.

37 (1957) 156 F Supp. 350.
38 *Ginsberg* v. *New York* 390 U.S. 629, at pp. 634 & 636 per Justice Brennan.
39 *Shaw* v. *DPP* (1962] A.C. 220, at p. 228.
40 *DPP* v. *Whyte* [1972] 3 All E.R. 12, at p. 19.
41 [1969] 1 Q.B. 151, at p. 168.
42 *DPP* v. *Whyte* [1972] 3 All E.R. 12, at pp. 24 (h), 25 (g–j).
43 ibid, at p. 24.
44 Lord Pearson argued that the 'significant proportion' test was only appropriate to individual books, like *Last Exit to Brooklyn*, which were on sale throughout the country: in the case of a bookseller, 'persons' in the Act simply meant 'some persons'. Only 'if the number of persons likely to be affected is so small as to be negligible – really negligible – the *de minimis* principle might be applied. But if a seller of pornographic books has a large number of customers who are not likely to be corrupted by such books, he does not thereby acquire a licence to expose for sale or sell such books to a small number of customers who are likely to be corrupted by them.' (*Whyte*, supra, p. 22.) On this point he was not followed by Lords Cross, Simon and Salmon, with Lord Wilberforce expressing no opinion either way.
45 *Paget Publications Ltd.* v. *Watson* (1952) 1 T.L.R. 1189.
46 *Report of the Select Committee on Obscene Publications* (1958), para. 18.
47 Rolph, *Lady Chatterley*, p. 39.
48 *R.* v. *Calder & Boyars* [1969] 1 Q.B. 151, at p. 155.
49 *R.* v. *Anderson* [1971] 3 All E.R. 1152, at p. 1158.
50 Robertson, 'Obscenity', *New Statesman*, 17 November 1972.
51 Indictment Rules 1971, Rule 5 (1).
52 In *R.* v. *Hicklin* (1868) L.R. 3 Q.B. 360, at p. 371, the court considered that the common law of obscene libel afforded no defence of 'public benefit'. The defendant had published an obscene book with an honest and possibly laudable purpose, but this was no justification for his transgression. The ratio of the decision was simply 'you shall not do evil that good may come.' The court assumed that the defendant 'knew perfectly well' that his publication would tend to deprave, although this finding was assisted by the presumption that a man knows the natural and probable consequences of his acts, a presumption abolished by the 1967 Criminal Justice Act. The court did not consider what the position would be if Hicklin had not known that his publication was obscene.
Compare *R.* v. *Thomson* (1900) 64 J.P. 456 and *R.* v. *Barraclough* [1906] 1 K.B. 201 with *R.* v. *De Montalk* (1932) 23 Cr. App. Rep. 182.
See generally Smith & Hogan, *Criminal Law*, 4th edn (London 1978), pp. 701–3.
53 *Shaw* v. *DPP* [1962] A.C. 220, at p. 227.
54 [1969] 1 Q.B. 151, at pp. 168–9.

55 Rolph, *Lady Chatterley*, pp. 121–2.
56 *R.* v. *Love* (1955) 39 Cr. App. Rep. 30.
57 See *Emmens* v. *Pottle* (1885), 16 Q.B.D. 354; *Sun Life Assurance Co. of Canada* v. *W.H. Smith & Co.* (1933), 150 L.T. 211.
58 Hansard, 7 July 1964, Col. 302 (H. of Commons).
59 *Ginzberg* v. *U.S.*, 383 U.S. 463 (1966).
60 Lord Reid, *Knuller* v. *DPP* [1973] A.C. 435, at p. 457.
61 Lord Justice Salmon, *R.* v. *Calder & Boyars* (1969) 1 Q.B. 151, at p. 172.
62 *R.* v. *Hicklin* L.R. 3 Q.B., at p. 365.
63 [1954] 2 Q.B. 16.
64 1953 S.C. (J) 16, at pp. 26–27.
65 Rolph, *Lady Chatterley*, p. 127.
66 Reported by Dennis Barker, 'Obscenity – Where to Draw the Line', the *Guardian*, 13 March 1971. Included in *Law and Morality*, ed. Blom-Cooper & Drewry (London 1976), pp. 231–2.
67 *Knuller* v. *DPP* [1973] A.C. 435, at pp. 456–7.
68 *R.* v. *Staniforth & Jordan* [1976] 2 W.L.R. 849 at p. 856.
69 [1961] Crim. L.R. 175.
70 [1976] 2 All E.R. 753.
71 Transcript of Court of Appeal (Lawton LJ, Thompson and Shaw JJ) judgment, 19 June 1975, p. 5. See [1976] Crim.L.R. 514.
72 [1969] 1 Q.B., at p. 769.
73 *R.* v. *Leong* (1961) 132 C.C.C. 273 (B.C.S.C.).
74 *Stanley* v. *Georgia* 394 US 557, at p. 565 (1969).
75 *R.* v. *Salter, Barton* (above, note 71), at p. 7 of the transcript.
76 *DPP* v. *Humphrys* [1976] 2 All E.R. 497.
77 Op. cit., per Lord Salmon at p. 528. Lord Salmon's belief in the inherent power of a court to prevent vexatious prosecutions was shared by Lord Edmond-Davies (pp. 533–5) but doubted by Viscount Dilhorne (pp. 507–11).
78 *Shaw* v. *DPP* [1962] A.C. 220.
79 *R.* v. *Greenfield & others*, [1973] 3 All E.R. 1050.
80 Practice Direction, 9 May 1977 [1977] 2 All E.R. 540.
81 *R.* v. *De Marney* [1907] 1 K.B. 388, criticized by Glanville Williams, *Criminal Law – The General Part*, 2nd edn (Stevens 1961), p. 381.
82 *R.* v. *Clayton & Halsey* [1963] 1 Q.B. 163.
83 [1962] A.C. 220, per Lord Tucker at p. 290.
84 [1973] A.C. 435, at p. 456.
85 See Theatres Act, 1968 s. 2 (4) and Criminal Law 1977, s. 53 (3).
86 Hansard (1964) Vol. 695 (H.C.) Col. 1212.
87 *R* v. *Lindsay* (Birmingham Crown Court, 1974), ruling of Mr Justice Ashworth.
88 *DPP* v. *Nock & Ashford* (1978) 67 Cr. App. Rep. 116.

CHAPTER 4

1 Confidential Memorandum, Assistant Commissioner (Crime) to Commander C1 Division, 15 March 1970.

2 'Police Seize £1m Porn Magazines', the *Guardian*, 19 May 1978.

3 Palmer, *The Trials of Oz*, p. 66.

4 See *The Report of the Commission on Obscenity and Pornography* (Bantam Books 1970), 'Erotic Stimuli and Satiation', p. 214.

5 *Evening Standard*, 2 November 1973, p. 5.

6 *Adams Tale* – as told to Gordon Honeycombe by D.C. Adam Acworth (Hutchinson 1974), pp. 199–202.

7 Prosecution of Offences Act, 1879 (42 & 43 Vict c. 22).

8 S.R. & O. (1946) No. 1467.

9 *R. v. Metropolitan Police Commissioner ex p Blackburn* (1973) 2 W.L.R. 43, at p. 51 (Lord Denning) and p. 57 (Roskill L.J.).

10 Minutes of Evidence, H.C. Paper 122 of 1958, pp. 25, 27, 32–33.

11 ibid, 3 June 1957.

12 The *Guardian*, 27 November 1973, p. 18: 'Public Prosecutor Number One.'

13 *R. v. Calder & Boyars* [1968] 1 Q.B. 151, at p. 165.

14 Letter dated 24 June 1976 to Mr Graham Baker, from the DPP's office.

15 Quoted in Wilcox, *The Decision to Prosecute* (Butterworth 1972), p. 6.

16 Memorandum to Select Committee on Obscene Publications, H.C. Paper 123–1, pp. 23–4. See generally Edwards, *The Law Officers of the Crown* (Sweet & Maxwell 1974), pp. 238–41.

17 Joint Committee on Censorship of The Theatre, *Report* (1967) H.L. 255 H.C. 503, Appendix 19, p. 172.

18 Criminal Law Act 1977, s 53.

19 Royal Commission on the Press, *Report* (1977), Cmnd 6810, Chapter 19, paras 48 & 50.

20 *R. v. Metropolitan Police Commissioner, ex parte Blackburn* [*1973*] 2 W.L.R. 43.

21 See L.H. Leigh, *Police Powers in England and Wales* (Butterworth 1975), p. 175.

22 *Ghani* v. *Jones* [1969] 3 All E.R. 1700, per Lord Denning, at p. 1703.

23 *Chic Fashions* v. *Jones* [1968] 1 All E.R. 229. See also *M.* v. *Metropolitan Police Commissioner* [1979] Crim. L.R. 53.

24 Hansard, H.L. Debate, 24 February 1970. H.C. Debate, Vol. 794 Col. 1548 (12 March 1970). See generally G. Zellick, 'Two Comments on Search and Seizure under the Obscene Publications Act' [1971] Crim. L.R. 504.

25 *Ghani* v. *Jones* [1970] 1 Q.B. 693, at 709, per Lord Denning.

26 *Oz*, edition No. 29.

27 Defence of Literature and The Arts Society Bulletin, 1972.

28 Separate opinion of Judge Mosler, European Court of Human Rights, *Handyside case*, 7 December 1976.

29 *Pringle* v. *Bremner and Stirling* (1867) 5 Macph, H.L. 55, at p. 60 (per Lord Chelmsford LC); *Chic Fashions Ltd.* v. *Jones* [1968] 1 All E.R. 299.

30 See also article 5 (3) – Right to trial within a reasonable time.

31 [1951] 2 Q.B. 1021, at p. 1025.

32 ibid, p. 1027.

33 *Report from the Select Committee on Obscene Publications* (H.C. 123, 1958), paras. 27–30.

34 *R.* v. *Metropolitan Police Commissioner, ex p. Blackburn* [1973] 2 W.L.R. 43, at p. 53 (per Phillimore L.J.).

35 *Morgan* v. *Bowker* [1964] 1 Q.B. 507, at p. 515.

36 H. Montgomery Hyde, *A History of Pornography* (Heinemann 1964), pp. 229–30.

37 See generally, Rolph, *Books in The Dock* (Andre Deutsch 1969), pp. 60–1.

38 Letter from Solicitor-General (Mr Peter Archer QC) to Sir Geoffrey Howe, 22 May 1975.

39 *Thomson* v. *Chain Libraries Ltd* [1954] 2 All E.R. 616, at p. 618. In this case Lord Goddard suggests that the police have no real function at the hearing of a forfeiture summons – the matter is, in effect, an argument between the justices and the respondent. This is certainly not a view normally adopted by police prosecuters, who invariably attend section 3 hearings and adduce evidence of the circumstances of publication, argue points of law, and cross-examine the respondent's witnesses. This conduct was specifically approved by the Divisional Court in *Burke* v. *Copper* [1962] 2 All E.R. 14 which decided that Metropolitan police officers were entitled to be present and to participate in section 3 proceedings in respect of books which they had seized.

40 [1954] 2 All E.R. at p. 619.

41 [1964] 1 Q.B. 507, at pp. 516–17.

42 *Olympia Press* v. *Hollis and others* [1974] 1 All E.R. 108, at p. 111.

43 ibid.

44 ibid.

45 [1962] 2 All E.R. 14, at p. 18.

46 *Re. Figcrest Limited*, Snaresbrook Crown Court, 7 November 1977.

47 Dicey, *An Introduction to Study of the Law and of the Constitution*, 10th edn. (London 1961), p. 246.

48 *Shaw* v. *DPP* [1962] A.C. 292.

49 Mr Justice Hart, *Herbert* v. *Guthrie*, Supreme Court of Queensland (1970) Qd.R. 16.

50 Quoted in H. Montgomery Hyde, *A History of Pornography*, p. 209.

51 Hansard, 7 July 1964, Col. 296.

52 ibid, Col. 302.

53 ibid, Col. 358.

54 Letter from Solicitor-General (Mr Peter Archer QC) to Sir Geoffrey Howe, 22 May 1975.

55 Niall Macdermott QC seems to have expressed the contemporary understanding of the undertaking when he told the House: 'Normally, when the Director of Public Prosecutions or the police, on his advice, are investigating a book about which there have been complaints, it is the practice, if the book is published in this country, to call on the publisher and interview him. If, at that stage, he affects surprise and indicates that, in view of the objections of the police, he will hold up publication or will not publish the work any further, he does not provide any material on which he can be prosecuted under the terms of this assurance.

What it amounts to is that a publisher who wants to ensure trial by jury has to make up his mind to stick to his guns, if he is genuinely publishing a work that he considers to be justifiable owing to literary merit. He must make up his mind to see the thing through, and must make clear that he intends to do so and will, if necessary, welcome having the matter decided by a jury. If he does that, it is the effect of the assurance we have been given that he will be prosecuted and will consequently have the right to elect for trial by jury.'

Hansard, 7 July 1964, Col. 332.

56 ibid, Col. 293.

57 Committee on Distribution of Criminal Business between Crown Courts and Magistrates' Courts, chaired by Lord Justice James (HMSO 1975), Cmnd 6323, p. 73.

58 Roger Hood, *Sentencing the Motoring Offender* (Heinemann 1972). See also David Lewis and Peter Hughman, *Just How Just* (Secker & Warburg 1975), Chapter 1.

59 *The Times*, 13 April 1973, reporting a survey in *New Society*.

CHAPTER 5

1 *R.* v. *United Artists*, Divisional Court, 21 May 1974.

2 *The Obscenity Laws*, a report by the Working Party set up by a Conference convened by the Chairman of the Arts Council of Great Britain (Andre Deutsch 1969), p. 27.

3 That is, if the court accepts that the case is 'one of exceptional difficulty, gravity or complexity and that the interests of justice require that the legally assisted person shall have the services of two counsel'. See Legal Aid in Criminal Proceedings Regulations, 1968, section 13 (2) (6).

4 *R.* v. *Waterfield* [1975] 2 All E.R. 40.

5 Bernard Levin, *The Pendulum Years* (Pan Books 1970), p. 287.

6 *The Times*, 30 January 1976.

7 Letter to *The Times*, 3 February 1976. And see Lord Pearce in *Rondel* v. *Worsely* [1969] 1 A.C. 191, at p. 274:

> From the moment that any advocate can be permitted to say that he will or will not stand between the Crown and the subject arraigned in the court where he daily sits to practise, from that moment the liberties of England are at an end.
> It is easier, pleasanter and more advantageous professionally for barristers to advise, represent or defend those who are decent and reasonable and likely to succeed in their action or their defence than those who are unpleasant, unreasonable, disreputable, and have an apparently hopeless case. Yet it would be tragic if our legal system came to provide no reputable defenders, representatives or advisers for the latter. And that would be the inevitable result of allowing barristers to pick and choose their clients.

8 'London Diary', *New Statesman*, July 1978.

9 Indictment Rules, Rule 5 (1).

10 e.g., *R.* v. *Barraclough* [1906] 1 K.B. 201.

11 *R.* v. *Anderson* 1971 3 W.L.C. 939.

12 Transcript of summing up of Mr Justice Ashworth, Birmingham Crown Court, 19 November 1974, pp. 5 & 16.

13 See *R.* v. *Byrne* (1953) 36 Cr. App. Rep. 125.

14 Lord Simon in *R.* v. *Knuller* [1973] A.C., at p. 489.

15 Robertson, 'Obscenity – A Jury Decides', *New Statesman*, 17 November 1972, p. 716.

16 Practice Direction, 1973 1 All E.R.

17 See, for example, Lord Atkins' speech in *Res Behari Lal* v. *King Emperor* (1933) 50 T.L.R. 1, and Lord Justice Bankes' comments in *R.* v. *Syme* (1914) 30 T.L.R. 691.

18 Robertson, 'Obscenity', *New Statesman*, p. 716.

19 Mary Whitehouse, *Whatever Happened to Sex* (London 1977), p. 146.

20 *The Times*, 3 February 1976.

21 *Report of the Commission on Obscenity and Pornography* (Bantam Books 1970), p. 247.

22 Letter to *The Times* from Mr Nicholas de Jongh, 3 February 1976.

23 *R.* v. *Penguin Books Ltd.*, 20 October 1960. Transcript of trial, pp. 20-6.

24 ibid, pp. 49–51.

25 *R.* v. *Waterfield* (1975) 1 W.L.R. 711, at p. 714.

26 *Scott* v. *Scott* [1913] A.C. 417, per Lord Halsbury.

27 ibid, p. 445.

28 *R.* v. *Waterfield*, supra note 25, at p. 715.

29 Ruling of Mr Justice Wien, *R.* v. *Lindsay*, Birmingham Crown Court, 17 October 1974.

30 [1973] 1 Q.B. 629.

31 *R.* v. *Waterfield*, supra, note 25, at p. 715.

32 *John Calder* (*Publications*) *Ltd* v. *Powell* [1965] 1 Q.B. 509.

33 *R.* v. *Calder & Boyars Ltd* [1969] 1 Q.B. 151, at p. 156.
34 *DPP* v. *A.&B.C. Chewing Gum Ltd* [1968] 1 Q.B. 159.
35 See *R.* v. *Anderson* [1971] 3 W.L.R. 939, and *DPP* v. *Jordan*, [1977] A.C. 699.
36 *Shaw* v. *DPP* [1962] A.C. 220, at p. 227 (Court of Appeal).
37 *DPP* v. *Jordan* [1977] A.C. 699, at p. 717.
38 *R.* v. *Anderson* [1971] 3 W.L.R. 939.
39 *DPP* v. *Jordan*, above note 37, at p. 718.
40 *DPP* v. *A.&B.C. Chewing Gum Ltd*, above, note 34.
41 *Jordan*, above, p. 718.
42 *R.* v. *Reiter* [1954] 2 Q.B. 16.
43 *R.* v. *Penguin Books Ltd.* [1961] Crim.L.R. 176. See Rolph, *Lady Chatterley*, p. 127.
44 ibid.
45 *R.* v. *Calder & Boyars* [1969] 1 Q.B. 151.
46 *DPP* v. *Jordan* above note 37, at p. 719.
47 *John Calder* (Publications) *Ltd* v. *Powell* [1965] 1 Q.B. 509.
48 *R.* v. *Calder & Boyars Ltd* [1969] 1 Q.B. 151, at p. 156.
49 *R.* v. *Staniforth & Jordan* (Court of Appeal) [1976] 2 W.L.R. 849, at p. 855.
50 per Lord Simon, *Knuller* v. *DPP* [1973] A.C. 435, at p. 489 and p. 495.
51 See W.R. Cornish, *The Jury* (Pelican 1971), pp. 160–2.
52 James Fitzjames Stephen, *Liberty, Fraternity and Equality* (1873), pp. 173–4.
53 HMSO 5205. See *The British Jury System*, ed. Nigel Walker (Cambridge 1975), p. 106.
54 Rolph, *Lady Chatterley*, p. 7.
55 See *Ellis* v. *Deheer* [1922] 2 K.B. 113.
56 After his conviction by a jury which had evinced difficulty in reading, let alone evaluating, *Last Exit to Brooklyn*, Mr John Calder complained: 'In the new climate in which publishers and writers now find themselves, where highly complex literary concepts will be argued out in criminal courts, it is essential that the framers of the Obscene Publications Act should bring in a new provision that enables juries to be selected from those who have at least A-levels in their education and who can show to the satisfaction of the court that they are capable of reading and understanding the book they have to judge.' Letter to *The Times*, 2 December 1967.
57 See *R.* v. *O'Donnell* (1917) 12 Cr. App. Rep. 219; *R.* v. *Canny* (1945) 30 Cr. App. Rep. 143.
58 *R.* v. *Farren & ors The Times*, January 1973.
59 *R.* v. *Taylor* [1977] 1 W.L.R. 612, at p. 615.
60 Rolph, *Lady Chatterley*, p. 226.
61 Quoted in Richard Michael, *The A.B.Z. of Pornography* (Panther 1972), pp. 117–18.

62 *R.* v. *Anderson* [1971] 3 All E.R. 1152, p. 1161.

63 *R.* v. *Collingbourne*, St Albans Crown Court, 5 June 1974.

64 *R.* v. *Ransom*, Southampton Crown Court, 10 October 1975.

65 'Obscenity cases prosecuted by the DPP and the Police': a résumé prepared by the DPP for the Court of Appeal in *R.* v. *Anderson*.

66 *R.* v. *Anderson* [1971] 3 W.L.R. 939, at p. 950.

67 *R.* v. *Metropolitan Police Commissioner, ex parte Blackburn* [1973] 2 W.L.R. 43, at p. 48.

68 [1974] 3 W.L.R. 430, at p. 437.

69 See *R.* v. *Stamford* [1972] 2 All E.R. 427, at p. 432.

70 *R.* v. *Staniforth & Jordan* [1976] 2 W.L.R. 849, at p. 856. But see *R.* v. *John Kelly* (12 June 1975) where the Court approved a suspended sentence for a first offence.

71 Practice Direction, 5 June 1973, reported in [1973] 2 All E.R. 592.

72 Sir Robert Mark, *Dimbleby Lecture* (BBC Publications 1973), p. 7.

73 See 'Courthouse Folklore' (Irving Wardle, *The Times*) and 'Oz Proves a Delightful Ding-Dong' (John Barber, *Daily Telegraph*), 22 November 1971.

CHAPTER 6

1 *R.* v. *Hicklin* [1868] L.R. 3 Q.B. 360, at p. 371. cf. Glanville Williams, *Criminal Law, The General Part* 2nd edn., p. 70, and the judgment of Mr Justice Windeyer in *Crowe* v. *Graham* [1968] 121 C.L.R. 375, at pp. 395–6.

2 *Roth* v. *U.S.* (1957) 237 F 2d 796, at pp. 819–20.

3 Santayana, *Reason in Art* (Vol. 4 of *The Life of Reason*) (London 1912), pp. 170–1.

4 *DPP* v. *Jordan* [1977] A.C. 699.

5 *R.* v. *Metropolitan Police Commissioner, ex p. Blackburn*.

6 See Kutchinsky, 'An Analysis of the Recent Decrease in Registered Sexual Offences in Denmark' (Paper delivered to Anglo-Scandinavian Seminar on Criminology, Oslo, September 1971), 'Eroticism without Censorship' (19th Congress of International Publishers Association, Paris 1972) and 'The Effect of Easy Availability of Pornography on the Incidence of Sex Crimes: The Danish Experience', *Journal of Social Issues*, 1972.

7 Anthony Storr, *The Obscenity Laws* (Andre Deutsch 1969), p. 83.

8 *Pornography – The Longford Report* (Coronet Books 1972), p. 460.

8 ibid, p. 460.

9 Helena Campbell, 'Sexual Offences and the Trend in Crime 1949–76'; [1978] *New Law Journal* 748.

10 See F.E. Kenyon, 'Pornography, The Law and Mental Health', *British Journal of Psychiatry* (1975), pp. 225–33.

11 *Report of the US Commission on Obscenity and Pornography* (Bantam Books 1970). For a trenchant critique, see Victor Cline, *Where Do You Draw the Line* (New York 1974).

12 Michael J. Goldstein and Harold S. Kant, *Pornography and Sexual Deviance* (University of California Press), 1973.

13 Reported by Maurice Yaffe, 'Pornography & Violence', *Maundsley Gazette*, Autumn 1976.

14 Davis & Braucht, 'Relationship between Exposure to Erotica and Character' (1970), see *Report of US Commission*, above, note 11, pp. 466–7.

15 See Court, *Law Light and Liberty* (Lutheran Publishing House, Adelaide 1975), and 'Time to Speak Out Against the Idea That Pornography can be a Good Thing', *The Times*, 3 August 1976.

16 See Robert J. Stoller, 'Pornography & Perversion', in Holbrook (ed.) *The Case Against Pornography* (Tom Stacey 1972). For a good summary of the 'effect' arguments against pornography, see Harry M. Clor, *Obscenity and Public Morality* (University of Chicago Press 1969), Chapter 4.

17 Eysenck & Nias, *Sex, Violence and the Media* (Temple Smith 1978), p. 221.

18 *R.* v. *Ransom*, Southampton Crown Court 10 October 1975.

19 *DPP* v. *Jordan* [1977] A.C. 699, at p. 721.

20 *R.* v. *Turner* (Terence) [1975] Q.B. 834, at 841, per Lawton LJ.

21 *R.* v. *Reiter* [1954] 2 Q.B. 16.

22 *Transport Publishing Co.* v. *Literature Board of Review* (1956) 99 C.L.R. 111, at p. 119, per Dixon CJ. Kitto & Fullagher JJ.

23 [1968] 1 Q.B. 159, at p. 164.

24 [1969] 1 Q.B. 151, at 170.

25 [1971] 3 All E.R. 1152, at 1159.

26 *DPP* v. *Jordan* (1977) A.C. 699, at p. 722.

27 ibid, p. 718.

28 A similar position has been reached in US Courts. Whether material is obscene is generally decided by viewing it, unless 'materials are directed at such a bizarre deviant group that the experience of the trier of fact would be plainly inadequate to judge whether the material appeals to the (particular) prurient interest': *Paris Adult Theatre* v. *Slaton* 413 U.S. 49 (1973) at p. 56.

29 *R.* v. *Martin Secker & Warburg* [1956] 2 All E.R. 683.

30 *Shaw* v. *DPP* [1960] A.C. 220, at p. 292.

31 *R.* v. *Stamford* [1972] 2 All E.R. 427, at p. 432.

32 *R.* v. *Cameron* Ontario Court of Appeal, 1966 4. CCC. 273.

33 *R.* v. *Prairie Schooner News & Powers* (1970), Manitoba Court of Appeal 75 W.W.R. 585, per Dickson J.A., at p. 599.

34 loc. cit.

35 *R.* v. *Times Square Cinema Ltd.*, Ontario Reports 1971, Vol. 3, p. 688, at p. 694 per Jessup J.A.

36 *R.* v. *Staniforth* [1976] 2 W.L.R. 849, at p. 856.

37 [1968] 1 Q.B. 159, at p. 164.

38 [1971] 3 All E.R. 1152, at p. 1159.

39 *R.* v. *Henn & Darby,* [1978] 1 W.L.R. 1031.

40 Wigmore, *A Treatise on the Anglo-American System of Evidence in Trials at Common Law* (1940), para 1920. See also Cowen and Carter, *Essays in Evidence* (Oxford University Press, 1955), pp. 169–70.

41 *Cross on Evidence,* 4th edn. (Butterworth 1974), p. 382.

42 *H.M. Advocate* v. *Brown* 1907 S.C. (J), at p. 77 and see Richard Fox, *The Legal Control of Obscenity* (Melbourne University Press 1966).

43 Clause 2 of Bill No. 56, 1954/55, Hansard, Commons Debate, Vol. 538, Col. 1130.

44 1958–9, Bill No. 34. Hansard Vol. 595, Col. 1027.

45 See for example C.D.L. Clarke, 'Obscenity, The Law and Lady Chatterley' (1961) 156 *Criminal Law Review,* p. 162.

46 9th edn., p. 173.

47 Rolph, *Lady Chatterley,* pp. 226, 232–3.

48 *DPP* v. *Jordan* [1977] A.C. 699, at pp. 726–7.

49 *R.* v. *Calder & Boyars* [1969] 1 Q.B. 151, at p. 172.

50 *Jordan,* supra, p. 710 (arguendo).

51 *The Obscenity Laws* (Deutsch 1969), p. 23.

52 *R.* v. *Calder & Boyars* [1969] 1 Q.B. 151, at p. 171.

53 Dennis Barker, the *Guardian,* 10 March 1971, commenting on the trial of Paul Ableman's book *The Mouth and Oral Sex.*

54 Rolph, *Lady Chatterley,* pp. 68–73.

55 *The Times,* 6–16 March 1971.

56 *R.* v. *Calder & Boyars* [1969] 1 Q.B. 151, at p. 172.

57 383 US 413 (1966). See also Charles Rembar, *The End of Obscenity* (Bantam Books 1968), pp. 428–61.

58 See Viscount Dilhorne's speech in *DPP* v. *Jordan* (supra) and Graham Zellick, 'Obscene or Pornographic? Obscenity and the Public Good', 1969 *Cambridge Law Journal,* p. 177.

59 Law Commission Report No. 76, *Report on Conspiracy and Criminal Law Reform* (HMSO 1976), Chapter 3, paras 69–76.

60 See the judgment of Kenneth Jones J., *Attorney General's Reference (No. 2 of 1975),* [1976] 2 All E.R. 753, at p. 759.

61 See the argument in *DPP* v. *Jordan* [1977] A.C. 699, at p. 711.

62 Hyde, *A History of Pornography,* p. 216.

63 *R.* v. *Staniforth and Jordan* [1976] 2 W.L.R. 849, at 854.

64 *DPP* v. *Jordan* [1977] A.C. 699, at pp. 718–19.

65 *R.* v. *Anderson* [1971] 3 All E.R. 1152.

66 *Attorney General's Reference (No. 3 of 1977)* [1978] 1 W.L.R. 1123.

67 See, for example, *Ladbroke (Football) Ltd* v. *William Hill (Football) Ltd,* (1964) 1 W.L.R. 273.

68 *Hensher (George) Ltd* v. *Rest a while Upholstery (Lancs) Ltd*, [1976] A. C. 64. See generally P.H. Karlen, 'What is Art? A Sketch for a Legal Definition,' 94 *Law Quarterly Review*, 383.

69 Palmer, *The Trials of Oz*, pp. 170–1.

70 *P. S. Johnson & Associates Ltd* v. *Bucko Enterprises Ltd* [1975] 1 N.Z.L.R. 311.

71 *Jordan*, supra at p. 719 per Lord Wilberforce.

72 Rolph, *Lady Chatterley*, p. 70.

73 *R.* v. *Calder & Boyars* [1969] 1 Q.B. 151, at p. 171.

74 Rolph, *Lady Chatterley*, p. 122.

75 ibid, p. 126.

76 ibid, p. 127.

77 ibid, p. 73.

78 *John Calder (Publications) Ltd* v. *Powell* (1965) 1 Q.B. 509.

79 Canada Evidence Act 1970, section 7.

CHAPTER 7

1 See H.L.A. Hart, *Law, Liberty and Morality* (Oxford University Press 1967), p. 44.

2 The New South Wales Court of Appeal (Holmes & Jacobs, JJ) *Ex parte McKay and others, Re. Crowe.* 85 WN pt 1 (NSW), p. 438.

3 *R.* v. *GLC ex p. Blackburn* [1976] 1 W.L.R. 550, at p. 556. Lord Denning made a similar remark in *R.* v. *Metropolitan Police Commissioner, ex. p. Blackburn* [1973] 2 W.L.R. 43, at p. 50.

4 *R.* v. *GLC*, supra, at p. 567.

5 Sir Robert Megarry, *A Second Miscellany-at-Law*, p. 316.

6 Hansard, Commons, 9 May 1974.

7 [1965] 1 All E.R. 1035, at p. 1038.

8 *Knuller* v. *DPP* [1973] A.C. 435, at p. 458.

9 *R.* v. *Stamford* [1972] 2 W.L.R. 1055, at p. 1057.

10 *R.* v. *Reynolds*, 8 December 1971. Cited by Home Office Working Party on Vagrancy and Street Offences (Working Paper, 1974, HMSO, p. 42).

11 *R.* v. *Grey* (1864) 4 F & F 72.

12 *Knuller* v. *DPP* [1973] A.C. 435, at p. 458.

13 Home Office Working Party, supra note 10.

14 From Mr Justice Bristow's charge to the jury in *Commissioners of Customs and Excise* v. *Paul Raymond Publications Ltd*, High Court, 6 February 1974, transcript, p. 6.

15 *A.G., ex parte McWhirter*, v. *IBA* [1973] 1 Q.B. 629, at pp. 634 and 637.

16 *Paris Adult Theatre* v. *Slaton* (1973) 413 U.S. 49, at p. 71.

17 *The Obscenity Laws* (Andre Deutsch 1969), p. 15.

18 *R.* v. *Anderson* [1971] 3 W.L.R. 939, at p. 949.

19 *R.* v. *Stanley* [1965] 1 All E.R. 1035, at p. 1038.

20 *McGowan* v. *Langmuir* (1931) S.C. (J) 10, at p. 13.
21 *Knuller*, supra, at p. 495, per Lord Simon.
22 *R.* v. *Stamford* [1972] 2 W.L.R. 1055, at p. 1060, citing the dictum of Lord Morris of Borth-y-Gest in *Shaw* v. *DPP* (1962) A.C. 220, at p. 292.
23 *Abrahams* v. *Cavey* [1967] 3 All E.R. 179.
24 See *Evening Standard* 21 January 1977, p. 10.
25 *R.* v. *Waterfield* (no. 2), 17 February 1975, pp. 6 and 8. See also *R.* v. *Farmer* (1973) 58 Crim. App. R. 229.
26 *R.* v. *Marion Smith*, Court of Appeal, 20 February 1976.
27 *R.* v. *Armstrong* (1885) 49 JP 745. *Beal* v. *Kelly* [1951] 2 All E.R. 763.
28 *R.* v. *Straker*, Court of Criminal Appeal 16 February 1965. See [1965] Crim. L.R., p. 239, and Memorandum by Jean Straker to Arts Council Working Party on the Obscenity Laws, supra note 17, pp. 84–96.
29 *R.* v. *Stamford* [1972] 2 W.L.R. p. 1055, at 1058.
30 [1975] Crim. L.R., p. 345.
31 *Knuller* v. *DPP* [1973] A.C. 435, at pp. 458–9.
32 (1968) 112 Sol. J. 656; [1968] Crim. L.R., p. 503.
33 *Lees* v. *Parr* [1967] 3 All E.R. 181 (note).
34 *Abrahams* v. *Cavey* [1967] 3 All E.R. 179, quoting Baron Parke in *Worth* v. *Terrington* (1845) 13 M&W 781.
35 *Jordan* v. *Burgoyne* [1963] 2 All E.R. 225.
36 *Cozens* v. *Brutus* [1973] 854 A.C., at p. 861, per Lord Reid.
37 [1973] 1 Q.B. 629, at p. 643 (argument of Mr Roger Parker QC for the IBA).
38 ibid, p. 659.
39 *Knuller* v. *DPP* [1973] A.C. 435, at p. 458, per Lord Reid.
40 *Crowe* v. *Graham* (1968) 41 ALJR 402, per Mr Justice Windeyer, and see also *Chance International Pty Limited* v. *Forbes* (1968), 69 W.N. (NSW), p. 19 (Mr Justice Helsham).
41 *US* v. *31 Photographs* (1957), 156 F Supp 350.
42 *Galletly* v. *Laird* 1953 S.C. (J) 16, p. 26, per Lord Justice Cooper.
43 *Report of the Committee on Privacy*, chaired by Sir Kenneth Younger (1972) Cmnd. 5012, paras 413, 421.
44 An opinion poll conducted in 1973 found that ninety-two per cent agreed with the proposition that 'there should be a law against sending indecent or suggestive material through the post to people who have not asked for it'. See *Sunday Times*, 30 December 1973, p. 1.
45 *Report of the US Commission on Obscenity*, p. 21.
46 James Committee on Distribution of Criminal Business between Crown Courts and Magistrates Courts (HMSO 1975), Cmnd 6323, para. 162.
47 *DPP* v. *Beate Uhse (UK) Ltd* [1974] 2 W.L.R. 50, at p. 52.
48 Younger Committee, Cmnd. 5012, paras. 423–4.
49 *Report of US Commission*, Minority Statement by Otto N. Larsen & Marvin E. Wolfgang, p. 447.

50 Canadian Criminal Code, s. 164. Canadian Post Office Act, s. 57.

51 [1972] 1 All E.R. 993.

52 *Evening Standard*, 18 September 1973.

53 The *Guardian*, 'London Letter', 20 February 1976.

54 Judge Marvin E. Frankel, *Argos Films* v. *Boyett*. See 'In the Realm of the Censors', James Bouras, *Film Comment* Jan/Feb 1977.

55 Customs and Excise Act, 1952, sections 44 (b) and 275, and the seventh schedule.

56 ibid, section 228 (a) and (b).

57 United Artists were permitted to import the Pasolini film *Salo*, but were subsequently asked to send it out of the country when its indecent content was publicized. The company refused to comply with the request, because they had been paid the duty on the film and considered it to have been legally imported. See 'Customs in the Cutting Room', *Sunday Times*, 1 May 1977.

58 See Customs and Excise Act 1952, sections 45 and 305.

59 (1972) *Criminal Law Review* 551.

60 See *R.* v. *Ardalan* [1972] 2 All E.R. 257.

61 *Frailey* v. *Charlton* [1920] 1 K.B. 147, and see *R.* v. *Waterfield* (No. 2), Court of Appeal, 17 February 1975, transcript, p. 3.

62 High Court, 6 February 1974, transcript, p. 304.

63 *R.* v. *Waterfield* (No. 2), Court of Appeal, 17 February 1975, transcript, p. 4.

64 *R.* v. *Henn* [1978] 1 W.L.R. 1031. See also *R.* v. *Johnson* [1977] Crim. L.R. 214.

65 *R.* v. *Knuller* [1973] A.C. 435, at p. 495, per Lord Simon.

66 Working Party on the Vagrancy Laws, HMSO 1974, p. 40.

67 *R.* v. *Mayling* [1963] 2 Q.B. 717.

68 *Smith* v. *Hughes* [1960] 2 All E.R. 859, at 861.

69 See *Brabham* v. *Wookey* (1901) 18 T.L.R. 99.

70 Paul O'Higgins, *Censorship in Britain* (Thomas Nelson 1972), p. 31.

71 See *Hoogstraten* v. *Goward* (1967) 111 Sol.J.581. Section 28 is applied to urban districts by the Public Health Act 1875, s. 171.

72 See *Abrahams* v. *Cavey* [1967] 3 All E.R. 179, and the cases collected in Brownlie, *The Law Relating to Public Order* (London 1968), pp. 176–8.

73 *A. G. ex parte McWhirter* v. *IBA* (1973) 1 Q.B. 629, at p. 637.

74 Notwithstanding its fate in 1974, the Bill was revived almost word for word by Mr Hugh Rossi MP and received a second reading as a private member's bill in January 1979.

75 See Geoffrey Robertson, 'How to catch Rubens in a draft', the *Guardian*, 13 November 1973, p. 13.

76 Mayor's Office, Houston 28 June 1977, ordinance 77–1259.

77 *R.* v. *Metropolitan Police Commissioner, ex parte Blackburn* [1973] 2 W.L.R. 43, at p. 48.

78 Poll conducted by Opinion Research Centre for *The Sunday Times*, 30
   December 1973, p. 1.
79 Working Party on the Vagrancy Laws, HMSO 1974, p. 37.
80 Cinematograph & Indecent Displays Bill, Standing Committee B, 3rd
   sitting, 29 November 1973, Col. 130, Mr Alex Lyon.
81 ibid, 8th sitting, 18 December 1972, Col. 351, Mr Michael McNair-
   Wilson.

CHAPTER 8

1 William Lambard, *Lambard Archeion* (1591) cited by Lord Diplock,
   Knuller v. *DPP* [1973] A.C. 435, at p. 471.
2 *R.* v. *Quinn & Bloom* [1962] 2 Q.B. 245, at p. 259.
3 See Professor Francis Sayre, (1922) *Harvard Law Review*, p. 393.
4 *The Poulterer's Case* 9 Co. Rep. 55b.
5 *Bagg's Case* (1616) 11 Co Rep. 936.
6 *R.* v. *Sedley* (1663) 1 Sid. 168.
7 *R.* v. *Curl* (1727) 2 Stra. 788; 1 Barn K.B. 29.
8 *R.* v. *Delaval* (1763) 3 Burr 1434.
9 *Jones* v. *Randall* (1774) 1 Cowp. 17.
10 *Shaw* v. *DPP* [1962] A.C. 220, at 267.
11 'Report on Homosexual Offences and Prostitution' (Wolfenden Committee) (1957), Cmnd 247, para. 102.
12 *Shaw* v. *DPP* [1962] A.C. 220, at p. 268.
13 *Shaw* v. *DPP* [1962] A.C. 220, at p. 275.
14 ibid, p. 292.
15 ibid, p. 294.
16 op. cit.
17 *Knuller* v. *DPP* [1973] A.C. 435, at p. 460.
18 *Kamara* v. *DPP* [1974] A.C. 104, at p. 132.
19 See, for example, 1975 Harvard Law Review 1652; 24 M.L.R. 626;
   (1964) 42 Canadian Bar Review 561; H.L.A Hart, *Law, Liberty and
   Morality*; Presidential Address to the Society of Public Teachers of Law,
   (1961) 6 J.S.P.T.L 104; and Law Commission Working Paper No. 50
   (1973), p. 13.
20 Answer given by Attorney-General to Parliamentary question, Hansard
   30 June 1972, Col. 42.
21 Law Commission Working Paper No. 57, 'Conspiracies Relating to
   Morals and Decency', HMSO 1974, para 56.
22 *Shaw*, op. cit., p. 268. See also observations of Lord Tucker at p. 285.
23 See *R.* v. *Knuller* (Court of Appeal) [1971] 3 All E.R. 314, at 317, per
   Fenton Atkinson LJ.
24 *Knuller* v. *DPP* [1973] A.C. 435, at p. 480.
25 ibid, p. 455.

26 ibid, p. 486.
27 *R.* v. *Bateman* (1925) 28 Cox CC 33, at p. 36.
28 *Knuller* v. *DPP* [1973] A.C. 435, at p. 460, per Lord Morris.
29 *Shaw* v. *DPP* [1962] A.C. 220 at 228 (Court of Appeal).
30 *Knuller* v. *DPP* [1973] A.C. 435, at p. 457, per Lord Reid.
31 ibid, p. 460, per Lord Morris.
32 ibid, p. 491, per Lord Simon.
33 ibid, p. 446 (arguendo); p. 497, per Lord Kilbrandon.
34 ibid, p. 490, per Lord Simon.
35 ibid, p. 455, per Lord Reid.
36 ibid, p. 490, per Lord Simon.
37 3 June 1964. Hansard, Vol. 695, Col. 1212. See *Knuller*, p. 459 (Lord Reid), p. 466 (Lord Morris), p. 480 (Lord Diplock), p. 494 (Lord Simon).
38 *Knuller*, op. cit., p. 465, per Lord Morris. See Court of Appeal comments on admissibility of expert evidence on a 'conspiracy to corrupt public morals' charge in *R.* v. *Anderson* [1971] 3 W.L.R. 939.
39 *Knuller* [1973] A.C. 435, at p. 446 (arguendo).
40 *R.* v. *Anderson* [1971] 3 W.L.R. 939.
41 Michael de la Noy, 'Miscellany', *Guardian*, 22 August 1975.
42 *Knuller*, op. cit., p. 481, per Lord Diplock.
43 See *R.* v. *Christian* (1913) 78 J.P. 112.
44 See Geoffrey Robertson, 'All Our Conspirators', *New Statesman*, 23 February 1973, p. 265.
45 *John Calder (Publications) Ltd* v. *Powell* [1965] 1 Q.B. 509.
46 *R.* v. *Crunden* (1809) 2 Camp 89.
47 *R.* v. *Elliot & White* (1861) Le & Ca 103.
48 *R.* v. *Reed* (1871) 12 Cox CC 1.
49 *R.* v. *Howell* (1864) 4 F & F 160; *R.* v. *Mears & Chalk* (1851) 4 Cox CC 423.
50 *R.* v. *Lynn* (1788) 2 Term. Rep. 733.
51 *Herring* v. *Walround* (1681) 2 Chan Cas 110.
52 Cited by Lord Mansfield in *R.* v. *Delaval* (1763) 3 Burr 1434, at 1438.
53 (1864) 4 F & F 73.
54 (1875) 1 Q.B.D. 15.
55 *Knuller* [1973] A.C. 435, at p. 469, per Lord Morris.
56 op. cit.
57 ibid, p. 495, per Lord Simon.
58 ibid, pp. 494–5, per Lord Simon.
59 op. cit.
60 ibid, p. 469, per Lord Morris.
61 ibid, p. 468 (Lord Morris) and p. 494 (Lord Simon). Contra Lord Reid at p. 458.
62 Theatres Act 1968, section 2 (4); Criminal Law Act 1977, section 53 (3).

63 *Knuller* [1973] A.C. 435, at pp. 458–9.

64 Preamble to Disorderly Houses Act, 1751.

65 *R.* v. *Higginson* (1762) 2 Burr 1233.

66 *R.* v. *Quinn & Bloom* [1962] 2 Q.B. 245.

67 *Knuller* [1973] A.C. 435, at p. 493.

68 *R.* v. *Brady & Ram* (1963) 47 Cr. App. Rep. 196; see also *Marks* v. *Benjamin* 1839 5 M&W 565, and *R.* v. *Davies* [1897] 2 Q.B. 199.

69 *R.* v. *Cinecentre Ltd*, Birmingham Crown Court, 15 March 1976. Summing up of Mr Justice Bush, transcript, p. 4.

70 *R.* v. *Berg & Others* (1927), 20 Cr. App. Rep. 38.

71 *R.* v. *Brady & Ram* (1963) 47 Cr. App. Rep. 196.

72 *R.* v. *Quinn & Bloom* [1962] 2 Q.B. 245, at p. 257.

73 *Shaw*, op. cit., p. 292, per Lord Reid; *Knuller*, op. cit., p. 495, per Lord Simon.

74 *Knuller*, op. cit., p. 495.

75 *R.* v. *Cinecentre Ltd*, Birmingham Crown Court, 15 March 1976. Transcript, pp. 3–4.

76 *R.* v. *Stannard* (1863) Crim Law Cases 405; *R.* v. *Barrett* (1862) Crim. Law Cases 255.

77 *Abbott* v. *Smith* [1964] 3 All E.R. 762.

78 5 July 1851. *Law Times Reports*, p. 203.

79 *R.* v. *Goldstein*, Bar Library Transcript.

80 1973 Cr. App. Rep. 229.

81 Working Paper No. 50, para 10.

82 House of Commons, 7 July 1964.

83 See Geoffrey Robertson, 'Whose Conspiracy' (NCCL 1974), pp. 42–3.

84 See Law Commission, Working Paper No. 50 (5 June 1973) para 13–23; Working Paper No. 57 (1974); Report No. 76 on conspiracy & Criminal Law Reform (1976) section 3. 16–20.

85 Law Commission Report No. 76, pp. 114–17.

86 *R.* v. *Atwood* (1617) Cro Jac 421. See G.D. Nokes, *History of the Crime of Blasphemy* (London 1928), p. 22.

87 Journal of House of Lords, xii, p. 713, 717. See Nokes, p. 47.

88 1 Ventris 293.

89 *R.* v. *Gathercole* (1838) 168 E.R. 1140.

90 See *R.* v. *Williams* (1797) 26 S.T. 653, *R.* v. *Richard Carlile* (1819) 1 St.T. (N.S.) 1387, *R.* v. *Mary Carlile* (1821) 1 St. T. (N.S.) 1033, *R.* v. *Waddington* (1822) 1 B&C 26.

91 *A full Report of the Trial of Henry Hetherington* (London 1840), p. 22; *R.* v. *Hetherington* (1840) 4 St. Tr (N.S.) 563.

92 *R.* v. *Moxon* (1841) 4 St. Tr (N.S.) 693.

93 See Paul O'Higgins, *Censorship in Britain*, p. 22.

94 Quoted by Professor Kenny, 'The Evolution of the Law of Blasphemy', 1922 *Cambridge Law Journal*, p. 123.

95 *R.* v. *Hetherington* (1840) 4 St. T. (N.S.) 563, at p. 591.
96 *R.* v. *Ramsay & Foote* (1883) 48 L.T. 733.
97 *Bowman* v. *The Secular Society Ltd.* [1917] A.C. 406, at p. 446.
98 *R.* v. *Gott* (1922) 16 Cr. App. Rep. 87.
99 *Freedom Under the Law*, Hamlyn Lecture (Stevens & Co 1949), p. 46.
100 *Crowe* v. *Graham*, (1968) 41 A.L.J.R. 409, per Windeyer J.
101 *R.* v. *Wicks* (1936) 25 Cr. App. Rep. 168.
102 *R.* v. *Lemon & Gay News Ltd.* (1978) 67 Cr. App. R. 70, at p. 82.
103 *R.* v. *Boulter* (1908) J.P. 188.
104 Transcript of summing up by Judge King-Hamilton in *R.* v. *Lemon*, Central Criminal Court 11 July 1977, p. 15.
105 See *R.* v. *Holbrook* (No. 1) (1877) 3 Q.B.D. 60; *R.* v. *Holbrook* (No. 2) (1878) 4 Q.B.D. 42.
106 *Goldsmith* v. *Pressdram Ltd.* [1976] 3 W.L.R. 191.

CHAPTER 9

1 *Report from the Joint Select Committee of the House of Lords and the House of Commons on the Stage Plays (Censorship)* 2 November 1909.
2 Richard Findlater, *Banned! – a Review of Theatrical Censorship in Britain* (Macgibbon & Kee 1967), p. 175.
3 Notes by the Lord Chamberlain's office on the Theatres Act 1843 and on the Administration of the Act, Appendix 22, *Report of Joint Committee on Censorship of the Theatre*, HMSO 1967 (H.C. 255; H.C. 503), p. 185.
4 ibid.
5 Memorandum submitted by the Director of the Royal Shakespeare Company to the Joint Committee, ibid, p. 67.
6 ibid, p. 98, Minutes of Evidence from Society of West End Theatre Managers.
7 *Report on Censorship of the Theatre*, p. xiii.
8 *Wigan* v. *Strange* (1865) L.R. 1 C.P. 175, per Erle CJ.
9 The Law Commission, *Report on Conspiracy and Criminal Law Reform* (Law Comm. Rep. No. 76) (HMSO 1976), part III, para. 93.
10 Theatres Act, 1968, section 18 and Public Order Act 1936, section 9.
11 *R.* v. *Hochhauser* [1964] 47 W.W.R. 350; *R.* v. *Benson* [1928] 3 W.W.R. 605.
12 *R.* v. *Mayling* [1963] 2 All E.R. 687.
13 *R.* v. *Holmes* (1853) Dears CC 207, at p. 209. *Languish* v. *Archer* (1882) 10 Q.B.D. 44.
14 See generally Brownlie, *The Law Relating to Public Order* (Butterworths 1968), p. 61.
15 Theatres Act 1968, section 7.
16 Section 7 (2) which exempts rehearsals etc. from the provisions of the

Theatres Act, also removes from these occasions the protection of section
2 (4), namely the restriction on proceedings at common law.

17 *Report on Censorship*, para. 48.
18 ibid, Appendix 19 (written opinion of the Solicitor-General), p. 172.
19 *Report on Censorship*, para 50.
20 ibid, para 51.
21 ibid, p. 56, question 314 (Evidence of Sir Dingle Foot QC).
22 ibid, p. 81, question 434 (Evidence of Mr Kenneth Tynan).
23 ibid, para 52.
24 *R.* v. *Brownson* [1971] Crim. L.R., 551.
25 Criminal Law Act 1977, Schedule 1.
26 *R.* v. *Brownson* [1971] Crim. L.R., 551.
27 *Grade* v. *Director of Public Prosecutions* [1942] 2 All E.R. 118.
28 See Leslie E. Cotterell, *Performance* (London 1977), p. 28.
29 *Report on Censorship*, p. 54.
30 *R.* v. *Quinn & Bloom* [1962] 2 Q.B. 245.
31 *R.* v. *Penguin Books* (1961); see Rolph, *Lady Chatterley*, p. 127.
32 See *Gould* v. *Evans & Co.* (1951) 2 T.L.R. 1189 and *Buckingham* v. *Daily News* [1956] 2 Q.B. 534.
33 *Jordan* v. *Burgoyne* [1963] 2 Q.B. 744.
34 *London County Council* v. *Bermondsey Bioscope Co. Ltd.* [1911] 1 K.B. 445, at p. 451.
35 See Neville March Hunnings, *Film Censors and the Law* (Allen & Unwin 1967), p. 50.
36 Ibid, p. 51.
37 ibid, p. 54.
38 *Ellis* v. *Dubowski* [1921] 3 K.B. 621, at 626.
39 *Mills* v. *London County Council* [1925] 1 K.B. 213.
40 *R.* v. *G.L.C. ex parte Blackburn* [1976] 1 W.L.R. 550, per Lord Denning, at pp. 554–5.
41 (1942), 385 H.C. Deb 504.
42 *Report of the Departmental Committee on Children and the Cinema* (HMSO 1950), Cmnd. 7945.
43 *G.L.C.* v. *Langian Ltd*, decision of Judge Bruce Campbell QC, Inner London Crown Court, 16 November 1977.
44 See *R.* v. *Liverpool Corporation, ex parte Liverpool Taxi Fleet Operators Association* [1972] 2 Q.B. 299.
45 *Film Censorship – The Cinema and the Williams Committee*, R.S. Camplin, Cinematograph Exhibitors' Association of Great Britain and Ireland, 1978, pp. 6, 18.
46 *G.L.C.* v *Langian*, Transcript of Judgment, p. 5.
47 Viscount Kilmuir, House of Lords, 22 June 1959, Vol. 217, Col. 74.
48 See John Trevelyan, *What the Censor Saw* (Michael Joseph 1973), p. 141.
49 ibid, pp. 66–7.

50 *R.* v. *G.L.C. ex parte Blackburn* [1976] 1 W.L.R. 550, at p. 560.
51 See 'Film Censors facing the Crunch', *Guardian*, 2 August 1975, p. 18.
52 *The Times*, 9 July 1976, p. 1.
53 For an account of GLC tergiversation on film censorship, see Enid Wistrich, *I don't mind the sex it's the violence – Film Censorship Explored* (Marion Boyers 1978).
54 The Law Commission, *Report on Conspiracy and Criminal Law Reform*, HMSO 1976, Part III, para. 58.
55 ibid, para. 67.
56 British Board of Film Censors, monthly *Report* for February 1976, p. 18.
57 See section 53 (3): As the result of a drafting oversight, it may still be possible to prosecute these offences as conspiracies to contravene the statute, although this would be contrary to Parliamentary intentions. See Edward Griew, *The Criminal Law Act 1977* (Sweet and Maxwell 1978), notes on section 5 (3) and section 53.
58 Section 53 (2) and (5): The DPP's consent should be obtained before application for a summons: see *R.* v. *Angel* (1968) 52 Cr. App. Rep. 280; *Price* v. *Humphries* [1959] 2 All E.R. 725.
59 Law Commission, *Report on Conspiracy*, para. 82.
60 *Report on Conspiracy*, para. 78.
61 *Attorney-General's Reference* (No. 3 of 1977) [1978] 3 All E.R. 1166.
62 1977 H.C. Vol. 935, Col. 458.
63 *Report of the Committee on the Future of Broadcasting*, chaired by Lord Annan (HMSO 1977), Cmnd. 6753, Chapter 16, para. 3.
64 Obscene Publications Act 1959, proviso to section 1 (3).
65 *Knuller* v. *DPP* [1973] A.C. 435, at p. 495.
66 Letter from Lord Normanbrook (Chairman, BBC) to Postmaster General, 19 June 1964. This undertaking was reaffirmed when the BBC Licence was renewed in 1969, and the contents of the letter are noted in the prescribing memorandum under Clause 13 (4) of the Licence and Agreement.
67 BBC's Royal Charter, Article 3 (a); Lord Normanbrook's letter; IBA Act 1973 section 2 (2) and 4 (1) (b) and (f).
68 *Annan Report*, supra note 63, pp. 260, 261.
69 C.A. Lewis, *Broadcasting from Within* (1924); quoted in Anthony Smith, *British Broadcasting* (David & Charles 1974), pp. 43–4.
70 P.P. Eckersley, *The Power Behind the Microphone* (1942), quoted in Smith, *British Broadcasting*, p. 470.
71 Hansard, House of Lords, 22 May 1952, Col. 1297.
72 Sir Hugh Greene, *The Third Floor Front: a view of Broadcasting in the Sixties* (1969) quoted Smith, *British Broadcasting*, p. 182.
73 Mary Whitehouse, *Whatever Happened to Sex* (Wayland Publishers 1977), p. 18.

74 *A.G. ex parte McWhirter* v. *IBA* [1973] 1 Q.B. 629, per Lord Denning, at p. 652.

75 *Sunday Times*, 30 December 1973.

76 *Annan Report*, Chapter 8, para. 8.

77 *Report of Joint Committee on Censorship of The Theatre*, Appendix 3, 'Control over the subject matter of programmes in BBC Television', p. 113.

78 *Report on Censorship*, Appendix 2, 'Control over the Subject matter of programmes in BBC Radio', p. 112.

79 *Annan Report*, Chapter 16, para. 38.

80 Letter from Mr Alasdair Milne (Director of Programmes, BBC) to Dennis Potter, 19 March 1976.

81 Letter from Sir Michael Swann (Chairman, BBC) to Mr Ben Whitaker (Chairman, Defence of Literature and the Arts Society), 25 March 1976.

82 Peter Fiddick, 'Brutal truth barred from the screens', *Guardian*, 23 January 1978, p. 8.

83 *A.G. ex parte McWhirter* v. *IBA* [1973] 1 Q.B. 629, per Lord Denning, at p. 650.

84 ibid, per Lord Justice Lawton, at p. 658.

85 *Gouriet* v. *Union of Post Office Workers* [1978] A.C. 435.

86 *Annan Report*, Chapter 12, para 4.

87 ibid, paragraphs 7 and 10.

88 *The Times*, 23 November 1977, letter to Editor from Jonathan Dimbleby and other employees of Thames Television.

89 'How Mason leaned on Thames Television', *Guardian*, 9 June 1978, p. 11.

90 See *Annan Report*, chapter 4 paras. 29–31 and chapter 13. The Committee thought that 'the statutory obligations placed upon the IBA to supervise programme content should stand' (13.11), apparently unaware that those obligations, as interpreted in *McWhirter's case*, require precisely the kind of intermeddling which the Committee went on to deplore.

91 *The Annan Report*, The Authorities' Comments, *Independent Broadcasting*, No. 12, July 1977.

92 'Broadcasting', Cmnd 7294, HMSO, July 1978.

93 'Publish or be Slammed', *Sunday Times*, 18 June 1978.

94 *Annan Report*, Chapter 16, para. 10.

95 Professor J.D. Halloran, 'Research Findings on Broadcasting', *Annan Report* Appendix F. See the discussion of the views of Professors Halloran and Himmelweit in Chapter 16 of the *Report*. A recent study of psychological research by Eysenck & Nias concludes that greater restraints should be imposed upon media violence: *Sex Violence and the Media* (Temple Smith 1978). Compare Anthony Smith, 'Censoring violence on TV isn't so simple', *Observer*, 24 September 1978.

96 See 'Violence in Television Programmes – the ITV Code' and 'The Portrayal of violence in television programmes – a note of guidance (BBC)' in Smith, *British Broadcasting*, pp. 239–45.

97 Report commissioned for Pye Television. See 'Homework Between TV Shows', *The Times*, 10 May 1978.

98 ibid.

99 'IBA Code of Advertising Standards and Practice'. See 'IBA as an Appeal Court', *Evening Standard*, 22 June 1978.

100 See Suzie Hayman, *Advertising and Contraception*, Birth Control Trust, 1977.

101 Section 8 (3) and Schedule 2, para. 8.

102 See T.C. Hartley & J.A.G. Griffith, *Government and Law* (Weidenfeld & Nicolson 1975), pp. 256–61.

103 *Annan Report*, Chapter 4, para. 30.

104 ibid, Chapter 15, para. 20.

105 *Broadcasting* (HMSO 1978), Cmnd 7294, para. 100.

106 *Annan Report*, chapter 6, para. 30; chapter 16, para. 50.

CHAPTER 10

1 *R.* v. *Calder & Boyars* [1968] 1 Q.B. 151, at p. 172.

2 Op. cit., at p. 172.

3 *Report of US Presidential Commission* (Minority Report) p. 458.

4 *Holborn* v. *Holborn* [1947] 1 All E.R. 32, per Lord Merriman.

5 *R.* v. *Metropolitan Police Commissioner ex p. Blackburn* [1973] 2 W.L.R. 43, at p. 46.

6 *R.* v. *Anderson* [1971] 3 W.L.R. 939, at p. 944.

7 See Palmer, *The Trials of Oz* (Blond & Briggs 1971), p. 148.

8 Anthony Storr, *Sexual Deviations* (Pelican 1964), p. 96.

9 *Inside Linda Lovelace* (Heinrich Hanan Publications 1974). (London 1974.)

10 See Bel Mooney, 'Sex After Marriage', *Cosmopolitan*, July 1977, p. 102.

11 See Bernard Levin, *The Pendulum Years* (Pan Books 1970), Chapter 17.

12 See Robertson, 'Obscenity: A Jury Decides', *New Statesman*, 17 November 1972.

13 See Geoffrey Robertson, 'The Abominable Crime', *New Statesman*, 1 November 1974, p. 611.

14 Coke, 3 Institutes, 59. See *R.* v. *Wiseman*, 1718, Fortescues Reports, p. 91.

15 *R.* v. *Harris* (1971) 55 Cr. Ap. Rep., p. 290.

16 Storr, *Sexual Deviations*, pp. 98–9.

17 *Knuller* v. *DPP* [1973] A.C. 435, at p. 457.

18 *See Re D* [1977] 2 W.L.R. 79.

19 *R.* v. *Anderson*, supra note 6, at p. 944.

20 Tony Honore, *Sex Law* (Duckworths 1978), p. 109.

21 *Report on Homosexual Offences and Prostitution* (1957) Cmnd 249, para 286.

22 Palmer, *The Trials of Oz*, p. 179.

23 See *R.* v. *Bourne* (1952) 36 Cr. App. Rep. 125.

24 *Pornography – The Longford Report*, p. 381.

25 Palmer, *The Trials of Oz*, p. 66.

26 *Appeal of Richard Handyside*, Inner London Crown Court, 29 October 1971, transcript, pp. 13 and 17.

27 *John Calder (Publications) Ltd* v. *Powell* [1965] 1 Q.B. 509, at p. 515.

28 *Report of the Advisory Committee on Drug Dependence*, 'Cannabis', HMSO (Wootton Report) (1969). See also Michael Scholfield, *The Strange Case of Pot* (Pelican 1971), and Lester Grinspoon *Marihuana Reconsidered*, 2nd edn. (Harvard University Press 1977).

29 *Shaw* v. *DPP* [1961] 2 All E.R. 446, at p. 465 (g–h).

30 Gillian Freeman, *The Undergrowth of Literature* (Panther 1967), p. 79.

31 Storr, *Sexual Deviations*, pp. 44–5.

32 *DPP* v. *A.&B.C. Chewing Gum* [1968] 1 Q.B. 159.

33 *R.* v. *Calder & Boyars* [1968] 3 W.L.R., at 984.

34 Anthony Burgess, 'What is Pornography', reprinted in Hughes, *Perspectives on Pornography* (London 1970), pp. 6–7. For a recent evaluation of experiments linking media violence to real-life aggression, see Eysenck & Nias, *Sex, Violence and the Media*, London 1978.

35 Hansord (1955), Vol. 539, Col. 63.

36 Mr Justice Griffiths in *R.* v. *Neville and others*, a bail application by the *Oz* editors, reported in *The Times* law report, 8 August 1971.

37 See Rolph, *Lady Chatterley*, p. 17.

38 Palmer, *The Trials of Oz*, p. 194.

39 *Report of U.S. Commission on Obscenity*, pp. 63, 467. See Eysenck & Nias, supra note 34, Chapter 5.

40 See Gaylin, 77 *Yale Law Journal* 570, especially p. 594; and *Ginsberg* v. *New York*, 390 US 629 (1968) at pp. 636 and 639.

41 *R.* v. *Sutton* [1977] 1 W.L.R. 1086, at p. 1089.

42 See *Sutton*, ibid. and *R.* v. *Hart & others*, Bristol Assizes 22/6/66, cited in Law Commission Report No. 76, on Conspiracy and Criminal Law Reform, Chapter 3, para 117.

43 Hansard, House of Lords, Wednesday 28 June 1978, Vol. 394, No. 103, Cols. 330–1.

44 Royal Courts of Justice, 29 March 1973, transcript, pp. 5, 6.

45 Lord Harris of Greenwich, 18 May 1978, Vol. 392, No. 81, Col. 563.

46 Hansard, House of Lords, Vol. 394, No. 103, Col. 334.

47 *R.* v. *Stamford* [1972] 2 All E.R. 427.

48 *R.* v. *Stanley* (1965) 2 Q.B. 327. *R.* v. *Straker* [1965] Crim. L.R. 239.

49 *Kosmos Publications Ltd* v. *DPP* [1975] Crim. L.R. 345.

50 *Brutus* v. *Cozens* [1973] A.C. 854.

51 Hansard, House of Lords, Vol. 392, No. 81, Col. 545–6.

52 Mr Brynmor John, Minister of State for the Home Office, reported in *The Times* 15 July 1978. See also Lord Harris in the House of Lords

debate, 28 June 1978, Hansard Vol. 394, No. 103, Col. 335, and Lord Scarman, 20 June 1978, Vol. 393, No. 97, at Cols. 1083–4.

CHAPTER 11

1 Fox R.G., *Study Paper on Obscenity*, prepared for the Law Reform Commission of Canada, Information Canada, 1972, pp. 43–4.
2 *Roth* v. *US* 354 US 463 (1957). See Justice Brennan at p. 470: 'All ideas having even the slightest redeeming social importance – unorthodox ideas, controversial ideas, even ideas hateful to the prevailing climate of opinion – have the full protection of the guaranties, unless excludable because they encroach upon the limited area of more important interests. But implicit in the history of the First Amendment is the rejection of obscenity as utterly without redeeming social importance.... There are certain well-defined and narrowly limited classes of speech, the prevention and punishment of which have never been thought to raise any constitutional problem. These include the lewd and obscene.... It has been well observed that such utterances are no essential part of any exposition of ideas, and are of such slight social value as a step to truth that any benefit that may be derived from them is clearly outweighed by the social interest in order and morality.... We hold that obscenity is not within the area of constitutionally protected speech or press.'
3 *Memoirs* v. *Massachusetts*, 383 US 413 (1966).
4 *Miller* v. *California*, (1973). 413 US 15.
5 *Pinkus* v. *US*, judgment delivered 23 May 1978.
6 *Pairs Adult Theatre* v. *Slaton*, 413 US 49 (1973), at p. 84.
7 *Jerry Lee Smith* v. *US* 23 May 1977, dissenting opinion.
8 Indecent Publications Act (1963) section 2 and section 11. For an over-enthusiastic account of the Tribunal's operation, see Stuart Perry, *The Indecent Publications Tribunal – A Social Experiment* (New Zealand 1965).
9 Mr Peter Coleman, New South Wales House of Representatives, Hansard 1974, 4587–8. See the Indecent Articles and Classified Publications Act 1975 (N.S.W.).
10 Richard Fox, *Cases and materials on Obscenity*, (Monash University Faculty of Law.
11 See Rolph, *Books in the Dock*, pp. 132–3.

Appendix:
Major statutory provisions relating to indecency and obscenity

OBSCENE PUBLICATIONS ACT 1959

An Act to amend the law relating to the publication of obscene matter; to provide for the protection of literature; and to strengthen the law concerning pornography.

Test of obscenity

1.–(1) For the purposes of this Act an article shall be deemed to be obscene if its effect or (where the article comprises two or more distinct items) the effect of any one of its items is, if taken as a whole, such as to tend to deprave and corrupt persons who are likely, having regard to all relevant circumstances, to read, see or hear the matter contained or embodied in it.

(2) In this Act 'article' means any description of article containing or embodying matter to be read or looked at or both, any sound record, and any film or other record of a picture or pictures.

(3) For the purposes of this Act a person publishes an article who:
(a) distributes, circulates, sells, lets on hire, gives, or lends it, or who offers it for sale or for letting on hire; or
(b) in the case of an article containing or embodying matter to be looked at or a record, shows, plays or projects it:

Provided that paragraph (b) of this sub-section shall not apply to anything done in the course of television or sound broadcasting.

Prohibition of publication of obscene matter

2.–(1) Subject as hereinafter provided, any person who, whether for gain or not, publishes an obscene article shall be liable:
(a) on summary conviction to a fine not exceeding one thousand pounds or to imprisonment for a term not exceeding six months;
(b) on conviction on indictment to a fine or to imprisonment for a term not exceeding three years or both.

(2) ... summary proceedings for an offence against this section may be brought at any time within twelve months from the commission of the offence....

(3) A prosecution on indictment for an offence against this section shall not be commenced more than two years after the commission of the offence.

(4) A person publishing an article shall not be proceeded against for an offence at common law consisting of the publication of any matter contained or embodied in the article where it is of the essence of the offence that the matter is obscene.

(5) A person shall not be convicted of an offence against this section if he proves that he had not examined the article in respect of which he is charged and had no reasonable cause to suspect that it was such that his publication of it would make him liable to be convicted of an offence against this section.

(6) In any proceedings against a person under this section the question whether an article is obscene shall be determined without regard to any publication by another person unless it could reasonably have been expected that the publication by the other person would follow from publication by the person charged.

Powers of search and seizure

3.—(1) If a justice of the peace is satisfied by information on oath that there is reasonable ground for suspecting that, in any premises in the petty sessions area for which he acts, or on any stall or vehicle in that area, being premises or a stall or vehicle specified in the information, obscene articles are, or are from time to time, kept for publication for gain, the justice may issue a warrant under his hand empowering any constable to enter (if need be by force) and search the premises, or to search the stall or vehicle, within fourteen days from the date of the warrant, and to seize and remove any articles found therein or thereon which the constable has reason to believe to be obscene articles and to be kept for publication for gain.

(2) A warrant under the foregoing sub-section shall, if any obscene articles are seized under the warrant, also empower the seizure and removal of any documents found in the premises or, as the case may be, on the stall or vehicle which relate to a trade or business carried on at the premises or from the stall or vehicle.

(3) Any articles seized under sub-section (1) of this section shall be brought before a justice of the peace acting for the same petty sessions area as the justice who issued the warrant, and the justice before whom the articles are brought may thereupon issue a summons to the occupier of the premises or, as the case may be, the user of the stall or vehicle to appear on a day specified in the summons before a magistrates' court for that petty sessions area to show cause why the articles or any of them should not be forfeited; and if the court is satisfied, as respects any of the articles, that at the time when they were seized they were obscene articles kept for publication for gain, the court shall order those articles to be forfeited:

Provided that if the person summoned does not appear, the court shall not make an order unless service of the summons is proved. Provided also that this sub-section does not apply in relation to any article seized under sub-section (1) of this section which is returned to the occupier of the premises or, as the case may be, to the user of the stall or vehicle in or on which it was found.

(4) In addition to the person summoned, any other person being the owner, author or maker of any of the articles brought before the court, or any other person through whose hands they had passed before being seized, shall be entitled to appear before the court on the day specified in the summons to show cause why they should not be forfeited.

(5) Where an order is made under this section for the forfeiture of any articles, any person who appeared, or was entitled to appear, to show cause against the making of the order may appeal to quarter sessions; and no such order shall take effect until the expiration of fourteen days after the day on which the order is made....

(6) If as respects any articles brought before it the court does not order forfeiture, the court may if it thinks fit order the person on whose information the warrant for the seizure of the articles was issued to pay such costs as the court thinks reasonable to any person who has appeared before the court to show cause why those articles should not be forfeited; and costs ordered to be paid under this sub-section shall be enforceable as a civil debt.

(7) For the purposes of this section the question whether an article is obscene shall be determined on the assumption that copies of it would be published in any manner likely having regard to the circumstances in which it was found, but in no other manner....

Defence of public good

4.—(1) A person shall not be convicted of an offence against Section two of this Act, and an order for forfeiture shall not be made under the foregoing section, if it is proved that publication of the article in question is justified as being for the public good on the ground that it is in the interests of science, literature, art or learning, or of other objects of general concern.

(2) It is hereby declared that the opinion of experts as to the literary, artistic, scientific or other merits of an article may be admitted in any proceedings under this Act either to establish or to negative the said ground.

OBSCENE PUBLICATIONS ACT 1964

An Act to strengthen the law for preventing the publication for gain of obscene matter and the publication of things intended for the production of obscene matter.

1.–(1) In Section two (1) of the Obscene Publications Act, 1959 (under which it is an offence punishable on summary conviction or on indictment to publish an obscene article, whether for gain or not) after the words 'any person who, whether for gain or not, publishes an obscene article' there shall be inserted the words 'or who has an obscene article for publication for gain (whether gain to himself or gain to another)'.

(2) For the purpose of any proceedings for an offence against the said Section two a person shall be deemed to have an article for publication for gain if with a view to such publication he has the article in his ownership, possession or control.

(3) In proceedings brought against a person under the said Section two for having an obscene article for publication for gain the following provisions shall apply in place of sub-sections (5) and (6) of that section, that is to say,

(a) he shall not be convicted of that offence if he proves that he had not examined the article and had no reasonable cause to suspect that it was such that his having it would make him liable to be convicted of an offence against that section; and

(b) the question whether the article is obscene shall be determined by reference to such publication for gain of the article as in the circumstances it may reasonably be inferred he had in contemplation and to any further publication that could reasonably be expected to follow from it, but not to any other publication.

(4) Where articles are seized under Section three of the Obscene Publications Act, 1959 (which provides for the seizure and forfeiture of obscene articles kept for publication for gain), and a person is convicted under Section two of that Act of having them for publication for gain, the court on his conviction shall order the forfeiture of those articles....

(5) References in Section three of the Obscene Publications Act, 1959, and this section to publication for gain shall apply to any publication with a view to gain, whether the gain is to accrue by way of consideration for the publication or in any other way.

2.–(1) The Obscene Publications Act, 1959 (as amended by this Act) shall apply in relation to anything which is intended to be used, either alone or as one of a set, for the reproduction or manufacture therefrom of articles containing or embodying matter to be read, looked at or listened to, as if it were an article containing or embodying that matter so far as that matter is to be derived from it or from the set.

(2) For the purposes of the Obscene Publications Act, 1959 (as so amended) an article shall be deemed to be had or kept for publication if it is had or kept for the reproduction or manufacture therefrom of articles for publication; and the question whether an article so had or kept is obscene shall:

(a) for purposes of Section two of the Act be determined in accordance with Section one (3) (b) above as if any reference there to publication of the article were a reference to publication of articles reproduced or manufactured from it; and

(b) for purposes of Section three of the Act be determined on the assumption that articles reproduced or manufactured from it would be published in any manner likely having regard to the circumstances in which it was found, but in no other manner.

THEATRES ACT 1968

An Act to abolish censorship of the theatre and to amend the law in respect of theatres and theatrical performances

1. Abolition of censorship of the theatre

(1) The Theatres Act 1843 is hereby repealed; and none of the powers which were exercisable thereunder by the Lord Chamberlain of Her Majesty's Household shall be exercisable by or on behalf of Her Majesty by virtue of Her royal prerogative.

(2) In granting, renewing or transferring any licence under this Act for the use of any premises for the public performance of plays or in varying any of the terms, conditions or restrictions on or subject to which any such licence is held, the licensing authority shall not have power to impose any terms, condition or restriction as to the nature of the plays which may be performed under the licence or as to the manner of performing plays thereunder:

Provided that nothing in this subsection shall prevent a licensing authority from imposing any term, condition or restriction which they consider necessary in the interests of physical safety or health or any condition regulating or prohibiting the giving of an exhibition, demonstration or performance of hypnotism within the meaning of the Hypnotism Act 1952.

Prohibition of presentation of obscene performances

2.–(1) For the purposes of this section a performance of a play shall be deemed to be obscene if, taken as a whole, its effect was such as to tend to deprave and corrupt persons who were likely, having regard to all relevant circumstances, to attend it.

(2) Subject to sections 3 and 7 of this Act, if an obscene performance of a play is given, whether in public or private, any person who (whether for gain or not) presented or directed that performance shall be liable....

(3) A prosecution on indictment for an offence under this section shall not be commenced more than two years after the commission of the offence.

(4) No person shall be proceeded against in respect of a performance of a play or anything said or done in the course of such a performance –

(a) for an offence at common law where it is of the essence of the offence that the performance or, as the case may be, what was said or done was obscene, indecent, offensive, disgusting or injurious to morality; or

(b) for an offence under section 4 of the Vagrancy Act 1824....

and no person shall be proceeded against for an offence at common law of conspiring to corrupt public morals, or to do any act contrary to public morals or decency, in respect of an agreement to present or give a performance of a play, or to cause anything to be said or done in the course of such a performance.

Defence of public good

3.–(1) A person shall not be convicted of an offence under section 2 of this Act if it is proved that the giving of the performance in question was justified as being for the public good on the ground that it was in the interests of drama, opera, ballet or any other art, or of literature or learning.

(2) It is hereby declared that the opinion of experts as to the artistic, literary or other merits of a performance of a play may be admitted in any proceedings for an offence under section 2 of this Act either to establish or negative the said ground.

Incitement to racial hatred

5.–(1) Subject to section 7 of this Act, if there is given a public performance of a play involving the use of threatening, abusive or insulting words, any person who (whether for gain or not) presented or directed that performance shall be guilty of an offence under this section if –

(a) he did so with intent to stir up hatred against any section of the public in Great Britain distinguished by colour, race or ethnic or national origins; and

(b) that performance, taken as a whole, is likely to stir up hatred against that section on grounds of colour, race or ethnic or national origins.

Provocation of breach of the peace

6. – (1) Subject to section 7 of this Act, if there is given a public performance of a play involving the use of threatening, abusive or insulting words or behaviour, any person who (whether for gain or not) presented or directed that performance shall be guilty of an offence under this section if –

(a) he did so with intent to provoke a breach of the peace; or

(b) the performance, taken as a whole, was likely to occasion a breach of the peace.

Exceptions

7. – (1) Nothing in sections 2 to 4 of this Act shall apply in relation to a performance of a play given on a domestic occasion in a private dwelling.

(2) Nothing in sections 2 to 6 of this Act shall apply in relation to a performance of a play given solely or primarily for one or more of the following purposes, that is to say –

(a) rehearsal; or

(b) to enable –

(i) a record or cinematograph film to be made from or by means of the performance; or

(ii) the performance to be broadcast; or

(iii) the performance to be transmitted to subscribers to a diffusion service;

but in any proceedings for an offence under section 2, 5 or 6 of this Act alleged to have been committed in respect of a performance of a play . . . if it is proved that the performance was attended by persons other than persons directly connected with the giving of the performance or the doing in relation thereto of any of the things mentioned in paragraph (b) above, the performance shall be taken not to have been given solely or primarily for one or more of the said purposes unless the contrary is shown.

(3) In this section –

'broadcast' means broadcast by wireless telegraphy (within the meaning of the Wireless Telegraphy Act 1949), whether by way of sound broadcasting or television;

'cinematograph film' means any print, negative, tape or other article on which a performance of a play or any part of such a performance is recorded for the purposes of visual reproduction;

'record' means any record or similar contrivance for reproducing sound, including the sound-track of a cinematograph film;

Restriction on institution of proceedings

8. – Proceedings for an offence under section 2, 5 or 6 of this Act or an offence at common law committed by the publication of defamatory matter in the course of a performance of a play shall not be instituted in England and Wales except by or with the consent of the Attorney-General.

Script as evidence

9. – (1) Where a performance of a play was based on a script, then, in any proceedings for an offence under section 2, 5 or 6 of this Act alleged to have been committed in respect of that performance –

(a) an actual script on which that performance was based shall be admissible as evidence of what was performed and of the manner in which the performance or any part of it was given; and

(b) if such a script is given in evidence on behalf of any party to the proceedings then, except in so far as the contrary is shown, whether by evidence given on behalf of the same or any other party, the performance shall be taken to have been given in accordance with that script.

(2) In this Act 'script', in relation to a performance of a play, means the text of the play (whether expressed in words or in musical or other notation) together with any stage or other directions for its performance, whether contained in a single document or not.

18. Interpretation

'play' means –

(a) any dramatic piece, whether involving improvisation or not, which is given wholly or in part by one or more persons actually present and performing and in which the whole or a major proportion of what is done by the person or persons performing, whether by way of speech, singing or action, involves the playing of a role; and

(b) any ballet given wholly or in part by one or more persons actually present and performing, whether or not it falls within paragraph (a) of this definition;

'public performance' includes any performance in a public place within the meaning of the Public Order Act 1936 and any performance which the public or any section thereof are permitted to attend, whether on payment or otherwise;

(2) For the purposes of this Act –

(a) a person shall not be treated as presenting a performance of a play by reason only of his taking part therein as a performer;

(b) a person taking part as a performer in a performance of a play directed by another person shall be treated as a person who directed the performance if without reasonable excuse he performs otherwise than in accordance with that person's direction; and

(c) a person shall be taken to have directed a performance of a play given under his direction notwithstanding that he was not present during the performance; and a person shall not be treated as aiding or abetting the commission of an offence under section 2, 5 or 6 of this Act in respect of a performance of a play by reason only of his taking part in that performance as a performer.

CRIMINAL LAW ACT 1977

Amendments of Obscene Publications Act 1959 with respect to cinematograph exhibitions

(2) In section 2 of that Act (prohibition of publication of obscene matter) at the end of subsection (3) there shall be inserted the following subsection –

' "(3A) Proceedings for an offence under this section shall not be instituted except by or with the consent of the Director of Public Prosecutions in any case where the article in question is a moving picture film of a width of not less than sixteen millimetres and the relevant publication or the only other publication which followed or could reasonably have been expected to follow from the relevant publication took place or (as the case may be) was to take place in the course of a cinematograph exhibition; and in this subsection 'the relevant publication' means –

(a) in the case of any proceedings under this section for publishing an obscene article, the publication in respect of which the defendant would be charged if the proceedings were brought; and

(b) in the case of any proceedings under this section for having an obscene article for publication for gain, the publication which, if the proceedings were brought, the defendant would be alleged to have had in contemplation." '

(3) In section 2 of that Act after subsection (4) there shall be inserted the following subsection –

'(4A) Without prejudice to subsection (4) above, a person shall not be proceeded against for an offence at common law –

(a) in respect of a cinematograph exhibition or anything said or done in the course of a cinematograph exhibition, where it is of the essence of the common law offence that the exhibition or, as the case may be, what was said or done was obscene, indecent, offensive, disgusting or injurious to morality; or

(b) in respect of an agreement to give a cinematograph exhibition or to cause anything to be said or done in the course of such an exhibition where the common law offence consists of conspiring to corrupt public morals or to do any act contrary to public morals or decency.'

(6) In section 4 of that Act (defence of public good) at the beginning of subsection (1) there shall be inserted the words 'Subject to subsection (1A) of this section' and at the end of that subsection there shall be inserted the following subsection –

'(1A) Subsection (1) of this section shall not apply where the article in question is a moving picture film or soundtrack but –

(a) a person shall not be convicted of an offence against section 2 of this Act in relation to any such film or soundtrack, and

(b) an order for forfeiture of any such film or soundtrack shall not be made under section 3 of this Act,

if it is proved that publication of the film or soundtrack is justified as being for the public good on the ground that it is in the interests of drama, opera, ballet or any other art, or of literature or learning.'

(7) At the end of section 4 of that Act there shall be added the following subsection –

'(8) In this section "moving picture soundtrack" means any sound record designed for playing with a moving picture film, whether incorporated with the film or not.'

POST OFFICE ACT 1953

11. Prohibition on sending by post of certain articles

(1) A person shall not send or attempt to send or procure to be sent a postal packet which –

(a) save as [the authority] may either generally or in any particular case allow, encloses any explosive, dangerous, noxious or deleterious substance, any filth, any sharp instrument not properly protected, any noxious living creature, or any creature, article or thing whatsoever which is likely to injure either other postal packets in course of conveyance or [a person engaged in the business of the authority]; or

(b) encloses any indecent or obscene print, painting, photograph, lithograph, engraving, cinematograph film, book, card or written communication, or any indecent or obscene article whether similar to the above or not; or

(c) has on the packet, or on the cover thereof, any words, marks or designs which are grossly offensive or of an indecent or obscene character.

CUSTOMS LAWS CONSOLIDATION ACT 1876

Section 42. Goods prohibited to be imported.

... Indecent or obscene prints, paintings, photographs, books, cards, lithographic or other engravings, or any other indecent or obscene articles.

PROTECTION OF CHILDREN ACT 1978

An Act to prevent the exploitation of children by making indecent photographs of them; and to penalise the distribution, showing and advertisement of such indecent photographs.

1.– (1) It is an offence for a person –

(a) to take, or permit to be taken, any indecent photograph of a child (meaning in this Act a person under the age of 16); or

(b) to distribute or show such indecent photographs; or

(*c*) to have in his possession such indecent photographs, with a view to their being distributed or shown by himself or others; or

(*d*) to publish or cause to be published any advertisement likely to be understood as conveying that the advertiser distributes or shows such indecent photographs, or intends to do so.

(2) For purposes of this Act, a person is to be regarded as distributing an indecent photograph if he parts with possession of it to, or exposes or offers it for acquisition by, another person.

(3) Proceedings for an offence under this Act shall not be instituted except by or with the consent of the Director of Public Prosecutions.

(4) Where a person is charged with an offence under subsection (1) (*b*) or (*c*), it shall be a defence for him to prove –

(*a*) that he had a legitimate reason for distributing or showing the photographs or (as the case may be) having them in his possession; or

(*b*) that he had not himself seen the photographs and did not know, nor had any cause to suspect, them to be indecent. . . .

6. – (1) Offences under this Act shall be punishable either on conviction on indictment or on summary conviction.

(2) A person convicted on indictment of any offence under this Act shall be liable to imprisonment for a term of not more than three years, or to a fine or to both.

(3) A person convicted summarily of any offence under this Act shall be liable –

(*a*) to imprisonment for a term not exceeding six months; or

(*b*) to a fine not exceeding the prescribed sum for the purposes of section 28 of the Criminal Law Act 1977 (punishment on summary conviction of offences triable either way: £1,000 or other sum substituted by order under that Act), or to both.

7. – (1) The following subsections apply for the interpretation of this Act.

(2) References to an indecent photograph include an indecent film, a copy of an indecent photograph or film, and an indecent photograph comprised in a film.

(3) Photographs (including those comprised in a film) shall, if they show children and are indecent, be treated for all purposes of this Act as indecent photographs of children.

(4) References to a photograph include the negative as well as the positive version.

(5) 'Film' includes any form of video-recording.

CHILDREN AND YOUNG PERSONS (HARMFUL PUBLICATIONS) ACT 1955

An Act to prevent the dissemination of certain pictorial publications harmful to children and young persons

1. Works to which this Act applies

This Act applies to any book, magazine or other like work which is of a kind likely to fall into the hands of children or young persons and consists wholly or mainly of stories told in pictures (with or without the addition of written matter), being stories portraying –

(*a*) the commission of crimes; or

(*b*) acts of violence or cruelty; or

(*c*) incidents of a repulsive or horrible nature;

in such a way that the work as a whole would tend to corrupt a child or young person into whose hands it might fall.

2. Penalty for printing, publishing, selling, etc., works to which this Act applies

(1) A person who prints, publishes, sells or lets on hire a work to which this Act applies, or has any such work in his possession for the purpose of selling it or letting it on hire, shall be guilty of an offence and liable, on summary conviction, to imprisonment for

a term not exceeding four months or to a fine not exceeding one hundred pounds or to both:

Provided that, in any proceedings taken under this subsection against a person in respect of selling or letting on hire a work or of having it in his possession for the purpose of selling it or letting it on hire, it shall be a defence for him to prove that he had not examined the contents of the work and had no reasonable cause to suspect that it was one to which this Act applies.

(2) A prosecution for an offence under this section shall not, in England or Wales, be instituted except by, or with the consent of, the Attorney General.

DISORDERLY HOUSES ACT 1751

An Act for the better preventing Thefts and Robberies, and for regulating Places of publick Entertainment, and punishing Persons keeping disorderly Houses

8. Who shall be deemed the keeper of such bawdy-house, etc.

And whereas, by reason of the many subtle and crafty contrivances of persons keeping bawdy houses, ... or other disorderly houses, it is difficult to prove who is the real owner or keeper thereof, by which means many notorious offenders have escaped punishment: Be it enacted by the authority aforesaid, that any person who shall at any time hereafter appear, act, or behave him or herself as master or mistress, or as the person having the care, government, or management of any bawdy-house, ... or other disorderly house, shall be deemed and taken to be the keeper thereof, and shall be liable to be prosecuted and punished as such, notwithstanding he or she shall not in fact be the real owner or keeper thereof.

INDECENT ADVERTISEMENTS ACT 1889

3. Whoever affixes to or inscribes on any house, building, wall, hoarding, gate, fence, pillar, post, board, tree, or any other thing whatsoever so as to be visible to a person being in or passing along any street, public highway, or footpath, and whoever affixes to or inscribes on any public urinal, or delivers or attempts to deliver or exhibits, to any inhabitant or to any person being in or passing along any street, public highway, or footpath, or throws down the area of any house, or exhibits to public view in the window of any house or shop, any picture or printed or written matter which is of an indecent or obscene nature, shall, on summary conviction in manner provided by the Summary Jurisdiction Acts, be liable to a penalty not exceeding forty shillings, or, in the discretion of the Court, to imprisonment for any term not exceeding one month, with or without hard labour.

4. Whoever gives or delivers to any other person any such pictures, or printed or written matter mentioned in section three of this Act, with the intent that the same, or some one or more thereof, should be affixed, inscribed, delivered, or exhibited as therein mentioned, shall, on conviction in manner provided by the Summary Jurisdiction Acts, be liable to a penalty not exceeding five pounds, or, in the discretion of the Court, to imprisonment for any term not exceeding three months, with or without hard labour.

5. Any advertisement relating to syphilis, gonorrhœa, nervous debility, or other complaint or infirmity arising from or relating to sexual intercourse, shall be deemed to be printed or written matter of an indecent nature within the meaning of section three of this Act, if such advertisement is affixed to or inscribed on any house, building, wall, hoarding, gate, fence, pillar, post, board, tree, or other thing whatsoever, so as to be visible to a person being in or passing along any street, public highway, or footpath, or is affixed to or inscribed on any public urinal, or is delivered or attempted to be delivered to any person being in or passing along any street, public highway, or footpath.

6. Any constable or other peace officer may arrest without warrant any person whom he shall find committing any offence against this act.

VAGRANCY ACT 1838

An Act to amend an Act for punishing idle and disorderly Persons and Rogues and Vagabonds
2. – **Persons exposing obscene prints, etc., in shop windows liable on conviction to punishment**

... Every person who shall wilfully expose or cause to be exposed to public view in the window or other part of any shop or other building situate in any street, road, highway, or public place, any obscene print, picture, or other indecent exhibition, shall be deemed to have wilfully exposed such obscene print, picture, or other indecent exhibition to public view within the intent and meaning of the said Act, and shall accordingly be liable to be proceeded against, and on conviction to be punished, under the provisions of the said Act.

INDEPENDENT BROADCASTING AUTHORITY ACT 1973

4. – **General provisions with respect to content of programmes**
(1) It shall be the duty of the Authority to satisfy themselves that, so far as possible, the programmes broadcast by the Authority comply with the following requirements, that is to say –

   (*a*) that nothing is included in the programmes which offends against good taste or decency or is likely to encourage or incite to crime or to lead to disorder or to be offensive to public feeling;

   (*b*) that a sufficient amount of time in the programmes is given to news and news features and that all news given in the programmes (in whatever form) is presented with due accuracy and impartiality;

   (*c*) that proper proportions of the recorded and other matter included in the programmes are of British origin and of British performance;

   (*d*) that the programmes broadcast from any station or stations contain a suitable proportion of matter calculated to appeal specially to the tastes and outlook of persons served by the station or stations and, where another language as well as English is in common use among those so served, a suitable proportion of matter in that language;

   (*e*) in the case of local sound broadcasting services, that the programmes broadcast from different stations for reception in different localities do not consist of identical or similar material to an extent inconsistent with the character of the services as local sound broadcasting services; and

   (*f*) that due impartiality is preserved on the part of the persons providing the programmes as respects matters of political or industrial controversy or relating to current public policy.

In applying paragraph (*f*) of this subsection, a series of programmes may be considered as a whole.

5. Programmes other than advertisements
(1) The Authority –

   (*a*) shall draw up, and from time to time review, a code giving guidance –

   (i) as to the rules to be observed in regard to the showing of violence, and in regard to the inclusion in local sound broadcasts of sounds suggestive of violence, particularly when large numbers of children and young persons may be expected to be watching or listening to the programmes, and

   (ii) as to such other matters concerning standards and practice for programmes (other than advertisements) broadcast by the Authority as the Authority may consider suitable for inclusion in the code, and in considering what other matters ought to be included in the code in pursuance of sub-paragraph (ii) shall have special regard to programmes broadcast when large numbers of children and young persons may be expected to be watching or listening; and

(*b*) shall secure that the provisions of the code are observed in relation to all programmes (other than advertisements) broadcast by the Authority.

INDEX